The Historian's Huck Finn

To Jim, local literary luminary. Thanks so much for all you do.

The Historian's Huck Finn

Reading Mark Twain's Masterpiece as Social and Economic History

☙❧

ANNOTATED BY
RANJIT S. DIGHE

The Historian's Annotated Classics
Ranjit S. Dighe, Series Editor

 PRAEGER™

An Imprint of ABC-CLIO, LLC
Santa Barbara, California • Denver, Colorado

Library of Congress Cataloging-in-Publication Data

Names: Dighe, Ranjit S., 1965- author.
Title: The historian's Huck Finn : reading Mark Twain's masterpiece as social and economic history / annotated by Ranjit S. Dighe.
Description: Santa Barbara, California : Praeger, 2016. | Series: The Historian's Annotated Classics | Includes bibliographical references and index.
Identifiers: LCCN 2015041761 | ISBN 9781440833489 (hardback : acid-free paper) | ISBN 9781610699419 (paperback : acid-free paper) | ISBN 9781440833496 (Ebook)
Subjects: LCSH: Twain, Mark, 1835–1910. Adventures of Huckleberry Finn. | Literature and society—United States—History—19th century. | Literature and history—United States—History—19th century. | Economics and literature—United States—History—19th century. | Finn, Huckleberry (Fictitious character) | BISAC: BUSINESS & ECONOMICS / Economic History.
Classification: LCC PS1305 .D54 2016 | DDC 813/.4—dc23 LC record available at http://lccn.loc.gov/2015041761

ISBN: 978-1-4408-3348-9 (hardcover)
ISBN: 978-1-61069-941-9 (paperback)
EISBN: 978-1-4408-3349-6

20 19 18 17 16   1 2 3 4 5

This book is also available on the World Wide Web as an eBook.
Visit www.abc-clio.com for details.

Praeger
An Imprint of ABC-CLIO, LLC

ABC-CLIO, LLC
130 Cremona Drive, P.O. Box 1911
Santa Barbara, California 93116-1911

This book is printed on acid-free paper ∞

Manufactured in the United States of America

The source of the original text reprinted here is:

Mark Twain, *Adventures of Huckleberry Finn.* New York: Charles L. Webster and Company, 1885.

ॐ

Contents

præ

Preface

I have been a huge fan of Huck Finn the character ever since I saw a movie version of the Tom Sawyer and Huckleberry Finn stories when I was about 8 years old. The consensus among film reviewers is that none of the movie versions were all that good, which may be why I have been unable to track down the version first viewed in my youth. Just the same, 40-plus years later those mental images of Huck and Tom's adventures are still with me. Huck and Tom knew how to live, going out into the woods and the river at night with no adults around, just two kids making up the rules as they went along. Huck was my favorite of the two because he knew the outdoors and didn't have to answer to anyone. (His reprobate father must have been absent or toned down in the movie.)

On our family's next trip to the library I picked up *Adventures of Huckleberry Finn* and did not get far with it. If I recall correctly, the dialect was too much for me to penetrate at the time. My disappointment was probably typical of children my age. The book is said to be the most assigned novel in American schools, but it is taught only rarely at the middle school level and almost never at the elementary school level. Many scholars consider this a good thing (Leonard 1999, 1, 3). I don't remember when I first read it all the way through, but by now I have lost count of the number of times I've read it, and I enjoy it even more each time. That may be typical of people my age too.

Lovers of classic novels often end up as teachers and find ways to work those novels into classes. In history and the social sciences, many college professors add spice to their courses by assigning a novel as a supplementary text. (And some go even further, such as University of Michigan professor and recent Federal Reserve nominee Kathryn Dominguez, who has taught "Jane Austen and Economics.") Over the years my economic history students and I have read Upton Sinclair's *The Jungle,* L. Frank Baum's *The Wonderful Wizard of Oz,* Harriet Beecher Stowe's *Uncle Tom's Cabin,* John Steinbeck's *The Grapes of Wrath,* and Mark Twain's *The Tragedy of Pudd'nhead Wilson,* with varying degrees of success. The most successful was surely *The Wizard of Oz,* which I turned into an annotated version that related the book to economics, politics, and history. But probably none of these convey the sweep of American history so well as *Adventures of Huckleberry Finn.*

Huckleberry Finn is a historical novel. Twain wrote it as a Connecticut Yankee in 1876–1883 as a not quite nostalgic look back at his boyhood days in Hannibal, Missouri, a river town in a frontier slave state in antebellum America, circa 1845. Thus, it spans two vastly different eras. The novel follows Huck and his friend Jim, a runaway slave, through border states and into the Deep South along the nation's leading trade route at the time, the Mississippi River. By the time the novel was published slavery had been over for 20 years, and Twain's own views of African Americans had evolved considerably, but white America's views as a whole had changed decidedly less. Reconstruction had ended, and blacks were shunted into second-class status in the South and virtually shunned in the North, and the nation underwent a period of monumental economic growth and political corruption that Twain dubbed "the Gilded Age." Unlike *The Adventures of Tom Sawyer,* its predecessor, *Adventures of Huckleberry Finn* is ironic, edgy, and relatively difficult. *Tom Sawyer* is narrated smoothly in the third person, whereas its sequel is in Huck's semiliterate backwoods dialect. Issues of race and slavery were minor in *Tom Sawyer* but are close to the heart of *Huckleberry Finn.* Consider, for example, that the word "nigger" appears nine times in *Tom Sawyer,* always in dialogue, compared with 214 times in *Huckleberry Finn.* Aside from race and slavery, the novel touches on dozens of historical issues, such as women's roles in society, river transportation, early manufacturing, frontier life, Indian removal, metallic and paper money, temperance, speculation, Jacksonian democracy, education, and class (see Tables 1, 2, and 3 for more examples).

Twain's life was a remarkable piece of history as well, spanning diverse places, positions, and eras, all of which informed his prodigious output. Chapter 1 is a life-and-times essay on Samuel Clemens, the man who became Mark Twain, which focuses at least as much on the times as on the life. Perhaps even more than Twain's stories and essays, Clemens's biography tells the story of the American 19th century from lower-middle-class life in a frontier slave state to a dream career as a steamboat pilot on the Mississippi, mining camps in the Far West, literary fame, fortune in the East, and much more.

Chapter 2 offers a more direct approach to 19th-century American history. It is not a typical chronological history but rather an essay that discusses what I believe are four key themes of 19th-century U.S. history: prosperity, expansion, inequality, and commercialism. Chapter 2 overlaps with many of the annotations but goes into greater depth. It is mainly aimed at instructors who want to know more about the stories behind the annotations, but I hope that readers will find it useful and engaging in its own right. Likewise, while I hope that students will find the annotated *Adventures of Huckleberry Finn* to be a self-contained, coherent, and enjoyable history lesson, I hope they can get something out of this chapter as well. Students often find history bewildering in its never-ending parade of facts. At the start of every semester someone asks me, "Are we going to have to remember a lot of dates?" I tell them not exactly, because history is more about cause and effect, explaining how and why things happened. The basic facts and timeline can be found in a few seconds on the Internet. Making sense of those facts by organizing them into compelling yet accurate stories is what good history does. Chapter 2 is my attempt to tell four such stories.

The heart of this book is Twain's novel and the 170 annotations that accompany it. As beautifully as *Huckleberry Finn* conveys the sweep of 19th-century American history, it does so indirectly. The novel touches on historical controversies and developments, but nobody thinks that Twain was trying to teach history. The annotations in this book are there to make the historical connections more explicit. In addition, many references that would have been familiar to readers in the 1880s are obscure now, so some of the annotations are just basic explanations. Others are admittedly tangential but hopefully interesting. In general, I try not to assume what Twain's intent was and also try to leave room for individual interpretation.

WHAT A LESSON PLAN WITH *HUCKLEBERRY FINN* MIGHT LOOK LIKE

A frequent pitfall of assigning novels in a history or social science class is that the instructor devotes too little class time to a given novel. Even if students are willing to read a full-length novel for just a class meeting or two, they may not get a proper chance to digest and discuss it. Some books only pertain to one short unit in a long semester, but *Huckleberry Finn* straddles so much of 19th-century American history that it could be stretched out over most of a semester. It has 43 chapters, averaging about seven pages of text each.

Table 1 shows how *The Historian's Huck Finn* might work in a general American history class that runs from colonial times to Reconstruction. The table links nine consecutive chapters from the freely available Open-Stax *U.S. History* textbook to chapters in *Huckleberry Finn*. For each of these textbook chapters, there are several *Huckleberry Finn* chapters—a minimum of 3 and as many as 23—that relate to it. For example, Chapter 9 of *U.S. History*, "Industrial Transformation in the North, 1800–1850," deals with the transportation revolution, early manufacturing, consumerism, women's economic opportunity, and immigration. These issues also come up (not all at once) in *Huckleberry Finn* in Chapters 1–5, 7, 9,

Table 1. *Huck Finn* **keyed to an American history textbook (OpenStax College 2015)**

Textbook Chapter	Textbook Chapter Title	Relevant *Huck Finn* Chapters	Themes in Common	Suggested *Huck Finn* Chapters to Read with Textbook Chapter
9	Industrial Transformation in the North, 1800–1850	1, 2, 3, 4, 5, 7, 9, 12, 13, 14, 16, 17, 19, 24, 26, 27, 32, 38	Transportation revolution; early manufacturing; consumerism; women's economic opportunity; immigration	1–4
10	Jacksonian Democracy, 1820–1840	3, 6, 13, 17, 26, 39, Last	Political involvement of the working class; Andrew Jackson-Henry Clay feud; Jackson's political dominance; Indian removal	5–8
11	A Nation on the Move: Westward Expansion, 1800–1850	1, 8, 12, 16, 20, 24, 29, 35, 40	Missouri and slavery; Texas and slavery; free soil and blacks	9–13
12	Cotton Is King: The Antebellum South, 1800–1860	1, 2, 8, 11, 12, 13, 14, 15, 16, 17, 18, 20, 21, 24, 26, 28, 31, 32, 33, 35, 36, 41, 42	Slavery (all aspects); Southern society (honor, gender roles)	14–18
13	Antebellum Idealism and Reform Impulses, 1820–1860	1, 5, 6, 8, 12, 16, 17, 18, 19, 26	Religious revivalism; temperance; abolitionism; women's rights movement; phrenology	19–22
14	Troubled Times: The Tumultuous 1850s	6, 8, 16, 17, 32	Abolitionism; Henry Clay; blacks' rights under the Constitution	23–26
15	The Civil War, 1860–1865	8, 17, 27	Abolitionism; causes of the Civil War; Civil War deaths	27–30
16	The Era of Reconstruction, 1865–1877	8, 19, 29, 31, 35–Last	Emancipation; "carpet-baggers"; abandonment of Reconstruction; reenslavement; lynching	31–34
17	Go West Young Man! Westward Expansion, 1840–1900	1, 9, 12, 17, 20, 22, 24, 29, 39, 40, Last	Westward expansion; frontier life; Indian removal	35–Last

12–14, 16, 17, 19, 24, 26, 27, 32, and 38. So, if one read Chapter 9 of the textbook and the first 4 or 5 chapters of *The Historian's Huck Finn* together, they would be ideal complements, and the annotations would make the connections clear. The later chapters mentioned here from *Huckleberry Finn* (i.e., 7, 9, etc.) would reinforce the early material. The range of common themes in the textbook and the novel is considerable, from economic topics such as slavery, westward expansion, and long-distance transportation; political issues such as Jacksonian democracy and the Andrew Jackson–Henry Clay feud; to social issues such as temperance and frontier violence. The last column lists suggested pairings of textbook chapters with blocks of chapters from *Huckleberry Finn*. Eight of the 9 textbook chapters have one or more common themes with the *Huckleberry Finn* chapter blocks that have been grouped with them. The one exception, Chapter 14 of *U.S. History*, does not overlap with the assigned *Huckleberry Finn* chapters (23–26) but reinforces several previous chapters of the novel. Depending on the pace of the course, these 9 textbook chapters and all of *Huckleberry Finn* could be covered in anywhere from three weeks (in a class that meets three times a week) to nine weeks.

The book is also well suited to an American economic history course. Table 2 suggests how *The Historian's Huck Finn* might be used as a supplement to a leading economic history textbook, Gary M. Walton and Hugh Rockoff's *History of the American Economy*. Chapters 8–14 of this textbook cover topics that also appear, sometimes indirectly, in various chapters of *Huckleberry Finn*. The overlap with the *Huckleberry Finn* chapters is actually somewhat better for Walton and Rockoff's book than for the OpenStax *U.S. History* book, which is ordered chronologically, whereas Walton and Rockoff's chapters are ordered thematically. Not surprisingly, the greatest degree of overlap is with their slavery chapter, but all of their chapters here overlap with at least eight of Twain's chapters. Common themes include western settlement; Indian removal; the communications revolution; the rise of the factory; and consumerism, specie, and banknotes. My suggested *Huckleberry Finn* chapters to assign with each textbook chapter appear in the last column. All seven pairings include at least one direct overlap (i.e., a *Huckleberry Finn* chapter that deals with at least one topic in the corresponding Walton and Rockoff chapter). If one wanted even more overlap, one could teach Walton and Rockoff's Chapters 8–13 in a different order (12, 11, 9, 8, 10, 13) without much loss of clarity, as those chapters are fairly self-contained and could be taught in any sequence. Depending on the pace of the course, these 7 textbook chapters and all of *Huckleberry Finn* could be covered in anywhere from two and one-third weeks to 7 weeks.

Some topics that *Huckleberry Finn* raises are more tangential to the material in Walton and Rockoff's chapters but could still be very interesting to discuss in class. The textbook section "Land and the Early Western

Table 2. *Huck Finn* keyed to an American economic history textbook (Walton and Rockoff 2014)

Textbook Chapter	Textbook Chapter Title	Relevant *Huck Finn* Chapters	Themes in Common	Tangential Themes in *Huck Finn* Chapters	Suggested *Huck Finn* Chapters to Read with Textbook Chapter
8	Land and the Early Western Movements	1, 9, 12, 17, 20, 22, 24, 29, 39, 40, Last	Western land acquisition and settlement; frontier life; regional trade and specialization; Indian removal	The urban frontier (e.g., St. Louis)	1–4
9	Transportation and Market Growth	7, 9, 12, 13, 16, 18, 20, 42	Water transportation; steamboats; inefficiency of land transportation; ocean transportation; communications revolution	Rafts and flatboats in river trading	5–10
10	Market Expansion and Industry in First Transition	2, 3, 5, 14, 17, 19, 24, 32, 38	Early manufacturing; rise of the factory; factory-produced clothing; home production; mills	Southern manufacturing; spread of consumer goods; printer's shops	11–16
11	Labor during the Early Industrial Period	1, 3, 4, 5, 6, 11, 12, 17, 18, 23, 26	Immigration; inequality; political gains for working men; women's economic opportunity; public education	Entrepreneurialism; upward mobility; living standards; temperance; Jacksonian democracy; apprenticeships; social class distinctions	17–22
12	Money and Banking in the Developing Economy	1, 2, 4, 9, 10, 20, 25, 34	Gold, coinage, silver, banknotes; free banking; counterfeiting	Price conversions; financial investments; speculation; confidence men	23–28
13	The Entrenchment of Slavery and Regional Conflict	1, 2, 6, 8, 11, 12, 14, 15, 16, 17, 18, 20, 24, 26, 28, 31, 32, 33, 35, 36, 41, 42	Social acceptance of slavery; slave prices and profitability; slave sales and family breakups	Slavery in border states; slave escapes; treatment of slaves; free blacks in North and cities; manumission and self-purchase; racism as justification for slavery	29–34
14	War, Recovery, and Regional Divergence	8, 17, 27, 29, 31, 35–Last	Abolitionism; emancipation; Compromise of 1850; Civil War deaths; Reconstruction and its abandonment	Status of African Americans after Emancipation and end of Reconstruction	35–Last

Movements" could be enhanced by a discussion of the urban frontier, as exemplified by such cities as St. Louis and Cairo, Illinois. In learning about steamboats and the early transportation revolution, students may be intrigued to discover that rafts played an important role in antebellum commerce as well. The spread of markets and industry is repeatedly seen in *Huckleberry Finn* in the various shops and store-bought goods that recur throughout the novel. We also see the spread of cheap books as a popular consumer item. Nineteenth-century money and banking are illustrated through the appearances of gold and silver specie and dubious banknotes. The country's spectacular economic growth had its dark side in the profusion of scam artists and confidence men, two of whom (the Duke and the King) are prominent characters in the novel. Finally, the novel's last nine chapters—in which Tom Sawyer makes a surprise appearance and orchestrates an "evasion" in which Jim, who has been captured as a runaway, is subjected to all kinds of bizarre torture inspired by bad romantic novels—can be read as a parable on the abandonment of Reconstruction and African Americans by the nation's political leaders. See Table 2 for a more complete list of overlapping and tangential themes.

Many professors, preferring the flexibility of a customized set of readings, do not use regular textbooks anymore. Table 3 shows a possible lesson plan, organized by weekly topics, with the *Huckleberry Finn* chapters covered about six at a time over seven weeks. Twain's prefatory "Notice," threatening harm to anyone who looks for a motive or moral in the story, and the first paragraph of Chapter 1 are included in the first week's introductory readings, as they raise the issue of positive, normative, and moralistic approaches to history as well as that of conflicting interpretations and perspectives. Huck begins:

> You don't know about me, without you have read a book by the name of "The Adventures of Tom Sawyer," but that ain't no matter. That book was made by Mr. Mark Twain, and he told the truth, mainly. There was things which he stretched, but mainly he told the truth. That is nothing. I never seen anybody but lied, one time or another.

A better introduction to historiography or postmodernism can scarcely be found. It also helps set the stage for the semester, during which many of the readings will contradict each other to some degree. The reading of *Huckleberry Finn* proper is in weeks 6–12, when the course covers the period from 1790 to 1860 as well as the American Civil War, Reconstruction, and the rise of big business. The chapter blocks fit well with the thematic units and, once again, introduce a number of colorful details and tangents.

In all three lesson plans the largest block is the final nine *Huckleberry Finn* chapters (35–"The Last"). The rationale is Chapters 35–40, the

Table 3. *Huck Finn* keyed to a pre-1900 American economic history lesson plan (14-week class)

Week	Unit	Assigned *Huck Finn* Chapters	Themes in Common	Other Themes in *Huck Finn* Chapters
1	What Is American Economic History?	"Notice," "Explanatory," first paragraph of Chapter 1	Conflicting interpretations	Morality and history
6	Economic Life in the New Republic (I)	1–4	Rapid growth; money and coinage; women's economic role; cash crops; early manufacturing; uneven regional development; self-sufficiency; consumerism	Slavery; upward mobility; inflation and price conversions; available investments; early immigration; public education
7	Economic Life in the New Republic (II)	5–10	Manufacturing; uneven regional development; self-sufficiency; communications revolution and newspapers	Slavery; living standards; alcohol consumption; temperance movement; Jacksonian democracy; speculation; water transportation; frontier settlement; money and prices
8	The Political Economy of Slavery	11–16	Slavery (enforcement, escapes, sales, families); apprenticeships as involuntary servitude; expansion of slavery	The Age of Jackson; urbanization along the frontier; living standards and public health; women's economic opportunity; transportation revolution and steamboats; frontier settlement
9	Westward Expansion and the Transportation Revolution	17–22	Westward expansion and settlement; frontier life; regional and international trade	Living standards; income distribution; Henry Clay–Andrew Jackson feud; alcohol consumption and temperance; confidence men; slavery (escapes, punishment); price conversions; tobacco; consumption of entertainment
10	The Political Economy of the Civil War	23–28	Slavery and racism; American Indians; Civil War deaths; inflation (price conversions)	Immigration; consumer spending; westward settlement; women's economic opportunity
11	Regional Divergence after the Civil War	29–34	Reconstruction and "carpetbaggers"; slavery, racism, and social norms; spread of factory production	Westward expansion and frontier; paper money
12	The Rise of Big Business	35–Last	Early manufacturing; communications revolution	Slavery (conditions, escapes, manumission, social norms); Reconstruction's abandonment; westward expansion into Indian territory; class (hereditary privilege)

infamous evasion sequence that readers tend to find aesthetically subpar and inconsistent with the rest of the book (Saunders 2008, xx–xxi). So, one might want to speed through those chapters and get to the last three. Alternatively, one might want to devote a whole unit to the evasion precisely because it is so problematic and then do the last three chapters (41–43) separately. Either way, the novel's beautiful ending, where Huck says that he's "got to light out for the Territory" rather than let Aunt Sally "sivilize" him, deserves special attention.

Huckleberry Finn is commonly called the Great American Novel. Properly spaced out over several weeks and with the aid of annotations that highlight its connections to American history, it could also be the Great American History Teaching Tool.

Many people helped make *The Historian's Huck Finn: Reading Mark Twain's Masterpiece as Social and Economic History* happen. Doug Deal was the first to suggest that *Huckleberry Finn* could be an amazing book to use in my economic history class. Frank Byrne and Adam Rothman offered helpful insights into the antebellum South and the western trunk of the underground railroad as well as numerous excellent references. Jolene Callen led me to the rich literature by British travelers in antebellum America. Brad Korbesmeyer offered great insights into Twain the author and Clemens the person. Panel participants at the 2015 Economic and Business History Society conference in La Crosse, Wisconsin, offered helpful suggestions. The State University of New York at Oswego provided me with a timely sabbatical and consistently helpful library services. Julia Dighe improved the manuscript immensely through her outstanding editorial assistance. Judith and Shrikant Dighe fed me and put up with me during the homestretch of this project. Finally, I wish to thank my comrades in the *Huckleberry Finn* reading group that met in Oswego in early 2015: Chris Sinatra, Tom Kammerer, Randi Taylor, Terry Manion, and especially Anne Pagano, my primary sounding board throughout this project, editorial and art assistant, and partner in Twain tourism. May we paint the river red again.

Chronology

Date	Key Events in American History	Key Events in Mark Twain's Life
1775	The American Revolution begins.	
1776	The Declaration of Independence is signed.	
1781	The United States of America defeats Britain and adopts the Articles of Confederation.	
1788	The U.S. Constitution is ratified.	
1793	The cotton gin is invented.	
1801	Oliver Evans develops the high-pressure steam engine.	
1803	In the Louisiana Purchase, the United States acquires 827,000 acres of land west of the Mississippi River.	
1807	America and Britain end their involvement in the international slave trade.	
1811	Steamboat traffic on the Mississippi River begins.	
1820	The Missouri Compromise admits Missouri to the union as a slave state.	

Date	Key Events in American History	Key Events in Mark Twain's Life
1825	The Erie Canal begins operation and will eventually connect the East Coast to the Great Lakes region.	
1829– 1837	Andrew Jackson serves as president of the United States.	
1830	The Indian Removal Act is passed.	
	The Baltimore & Ohio Railroad opens.	
1832– 1836	President Andrew Jackson attempts to destroy the Bank of the United States and eventually succeeds.	
1835		Samuel Clemens is born in Florida, Missouri, on November 30.
1837	In the Panic of 1837 there are shortages of gold and silver coins, and numerous banks fail.	
1837– 1863	In the free banking era there is no central bank, and banks continue to issue their own money.	
1838– 1839	The forced westward relocation of eastern Indian tribes becomes known as the Trail of Tears.	
1839		The Clemens family moves to Hannibal, Missouri.
1844	The first intercity telegraph transmission ushers in the rapid rise of the telegraph.	
1845	Texas is admitted as a state.	
1846– 1848	In the Mexican-American War, the United States gains the entire Southwest. Status of slavery in new territories becomes a paramount political issue.	

Date	Key Events in American History	Key Events in Mark Twain's Life
1847		John Marshall Clemens (Samuel Clemens's father) dies.
1848		Samuel Clemens quits school and becomes a printer's apprentice.
1848–1855	The California Gold Rush occurs.	
1850	The Compromise of 1850 includes a tough new Fugitive Slave Act and allows new territories to adopt slavery if a majority of white male settlers favor it.	
1852	Harriet Beecher Stowe's *Uncle Tom's Cabin* is published.	
1853–1856		Clemens works as a printer in New York City, Philadelphia, Cincinnati, and St. Louis.
1854	The Kansas-Nebraska Act intensifies the controversy over slavery in territories and new states.	
1856		Clemens begins writing humor pieces for an Iowa newspaper.
1856–1861		Clemens works as a cub pilot and then as pilot on steamboats on the Mississippi River.
1857	In the *Dred Scott* decision, the U.S. Supreme Court extends slaveholders' rights and denies rights for blacks.	
1858		Henry Clemens, younger brother of Samuel Clemens, dies as the result of a steamboat explosion.

Date	Key Events in American History	Key Events in Mark Twain's Life
1859	John Brown's raid occurs at Harpers Ferry, Virginia.	
1860	Over 30,000 miles of railroad track are in operation, up tenfold from 1840.	
	Abraham Lincoln is elected president of the United States.	
1861		Samuel Clemens serves in a pro-Confederate militia for two weeks.
1861– 1864		Clemens joins brother Orion in Nevada Territory and works as a miner and a newspaperman.
1861– 1865	The American Civil War occurs.	
1863	The Emancipation Proclamation is issued.	Clemens adopts the pen name "Mark Twain."
1864		Clemens moves to San Francisco, where he works as a journalist, a fiction writer, and a travel writer.
1865	The Thirteenth Amendment freeing all slaves is passed.	The short story "The Celebrated Jumping Frog of Calaveras County" becomes successful.
	Black Codes are passed by southern legislatures.	
1866	The transatlantic telegraph cable is successfully laid.	Clemens travels to Hawaii as a correspondent and lectures for the first time.
1867– 1877	During Reconstruction, federal troops occupy former Confederate states to uphold rights of African Americans.	

Date	Key Events in American History	Key Events in Mark Twain's Life
1868	President Andrew Johnson is impeached by the House of Representatives but is acquitted by the Senate.	Clemens tours the United States as a lecturer.
1869	Jay Gould and James Fisk attempt to corner the gold market, the first of several major scandals during Ulysses S. Grant's administration. The transcontinental railroad opens.	*The Innocents Abroad* travelogue is published and becomes a best seller.
1870		Clemens marries Olivia Langdon, daughter of a wealthy industrialist and progressive in Elmira, New York.
1870–1871		Samuel and Olivia Clemens live in Buffalo, New York. In 1870 Olivia's father dies, and the Clemenses' son Langdon is born prematurely.
1871		The Clemens family moves to Hartford, Connecticut.
1872		*Roughing It* is published. Langdon Clemens dies at 19 months of age. Susy Clemens, the first of three daughters, is born.
1873		*The Gilded Age,* Twain's first novel, cowritten with Charles Dudley Warner, is published.
1874		Clara Clemens is born.
1876		*Adventures of Tom Sawyer* is published. Twain begins work on *Huckleberry Finn*.

Date	Key Events in American History	Key Events in Mark Twain's Life
1877	Reconstruction ends. The second-class status of African Americans will last for nearly 90 years.	
1880		Jean Clemens is born.
1880–1894		Samuel Clemens invests in a typesetting machine and ends up losing the equivalent of almost $9 million in today's money.
1881	The Chinese Exclusion Act is passed.	*The Prince and the Pauper* is published.
1882		*A Tramp Abroad* is published.
1883		*Life on the Mississippi* is published.
1884		Samuel Clemens founds a publishing company with nephew Charles Webster. *Adventures of Huckleberry Finn* is published in the United Kingdom.
1885		*Adventures of Huckleberry Finn* is published in the United States. Clemens's publishing company publishes the memoirs of Ulysses S. Grant.
1889		*A Connecticut Yankee in King Arthur's Court* is published.
1891		The Clemens family moves to Europe due to financial strain.
1894		*The Tragedy of Pudd'nhead Wilson* is published.

Date	Key Events in American History	Key Events in Mark Twain's Life
		Samuel Clemens files for bankruptcy.
1895		Clemens begins a world lecture tour to raise money to repay creditors.
1896		Susy Clemens (oldest daughter) dies.
1897		*Following the Equator* is published.
1898	The Spanish-American War begins the era of American involvement in Latin America and the Pacific.	Samuel Clemens repays his debts.
1899– 1902	In the Philippine-American War, the United States defeats Filipino insurgents and begins a decades-long occupation of the Philippines.	
1900		Clemens declares himself an anti-imperialist.
1901	Theodore Roosevelt becomes president.	
1904		Olivia Clemens dies.
1906		Samuel Clemens begins work on his autobiography.
1907	A worldwide financial panic occurs, the last one before the creation of the Federal Reserve System.	
1909		Jean Clemens (youngest daughter) dies.
1910		Samuel Clemens dies in Redding, Connecticut, on April 21.
1914	World War I begins in Europe. The United States will enter the war in 1917.	

CHAPTER 1

CS80

Samuel Clemens in His Times

> The 20th Century is a stranger to me. I wish it well, but my heart is all
> for my own century. I took 65 years of it, just on a risk, but if I had
> known as much about it as I know now I would have taken the whole
> of it.
>
> Mark Twain, *Mark Twain's Notebook,* 1900

One can find the sweep of 19th-century American history in *Adventures of Huckleberry Finn.* One can also find it in the life of Samuel Clemens, the Missouri frontier boy who became Mark Twain. In his travelogues, autobiography, interviews, letters, notebooks, and countless essays and sketches, Clemens shows himself to be a man of his times and then some. This chapter will show how he personally experienced key developments in American history, how they shaped him, and how he voiced his opinions on big issues of the time. Like Forrest Gump, Clemens was present at seemingly every great historical episode of his time.

Clemens's life, from 1835 to 1910, runs from the Age of Jackson to the Progressive Era. His American roots go back much farther. Both his father, John Marshall Clemens, and his mother, Jane Lampton Clemens, were third-generation Americans whose families had arrived in the colonies by the mid-18th century. Like many Americans, they proudly claimed an aristocratic heritage, including membership in the tribunal that sentenced Charles I to death, earls of Dunham, and first families of Virginia. Their actual relations to these figures were dubious at best. However, at least one branch of the family tree had become wealthy; John Marshall Clemens's maternal grandmother, Rachel Moorman, was the daughter of a Virginia planter who freed 33 of his slaves (Kaplan 2005, 6).

The family was well acquainted with downward mobility as well, especially in the early 19th century. Pamela Goggin, the daughter of Rachel Moorman and Stephen Goggin Jr., the son of an Irish immigrant, had married Samuel B. Clemens in 1797. He had done well enough to sell his prime farmland for $1,000 and buy a 199-acre farm in western Virginia in 1804. But a year later he was crushed to death when a log slipped during a house-raising. Pamela Goggin, now with five children—including 5-year-old John Marshall—was left with some land and several slaves but saw no better option than to move to Kentucky and stay with her brother. She remarried in 1809 to a man who insisted that the children repay him for their rearing costs. John Marshall dropped out of school at age 11 and worked as a clerk. In his 20s he was still deep in debt to his stepfather when he received $884 from the liquidation of his father's estate and used it to repay almost all of the debt (Kaplan 2005, 6–7).

John Marshall Clemens continued the family's downward mobility, becoming a classic example of so-called poor gentry. This is not to deny that he was hardworking and ambitious. Despite his stepfather's penuriousness, John lived up to his illustrious legal name by reading law under the guidance of an attorney in Columbia, Kentucky, and becoming a practicing lawyer in 1822. Perhaps in honor of the chief justice, he went by the name Marshall. He married Jane Lampton, who came from a well-to-do family of farmers and shopkeepers. He had inherited eight slaves, although economic pressures forced him to sell seven of them. He still had enough money, about $400, to purchase some 70,000 acres of land in thinly settled Fentress County, Tennessee, in the late 1820s and early 1830s. Land was a popular investment at the time, as rapid westward settlement, the expansion of cotton slavery, and new federal policies of Indian removal pointed to a high demand for lands in the south-central region. Recognizing the long-term nature of the investment, Marshall clung tenaciously to the Tennessee lands, refusing to sell even in hard times and instructing Jane and the children to hold on to the land for as long as possible. The land would never return a profit for Marshall or his children. Marshall made other questionable choices, such as moving from bustling Columbia to one tiny town and then another in Tennessee, neither of which brought his legal practice enough business to break even. He opened general stores to supplement his income, but what little money he made went into more Fentress County land (Kaplan 2005, 7–9).

The great American land boom of the mid-1830s bypassed the small Tennessee towns where Marshall and Jane lived. In 1835 economic and family reasons compelled them to move more than 500 miles northwest to a new frontier town, Florida, Missouri, about 50 miles west of the Mississippi River. Later that year, on November 30, Jane gave birth to their sixth child, Samuel. Jane's family had moved to Missouri earlier in the decade, and her brother-in-law, John Quarles, had already established a successful general store. Marshall saw opportunity in Missouri, with its diverse economy, eastern border on the Mississippi River, and gateway to the West that had been famous since the Lewis and Clark expedition. The state seemed ideally situated to capitalize on the nation's westward expansion and transportation revolution, and Marshall continued to buy small parcels of land.

Samuel Clemens was born in this two-room house in the small town of Florida, Missouri. His family lived in the house as renters for four years before seeking greater opportunity in Hannibal, 40 miles to the northeast. (Library of Congress)

He hoped that Florida, located on three forks of the Salt River, which emptied into the Mississippi, would become a booming trading center, but the river's rises and falls proved too inhospitable to trading boats. As in small-town Tennessee, he found little business for a lawyer and tried his hand at running a general store. The town did not appear big enough to support two general stores, and Marshall's dour personality apparently did not help the store's business (Kaplan 2005, 9–12).

The financial panic of 1837 and the ensuing economic crisis of 1839 slammed the brakes on the nation's expansion and threw countless American lives into turmoil. No longer hopeful that Florida would develop into a city, Marshall sold his Missouri lands and moved the family, including Jennie, their last remaining slave, 40 miles northeast to Hannibal, a Mississippi River town almost five times the size of Florida and rapidly growing (Kaplan 2005, 13; Powers 2005, 21). The family improved its economic standing only slightly. Marshall arrived already in debt from another land purchase and proceeded to borrow heavily to stake yet another doomed general store upon arriving in Hannibal (Powers 2005, 21–23). Marshall's legal practice earned a bit more income than before, and he earned some additional income as a justice of the peace. The family was able to pay a private school subscription (as it was called) for young Sam. As he put it later with some exaggeration, "There were no public schools in Missouri, but there were two private schools" (Twain 2010, 2:177).

Yet Marshall's business sense was as abysmal as ever, and he found himself chronically in debt and unable to collect on debts owed to him. Soon after the family's arrival in Hannibal, their oldest son, Orion, became a printer's apprentice at age 14. In 1841 the family lost their house; they owed their next house to the generosity of a Clemens cousin (Powers 2005, 34, 38–41; Twain 2010, 1:655).

Another notable aspect of the family's financial struggles was their sale of Jennie, a faithful slave who had been with them since their Tennessee days and had even saved Sam from drowning. Missouri, though technically a midwestern state, was southern in all but name: a slave state largely populated by transplants from Kentucky, Tennessee, and other southern states, many of whom had brought slaves with them. Although Marshall and Jane Clemens were not farmers, they had grown up with slaves, as would Samuel, who always considered himself a southerner. Slave ownership was common in Hannibal, more so than in the state or the South as a whole. In 1850 some 44 percent of white families in Marion County owned slaves, not counting families who leased them (Dempsey 2003, 78–79). In Hannibal the Clemens family had the services of Jennie as well as other slaves whom they had leased at various times. Thus, Samuel knew slavery firsthand from his childhood and most of his first 25 years. He wrote later that as a youth in Missouri he never questioned slavery and neither did anyone else he knew. It was justified in the pulpit and never criticized in the press. Most of his adult reminiscences about slavery are fairly benign, such as the idyllic visits to his rich uncle John Quarles's farm in Florida, Missouri, where Clemens enjoyed playing with the slave children and with an older slave, Uncle Dan'l, who was a master storyteller and became the model for Jim in *Huckleberry Finn* (Twain 2010, 1:210–212). Yet the exceptions are telling, as are the incidents that Twain scholars have uncovered. Clemens said that he rarely saw slaves abused, but in a later work, *Following the Equator* (1897), he said that certain physical abuse, such as the cuffing of slaves, was so common and accepted that people in Hannibal did not recognize it as abuse. He also recalled the following wanton murder of a slave:

> When I was ten years old I saw a man fling a lump of iron-ore at a slave-man in anger, for merely doing something awkwardly—as if that were a crime. It bounded from the man's skull, and the man fell and never spoke again. He was dead in an hour.

Clemens told at least two versions of the story. In this account the murderer was the slave's master, whom he "knew had the right to kill his slave if he wanted to" (Twain 1897, 352). In an earlier version he said that the town was indifferent about the slave but that "considerable sympathy was felt for the slave's owner, who had been bereft of valuable property by a worthless person who was not able to pay for it" (Twain 1989, 89). Marshall Clemens, by his son's recollection, was kindly and upright but cuffed the family's leased slave boy, Lewis, regularly (Twain 1897, 351–352). Clemens's mother, whom Samuel remembered as saintly, once tried to thrash Jennie with a whip, an act that Marshall completed with extra vigor after Jennie grabbed the whip away from her (Pettit 1974, 17). Jennie's sale was not to another family in town but to a crooked local businessman known as "the nigger-trader" who promptly sold her down the river, where she became a chambermaid on a steamboat (Powers 2005, 38–39). The family briefly owned an elderly slave named Charley whom Marshall received in the payment of a debt. Fourteen months later, he took Charley on a business trip and apparently traded him in Natchez, Mississippi, way down the river, for 10 barrels of tar valued at $40 (Pettit 1974, 17). Twain also recalled a leased slave boy, Sandy, who sang and laughed incessantly, to the point where the young Sam asked his mother to shut him up. She told Sam that Sandy had been forever separated from his mother and that he sang to forget his pain (Twain 2010, 1:212).

In March 1847 Marshall Clemens died of pneumonia at age 49, plunging the family into near poverty (Powers 2005, 41–42; Twain 2010, 1:654). Aside from having fathered Samuel Clemens, his greatest legacy was the Hannibal & St. Joseph Railroad, for which he had advocated as the chair of a business committee. Chartered a month before Marshall's death and completed in 1859, the railroad was the first to traverse the state and was wildly successful, helping both cities and northern Missouri's timber industry to prosper for the rest of the century (Powers 2005, 42). But having died nearly broke with no major assets except the nonperforming Tennessee land, he clearly has to be counted as a failure rather than a success. In an entrepreneurial culture that esteems risk taking, there will be many bad bets and much money lost. Success stories are repeated and published; failure stories generally are not. Yet failures on the order of those of Marshall Clemens vastly outnumbered success stories such as those of Mark Twain. One study suggests that one in five householders at the turn of the 19th century could not pay their debts. Another found that more than half of San Francisco merchants failed in the 1850s. Another found that 30–60 percent of small businesses in Poughkeepsie, New York, failed within 3 years. The most oft-repeated statistic of all, though probably bogus, was that 97 out of 100 merchants will fail. Beyond the outright failures, thousands of businessmen spent years just barely staying afloat. And many lost everything in the nation's periodic financial panics, which occurred roughly every 20 years (Sandage 2005, 7).

The family's straitened circumstances compelled Samuel to drop out of school and enter the workforce at an early age, just as Marshall and Orion had done before. Leaving school at age 11 may have been unusual for a judge's son, but overall it was fairly common. Only about half of white children ages 9 to 13 in the South in 1850 attended school. Even in the Northeast the number was only 80 percent, and fewer than half of children were still in school at age 16 (Goldin and Katz 2003, 51). With virtually no restrictions against child labor, Sam worked brief stints in several shops and as a paperboy until finally Jane apprenticed him to the publisher of the Hannibal *Courier.* He worked primarily as a typesetter, picking up a marketable but tedious skill. For Sam, like Orion before him, the newspaper was a "poor boy's college." Sam had hated school, mastering little more than spelling. But typesetting and the demands of writing copy for deadlines trained his ear to distinguish between good writing and bad (Powers 2005, 45–47, 50, 56; Levy 2014, 19). A few years later he went to work for the rival Hannibal *Journal,* a struggling newspaper that Orion had purchased. Orion quickly became bored with the enterprise and allowed the teenage Samuel considerable scope in editing the paper and writing satirical sketch stories and fake letters to the editor. Eventually Sam's barbs permeated all facets of the paper and were probably its strongest selling point (Powers 2005, 51–60).

Slavery was necessarily one of the big issues that the Hannibal newspapers covered. The Hannibal papers were predictably antiabolitionist and apoplectic that anyone would aid a fugitive slave. This included Orion's *Hannibal Journal and Union,* despite the fact that Orion would become an abolitionist himself by the start of the Civil War. A particularly galling case was the Jerry Rescue, the successful escape of a Marion County slave who was arrested as a fugitive in Syracuse, New York, and liberated from jail by an abolitionist mob on the day of his trial in 1851. Covering that incident, Orion, possibly with Sam's assistance, lamented the northern states' unwillingness to enforce the Fugitive Slave Act of 1850 and their "[hostility] to extending to Southern men rights guaranteed to them by the Constitution and the laws of the land" (October 16, 1851, qtd. in Dempsey 2003, 189). The case remained an open wound among Hannibal's whites for years. In August 1853, by which time Sam had left Hannibal and traveled to New York City by train, he wrote to his mother in a letter that he had seen the site of the Jerry Rescue in Syracuse and said, "I reckon I had better black my face, for in these Eastern states niggers are considerably better than white people." In another letter he described the children he saw in a few blocks of New York City as such: "Niggers, mulattoes, quadroons, Chinese, and some the Lord no doubt originally intended to be white, but the dirt on whose faces leaves one uncertain as to that fact, block up the little, narrow street; and to wade through this mass of human vermin, would raise the ire of the most patient person who ever lived" (Dempsey 2003, 233).

Sam was 17 years old when he wrote those words. Obviously, his views on slavery and race would evolve. In leaving Hannibal for New York City (after a short stint in St. Louis), he followed a path trodden by many

Sam as a printer's apprentice, at approximately age 15. He later wrote that his time in print shops exposed him to a vast array of writing and turned him into a writer. (Bancroft Library Pictoral Collections)

ambitious young men on farms and in frontier towns seeking greater op-portunity in America's fast-growing cities. His dream career had always been steamboat pilot, but first he needed to raise money to pay for the train-ing. Growing up, he and the other boys in Hannibal had been captivated by the steamboats and the men who piloted them up and down the Mississippi River. This job seemed adventurous and challenging, and it paid well. It was easy to see why it paid well: steamboats, complemented by canal boats, handled most of the growing nation's trade. As of 1850, boats carried six times as much freight as railroads. The rise of steamboats paralleled the rise of King Cotton: on the eve of the Civil War, steamboats carried more than half the nation's cotton crop, almost 2 million bales, down the Mississippi (Buchanan 2004, 6). For the time being, however, he plied his trade as a typesetter, first in St. Louis and then in New York and Philadelphia. He rejoined the family at its new home in Muscatine, Iowa, a Mississippi River town with a relatively large black community, including many fugitive slaves, and its next home in Keokuk, Iowa, where he worked in Orion's print shop and wrote satirical travel letters for a local newspaper. Sam educated himself further through frequent use of public libraries. But Keokuk was even sleepier than Hannibal, and Sam moved on once again, to Cincinnati, where he earned enough money as a printer to afford the down payment on his steamboat pilot training (Powers 2005, 72–75).

Sam became a cub pilot at age 21 and a licensed steamboat pilot two years later in 1859. Receiving his pilot's license was one of the proudest moments of his life. His regular route was between St. Louis and New Orleans, two emporiums of cotton and other crops, imported goods, and slaves. Legend has it that he picked up his legendary pen name, Mark Twain, from a steamboat call meaning that the water was 2 fathoms (12 feet) deep (Powers 2005, 118). He also learned firsthand the terrible price that came with the transportation revolution: the nation's earliest and deadliest major industrial accidents involved steamboats, including a steamboat explosion in 1858 that killed Sam's younger brother Henry, for which Sam never forgave himself. This may be why steamboat accidents, wrecks, and deaths are so common in *Huckleberry Finn* and why transportation disasters in general, including train wrecks, loom so large in Twain's writing. Yet in *Life on the Mississippi* and other writings, Twain gave every indication of having found fulfillment as a river pilot. If not for the indefinite interruption of the Mississippi River traffic by the Civil War, he might well have had a long and happy career as a steamboat pilot.

Sam's next vocation would be his strangest and shortest lived: two weeks as a soldier in a pro-Confederate militia. The confusion surrounding Clemens's military experience, if it can be called that, says something about the divided loyalties and motivations of many Americans during the Civil War, especially in border states such as Missouri. The outbreak of war all but grounded Mississippi River commerce, and many displaced steamboat pilots joined the military, then composed largely of state and local militia units. Clemens, at age 25, joined a pro-Confederate militia in Marion County for reasons that are not entirely clear. Despite his earlier racism and outrage over abolitionists, we know virtually nothing about where he stood on slavery and secession in 1861, and it appears that he gave them little thought at the time (Powers 2005, 82). Missouri was a slave state but rejected secession almost unanimously at a state convention in March 1861.

Missouri slaveholders actually felt that their property would be safer in the Union on account of the state's unusual geography: it was already bordered on three sides by free states or territories, and secession would cause it to be nearly surrounded by another country, a potential haven for runaway slaves. The state's voters in 1860 had issued a split verdict, giving less than 20 percent of the vote to the secessionist presidential candidate who had carried the Lower South but electing a fiery secessionist governor, Claiborne Jackson. Governor Jackson provoked a confrontation with the commander of a federal arsenal in St. Louis, which led to a riot and the deaths of several bystanders. Following that debacle, the state reconstituted its militia as the Missouri State Guard, an anti-invasion force. This was the militia that Sam Clemens joined just days after federal forces had occupied the state capital and Governor Jackson had gone into exile (Dempsey 2003, 257–266). In his somewhat fictionalized essay "The Private History of a Campaign That Failed," Sam wrote that he and 14 friends and acquaintances formed their company one late spring night in Hannibal in response to the governor's call to repel the invasion. Sam described the company as something of a lark, similar to Tom Sawyer's gang, and said that they spent most of their time retreating. Their mission was ostensibly to defend Missouri against all invaders, Union or Confederate; however, a visit with an old colonel who preached neutrality but "knew quite clearly that he had invested us in the cause of the Southern Confederacy" seemed to bring home the reality of the situation (Twain 1979, 23). There was no neutral Missouri to defend. The climax of the essay is their shooting of a horseman who in hindsight appears to have been a civilian and whose death haunts Clemens and the rest of his unit, but the episode is uncorroborated and likely a fiction. He wrote that his unit disbanded upon hearing that a Union regiment was conducting a sweep of the area; offers of amnesty from Union officials may have made the decision an easy one (Dempsey 2003, 268–269).

Seeking a new situation, Sam moved west to a new frontier, the Nevada Territory, in the summer of 1861. He traveled there by stagecoach with Orion, who had campaigned for Abraham Lincoln in 1860 and, through a connection with a St. Louis lawyer who became Lincoln's attorney general, had secured a position as secretary of the Nevada Territory. One aspect of the western frontier life that made an impression on Sam was the condition of American Indians. The young Sam had had minimal contact with Indians other than a feckless "half-breed" he knew in Hannibal and on whom he based the "Injun Joe" character in *Tom Sawyer;* Indian territories bordered the other side of Missouri, but otherwise Indians were invisible to Sam. The Far West in the 1860s was a different story. With a larger standing army, a homestead act that encouraged Americans to settle in the West, and the railroads pushing ever farther west, the U.S. government was constantly at war with Indian tribes. U.S.-Indian battles became more frequent than ever, and most of the battles took place in the

West. Sam and Orion encountered no Indians on their stagecoach trip to Nevada but had been warned about recent Sioux and Apache attacks on travelers. Sam readily believed the worst about American Indians, having been scared as a youngster by his mother's stories of Indian atrocities that her Kentucky ancestors had supposedly witnessed. Although Clemens does not offer firsthand accounts of Indian violence in his writing, he had to have been well aware of the Snake War of 1864–1868, which killed 1,762 people and included battles close to where he had lived in Nevada. But Sam's attitude toward Indians in most of his writings displays not fear but rather contempt. In *Roughing It* (1872), his semifictionalized account of his time in the West, he describes all Indian tribes as "treacherous, filthy and repulsive," deserving of pity but only from a distance (169). That pity was absent in his appalling 1870 essay "The Noble Red Man," in which he dismissed all Indians as depraved and bloodthirsty— "a good, fair, desirable subject for extermination if ever there was one" and "The scum of the earth!" (Twain 2000, 104–105). The venom of his rhetoric is hard to account for other than as pandering to popular prejudice and swatting at James Fenimore Cooper, whose novels about "noble savages" Clemens had enjoyed as a child but had come to regard as bad writing and silly stereotyping (see the 1895 essay "Fenimore Cooper's Literary Offenses" in Twain 1994). Near the close of the century, if not earlier, Clemens had come around, mocking "the white man's notion that he is less savage than the other savages" and acknowledging Indian displacement and extermination as an "evil result" of European settlement (Twain 1897, 213; Twain 1979, 172). But his early writings are more emblematic of the era. A general's supposed comment that "the only good Indian is a dead Indian" was one of the most quoted lines of the century. Theodore Roosevelt said in a lecture in 1886 that "I don't go so far as to think that the only good Indians are dead Indians, but I believe nine out of ten are, and I shouldn't like to inquire too closely into the case of the tenth" (qtd. in Hagedorn 1921, 355).

Conflict between Indians and whites in the West was all but inevitable as railroads speeded the pace of white settlement and encroachment onto Indian lands. Among the new migrants were miners and prospectors. The 1849 California Gold Rush had been followed by a silver rush in Nevada in 1859. Silver mines in Nevada and other western states were so plentiful as to prompt a momentous change in the nation's longtime monetary system, from a gold and silver standard to a gold standard. At least one presidential election, that of 1896, would be fought over that issue. Yet not all silver miners were successful. Sam Clemens was among the unsuccessful. Dreaming of riches, he prospected for silver for almost a year but came up empty. The experience had to remind him of his father's failed land speculation: "We were always going to be rich next year—no occasion to work. It is good to begin life poor; it is good to begin life rich—these are wholesome; but to begin it *prospectively* rich! The man who has not experienced it cannot imagine the curse of it" (Twain 2010, 1:209). Tired of failure but wanting to stay in the West, he returned to the newspaper business.

Sam found work as a reporter and editor at the *Territorial Enterprise* in nearby Virginia City, a boomtown that had sprung up with the discovery of the Comstock Lode. The city was big enough to support an offbeat paper that was more like a literary magazine than a newspaper. It had already attracted several other writers whose wit and imagination outstripped their accuracy. Clemens began writing humorous sketches about the mining camps and the West, with imaginary recurring characters. In a dispatch that ran on February 3, 1863, his byline at the bottom, for the first time, was "Mark Twain" (Powers 2005, 110–117). By early 1864 Clemens had won over Artemus Ward, America's leading humorist at the time, and gotten sketches published in a prestigious New York weekly. But it was not quite the living Clemens had hoped for. Piloting a riverboat had paid much better. When he headed to San Francisco in 1864, it was with the intention of staying just long enough to sell some troubled mining stocks for Orion and then, with Union forces now protecting Mississippi River commerce, travel back to the big river to resume his old career. Unable to get much for the stocks or hold on to his new job as a reporter at a more serious newspaper, he could not raise the money for the trip (Powers 2005, 129–134, 146). Even aside from the fact that the steamboat was about to enter its waning days on account of the boom in railroad construction, these setbacks worked to Clemens's advantage, as he wrote some of his best dispatches for the *Enterprise* and latched on to a new literary journal, *The Californian,* coedited by another rising young star, Bret Harte. In late 1865 Twain's short story "Jim Smiley and His Jumping Frog" (later retitled "The Celebrated Jumping Frog of Calaveras County") was published to great acclaim in the *Saturday Press* of New York and subsequently republished all over the country. At age 27, Samuel Clemens had become Mark Twain. At age 30, Mark Twain had become a star (Powers 2005, 146–148, 152–154).

Sam Clemens was far from rich, however. In fact, he was still in debt and still plagued by the family's poor financial judgment. Orion was struggling again. Sam's older brother was a classic 19th-century reformer, an identity that helped him and then hurt him in the 1860s. Orion had become an abolitionist by 1860, and his strong support for Lincoln had landed him the territorial secretary job. When Nevada gained statehood, Orion was the obvious person to be elected its first secretary of state. But shortly before the Republican Party nominating convention of 1864, Orion announced his support of prohibition, a popular cause among reformers but a losing one in a hard-drinking mining state. With typical high-mindedness that drove Sam crazy, Orion also declined to attend the convention, saying that his presence might pressure people into voting for him. Orion lost (Kaplan 2005, 114). A year later Sam received an offer of $200,000 for the Tennessee land from a businessman who liked its potential for growing wine grapes. Orion, believing it immoral to prosper from alcoholic beverages, turned it down. Sam was livid. The land suddenly went back to being "worth what it was before—nothing, and taxes to pay," he wrote later (Powers 2005, 158–159). Orion's losing streak would continue throughout his life. His failed career turns included lawyer, journalist, and inventor; Sam criticized his brother's "capricious and ill-regulated mind" but supported him for years financially (Kaplan 2005, 82, 329–330).

Ocean steamships, as opposed to river steamboats, would soon make Mark Twain a best-selling author and an international celebrity. Improved steamship technology was a boon for international travel as well as a major factor in the great waves of immigration that America experienced after the Civil War. Clemens made two big trips in the mid-1860s that led to two books. The first was to the Sandwich Islands (now called Hawaii) as a guest of a steamship company eager to capitalize on Mark Twain's fame. The Sacramento *Union* agreed to pay him for his dispatches. He stayed four months and wrote 25 letters that were published in the *Union* (and later became chapters in *Roughing It*). He capped off the trip in the fall of 1866 with a wildly successful lecture tour of California and Nevada. By this time he was ready to leave California in favor of greater literary opportunity. He arranged another trip as a "Travelling Correspondent," this time for the *Alta California* newspaper on a voyage to Europe, Asia, and the Mediterranean, with the intention of relocating to the East Coast upon his return. A deadly cholera outbreak ended the trip prematurely, and Sam ended up in New York City. His early months in the city were frustrating, as he tried in vain to find a publisher for a book-length collection of sketches including the "Jumping Frog" story. But he found an ideal travel-writing opportunity in a six-month expedition to the Holy Land and other ancient sites on the Mediterranean, headed by the renowned preacher Henry Ward Beecher. Sam's sketches from that trip would become *The Innocents Abroad* (1869). The book was not only a best seller but would be the best selling of all of Mark Twain's books in his lifetime.

While on the Holy Land excursion in 1867 Sam bonded with 17-year-old Charley Langdon, the hard-drinking son of a wealthy and refined family in Elmira, New York, traveling on his own. After becoming entranced by a small picture of Charley's 22-year-old sister Olivia, Sam was determined to meet her. They met when the Langdons were in New York City for New Year's Eve. He would not see her again until the following summer when he visited Charley in Elmira. The Langdons were elegant, progressive, and successful in ways that had conspicuously eluded Sam's family. Jervis Langdon, Olivia's father, was the wealthiest man in Elmira, a prosperous small upstate city, and owned coal mines and railroads all over the Northeast and Canada. One of his ancestors had been a signer of the U.S. Constitution and governor of New Hampshire; another had been president of Harvard University. The couple had been among the founders of an abolitionist Congregational church and had aided fugitive slaves on the underground railroad. Olivia herself was well educated and had graduated from Elmira Female College, of which her father was a founding trustee. Through the Langdons, Sam met numerous activists and reformers. Sam was deeply in love with Olivia but felt he had to allay suspicions that he was after her family's money. His rapid completion of *The Innocents Abroad* as well as his ambitious lecture tour for it bolstered his prospects, but still he labored to convince Olivia's parents that he was worthy of her. After five months of relentless courtship, Sam and "Livy" became engaged in February 1869. They married a year later.

Despite the runaway success of *The Innocents Abroad* and his marriage into an aristocratic Yankee family, Clemens was not part of the eastern literary establishment just yet. His first experience in the East was in Buffalo, a long way from the East Coast, and involved an ill-fated return to journalism. With a $12,500 loan from his father-in-law, Sam bought a one-third share in the Buffalo *Express* and became its managing editor in the summer of 1869. His father-in-law also financed Sam and Livy's beautiful downtown house. Perhaps the most notable product of Sam's tenure at the paper, which included about 60 written pieces, was an angry column titled "Only a Nigger" in which he sarcastically defended the lynching of an innocent black man in Memphis. Breaking with his earlier bigoted racial remarks, he took to task anyone who rationalized that "the lives of a few 'niggers'" are unimportant. By this time, and starting two years earlier, he had stopped using the word "nigger" in print without quotation marks except in dialogue and dialect, as in *Huckleberry Finn* (Pettit 1974, 42–43). His interest in the paper faded after Livy joined him in Buffalo. Eager to get back to writing stories, he began work on *Roughing It*. The Clemenses' time in Buffalo became so tinged with tragedy that they did not stay long. Jervis Langdon died of cancer in June 1870. Livy, after a painful pregnancy, gave birth in October to a premature baby, Langdon Clemens, whom Sam did not expect to live. (He was correct; Langdon died after 19 months.) Livy came down with typhoid fever in February 1871. Forever associating Buffalo with torment, Sam hastily sold the house and his share of the newspaper.

After convalescing in Elmira, Livy and Sam bought a house in Hartford, Connecticut, and made it their primary residence. Hartford, then the most prosperous city in the nation, was well situated between Boston, the nation's literary capital, and New York City, the publishing capital. The Clemenses moved into a mansion in a tony, progressive community called Nook Farm. Harriet Beecher Stowe lived next door. Livy gave birth to three daughters on whom Sam doted. At last he had found a domestic paradise. The Clemenses lived lavishly, decorating their house opulently and employing many servants, but with Sam's literary successes and lecture tours, they seemed able to afford it. Fascinated by technology, Sam tried

Twain and his family moved into this mansion in Hartford, Connecticut, in 1871, shortly after his travelogue *The Innocents Abroad* became a bestseller. The lavishly furnished house reflected his and his wife's expensive tastes, as well as his financial mismanagement. Twain and most of the family moved out of the house in 1891; they finally sold it in 1903. (Library of Congress)

his hand at inventing, patenting three inventions, one of which—a self-pasting scrapbook in 1872—actually made him some money. Yet Sam was as restless as ever with his finances. He suspected that his publisher was cheating him out of royalties or at least failing to maximize the book's sales. Sam would later establish his own publishing company, another business move that ended in disaster.

By this time the nation had recovered from the devastation of the Civil War and had begun a true industrial revolution. The nation was building factories, machines, railroads, and all manner of goods at unprecedented rates. The frontier was rapidly moving west, as the federal government subsidized western development by giving away land to homesteaders and much more land to railroad companies. The spread of the railroads, which by now stretched all the way to the Pacific Ocean, was putting new cities and towns on the map. The intersection of big profits, American commercial ambitions, and increased government involvement created greater scope for corruption than ever before. Confidence swindles, speculative bubbles, and rash investments had existed before but not on this scale. Clemens dubbed the era "the gilded age" to represent the glossy, deceptive veneer of so many bad ventures and made it the title and theme of his first novel, cowritten with his friend William Dean Howells. (Ironically, the presidential administration most associated with the corruption was that of Twain's friend and favorite president, Ulysses S. Grant.) The novel's publication coincided with one of America's greatest financial crises, the Panic of 1873, which was perfect timing except that the ensuing economic slump, called "the great depression" at the time, cut into the book's sales.

Clemens made history as much as he lived it. Mark Twain, with his distinctive white suit, cigar, mustache, drawl, and endless quips, was perhaps the most famous man in America, at least after the publication of *Tom Sawyer* in 1876. Twain was not the first literary celebrity, but the term "celebrity" itself was fairly new, dating back to midcentury, and in America his only apparent predecessors were an Englishman, Charles Dickens, and a poet, Walt Whitman (Moran 2000, 16). In an age without radio, television, movies, or recordings, celebrities were fewer and generally less known than their counterparts today, which makes Twain's fame all the more exceptional. A recent book titled *100 Entertainers Who Changed America* (2013) includes only a handful from the 19th century and only two authors, Twain and Kurt Vonnegut. Twain was popular as an entertainer—a "humorist" whose lectures were like a cross between one-man shows and stand-up comedy—long before he received his due as a literary giant. His comical, dialect-heavy performances and prose drew on the minstrel shows that had enthralled Sam as a boy and had been America's most popular form of entertainment for much of the century. He chafed sometimes at being seen as "just" a humorist but otherwise seemed happy to market his image. He trademarked his pen name and allowed it to be used in brand names such as Great Mark Cigars, Mark Twain Cigars, and Mark Twain Flour (Ketcham 2001). Clemens granted perhaps more interviews than any other author of his era (Scharnhorst 2006, ix). He socialized with presidents, tycoons, and figures as diverse as P. T. Barnum and Frederick Douglass. Practically anything Clemens did in public was news.

Despite his success as an author and lecturer, Clemens remained a poor investor and money manager. He and Livy spent money practically as fast as he earned it. Rather than invest his money conservatively, he could not resist the temptation to put most of his eggs in highly speculative baskets. "Sam's reputation as a soft touch was . . . detectable by main-chance bloodhounds for hundreds of miles," wrote a biographer (Powers 2005, 451–452). For 14 years through 1894, Sam invested millions in the Paige Compositor, a mechanical typesetter that may have attracted him because of his own tedious work as a manual typesetter. The Paige Compositor had so many thousands of parts that it broke down easily and was hard to repair. During that time a competitor, the Linotype machine, demonstrated its superiority and gained widespread use. Twain also believed that he could capture more of the profits from his books if he had his own

This *Puck* magazine cartoon from 1885, subtitled "America's Best Humorist," is from shortly after Twain's wildly successful lecture tour for *Adventures of Huckleberry Finn*. Twain was a gifted performer whose lectures were more like one-man-shows. (Library of Congress)

publishing company. He marketed the books aggressively, having agents sell them door-to-door like encyclopedias, but finding capable managers for such a large-scale endeavor was difficult. His choice of his niece's husband, Charles Webster, worked out poorly. The company's initial successes with *Adventures of Huckleberry Finn* and the memoirs of Ulysses S. Grant may have made Clemens and Webster overconfident. They had a string of failures, notably a priest's biography of Pope Leo XIII. Clemens and Webster blamed each other for the company's ruin. In 1894 Clemens filed for bankruptcy. With the aid of a wealthy benefactor, Henry H. Rogers of Standard Oil, Clemens reorganized his finances and commenced a world lecture tour.

From the proceeds of the tour Clemens was able to repay his creditors in full, but his remaining years were hard. Susy, his eldest daughter, died in 1896. Olivia died in 1904. Jean, his youngest daughter, died in 1909. Clemens was decidedly less prolific, generating no novels of particular note and injecting even more cynicism and misanthropy into his stories and essays than before. Some of his cynicism reflected disenchantment with American politics and foreign policy. He had generally voted Republican, making an exception for Democrat Grover Cleveland, and backed William McKinley in 1896. Clemens had supported the Spanish-American War of 1898 as a noble attempt to assist the natives of Cuba, Puerto Rico, and the Philippines against Spanish colonialism, but he was appalled by America's prolonged occupation of those countries. He declared himself an anti-imperialist in 1900 and became an officer in the Anti-Imperialist League. "Progressive" Republican president Theodore Roosevelt, who presided over the suppression of the Philippine independence movement, earned some of Clemens's greatest scorn. He said that Roosevelt was the Tom Sawyer of American politics, which apparently was his way of saying that Roosevelt was callous and greedy for attention. Notably, Clemens's later works show considerably more compassion for marginalized groups such as Native Americans and blacks.

Virtually all of Clemens's works have historical content. His classic Mississippi River books—*Tom Sawyer, Life on the Mississippi, Huckleberry Finn,* and *Pudd'nhead Wilson*—paint a vivid picture of antebellum society and culture on the big river and in its towns. Those works and *The Gilded Age* also offer a window into the corruption and racial regression of the postemancipation era in which he wrote them. His most explicitly historical novels—*The Prince and the Pauper, A Connecticut Yankee in King Arthur's Court,* and the little-read *Joan of Arc*—tell us a little about the Middle Ages and even more about the progressive Enlightenment mindset, which Clemens clearly had imbued, with a love of technology and a deep disdain for slavery, monarchy, and religion. But Clemens's greatest history was his life. From a frontier boyhood to fame and fortune, from the bigotry of a slave society to condemnations of lynching and imperialism,

Twain in an iconic shot from May 1907. By this time the public was accustomed to this image of Twain, with his bushy mustache, mane of white hair, and light-colored clothing. He said light-colored clothing enlivened the spirit and was more pleasing to the eye. (Library of Congress)

from prospering with old steam-powered technology to bankrupting himself with speculation in new technology, and from his failed ventures in mining and publishing to the success of his world lecture tours, Sam Clemens lived an extraordinary yet quintessentially American life.

CHAPTER 2

∞

"The Raging, Tearing, Booming Nineteenth Century"

Mark Twain promised to punish anyone looking for a moral, motive, or plot in *Huckleberry Finn*. Scholars tend to feel the same way about American history, regarding the notion of a single all-encompassing narrative as an oversimplification. Yet there are several compelling themes that I would argue are indispensable to an understanding of 19th-century American history. *Adventures of Huckleberry Finn* and my annotations touch on these themes. This chapter makes them more explicit.

History rarely fits neatly with the calendar, so historians often speak of a "long 19th century" from 1789 to 1914—from the first year of the French Revolution and American life under the Constitution to the outbreak of World War I. Twain's life (1835–1910) straddles much of that epoch. *Huckleberry Finn* has an even longer reach, as Huck relates fractured accounts of King George III and the French Revolution, a con man in his party pretends to be descended from the guillotined French king, and Tom Sawyer takes his cues from historical romance novels set in feudal Europe. So, reading *Huckleberry Finn* as history will inevitably cover a lot of ground.

Different historians will emphasize different themes. As an economic historian I naturally gravitate toward economic themes, and the four I have identified for America's long 19th century are prosperity, expansion, inequality, and commercialism. Many other traits often associated with America—such as freedom, opportunity, and even disunion—can be considered their corollaries. None of them is unique to America, but 19th-century America arguably epitomized each of them more than any other leading country of the time. Sometimes they contradict each other, but American history is full of contradictions, as Walt Whitman says in his American epic "Song of Myself":

> Do I contradict myself?
> Very well then I contradict myself,
> (I am large, I contain multitudes.)

Those contradictions provide much of the drama that makes American history so exciting: slavery in a land of freedom, a racial caste system in a land where "all men are created equal," a constitution that has been a model for much of the world but could not enforce its own words on voting rights and equal protection, and a transportation and communication revolution that furthered national prosperity but inadvertently helped overthrow King Cotton, the longtime foundation of that prosperity.

PROSPERITY

Even before the American Revolution, the American colonies had one of the highest standards of living in the world. Although the colonies paid a high price for their independence, losing much of their prosperity during the war and the chaotic decade that followed, the new American republic was still among the world's richer nations and grew rapidly after 1790. By 1820, American per capita income had edged ahead of Britain's (Lindert and Williamson 2013, 727, 749–752; Johnston and Williamson 2015; S. Williamson 2015). The story of the American economy in the 19th century is one of a rich country growing richer still and also growing a whole lot bigger through massive increases in labor, physical capital, and land. America did not become the world's largest economy until late in the 19th century (and that expansion is the focus of the next section), but its high standard of living has deep roots.

These roots are so deep as to predate British settlement. Native American tribes had been inhabiting, adapting to, and migrating across North America for thousands of years before the first European colonists arrived. By the time British settlers arrived in the early 17th century, American Indians had cleared and settled a good portion of the eastern lands where the colonists would live, had learned the lay of the land, and had domesticated native crops. The agricultural economies of the Indians did much to pave the way for the prosperity of early colonial agriculture. Somewhat ghoulishly, the colonists benefited from plagues that killed many if not most of the Indians before the colonists even arrived, thereby gifting the colonists with vast amounts of precleared land and minimizing Indian resistance to colonial settlement and expansion. But there is much more to colonial-Indian relations than simply the dispossession of the Indians' land; the surviving Indians taught the colonists much about American agriculture and geography and traded with them.

By the end of the colonial era and probably fairly early in it, the colonists had a standard of living that rivaled or surpassed those of the

European nations. According to some recent estimates, per capita income was higher in the colonies than in Britain as early as 1650 (J. Williamson 2015). Abundant land arguably preceded all other factors. "Plenty of land" made America a land of plenty at a time when farming was by far the dominant occupation (Henriques 2015). Landownership was the path to freedom and prosperity, and colonial America offered many the opportunity to own one's farm and in particular a much larger farm than was available in densely populated Europe; 75 or more acres were the norm in most colonies (Perkins 1980, 146–147). The land was blessed with fertile soil and bountiful supplies of timber. It ranged over three distinct climatic zones, including a middle region that was ideal for grains and livestock and a southern region suitable for cash crops such as tobacco, sugar, and (later) cotton. Fish and game were plentiful as well. The flip side of abundant land was scarce labor, which meant high wages. Skilled workers in the cities were able to command higher wages than they could have in Europe. Navigable rivers, especially in the South, and a long coastline facilitated trade and allowed for efficient specialization in production. On the eve of the American Revolution all along the income distribution except at the very top, free white colonists had higher incomes than their English counterparts (Lindert and Williamson 2013, 758).

Economic historians have credited American prosperity to resourceful people as well as abundant resources. Generally speaking, colonial America's British settlers were a self-selected population of ambitious, hardworking immigrants willing to assume the risk of the transatlantic voyage and relocation in exchange for the riches they hoped to find. Although this description obviously does not fit the slaves who would come to make up one-fifth of the colonial population on the eve of the American Revolution, it does describe the overwhelming majority of indentured servants, who were roughly half of the white immigrants to the colonies. The servants assumed tremendous risk, as many did not even survive the voyage or their term of indenture and sacrificed several years of their freedom for long-term opportunity in America. Upon finishing their term of service, they typically received land or freedom dues to start their own farm or artisan shop. The entrepreneurial spirit of the colonists was remarkable, especially for a preindustrial society composed mostly of farmers. Colonists were saving money and taking on various economic risks in the hope of economic advancement: investing in new capital, buying new land and livestock, and generally dealing with markets a good deal more than in a traditional farm society. The abundance of land, notably on the western frontier, created considerable upward mobility such that even young "common" unskilled laborers could look forward to owning land (Perkins 1989).

The colonists, unlike their fellow British citizens across the Atlantic, could enjoy more of the fruits of their labor and spend less time in military service because they received virtually free military protection from Britain. Prior to the end of the Seven Years' War in 1763, the American colonists were among the most lightly taxed people in the world, whereas the British were among the most heavily taxed (Perkins 1980, 123, 129). The colonies did not have a global empire to maintain and did not participate in Britain's costly imperial wars. The nearest exception was the North American theater of the Seven Years' War, also known as the French and Indian War. The British and American victory in this war removed the French as an imperial threat to the colonies, apparently reducing colonial defense costs and paving the way for faster westward expansion. When the British sought to restrict westward expansion so as to avoid costly conflicts with Indians and attempted to tax the colonists to help pay for the policing of the frontier and therefore aid that restriction, the stage for revolt was set.

After more than 35 years of wars, political crises, and post–Revolutionary War chaos, the United States of America finally stabilized itself by the early 1790s with a constitution and early legislation that unified the states economically into a free trade zone with a single currency and minimal government interference. America's lack of imperial rivalries put the country in an excellent position to trade with Britain, France, and all the leading powers of Europe. American exports and imports soared, and the new republic reached new heights of prosperity. Eli Whitney's invention of the cotton gin in 1793 put the new nation on a path to cotton-driven prosperity, with the South becoming increasingly specialized in this profitable cash crop. Cotton dominated U.S. exports, and cheap southern cotton provided the raw material for northern textile factories, kicking off American industrialization.

Much of the growth in American prosperity reflected that industrialization. Just as Alexander Hamilton had hoped, much of the country moved, albeit gradually, from agriculture to the higher-earning manufacturing sector. America was late to the industrial revolution, which had begun in Europe around 1750, but the late start meant that the nation could play an exceptionally rapid game of catch-up. In some cases, American industrialists could simply copy the technology of the British industrial leaders, as Samuel Slater and Francis Cabot Lowell did in textiles; in other cases, they could adapt European breakthroughs for the American environment, as Oliver Evans did with the steam engine. Strategic use of tariffs helped America's infant textile industry become competitive with European textiles, and American industrialization in general got a unlikely kick start from President Thomas Jefferson, who in 1807 imposed a trade embargo on Britain, France, and other warring nations of Europe in response to their interference with American merchant ships. The embargo and then the War of 1812 effectively forced America to start producing its own goods. After the war, America went back to being open to foreign trade and investment. Much of the money for American investment in canals, railroads, and industry came from British and other European lenders.

The great inventions in canals, steamboats, and railroads that constituted the 19th-century transportation revolution were by no means confined to America, but no country was in a better position to capitalize on those transportation improvements. The boundaries of the original nation stretched all the way west to the Mississippi River, but land transportation was so expensive that most people lived along the East Coast, and almost nobody settled west of the Appalachian Mountains. Thus, most of the original U.S. territory was unutilized or barely utilized by the new nation. The Louisiana Purchase of 1803 doubled the size of the nation, but getting to the new territory was almost prohibitively costly. Even the Mississippi River, to which Americans now had unfettered access, was extremely expensive to travel upstream. With water transportation still the key to America's internal and external trade, the advent of the commercial steamboat in 1807 could hardly have been more timely. Steamboats drastically reduced upriver transportation costs and made settlement of inland areas near major rivers feasible. The completion of the Erie Canal in 1825 extended inland trade and settlement in the North, and before long all five of the Great Lakes were connected to the Atlantic Ocean. Northern and midwestern settlement and production boomed.

Even before the railroads, a true transportation revolution had taken place, allowing Americans to utilize most of what is now the eastern half of the continental United States. The Mississippi River had already been important, but the steamboat turned it into the nation's greatest economic thoroughfare and generated all kinds of economic activity in the nearby lands. Upriver transportation costs continued to fall as steamboats became more efficient, increasing their productivity (output per unit of input) on the Mississippi by an average of almost 4 percent per year from 1815 to 1860, a faster rate of growth than even railroads or canals managed over a long span. Upriver freight rates in the same span fell by 95 percent (Haites, Mak, and Walton 1975, 183–184; Atack and Passell 1994, 158). Former senator James Lanman said in 1841, "Steam navigation colonized the West!" Canals, dramatically cheaper than the alternative of horses and wagons, accomplished much the same thing for the Mid-Atlantic region, the North, and the Midwest (then the Northwest). All of this meant that a national market was now possible. As shipping costs plunged, non–locally produced goods became cheaper, so consumers had access to higher-quality, lower-cost goods from all over. The waterborne transportation revolution also allowed agriculture to expand into fertile areas such as the Midwest and especially the cotton Southwest, which had the best cotton yields and eventually the wealthiest cotton planters. Industry could expand into new cities where it was cheaper to build large factories and house the workforce. The country's natural resources, including iron and coal, were

This Currier and Ives print, although published after the Civil War, indicates the prosperity of the antebellum southwest. Prior to the Civil War and the rise of big business, the richest Americans tended to be cotton plantation owners with easy access to America's great freight highway, the Mississippi River. (Library of Congress)

now easier to access and ship to the companies and cities that demanded them.

Other than transportation, manufacturing was the nation's most dynamic sector even before the Civil War, when it was still small both in total and as regards the size of firms. Productivity growth in manufacturing averaged a remarkable 2 percent per year from 1820 to 1860; since this growth is exponential, this means that a factory in 1860 with the *same* amount of labor, capital, materials, and land could produce more than twice as much output as a factory in 1820. America was awash in small factories, with about 120,000 in 1860. Paper, furniture, woodwork, and textiles showed especially strong productivity growth. The growth of manufacturing helped agricultural productivity too, especially in the North with new technology such as the mechanical reaper. Southern agriculture remained labor-intensive but also saw a rapid rise in productivity, thanks to moving to more fertile land in the West and the development of new cotton varieties (Olmstead and Rhode 2008). Manufacturing was a strong growth sector and, with a rapidly growing domestic market, was poised for takeoff. More so than in any other country at midcentury, a very large portion of total U.S. manufacturing was capital goods—that is, tools and machinery to be used by *other* manufacturers. The "machine tool" industry originated in America, and American manufacturing was notably more mechanized than British manufacturing (Atack and Passell 1994, 201–205). With the new telegraph creating an information revolution that connected the country like never before and the new railroads raising the possibility of cheap shipping to every corner of the nation, a new era of superproductive manufacturing firms that could supply the whole nation at low cost was at hand.

America's 19th-century transportation revolution and prosperity are commonly associated with the railroads. Economic historians generally regard the railroads as the most important contributor to that century's growth but do not regard it as indispensable (Whaples 1995, 143, 149). Railroads were cheaper to construct and ship freight on than canals, but canals and steamboats had already lowered transportation costs dramatically, and the economy had grown mightily without the railroad. Even the so-called forty-niners of the California Gold Rush had gotten there largely without the aid of railroads. But railroads clearly were the future, and their contributions were massive. A telling pair of statistics is that at midcentury boats still carried six times as much freight as the railroads, but there were well over twice as many miles of railroad tracks as there were miles of canals. Railroads were famously "built ahead of demand." And the demand was certainly there after the Civil War; from 1865 to 1900, railroad passenger traffic grew 500 percent, and railroad freight traffic grew 6,000 percent. The other greatest midcentury innovation, the telegraph, had a symbiotic relationship with the railroads, as telegraph lines were built along railroad lines and vice versa. The telegraph enabled better coordination and safety on the railroads, and the trains shipped newspapers whose coverage and timeliness had improved dramatically thanks to telegraphic transmission of information. The railroads and telegraph facilitated the rise of American stock exchanges, where railroad company stocks were by far the biggest. The railroads were not only cheaper than canals but could be run all year long and into areas with no nearby water sources. Railroads were also the nation's first big businesses, and as such they aided America's postwar mass production not only in enabling things to be shipped more cheaply and to more places but also in providing the new industries with a wealth of engineering and organizational experience. Andrew Carnegie was among those who got his start in the railroads.

In many ways cotton slavery had been the linchpin of American prosperity through 1860. Yet although it had directly enriched southern plantation owners and indirectly enriched northern textile industrialists, bankers, and shipping merchants, King Cotton was not enough to hold the North and South together. The Civil War, like the American Revolution, damaged American prosperity. (Economic historians generally regard the commonplace observation that wars are good for the economy as a myth.) The deaths of over 620,000 Americans gutted the labor force; much of the

South's capital stock, farmland, and livestock was destroyed; rapid war-time inflation in the North caused the purchasing power of wages to fall; and hyperinflation in the South reduced the region to barter. For a decade and a half after the war, the North and the South experienced "regional divergence." The North's economy entered a new era of spectacular indus-try-led growth, while the South remained rural and grew more slowly. Comparisons of the southern economy before and after emancipation are in any event difficult. Once free, African Americans no longer had to work from sunup to sundown and could set their own hours just as whites did; in particular, women and children no longer had to work all day in the fields. The free blacks worked about one-third less than they did as slaves, a decision that surely enhanced their well-being but would have reduced total output and made it appear that living standards had fallen (Ransom and Sutch 2001, 46). An unequivocal problem for the South was the lower price of cotton. In a sense the war had overthrown King Cotton by forcing Europe to look elsewhere for cotton and aiding the emergence of India, Brazil, and Egypt as major cotton producers, causing the world price to fall. The South continued to produce more and more cotton, to the point of overproduction (Atack and Passell 1994, 377, 381). Surprisingly, the South grew just as fast as the North from 1880 to 1900, partly because tariffs were lower in that period (Higgs 1971, 108, 114; Hummel 1996, 342); still, it was from a much lower base. By 1880 the North was much richer and had become the main driver of the nation's prosperity.

The years from 1865 to 1914 are often called America's industrial revolution, the age of mass production, the age of enterprise, and the rob-ber baron era. It is obvious that American industry, retailing, and finance got much bigger and that a few people became astoundingly rich during this time, but since the focus of the section is the *nation's* prosperity, we will start with gross domestic product (GDP) per person. From 1870 to 1920 GDP per person more than doubled, growing at an average rate of 1.7 percent per year, faster than ever before in U.S. history (Carter et al. 2006, 3:5). What accounts for the country's postwar prosperity? Part of it was simply the continuing shift from agriculture to manufacturing. In 1869 agriculture still accounted for more than half of U.S. commodity output; by 1890 manufacturing was the largest sector of the economy. Manufac-turing was not only expanding but was making extraordinary gains in ef-ficiency. New industries, such as steel, petroleum, chemicals, and later automobiles, had entered the picture. The spread of the railroads to practi-cally every corner of the nation made America's mineral and agricultural resources more accessible to the factories and gave the factories a huge national market for their goods. The national market was bolstered by fur-ther waves of immigration, which also provided the necessary labor for industry to produce at a vast scale. Profits and profit opportunities soared, and American entrepreneurs responded. The period saw the rise of the inventor-entrepreneur, epitomized by Thomas Edison, as the number of patents skyrocketed and technology made great advances (Lamoreaux 2010, 367–368, 391). Industry expanded to untold heights and became more concentrated, including the formation of near monopolies and trusts in many industries. Yet prices fell, thanks mainly to the improved technology and cheaper costs associated with mass production. While not all Americans shared in the nation's bounty, the American standard of living was higher than world history had ever known. The real (inflation-adjusted) wages of factory workers grew roughly as fast as per capita GDP, averaging 1.6 percent growth per year, with total growth of 121 percent, from 1865 to 1914 (Miller and Sexton 2005, 175; Licht 1995, 183).

EXPANSION

At the time of George Washington's inauguration in 1789, the United States consisted of 13 predominantly rural colonies-turned-states with a small population concentrated on the East Coast. By 1900 the United States had not just the richest economy but also by far the largest. Combine the world's third-largest population with the highest standard of living, and that's what you get. Some contributions to that high standard of living, as noted in the previous section, were abundant land (America was the third-largest country in the world in terms of land), the world's best technology, and the world's largest stock of industrial capital (machinery, tools, and other means of production). The nation grew at an astounding rate. American growth is perhaps best seen through a comparison with Great Britain, the world's leading economy in 1800. The U.S. economy was one-sixth the size of Britain's in 1800, one-third in 1860, and two-thirds in 1880 and zoomed past it in the next two decades. In 1900 the U.S. economy was 125 percent as large as Britain's, and in 1913 it was more than twice as large (Morris 2006, 272). Economists decompose the sources of economic production and growth into land, labor, materials, and capital. Let us look at each of those factors in turn.

Although early America had fairly little settlement beyond the East Coast, Americans had been looking west for a long time. Several of the original colonies, notably Virginia and Massachusetts, claimed land all the way to the Mississippi River. The western lands were inhabited, of course, by Native American tribes, but the natives' ability to defend those lands was limited. Many transfers in fact took place peacefully. As historian Eric Foner notes, "Especially after epidemics caused by contact with European diseases led to a disastrous population decline, Indians owned more land than they could possibly use, so selling some of it made sense" (2006, 17). Meanwhile, the very rapid population growth in the colonies and then in the United States created enormous pressure for westward expansion into Indian lands. In the colonial era the pace of westward movement was gradual because of the prohibitively high cost of overland travel and also Britain's reluctance, as an imperial power with many costly entanglements, to get drawn into costly, drawn-out conflicts with the Indians. The British had supported their American colonies' encroachments onto Indian territory only up to a point and much less so than many colonists would have liked. In the case of Bacon's Rebellion in 1676, for example, a colonist named Nathaniel Bacon led an insurrection against the Virginia colonial government over its unwillingness to provide military support for Bacon and his band of warrior-settlers. When the Seven Years' War ended in 1763, a treaty restricted colonial American settlement beyond a proclamation line. Many Americans ignored the line, including land speculators such as George Washington, while others fumed that Britain was hemming the colonies in. Economic historian Marc Egnal (1988) has identified an "expansionist" ideology that took hold among many colonial and future revolutionary leaders. The expansionists believed that the colonies were destined to expand all the way west, with or without Britain. The Quebec Act of 1774, which enlarged the British province of Quebec to the west and the south to placate the French Canadians still living in those areas, outraged the expansionists, even though virtually no colonists lived there. Although expansionism was not the sole cause of the American Revolutionary War, the new American government was far more committed to westward expansion and far less inclined to avoid conflict with Indians than the British had been. (Indian tribes, sensing that they would get a better deal from the British, tended to fight on the British side of both the Revolution and the War of 1812.)

In the 19th century expansionism received a fancier name: manifest destiny. Federal policy proceeded as if it were God's will that the United States should occupy all the land stretching from the original colonies to the Pacific. Early in the century Thomas Jefferson purchased the Louisiana Territory from a cash-strapped Napoleon for the United States, doubling the size of the United States, or rather extending the nation's claims to the continent. (The Indian tribes that inhabited that territory had claimed the land much earlier.) America's invasion of Spanish Florida in the First Seminole War of 1817–1818 resulted in Spain's cession of Florida to the United States. American expansion over the next quarter century was mostly a matter of peopling in the land that America had already claimed, including the vast area west of the Appalachians. Northerners and many immigrants headed for the Midwest, which was now linked to the Atlantic Ocean and the Great Lakes by means of canals, and southerners moved west to the nation's best cotton-growing country with the aid of steamboats that could easily travel upriver. Much of this expansion was assisted by the U.S. government's deliberate expulsion of key eastern Indian tribes from their land. The 1830s, which began with the Indian Removal Act and ended with the Trail of Tears, epitomized this policy, as did the president for most of that decade, the veteran Indian fighter Andrew Jackson.

This 1872 painting by John Gast depicts several aspects of American westward expansion. The religious overtones of "manifest destiny" are evident in the goddess who glides over the settlers. On the ground we see all forms of transportation, from covered wagons to trains, as well as Native Americans being driven even farther west. (Library of Congress)

Spain's experience with Florida would be echoed in Mexico's attempts to hold on to Texas and its entire holdings in the American Southwest. In all three cases a sparse population was outnumbered and overrun by acquisitive, ambitious Americans. Spain had lacked the resources to defend its Florida colonies, and the American government, arguing that Florida had become a haven for escaped slaves and a base for Seminole attacks, invaded and quickly wrested the territory for itself. Mexico won its independence from Spain in 1821 but was far too weak a country to have much of a chance against an expanding United States that wanted much of its land. Mexico's abolition of slavery in 1829 was laudable but did not help its chances with the American settlers who had moved with their slaves into the prime cotton-growing country of Texas. Mexico closed Texas off to further U.S. immigration in 1830, another measure that was widely flouted. Americans in Texas declared independence in 1835 and successfully fought for it, becoming an independent republic but seeking to be part of the United States. The United States under President James K. Polk annexed Texas in 1845 and provoked a war with Mexico. The war was a smashing military success for the United States; it was over in 21 months with under 14,000 U.S. deaths and resulted in the acquisition of what is now California, Arizona, New Mexico, Nevada, Utah, and Colorado. (At the same time the Polk administration acquired what is now Washington, Oregon, Idaho, and parts of Montana and Wyoming through a treaty with Britain.) While the war was a great victory for expansionism, the victory deepened the conflict between free-soil expansionists, who did not own slaves and did not want to compete with slave plantations for land or jobs, and slaveholding expansionists.

The Mexican War was also significant for how it changed the nature of American expansion as regarded Native Americans. Indian resistance had been a significant obstacle to American expansion in the early decades of the republic; just as British authorities had avoided unnecessary conflicts with Indians in colonial times, President Jefferson said that "an Indian war was too serious a thing, to risk incurring one merely to gratify a few intruders with settlements" (qtd. in Anderson and McChesney 1999, 211). The Mexican-American War, and later the Civil War, left America with a much-enlarged standing army that could more easily defeat Indian warriors on the battlefield. In every decade of the first half century of the nation's existence, there were more U.S.-Indian treaties than battles. Even in the Trail of Tears decade of the 1830s, treaties outnumbered battles by 84 to 63. To be sure, many of these treaties had involved unrepresentative factions of tribes, were signed under duress, or were not fairly implemented, but at least on paper they allotted significant land for the tribes and slowed the pace of American expansion (Perdue and Green 2010, 42–43, 55–60). In every decade from the 1840s through the end of the century, however, battles outnumbered treaties. In the 1840s and 1850s, battles outnumbered treaties 243 to 76. In the 1860s, it was 786 to 61. From 1870 through 1897, it was 674 to 0 (Anderson and McChesney 1999, 211–215). Together with the lack of Indian resistance, the transportation revolution and rapid population growth ensured that Americans would not hesitate to populate and use all this land.

America had established an empire entirely on its own continent, a vast nation that stretched from the Atlantic Ocean to the Pacific. But the nation was not done expanding. The Guano Islands Act of 1856 authorized the country to annex any of the dozens of uninhabited, unclaimed fertilizer-rich islands in an area of the Pacific southwest of Hawaii. The first annexations began in 1857, and 94 had been annexed by 1903. Alaska was purchased from Russia shortly after the Civil War and became economically important to the United States three decades later, when the Klondike Gold Rush began in 1897. The Samoan island of Tutuila, in the South Pacific, became a U.S. naval base. Hawaii, long before its U.S. annexation in 1898, resembled a U.S. colony as early as the 1860s, when most of the plantations, whaling ships, and merchant ships were owned by Americans.

Finally, U.S. entry into a war with Spain in 1898 over its intervention in Cuba and the Philippines left America in possession of the Philippines, a custody that it did not relinquish until the 1930s; the nearby island of Guam, which remains a U.S. naval base; and Puerto Rico. The commercially vital Panama Canal Zone became a de facto U.S. holding, as the United States wrote itself a perpetual lease and obtained ratification in 1904 from Panama, a new republic whose secession from Colombia had received U.S. military support. Most of the remaining countries in the Caribbean had become U.S. protectorates by 1910, with governments that were friendly to U.S. business interests (Nugent 2009, 240, 249–268, 273, 281, 286, 293–294).

Compared with America's territorial expansion, the expansion of its population and workforce is simple to grasp. The country went from just under 4 million people in its first census year, 1790, to almost 92 million in 1910. To put these numbers into perspective, consider that if the U.S. population had grown as fast after 1910 as it did before, the U.S. population today (in 2015) would be almost 1.5 billion, larger than that of India or China. Instead, the current U.S. population is about 321 million. Population growth over the past century has not come close to 19th-century rates and has been particularly slow in recent decades, averaging just under 1 percent per year. Two factors stand out in regard to America's astounding population growth in 1790–1910: rapid immigration and a high rate of natural increase.

America had been an attractive place for ambitious Europeans dating back to the colonial era, to the point that roughly half of white immigrants to the colonies had been willing to sell themselves into several years of indentured servitude in order to pay for their transatlantic voyage to America. (About 10 percent of the indentured servants came not of their own volition but as expelled convicts.) As voyage costs fell, more and more Europeans could afford to pay for their own trip, and indentured servitude all but died out. But white immigration before the 1830s was modest, and the great waves of immigration did not begin until about 1845. More notable was the spike in slave imports in the 15 years from the invention of the cotton gin to the ban of the transatlantic slave trade. As repugnant as the slave system was, slaves in the American South, compared with slaves in the tropics, stayed remarkably healthy, with low mortality rates and high birth rates. Just as had been true during colonial times even before the ban on further slave imports, slaves were valuable chattel, and planters had every incentive to encourage their slaves to marry and raise the next generation of slave laborers. In the South the slave population actually grew slightly faster (2.6 percent per year) in 1800–1860 than the free population did. On the eve of the Civil War, slaves were more than a third of the southern population and more than half the population in two states (South Carolina and Mississippi).

White Americans also had a remarkable rate of natural increase, coupled with high immigration from Europe. (Not all European immigrants were initially accepted as white, however; the nativist backlash to the new Americans is discussed in the next section.) Although the century's trend was toward urbanization, most of the population still lived in rural areas or small towns with considerable elbow room, with the result that communicable diseases were easier to avoid. Food was cheap and plentiful, and nutritious protein-rich diets were common. Infant and child mortality rates were low, family sizes were large, and life expectancy was high. Immigrants accounted for much of the population increase in the North. The Irish Potato Famine and the repression that followed the failed German revolutions in the 1840s kicked off the first big wave of immigration. The next big wave was in the decade after the Civil War; Irish and Germans continued to come over in large numbers, as did Scandinavians and English (Dinnerstein and Reimers 1999, 18–19). Religious and political persecution often motivated Europeans to immigrate, but more often economic distress was the key factor. The late 19th century was a great age of international migration, and immigrants sought opportunities in many countries including Canada and Australia, but by far the largest number went to the United States. Economic opportunity in the United States appears to have been the main draw. Another factor was the lack of restrictions on immigration. Prior to World War I, the nation's only immigration restrictions pertained to contract laborers, prostitutes, convicts, various undesirables, and East Asians (Dinnerstein and Reimers 1999, 222). Falling voyage costs, economic depression in Europe, and the availability of relatively high-wage factory work in American cities touched off even bigger waves of immigration in the late 19th and early 20th centuries. Nearly 9 million immigrants came to America in the first decade of the 1900s, an all-time record that was nearly as high as the previous two decades combined. The new immigrants came largely from Italy, Austria-Hungary, Russia, and the Baltic States.

In relating this massive population increase to a similarly massive increase in the labor force and American output, we can think of three great migrations in the long 19th century: to America, to the cities, and westward. Many made all three of these migrations at once, as with immigrants who took a steamship across the Atlantic and immediately headed to Chicago or another city in the industrial heartland in search of factory work. Immigrants tended to be young unmarried males seeking work. Not all of them intended to stay or ended up staying, but their labor was vital to American expansion. These migrations were greatly facilitated by the transportation revolution, including improvements in ocean steamship technology and productivity that allowed for cheaper, faster voyages. Railroads and canals made it easier than ever before for people to choose where they wanted to live. Many midwestern and western states, along with the railroads that owned much of the land in those states, worked tire-lessly to entice immigrants, sometimes even sending agents to Europe to recruit them (Dinnerstein and Reimers 1999, 27–28).

The transportation revolution, especially the railroads, did much to facilitate the flow of material and physical capital to America's great industrial plants. As transport costs fell, firms had more choices about where to locate their plants and could build at the most efficient scale, however big that might be, knowing that they could ship all over the nation and the world. To a greater degree than in Europe, American firms had often purchased tools and machines from other firms. Now this could done on a much larger scale, with heavy machinery being produced in one state and shipped to another. Setting up new factories, expanding existing ones, and even relocating became easier than ever before. Likewise, producers were better able to tap into America's bounty of minerals and other natural resources. With access to oil fields and coal deposits in Pennsylvania, iron ore ranges along the Great Lakes, copper in Michigan and Montana, zinc and lead from various states, and a host of other minerals, American manufacturers resourcefully made extensive use of these cheap American resources and gave themselves a leg up on their foreign competition. Many of the new industries and products, such as steel and automobiles, drew heavily on natural resources that America had always possessed (Wright 1990). The increasingly huge scale of American manufacturing and the concomitant opportunity for big profits continued to stimulate the invention of new machinery and the development of new factories. So did America's comparatively high wages, which provided an incentive for companies to mechanize their operations further.

INEQUALITY

One of the great paradoxes of America for most of its history is that it is the land of opportunity but also a land of profound inequality. Much of that inequality simply reflects the vast scale of operations in America that generated some of the world's biggest fortunes, including the land-based riches of the Astors and the shipping-based riches of the Girards early on and moving into the stratosphere with the rise of big business and big finance in the late 19th century, as led by such magnates as John D. Rockefeller, Andrew Carnegie, J. P. Morgan, Cornelius Vanderbilt, and Jay Gould. Yet American inequality runs much deeper than "the rich getting richer." On the eve of the American Revolution, colonial America had greater income equality than anyplace else in the world (J. Williamson 2015), but the source of much of that equality and opportunity—the frontier—was largely a by-product of plagues, military defeats, and dubious treaties that pushed the land's original inhabitants out of the picture. One-fifth of the pre-Revolution population was black slaves, whose contributions to American prosperity and expansion were monumental but who obviously lacked basic rights and saw little of the fruits of that prosperity. Women shared in their families' economic gains but, once married, had few economic freedoms. Middle- and upper-class married women were expected to stop working outside the home. Although Yankee farm girls had comprised most of the workforce at the pioneering New England textile mills, the mill owners wasted little time in replacing them with Irish immigrants in the 1840s. Until midcentury—or later in many states—married women had no legal right to own property independently, keep their earnings, or do business at all without the consent of their husbands (Khan 2005, 167–168). Had women had the right to vote, serve on juries, or practice law, greater economic liberty might have come sooner. Economic prosperity, expansion, and opportunity in America were such that American exceptionalism was real, but so were the American exceptions, who constituted a majority of the population.

Even among white males, prosperity and growth bypassed many. Although late colonial America had more economic equality that anywhere in Europe, the conditions that made that possible—the frontier and America's relatively more rural, agricultural economy—would not last through the 19th century. America's urbanization and industrialization were slow but strong in the first six decades of the century and blisteringly rapid in the half century after the Civil War. The 1890 census reported that a "frontier line" no longer existed, and an endlessly quoted historical essay three years later bemoaned the "closing" of the frontier. By the late 19th century the rural frontier held little promise anyway, as farmers were visibly and vocally in distress over fluctuating prices, being at the mercy of railroads and banks, and the marginal farmland that remained. By the Civil War inequality had returned to European levels, and thereafter it steadily moved past them (J. Williamson 2015). Economic historians have long noted the "antebellum puzzle" of rapid per capita income growth at the same time, 1830–1860, that life expectancies and average heights were declining. Urbanization and increased ease of transportation were good for American incomes but not so good for American health (Haines, Craig, and Weiss 2003, 382). The early urban factory workers and the canal, steamboat, and railroad workers likely bore the brunt of those by-products of economic progress.

The Civil War was surely good for munitions producers and other military contractors, but factory workers saw their wage gains eroded by rampant wartime inflation, with the result that the purchasing power of their earnings actually fell. The human costs of war fell much more severely on poor and middle-class Americans as well. Despite the draft, wealthier Americans could avoid Union service by paying $300 (about $6,000 in today's money) for a substitute. The Confederacy's "twenty-nigger rule" allowed plantations with at least 20 slaves to leave someone behind, typically the master of the house, to keep order. The war's casualties were astounding: an estimated 800,000 dead (620,000 counted soldiers plus at least 130,000 uncounted soldiers and 50,000 civilians, mostly southern) (Hacker 2011; McPherson 1988, 619n53); nearly 500,000 injured, not counting cases of post-traumatic stress disorder; and perhaps 400,000 missing.

The half century after the Civil War would seem on the surface to have been a good one for American factory workers, who were paid more than their European counterparts and saw their inflation-adjusted wages more than double, yet the large amount of strikes and union activity suggests some grounds for dissatisfaction. To begin with, their wages, although high compared with Europe, appear to have been too low to support a decent standard of living. According to historian Walter Licht, "For the great majority of working people . . . the late nineteenth century was a time of just making ends meet." Typical working-class families lived in crowded, dismal tenements in cheap apartment buildings that were often firetraps. For necessary extra income they often overcrowded their apartments further by taking in boarders and depended on the labor of their children, who often had to drop out of school (Licht 1995, 184). Adequate urban public sanitation was sorely lacking for much of this time. "Whole neighborhoods were filthy, foul smelling, and overcrowded" (Dinnerstein and Reimers 1999, 62). Workdays and workweeks were long, with 12-hour days and 60-hour weeks not uncommon. Factories were frequently unsafe, with accidents assumed to be the fault of workers; worker's compensation laws were rare at the state level and nonexistent at the federal level. As the scale of industry grew and the era's industrial magnates became rich beyond comprehension, workers naturally figured that money could be found to improve their wages and working conditions.

Industrialization, urbanization, and mass immigration also brought a new phenomenon: mass unemployment. While farmers were subject to economic fluctuations, they could still feed and house themselves in hard times. Industrial laborers who could not find work had no means of support. A large fraction, perhaps one-third, of the immigrants who came to America (and other countries) during this time eventually returned home (Nugent 1995, 35). Some had not intended to stay, preferring to accumulate some savings and bring them back home, but others were disappointed by the working and living conditions in America. This was particularly true during economic depressions, which had become more common and more severe than before. Although immigration generally fell sharply during economic slumps, perfect coordination between the choice to immigrate and the availability of work in America was not possible. In fact, 1907, the year that set the all-time record total for immigration to America, was also the year of one of the nation's most infamous financial panics. Nonfarm unemployment was generally high even in good times. In the

THE PROTECTORS OF OUR INDUSTRIES.

This 1889 cartoon from *Puck* magazine shows four great capitalists of the day sitting on bags of money on a raft held up by underpaid laborers. While American laborers actually earned higher wages than their European counterparts, wages were still low. (Library of Congress)

period from 1897 to 1905, after the depression of the 1890s and before the Panic of 1907, a period of remarkably rapid and steady industrial growth, the nonfarm unemployment rate averaged well over 10 percent (roughly double its 2015 level) with little downward trend. Production quickly recovered after the 1907 recession, but nonfarm unemployment remained high, averaging over 12 percent from 1908 through 1915 (U.S. Department of Commerce 1975, D10, D86).

The immigrants who stayed in America typically managed to improve their economic lot, but discrimination against them was common and severe. The first wave of Irish was regularly portrayed as apelike shanty dwellers, and Catholics were the prime target of nativist groups, including the "Know-Nothing" political party. Chinese immigrants in California brought a violent backlash and the only American immigration law that specifically restricted a particular nationality, the Chinese Exclusion Act of 1882. Similar resistance to Japanese immigrants in California led to the Gentlemen's Agreement of 1907, in which Japan agreed to limit exit visas to the United States. Like their Irish predecessors, the southern and eastern Europeans who came over in the late 19th and early 20th centuries were not considered "white" and incurred a racist backlash that led to general immigration restrictions based on "national origins" shortly after World War I. Of the new immigrants, Jews faced the most intense discrimination, notably in housing and employment, but discrimination against Slavs and Italians was pervasive as well (Dinnerstein and Reimers 1999, 56, 78–82).

Outside of the cities, the farm sector was not quite the bastion of equality that one might imagine. Although the opportunity to start one's own farm on the frontier was the essence of early American equality, that opportunity became somewhat less meaningful over time, at least for poor and middle-class people. Despite the nation's vast unsettled landholdings, easily accessible unclaimed fertile frontier land had become hard to come by. The federal government, after a classic Jefferson-Hamilton debate over how to dispose of its massive landholdings, rejected Jefferson's plan to give them away to settlers in favor of Hamilton's plan to sell them. Poor and middle-class individuals, had they attempted to buy available land, would generally have been outbid. A substantial portion of the nation's farmland was owned by landlords or speculators and cultivated by tenant farmers in a situation that somewhat resembled European serfdom. New York state, for example, had almost as many tenant farmers as farm freeholders in 1821, and tenant farming had become common in much of the nation by 1860 (Gates 1960, 36, 96). Prospective frontier farmers still had the option to squat on newly owned unsettled land, to which they could obtain title if they made sufficient improvements, but that required a considerable and time-consuming investment in clearing and planting the land, building a dwelling, and defending the homestead against Indians and rival squatters. Homesteaders often called these early years their "starving times," and many finally gave up. Even after the federal government passed the Homestead Act to give away land to prospective farmers, two-thirds of the homesteaders before 1890 failed to improve the land sufficiently to earn title to it (Anderson and Hill 1993, 110–111). Many struggling homesteaders ended up as tenant farmers. Not surprisingly, tenant farms made less money than owner-occupied farms, only half as much in 1860. One out of every four farmers in America was a tenant in 1880, even before the acute agrarian distress and populist revolt of the late 19th century (Atack and Passell 1994, 295, 408–409). Those late decades were particularly hard on farmers in general due to volatile crop prices and yields, railroad and storage charges, and mortgage debt. Although farm incomes held their own on average during that period, so many farmers fared poorly that several agrarian protest organizations formed and eventually produced an important third party, the People's Party.

For Native Americans, the 19th-century United States was anything but a land of opportunity. While Indians had been indispensable to colonial economic development, white Americans had essentially no intention of opening their society to them or sharing the land with them. The closest the nation came was its pre-1828 policy of attempting to "civilize" Indian tribes by encouraging them to adopt family-based farming "instead of remaining in a state of hunters." The "hunter" designation was plainly false, as the tribes had been growing crops for centuries, but it fit a convenient rationalization about primitive Indians who impeded progress (Perdue and Green 2010, 43–44). The famous "Civilized Tribes"—Cherokee, Chickasaw, Choctaw, and Creek—were southern tribes that successfully switched from communal agriculture to family-based farming as urged. The Cherokees had private property rights, a constitution, livestock, a newspaper, small factories, cotton plantations and gins, and upward of a thousand slaves. Yet all of these tribes were forced to relocate in the 1830s when federal policy explicitly became one of Indian removal (Wishart 2003, 119). Tribal removal in early America was usually accomplished via treaty rather than outright warfare, but treaties offered negligible protection of Indian land rights. To begin with, many treaties were agreements with a corrupt faction of an otherwise unwilling tribe. Treaties were regularly sidestepped when the government wanted to expand into Indian lands, even when the U.S. Supreme Court ruled the action unconstitutional, as in the 1830s. By 1871 the federal government stopped making treaties with Indians altogether (Perdue and Green 2010, 42–43, 48, 52–60, 89). By the end of the long 19th century Native Americans had lost nearly all of their land, an estimated half of their population, and much of their culture (Thornton 2000, 24, 32).

Indian removal to the West did not spare the surviving Indians from further conflict. In fact, it intensified. American acquisition in the 1840s of what is now the western half of the Lower 48 as well as rapid railroad-aided westward migration meant renewed conflict with Indians, including western tribes whose previous contact with whites had mostly been with Spanish colonists in California and British Canadians in the Northwest. Those contacts had brought deadly epidemics as usual, but they had also brought a thriving fur trade in the Northwest and a revolutionary horse culture to the Indians of the Southwest and the Great Plains. The Plains Indians were the tallest people in the world in the 19th century, an indication of high living standards. Several of these horse-riding tribes, notably the Apache and Comanche tribes, had developed into exceptional cavalry and were in a better position than their eastern counterparts to resist the encroachment of new settlers (Wishart 2003, 119; Steckel and Prince 2001). At the same time, the enlarged U.S. standing army was better equipped than ever to battle Indians. As white westward settlement proceeded apace, warfare with the Indians was practically constant (Perdue and Green 2010, 52, 58, 76, 79). In the second half of the century the federal government acquired all of the western Indian land and designated parts of it as Indian reservations. As before, there were tribes that resisted

INDIAN LAND FOR SALE

GET A HOME

OF

YOUR OWN

❋

EASY PAYMENTS

PERFECT TITLE

❋

POSSESSION

WITHIN

THIRTY DAYS

FINE LANDS IN THE WEST

IRRIGATED
IRRIGABLE

GRAZING

AGRICULTURAL
DRY FARMING

The Dawes Act of 1887 sought to replace tribal ownership of Indian lands with individual allotments of 160 acres per family. The remaining land went to the federal government, which sold much of it, as in this 1910 advertisement from the Department of the Interior. In all, Native Americans lost some 90 million acres of land in the half-century after 1887. (Library of Congress)

moving to the new areas and finally did so at gunpoint. Indians on the reservations were isolated and lacked the protection of U.S. citizenship, yet federal Indian policy officially aimed at assimilation. The Dawes Act of 1887, which affected most but not all tribes, gave each Indian family title to 160 acres of land and gave the federal government the right to dispose of the remaining reservation land, causing Indians to lose roughly 90 million acres of their land in the next half century. Assimilation also meant reservation boarding schools with a guiding ethos of "kill the Indian, save the man" (Wishart 2003, 120; Banner 2005, 235, 239–240; Perdue and Green 2010, 80–82). Indians had become practically invisible: in 1800 roughly 1 in 9 persons in the current continental United States was an American Indian, whereas by 1910 it was 1 in 316.

African Americans spent most of the long 19th century as slaves. In the U.S. Supreme Court's infamous *Dred Scott* decision of 1857, Chief Justice Roger Taney, himself a slaveholder, wrote that blacks "had no rights which the white man was bound to respect." The best that can be said of American slavery is that the slaves survived it and had high natural rates of increase, unlike their counterparts in the tropics, who tended to die off early. The horrors of slavery, from physical abuse and forced separations from family to constant threats of both, have been well documented. Economically speaking, slaves were American exceptions in that they had no say over where or how much they worked and received little or no cash income. Even as the market price of slaves soared, their pay did not. Relative to productivity, slave incomes actually declined from 1774 to 1860 (J. Williamson 2015).

Both before and after emancipation, African Americans mostly missed out on high-wage industrial jobs. Those jobs were mostly in the North, where few blacks lived. Northern employers and communities were simply not welcoming to blacks, preferring instead to hire European immigrants. Stuck in the South, where industrialization remained minimal and skilled jobs were generally reserved for whites, most African Americans earned no more than a pittance, working as sharecroppers or tenant farmers. A lucky few—about one in five by 1910—advanced far enough up the economic ladder to full ownership of their farms, and southern blacks accumulated property at a healthy rate during that time, but it was from a low base, and opportunities remained limited (U.S. Department of Commerce 1975, K136–K137; Higgs 1982). The civil rights protections that the Reconstruction authorities had afforded the freedmen vanished in 1877 when the federal government pulled the last of its occupying troops out of the South. The citizenship, equal protection, and voting rights that were theirs under the Fourteenth and Fifteenth Amendments would not be seriously enforced until close to a century later. Even the Thirteenth Amendment, which outlawed slavery, had a gigantic loophole that southern employers would exploit, as it outlawed slavery and involuntary servitude "except as a punishment for crime whereof the party shall have been duly convicted." So the coerced labor of convicts was legal. Southern blacks were routinely arrested on trumped-up charges of vagrancy or for breach of contract if they tried to switch employers or farm landlords. Prisons used the forced labor of convicts for road building and other public works or leased out their labor to corporations and other employers (Blackmon 2009, 53–57). The second-class status of southern blacks was reinforced by the rise of antiblack terror groups such as the Ku Klux Klan, waves of lynchings, enforced segregation in the form of Jim Crow laws, and employers' refusal to hire blacks for all but the most menial jobs. Not until World War I and the attendant cutoff of European immigration forced northern employers to look south for new workers did the situation change much.

COMMERCIALISM

"The business of America is business," said President Calvin Coolidge. Historian Thomas C. Cochran made a similar claim, arguing that business

This 1867 cartoon from *Harper's Weekly* illustrates the limited gains for African Americans after emancipation. The illustration at left depicts a slave's sale as punishment for a crime, whereas the one on the right depicts a freedman being publicly whipped as punishment for a crime. Even closer to slavery was the postbellum South's system of convict labor, in which many blacks charged with petty crimes like vagrancy received long sentences and were hired out as prison laborers. (Library of Congress)

was the main social institution in the United States, ahead of religious, political, and other civic organizations. Business and commerce play vital roles in any modern society, but America and Britain stood out in their commercial orientation. When Adam Smith in *The Wealth of Nations* (1776) called England "a nation of shopkeepers," he seems to have been repeating a frequently leveled charge. England and its American colonies both underwent a consumer revolution in the 1700s as factory-produced consumer goods became wildly popular in households and began to re-place household production. Americans successfully put their consumer-ism aside in boycotting British goods in the decade before the American Revolutionary War, and the war and its depression-like aftermath put a further crimp in their consumption, which may have been long-lasting. As surprising as it may seem today, the Americans of the 19th century were big savers. American commercialism stayed strong; Americans seemed to enjoy making money even more than spending it. "I do not know a country where the love of money holds a larger place in the heart of man," French-man Alexis de Tocqueville wrote in 1835 in his legendary *Democracy in*

America (Tocqueville 2000, 50). And the art of acquiring wealth has been particularly prized in America.

"Commercialism" is a somewhat value-laden term, but it is not necessarily a pejorative one. It simply means "the principles, practices, and spirit of commerce" whereby commerce is business or the trading of goods or commodities. Thus, it could connote entrepreneurship, street smarts, business sense, and being good with money. Yet it could also connote a greedy, grasping, profiteering, and selfish mind-set. A second definition from the same source is "a commercial attitude in noncommercial affairs; inappropriate or excessive emphasis on profit, success, or immediate results" (Dictionary.com). One's politics and values will have some bearing on how one feels about a commercialist outlook. But few would dispute that the acquisition of wealth has been a greater priority among Americans than Europeans. Some of this may have reflected greater opportunities to indulge one's inner shopkeeper in America, where land and resources were abundant, the domestic market was large and growing, intervention from governments and guilds was minimal, and there was less competition from established firms in banking, manufacturing, and trade. Commercialism went hand in hand with the other three themes I have identified, as it is about getting rich (prosperity), then richer (expansion), and pulling away from the rest of the pack (inequality). It also goes with such classic American values as seeking economic opportunity and economic freedom, and it helped drive such 19th-century phenomena as industrialization (a shift into a more profitable sector), the rise of mass production and big business, and the consumer society that developed gradually before fully flowering in the late decades of the century.

Even in colonial times, the entrepreneurial spirit was strong, as noted earlier. Virtually all free colonists and early Americans had it. They saved much of their income not merely as a precaution but with an eye toward wealth accumulation, with which they had no qualms despite biblical warnings against the love of wealth. Even small farmers tried to produce a surplus and take it to market. Large cash-crop planters such as Thomas Jefferson obviously produced for the market and bought and sold slaves in another large market. Yet the rise of an American commercial culture in the 19th century went way beyond market-based agriculture. Like much of American history, it is related to the formative debates between Jefferson and Hamilton. Jefferson decried "the selfish spirit of commerce, which knows no country, and feels no passion or principle but that of gain." He idealized a nation of small yeoman farmers without the corrupting influences of large-scale industry, big financial institutions, and big cities. Hamilton argued the opposite, that the nation would be more prosperous and no less virtuous if it encouraged the development of manufacturing, banking, and finance as well as the urbanization that would be necessary to support such development. Debate over these issues continued long after both men had died, but as the 19th century went on, it became clear that Hamilton had prevailed. By 1900 America had become the world's leading industrial power, factories produced twice as much output as farms, investment banker J. P. Morgan was perhaps the most powerful man in America, and although rural dwellers still outnumbered urban dwellers, the city population had grown more than twice as fast over the course of the century. By 1920 a majority of Americans would live in cities (U.S. Department of Commerce 1975, A57, A69).

America's transformation into a Hamiltonian nation was gradual before the Civil War—although it is notable that the words "commercialism" and "capitalism" both entered the lexicon around 1850—and rapid afterward. Although American industrialization before the war was impressive, America was still by and large a farming nation. On the eve of the war every region of the nation, including the Northeast, had a majority rural population. At the state level the only exceptions were Massachusetts and Rhode Island (U.S. Department of Commerce 1975, A178–A179). Cotton, America's great cash crop, dominated the economy. Cotton textiles were the leading manufacturing sector, and much of northern shipping and finance revolved around the cotton crop. The slave plantation owners who dominated the South's economy and political leadership seemed to espouse Jefferson's philosophy, portraying themselves as gentleman farmers with a civilized way of life that was superior to the grimy, greedy factory and finance capitalism of the North. Yet they were as dependent on commerce as almost anyone, as they specialized in a cash crop with a worldwide market. Moreover, they employed full-time managers (overseers) and typically looked to expand in terms of both land and slaves. Then again, research by economic historians finds that these planters passed up numerous opportunities to enrich themselves further by investing in industry. Where manufacturing had been tried in the South, it had generally been highly profitable. Yet the South in the 19th century was overwhelmingly agricultural even after emancipation (Bateman and Weiss 1981; Licht 1995, 37, 38, 117–124). The South's surprisingly large number of middle-class yeoman farmers tended to produce for their own consumption and local markets (Atack and Passell 1994, 274).

In the North and on the nation's northwest frontier, passing up profit opportunities was relatively rare. Although farming remained by far the largest sector, with corn, wheat, and livestock among the region's biggest products, northern farmers regularly moved west in search of greater profits, bore considerable capital costs in setting up new farms, replaced wooden plows with superior iron ones, adopted mechanical threshers that tremendously sped up the process of gathering the grain, and adopted the mechanical reaper. By midcentury, 71 percent of northern farmers produced marketable surpluses and had an impressive rate of return of 12 percent (Atack and Passell 1994, 274–283, 291, 294). Many farm children moved into the trades, manufacturing, transportation, and professional services (Howe 2009, 525–526). The trade embargo of 1807 and the War of 1812, by removing the competition from European goods, made manufacturing more profitable than ever before, and there was a rush of new firms in such lines as textiles, clothing, and boots and shoes. By 1815, just after the war ended, the economy was starting to boom, and a great many American consumers, both rural and urban, were experiencing rising real incomes and were ready to spend more of that money. Home production of food, clothing, and even heat (from firewood) had been the norm, but increasingly Americans looked to buy the goods they consumed (Howe 2009, 5, 33–43). British and European imports were still seen as the best, but low-priced goods from American factories found ready buyers. Manufacturing and mining remained enticing profit sectors. America had bountiful resources and a growing domestic market, and the technology could be borrowed or stolen from Europe's ongoing industrial revolution, which had begun a half century before American industrialization had really begun. Producing for and facilitating a national market, as with the construction of the Erie Canal, which began in 1817, was even seen as patriotic, as it would help to unify the states, just as the framers of the U.S. Constitution and American nationalists had hoped. "For the United States the push to advance economically became an intrinsic part of its emerging national character" (Appleby 2010, 168). By 1860 America had over 120,000 factories, albeit few very large ones. The rise in consumer well-being was even more striking. People were not merely buying baubles but were benefiting from innovations that made a big impact in their lives. Home life by this time was more comfortable thanks to central heating (steam-powered radiator heat), oil lamps that one could read by, and cast-iron cookstoves. People at home were more connected, as they could read newspapers that covered news that had just happened, thanks to the telegraph, and could host visitors from far away, thanks to the railroads. In some big cities people had indoor plumbing and running water (Gordon 2004, 165–166).

America's antebellum commercialism also involved a high degree of speculation—that is, investing in long-shot projects or buying something not for its intrinsic value but with the hope of selling it at a profit later. "Every man is a speculator," wrote Jeremiah Church in an 1845 travelogue of the Midwest and the South, "from a wood-sawyer to a President, as far as his means will go, and credit also" (qtd. in Fraser 2006, vii). Economist John Kenneth Galbraith wrote that "the speculative imagination was in its most ardent form in the United States" (1994, 54). Once again, much of that speculative tendency predates the 19th century. Speculating in western lands was common in colonial times; famous speculators included George Washington and 11 of the other 55 delegates to the Constitutional Convention (Foner 2006; McGuire 2003, 53). Investors and speculators were naturally taken by the country's prosperity and rapid expansion, its opportunity to adopt European industrial technology, and such visible projects to expand the national market as the canals, the telegraph, and America's first big business and biggest stocks, the railroads. American expansion and speculation often led to overexpansion of credit, as in the "era of good feelings" that preceded the financial panic of 1819 and the speculative boom of the 1830s. Northern speculators in western lands tended to push for federal funding of railroads, canals, and other internal improvements, which would raise the value of their land. Even southern slaveholders, who generally avoided manufacturing and opposed federal funding of internal improvements, were speculators, namely in slaves. The planters saw their slaves as valuable capital investments and tradeable commodities, with an estimated value of $4 billion on the eve of the Civil War, and many speculated in slaves, selling them not merely to pay off debts but for profit (Tadman 1989, 211).

American acquisitiveness skyrocketed in the half century after the Civil War. Twain, no stranger himself to dubious investments, coined the phrase "the gilded age" early in the period. Numerous industrialists, developers, financiers, and speculators made extraordinary fortunes. While those fortunes and the unparalleled influence of the men who had them made many Americans nervous, Americans generally were inclined to agree with Andrew Carnegie's words: "It will be a great mistake for the community to shoot the millionaires, for they are the bees that make the most honey, and contribute most to the hive even after they have gorged themselves full" (Carnegie 1913, 93). Even taxing the millionaires was an idea that would have to wait until the 1910s. Upper- and middle-class Americans readily embraced the social Darwinism and materialism of philosopher Herbert Spencer (Cochran and Miller 1961, 119–128). After all, ordinary Americans aspired to wealth themselves. Most did not find it, of course, but they did find high-quality, inexpensive American manufactured goods within easy reach, thanks to mass production and distribution as well as plunging transportation costs. Cities continued to be production and trading centers but also became consumer emporiums, with department stores and popular shopping districts. Contemporary travelers consistently noted that Americans loved money more and pursued it more energetically than Europeans. Oscar Wilde, after visiting America in the 1880s, wrote that "At an age when we are still boys at Eton, or lads at Oxford, they are practising some important profession, making money in some intricate business" (Wilde 1887, 342).

Postbellum commercialism surely did not benefit all Americans—such as farmers who were often on the wrong side of fluctuations in crop prices, railroad rates, and interest rates—yet clearly it was here to stay. A notable example of the triumph of commercialism can be found in a surprising place: William Jennings Bryan's "Cross of Gold" speech. This speech,

This 1852 painting by Francis William Edmonds shows a sharp-dressed man who is trying to get a rural couple to buy land, presumably sight unseen. The scroll he is holding is a map labeled "1000 Valuable Lots" by "Railroad Avenue." Speculation in western lands was common and sometimes profitable, but cases of fraud were notorious and failures were rampant. (Smithsonian American Art Museum, Washington, DC/Art Resource, NY)

which Bryan gave at the 1896 Democratic National Convention where he was nominated for the presidency, is often seen as the last gasp of the Jeffersonian agrarian outlook, and Bryan's call to end the gold standard antagonized bankers as few politicians had done before. And yet Bryan's most famous sentence, which ends with "you shall not crucify mankind upon a cross of gold," begins with "Having behind us the producing masses of this nation and the world, *supported by the commercial interests* and the toilers everywhere" (Bryan 1896 [my emphasis]). Rather than bash business, Bryan insisted that the people he represented—farmers, wage workers, miners, small merchants, small-town attorneys—were also businessmen. Even Bryan, widely considered the most radical major-party candidate to date and on his way to a landslide defeat by conservative Republican William McKinley, draped his proposals in the rhetoric of business and commercial interests. Even the party of Jefferson was now the party of Hamilton.

CONCLUSION

Mark Twain called his times "the raging, tearing, booming nineteenth century" (Twain 1889, 244). This chapter runs through four themes—prosperity, expansion, inequality, and commercialism—that I believe are central to understanding America in those times. Twain's mention of "tearing" suggests a possible fifth theme: disunion. The Civil War was the most traumatic event in the nation's history and should be prominent in any account of America's 19th century. It can also be explained in terms of the other four themes. Slave labor contributed immensely to the nation's prosperity, as cotton became a great cash crop whose commercial potential was fully exploited by southern planters and northern businessmen alike. Cotton slavery enriched so many northerners as well as southerners that its survival had seemed assured for generations. But as perhaps the most unequal social system imaginable, slavery was unsustainable, at least amid the innovation of the 19th century. Innovations in transportation facilitated slave escapes, and innovations in communication brought news of the slaves' plight to whites, increasing numbers of whom resolved not to cooperate with slave catchers. The increased value of slave property made the planters some of the richest people in America and raised the stakes in their demands for tighter fugitive slave laws and other protections. One of the protections they sought was the territorial expansion of slavery. Indeed, expansion had always been at the heart of the sectional debate over slavery. Slaveholders looked to move into new states or, as speculators, profit from the rise in slave prices that expansion presumably would bring. Non-slaveholders in the North looked to establish their own farms, factories, or other businesses and did not want to compete with slave plantations for the land. The nation's massive land acquisitions of the 1840s brought the controversy over slavery's expansion to a new boil. Only through the crucible of the Civil War would the issue finally be resolved, and even then many issues remained. African Americans remained separate and unequal. So did the northern and southern economies. For the next 50 years the southern economy continued to revolve around plantation-based agriculture, while northern industry experienced an unprecedented boom.

Disunion, like this chapter's primary themes, relates to *Adventures of Huckleberry Finn,* especially as its main plot involves a fugitive slave. The annotated *Huckleberry Finn,* which is presented next, is the union of Twain's novel and 19th-century American history, two things that are complex, challenging, and contradictory but also captivating, especially as one spends more time with them.

CRANKO

*Adventures of Huckleberry Finn
(Tom Sawyer's Comrade)*

By Mark Twain

With Annotations
By Ranjit S. Dighe

NOTICE

PERSONS attempting to find a motive in this narrative will be prosecuted; persons attempting to find a moral in it will be banished; persons attempting to find a plot in it will be shot.[1]

BY ORDER OF THE AUTHOR
PER G. G., CHIEF OF ORDNANCE

EXPLANATORY

IN this book a number of dialects are used, to wit: the Missouri negro dialect; the extremest form of the backwoods South-Western dialect; the ordinary "Pike-County" dialect; and four modified varieties of this last.[2] The shadings have not been done in a hap-hazard fashion, or by guesswork; but pains-takingly, and with the trustworthy guidance and support of personal familiarity with these several forms of speech.

I make this explanation for the reason that without it many readers would suppose that all these characters were trying to talk alike and not succeeding.

THE AUTHOR.

---

1. Twain's words are ironic. Generations of readers have found all sorts of morals in *Huckleberry Finn.* Twain concluded one of his last short stories, "A Fable" (1909), with an explicit, all-purpose "moral": "You can find in a text whatever you bring, if you will stand between it and the mirror of your imagination" (Twain 2012, 635). In rejecting a moral, he may have been taking a swipe at the one-dimensional morality of countless popular stories of his time in which good boys were always rewarded and bad boys were always punished. In interviews and essays he lambasted those tedious tales, and two of his early stories, "The Story of the Bad Little Boy" (1865) and "The Story of the Good Little Boy" (1870), gleefully broke that mold, with the bad little boy becoming ever worse but also wealthy, "universally respected," and a member of the legislature, whereas the good little boy suffers one affliction after another and dies young in an explosion.

2. Missouri is the setting for much of the novel. Most of the geographical references are real, with the notable exception of Huck's fictitious hometown of St. Petersburg, which is closely modeled on Twain's own hometown of Hannibal, a town in the state's northeast corner and on the banks of the Mississippi River. Apparently Twain has placed St. Petersburg in Pike County, the real-life county about 20 miles south of Marion County, where Hannibal was located. Marion County and about a dozen other northeastern Missouri counties were carved out of Pike County, one of the earliest counties in the Missouri Territory, so in that sense many Missourians spoke in various Pike County dialects.

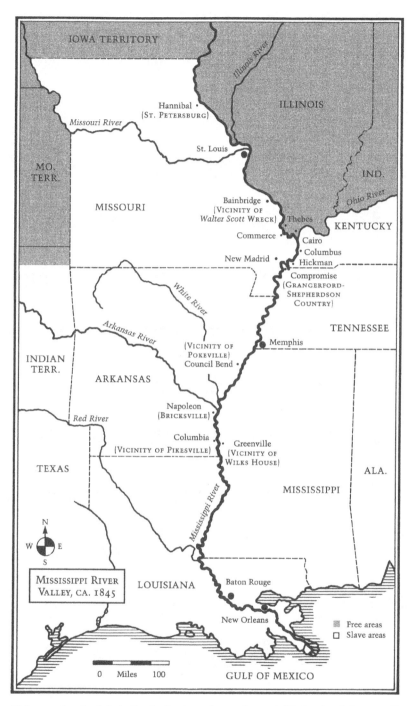

This map by the Mark Twain Project shows the real-life basis of the novel's partly fictional geography. From St. Petersburg, Missouri, based on Twain's hometown of Hannibal, Huck and Jim travel down the Mississippi River and get as far south as the Wilks House, near Greenville, Mississippi. At some points Huck refers to real cities by name, such as St. Louis and New Orleans. (The Mark Twain Project, Berkeley, California.)

CONTENTS.

ILLUSTRATIONS.[3]

Huckleberry Finn. *Frontispiece*
The Widow's
Learning about Moses and the "Bulrushers"
Miss Watson
Huck Stealing Away
They Tip-toed Along
Jim
Tom Sawyer's Band of Robbers
Huck Creeps into his Window
Miss Watson's Lecture
The Robbers Dispersed
Rubbing the Lamp
! ! ! ! !
Judge Thatcher surprised
Jim Listening
"Pap"
Huck and his Father
Reforming the Drunkard
Falling from Grace
Getting out of the Way
Solid Comfort
Thinking it Over
Raising a Howl
"Git Up"
The Shanty
Shooting the Pig
Taking a Rest
In the Woods
Watching the Boat
Discovering the Camp Fire
Jim and the Ghost

---

3. Most of these illustrations do not appear in this edition of the novel, but their names help convey the charm and specifics of the novel, so this list has been left in.

"I am the Late Dauphin"
Tail Piece
On the Raft
The King as Juliet
"Courting on the Sly"
"A Pirate for Thirty Years"
Another little Job
Practicing
Hamlet's Soliloquy
"Gimme a Chaw"
A Little Monthly Drunk
The Death of Boggs
Sherburn steps out
A Dead Head
He shed Seventeen Suits
Tragedy
Their Pockets Bulged
Henry the Eighth in Boston Harbor
Harmless
Adolphus
He fairly emptied that Young Fellow
"Alas, our Poor Brother"
"You Bet it is"
Leaking
Making up the "Deffisit"
Going for him
The Doctor
The Bag of Money
The Cubby
Supper with the Hare-Lip
Honest Injun
The Duke looks under the Bed
Huck takes the Money
A Crack in the Dining-room Door
The Undertaker
"He had a Rat!"
"Was you in my Room?"
Jawing
In Trouble
Indignation
How to Find Them
He Wrote
Hannah with the Mumps
The Auction

The Doctor
Uncle Silas in Danger
Old Mrs. Hotchkiss
Aunt Sally talks to Huck
Tom Sawyer wounded
The Doctor speaks for Jim
Tom rose square up in Bed
"Hand out them Letters"
Out of Bondage
Tom's Liberality
Yours Truly

ADVENTURES

OF

HUCKLEBERRY FINN

(TOM SAWYER'S COMRADE)

SCENE: THE MISSISSIPPI VALLEY
TIME: FORTY TO FIFTY YEARS AGO[4]

---

4. What year is the book set in? Twain finished it in 1883 and published it in 1884, so "forty to fifty years ago" could mean any year from 1833 to 1844. If Twain were trying to connect the story to his personal history, then the book is most likely set around 1845, when he turned 10 years old, nearly Huck's age. A date before 1840 seems unlikely, as Hannibal was not chartered as a town until 1839, and the Clemens family did not move there until late 1839. From a population of 30 in 1830, it grew large enough by the end of the decade to attract professionals such as Sam's father, a lawyer and retail businessman. Huck describes St. Petersburg in a later chapter as a "little town," but we soon learn that it is large enough to have a school, a church, a sawmill, a barrel shop, and at least two judges. Another clue comes later, with a mention of Texas as if it were already a state; Texas was admitted to the union in 1845.

CHAPTER I.

YOU don't know about me, without you have read a book by the name of "The Adventures of Tom Sawyer," but that ain't no matter. That book was made by Mr. Mark Twain, and he told the truth, mainly. There was things which he stretched, but mainly he told the truth. That is nothing. I never seen anybody but lied one time or another, without it was Aunt Polly, or the widow, or maybe Mary. Aunt Polly—Tom's Aunt Polly, she is—and Mary, and the Widow Douglas is all told about in that book, which is mostly a true book, with some stretchers, as I said before.

Now the way that the book winds up is this: Tom and me found the money that the robbers hid in the cave, and it made us rich. We got six thousand dollars apiece—all gold. It was an awful sight of money when it was piled up. Well, Judge Thatcher he took it and put it out at interest, and it fetched us a dollar a day apiece all the year round—more than a body could tell what to do with.[5] The Widow Douglas she took me for her son, and allowed she would sivilize me; but it was rough living in the house all

---

5. Six thousand dollars was a tremendous amount of money back then. Based on economic historians' estimates of 19th-century price indexes, prices today are roughly 30 times higher today than they were in 1840–1844, so the sum of money would be worth $180,000 (Officer and Williamson 2015). Or, considering that the coins were gold, valued then at $18.93 per ounce and today at about $1,100 per ounce (in mid-2015), they would have a market value of almost $350,000. Even that seems an underestimate considering how much lower incomes were back then. Households were much more self-sufficient at that time, growing, catching, and cooking much more of their own food; sewing more of their own clothing; and performing many more household tasks themselves. Six thousand dollars was more than most Americans at that time would ever see in their lifetime. The average yearly income in America in 1840 was about $111 and was less than $80 in the six-state census region that included Missouri (Lindert and Williamson 2013, 29).

Note that the money is in gold. Gold and silver coins circulated freely for most of the 19th century and were the basis of the nation's money supply. Banks could issue their own paper banknotes, with the expectation that they could be redeemed for gold or silver coins, also known as "hard money." Most banks did so responsibly, but the crooked exceptions were notorious. In other cases, the banknotes were legitimate but the bank was obscure, remote, or very new, causing the notes to be of low or uncertain value. And general financial panics, notably the Panic of 1837, brought numerous bank failures, causing the notes of many banks to become worthless. Deposit insurance existed only in a handful of states before the Civil War, all in the North, so holders of bad banknotes often lost everything (Federal Deposit Insurance Corporation 1998, 3, 5). A trove of gold coins obviously is "as good as gold," with no doubt about its value, authenticity, or convertibility.

the time, considering how dismal regular and decent the widow was in all her ways; and so when I couldn't stand it no longer, I lit out. I got into my old rags, and my sugar-hogshead again, and was free and satisfied.[6] But Tom Sawyer, he hunted me up and said he was going to start a band of robbers, and I might join if I would go back to the widow and be respectable. So I went back.

The widow she cried over me, and called me a poor lost lamb, and she called me a lot of other names, too, but she never meant no harm by it. She put me in them new clothes again, and I couldn't do nothing but sweat and sweat, and feel all cramped up. Well, then, the old thing commenced again. The widow rung a bell for supper, and you had to come to time. When you got to the table you couldn't go right to eating, but you had to wait for the widow to tuck down her head and grumble a little over the victuals, though there warn't really anything the matter with them. That is, nothing only everything was cooked by itself. In a barrel of odds and ends it is different; things get mixed up, and the juice kind of swaps around, and the things go better.

After supper she got out her book and learned me about Moses and the Bulrushers; and I was in a sweat to find out all about him; but by and by she let it out that Moses had been dead a considerable long time; so then I didn't care no more about him; because I don't take no stock in dead people.

Pretty soon I wanted to smoke, and asked the widow to let me. But she wouldn't. She said it was a mean practice and wasn't clean, and I must try to not do it any more. That is just the way with some people. They get down on a thing when they don't know nothing about it. Here she was

---

Interest of $1 a day on $6,000 principal equates to an effective yearly interest rate of 6.27 percent, roughly the same as the 6 percent rate at which the money was invested at the end of *The Adventures of Tom Sawyer.* Either is a healthy return in a time of near-zero inflation such as the 19th century. (Prices fluctuated, but periods of inflation were offset by periods of deflation, or falling prices, with the result that consumer prices were the same in 1890 as in 1830 [Officer and Williamson 2015].) The antebellum United States was a fast-growing emerging market, so returns on investments in growing sectors such as manufacturing, mining, and transportation were high, typically in the range of 8 to 12 percent, so the gold appears to have been invested conservatively.

6. A sugar-hogshead is a large barrel for storing sugar. Sugarcane had been the world's biggest cash crop for centuries, before being overtaken by cotton in the 19th century, and was harvested with slave labor. Sugar slavery was more arduous and had a much higher death rate than cotton slavery in the American South. Most of the sugar plantations in the Western Hemisphere were in the Caribbean or Latin America, but some existed in the southernmost part of the United States. The sugar plantations of Louisiana were notorious for their brutal practices, which partly explains the phrase "sold down the river," since New Orleans was at the base of the Mississippi River and was also the site of the largest slave auction market in antebellum America.

a-bothering about Moses, which was no kin to her, and no use to anybody, being gone, you see, yet finding a power of fault with me for doing a thing that had some good in it. And she took snuff, too; of course that was all right, because she done it herself.[7]

Her sister, Miss Watson, a tolerable slim old maid, with goggles on, had just come to live with her, and took a set at me now with a spelling-book. She worked me middling hard for about an hour, and then the widow made her ease up.[8] I couldn't stood it much longer. Then for an hour it was deadly dull, and I was fidgety. Miss Watson would say, "Don't put your feet up there, Huckleberry;" and "Don't scrunch up like that, Huckleberry—set up straight;" and pretty soon she would say, "Don't gap and stretch like that, Huckleberry—why don't you try to behave?" Then she told me all about the bad place, and I said I wished I was there. She got mad then, but I didn't mean no harm. All I wanted was to go somewheres; all I wanted was a change, I warn't particular. She said it was wicked to say what I said; said she wouldn't say it for the whole world; *she* was going to live so as to go to the good place. Well, I couldn't see no advantage in going where she was going, so I made up my mind I wouldn't try for it. But I never said so, because it would only make trouble, and wouldn't do no good.

Now she had got a start, and she went on and told me all about the good place. She said all a body would have to do there was to go around all day long with a harp and sing, forever and ever. So I didn't think much of it. But I never said so. I asked her if she reckoned Tom Sawyer would go there, and she said not by a considerable sight. I was glad about that, because I wanted him and me to be together.

---

7. Tobacco was the first big cash crop on the North American continent and contributed significantly to the growth of slavery in the southern colonies. Tobacco continued to be big long after cotton eclipsed it as the nation's top cash crop. Tobacco country was also notable for the widespread smoking of tobacco, including by children. Indian children commonly smoked it, and so did many white children in Missouri (Twain 2001, 20n18). Twain recounted that on his first day of school in Hannibal, an older girl asked him if he chewed tobacco. He said no, and she shamed him: "Here is a boy seven years old who can't chaw tobacco." He said that as a child he later "learned to smoke fairly well," however (Twain 2010, 1:216).

8. "Old maid" refers to a woman past the usual marrying age who has never married. Unmarried women typically lived with other family members, as Miss Watson does. Miss Watson's zeal to teach Huck his spelling suggests that she may have been a schoolteacher or tutor, which is period appropriate. Most occupations were closed to women, and upon marrying women who could afford to do so were expected to work only in the home. (Poorer married women, including free blacks and some immigrants, often worked as domestic servants.) Unmarried older women, such as the middle-aged spinsters in textile mills from whom that term derives, tended to work in a handful of pink-collar occupations, such as teacher or librarian.

Miss Watson she kept pecking at me, and it got tiresome and lone-some. By and by they fetched the niggers in and had prayers, and then everybody was off to bed.[9] I went up to my room with a piece of candle, and put it on the table. Then I set down in a chair by the window and tried to think of something cheerful, but it warn't no use. I felt so lonesome I most wished I was dead. The stars were shining, and the leaves rustled in the woods ever so mournful; and I heard an owl, away off, who-whooing about somebody that was dead, and a whippowill and a dog crying about somebody that was going to die; and the wind was trying to whisper some-thing to me, and I couldn't make out what it was, and so it made the cold shivers run over me. Then away out in the woods I heard that kind of a sound that a ghost makes when it wants to tell about something that's on its mind and can't make itself understood, and so can't rest easy in its grave, and has to go about that way every night grieving. I got so down-hearted and scared I did wish I had some company. Pretty soon a spider went crawling up my shoulder, and I flipped it off and it lit in the candle; and before I could budge it was all shriveled up. I didn't need anybody to tell me that that was an awful bad sign and would fetch me some bad luck, so I was scared and most shook the clothes off of me. I got up and turned around in my tracks three times and crossed my breast every time; and then I tied up a little lock of my hair with a thread to keep witches away. But I hadn't no confidence. You do that when you've lost a horse-shoe that you've found, instead of nailing it up over the door, but I hadn't ever heard anybody say it was any way to keep off bad luck when you'd killed a spider.

I set down again, a-shaking all over, and got out my pipe for a smoke; for the house was all as still as death, now, and so the widow wouldn't know. Well, after a long time I heard the clock away off in the town go boom—boom—boom—twelve licks—and all still again—stiller than ever.

9. From "fetched the niggers" we might infer that the Widow Douglas was one of the wealthier members of the community, since only about one-fourth of southern whites owned slaves and only about one-twenty-fifth owned 10 or more (Miller and Sexton 2005, 124). To be sure, however, not all of the millions of southerners who owned slaves were wealthy; one historian's study of midcentury census returns in several counties found that a sizable minority of slaveholding families, normally around 10 percent but sometimes as high as 30 percent, did not own any land (Owsley 1949, 150–229). Twain's own family never rose above the middle class yet owned or leased a few slaves while Twain's father was alive.

Including the slaves in religious activities, often with segregated services, was com-mon in the South. Here as elsewhere when Europeans encountered non-Christian peoples, the motives were mixed. A missionary imperative to save souls was surely present, but so was a desire for a "slave morality" in which the slaves meekly accepted their servitude. Scripture was often selectively mined to justify racial slavery as God's will. "Slaves, obey your earthly masters" and similar phrases appear in several books of the New Testament.

Pretty soon I heard a twig snap down in the dark amongst the trees—something was a stirring. I set still and listened. Directly I could just barely hear a "*me-yow! me-yow!*" down there. That was good! Says I, "*me-yow! me-yow!*" as soft as I could, and then I put out the light and scrambled out of the window onto the shed. Then I slipped down to the ground and crawled in amongst the trees, and sure enough there was Tom Sawyer waiting for me.

CHAPTER II.

WE went tip-toeing along a path amongst the trees back towards the end of the widow's garden, stooping down so as the branches wouldn't scrape our heads. When we was passing by the kitchen I fell over a root and made a noise. We scrouched down and laid still. Miss Watson's big nigger, named Jim, was setting in the kitchen door; we could see him pretty clear, because there was a light behind him.[10] He got up and stretched his neck out about a minute, listening. Then he says:

"Who dah?"

He listened some more; then he come tiptoeing down and stood right between us; we could a touched him, nearly. Well, likely it was minutes and minutes that there warn't a sound, and we all there so close together. There was a place on my ankle that got to itching, but I dasn't scratch it; and then my ear begun to itch; and next my back, right between my shoulders. Seemed like I'd die if I couldn't scratch. Well, I've noticed that thing plenty times since. If you are with the quality, or at a funeral, or trying to go to sleep when you ain't sleepy—if you are anywheres where it won't do for you to scratch, why you will itch all over in upwards of a thousand places. Pretty soon Jim says:

"Say, who is you? Whar is you? Dog my cats ef I didn' hear sumf'n. Well, I knows what I's gwyne to do: I's gwyne to set down here and listen tell I hears it agin."

So he set down on the ground betwixt me and Tom. He leaned his back up against a tree, and stretched his legs out till one of them most touched one of mine. My nose begun to itch. It itched till the tears come into my eyes. But I dasn't scratch. Then it begun to itch on the inside. Next I got to

---

10. Jim is Miss Watson's personal slave and apparently her only slave. What kind of work does he do for her? We never really find out, other than his guard duty in this scene and his cowherd duties mentioned later. The usual distinction between house servants and field slaves does not really apply here, but it was an imperfect fit in real life too. Even on the plantations, many slaves were skilled artisans such as carpenters and blacksmiths (Fogel and Engerman 1974, 38–43). Since Jim is Miss Watson's only slave, he likely performed a variety of tasks for her.

itching underneath. I didn't know how I was going to set still. This miserableness went on as much as six or seven minutes; but it seemed a sight
longer than that. I was itching in eleven different places now. I reckoned I
couldn't stand it more'n a minute longer, but I set my teeth hard and got
ready to try. Just then Jim begun to breathe heavy; next he begun to
snore—and then I was pretty soon comfortable again.

Tom he made a sign to me—kind of a little noise with his mouth—and
we went creeping away on our hands and knees. When we was ten foot off
Tom whispered to me, and wanted to tie Jim to the tree for fun.[11] But I said
no; he might wake and make a disturbance, and then they'd find out I
warn't in. Then Tom said he hadn't got candles enough, and he would slip
in the kitchen and get some more. I didn't want him to try. I said Jim might
wake up and come. But Tom wanted to resk it; so we slid in there and got
three candles, and Tom laid five cents on the table for pay. Then we got
out, and I was in a sweat to get away; but nothing would do Tom but he
must crawl to where Jim was, on his hands and knees, and play something
on him. I waited, and it seemed a good while, everything was so still and
lonesome.

As soon as Tom was back, we cut along the path, around the garden
fence, and by and by fetched up on the steep top of the hill the other side
of the house. Tom said he slipped Jim's hat off of his head and hung it on
a limb right over him, and Jim stirred a little, but he didn't wake. Afterwards Jim said the witches bewitched him and put him in a trance, and
rode him all over the State, and then set him under the trees again and
hung his hat on a limb to show who done it. And next time Jim told it he
said they rode him down to New Orleans;[12] and, after that, every time he

---

11. Tom, unlike Huck, is from the slave-owning class and tends to regard Jim as an
object for practical jokes. Along similar lines, the name "Jim" recalls Jim Crow. Long before
"Jim Crow" became the term for the post–Civil War South's system of segregation, Jim
Crow was the name of a stock character in minstrel shows. Minstrel shows were the most
popular form of entertainment in America from the 1840s to the 1890s, and they both reflected and perpetuated white stereotypes of blacks. In these shows white actors would
perform in blackface, talk in exaggerated Negro dialects, and act buffoonish. The Jim Crow
character was "a childlike plantation darky who loved to entertain whites" (Lemons 1977,
473). Edward Kemble's drawings of Jim, which strike many readers today as racist, play into
that stereotype. The drawings do not appear to have offended Twain, who adored the minstrel shows in his youth.

12. "Rode him down to New Orleans" apparently refers to being sold down the river,
away from one's family, into a harsher form of slavery in Louisiana or in the new cotton
plantations of the Southwest. Threats to sell a slave down the river or otherwise separate
him from his family were a cruel but common means of discipline. New Orleans was also the
site of the largest antebellum slave auction market, as noted earlier. When Jim says that he
was ridden by witches and saw the devil, it could be a metaphor for the real-life nightmare
for many slaves who were transported by slave traders and then sold in New Orleans.

JIM.

(Illustration by Edward W. Kemble. From Mark Twain, *Adventures of Huckleberry Finn*. New York: C. L. Webster, 1885. Digitized by the University of Virginia Library.)

Slave auctions took place in several southern cities, notably New Orleans. Sales
that broke up families were perhaps the ultimate punishment of slaves, a theme
that Twain revisited in *The Tragedy of Pudd'nhead Wilson* (1893). The mere
threat of such sales kept many slaves in a constant state of terror. (Library of
Congress)

told it he spread it more and more, till by and by he said they rode him all
over the world, and tired him most to death, and his back was all over
saddle-boils. Jim was monstrous proud about it, and he got so he wouldn't
hardly notice the other niggers. Niggers would come miles to hear Jim tell
about it, and he was more looked up to than any nigger in that country.
Strange niggers would stand with their mouths open and look him all over,
same as if he was a wonder. Niggers is always talking about witches in the
dark by the kitchen fire; but whenever one was talking and letting on to
know all about such things, Jim would happen in and say, "Hm! What you
know 'bout witches?" and that nigger was corked up and had to take a
back seat. Jim always kept that five-center piece[13] round his neck with a

---

13. The "five-center piece," using the multiply-by-30 conversion rule noted earlier,
would be equivalent to $1.50 today in terms of buying power. Nickels did not exist back then
in the United States, but silver "half dimes" (marked as such) did. The "five-center piece"
could also have been a foreign coin. Gold and silver coins were scarce in early America, so
much of the coinage in circulation was from other countries, especially Spain. (In fact, the
U.S. dollar is derived from the Spanish dollar.) Not until 1857 did Congress forbid the use of
foreign coins as legal tender (Dobeck and Elliott 2007, 40).

string, and said it was a charm the devil give to him with his own hands, and told him he could cure anybody with it and fetch witches whenever he wanted to just by saying something to it; but he never told what it was he said to it. Niggers would come from all around there and give Jim anything they had, just for a sight of that five-center piece; but they wouldn't touch it, because the devil had had his hands on it. Jim was most ruined for a servant, because he got stuck up on account of having seen the devil and been rode by witches.[14]

Well, when Tom and me got to the edge of the hill-top we looked away down into the village and could see three or four lights twinkling, where there was sick folks, maybe; and the stars over us was sparkling ever so fine; and down by the village was the river, a whole mile broad, and awful still and grand. We went down the hill and found Jo Harper and Ben Rogers, and two or three more of the boys, hid in the old tanyard. So we unhitched a skiff and pulled down the river two mile and a half, to the big scar on the hillside, and went ashore.

We went to a clump of bushes, and Tom made everybody swear to keep the secret, and then showed them a hole in the hill, right in the thickest part of the bushes. Then we lit the candles, and crawled in on our hands and knees. We went about two hundred yards, and then the cave opened up. Tom poked about amongst the passages, and pretty soon ducked under

---

14. The multiple usages of "nigger" in this paragraph, and in the book as a whole, demand comment. Just how common was that word in Huck's time and at the time of the book's publication? Although virtually every character in this novel says "nigger," upper-class whites in the antebellum South, at least in some areas, seldom did. Mary Chesnut, the wife of a South Carolina planter and politician, said she had never heard the word uttered by well-bred people before the end of the war, but "Now it is in everybody's mouth," perhaps as a show of defiance (qtd. in Litwack 1979, 255). Twain himself used it only rarely in his other writings except in quotations (nine times in *Tom Sawyer*, for example) or enclosed in quotation marks ("coarse, ragged 'nigger' clothes" in *Life on the Mississippi* [Twain 1963, 158]). Clearly, Twain used the word so heavily in this book for a reason.

Jim's becoming "stuck up" and "most ruined for a servant" goes with the common observation that docile slaves were the best kind. Slave owners used a variety of means, from religious instruction and positive incentives such as bonuses to threats and whippings, to keep their slaves tractable. People will not naturally submit to slavery, so the possibility of slave escapes or even revolts always existed. Yet slave escapes and revolts were very rare. Historians have long tried to explain why. The answer seems to be that the slaves knew that escapes were prohibitively difficult and insurrections futile. Slave owners had the backing of the government and the local white community, so open rebellion by slaves was almost certain to fail. Their masters, on the other hand, could issue credible threats of punishment, from whipping to permanently separating the rebellious slave from his or her family through slave sales. Just the threat of such punishments had the power to keep slaves in line.

a wall where you wouldn't a noticed that there was a hole. We went along a narrow place and got into a kind of room, all damp and sweaty and cold, and there we stopped. Tom says:

"Now, we'll start this band of robbers and call it Tom Sawyer's Gang. Everybody that wants to join has got to take an oath, and write his name in blood."

Everybody was willing. So Tom got out a sheet of paper that he had wrote the oath on, and read it. It swore every boy to stick to the band, and never tell any of the secrets; and if anybody done anything to any boy in the band, whichever boy was ordered to kill that person and his family must do it, and he mustn't eat and he mustn't sleep till he had killed them and hacked a cross in their breasts, which was the sign of the band. And nobody that didn't belong to the band could use that mark, and if he did he must be sued; and if he done it again he must be killed. And if anybody that belonged to the band told the secrets, he must have his throat cut, and then have his carcass burnt up and the ashes scattered all around, and his name blotted off of the list with blood and never mentioned again by the gang, but have a curse put on it and be forgot, forever.

Everybody said it was a real beautiful oath, and asked Tom if he got it out of his own head. He said, some of it, but the rest was out of pirate books and robber books, and every gang that was high-toned had it.[15]

Some thought it would be good to kill the *families* of boys that told the secrets. Tom said it was a good idea, so he took a pencil and wrote it in. Then Ben Rogers says:

"Here's Huck Finn, he hain't got no family—what you going to do 'bout him?"

"Well, hain't he got a father?" says Tom Sawyer.

---

15. Books were a big and growing business in 19th-century America, rising from an estimated $2.5 million in 1820 to $12.5 million in 1850 to $45 million in 1899 (Winship 2003, 12; United States Department of Commerce 1975). Twain was famously disdainful of the best sellers of his day and even wrote his first novel, *The Gilded Age: A Tale of Today*, with Charles Dudley Warner after their wives, tired of hearing their disparagement of the books they were reading, challenged them to write something better. The "pirate books and robber books" sound like the exploitative and controversial dime novels aimed at children, young adults, and unsophisticated adult readers (Twain 2001, 35–36n26). But that was not all that Tom and children of that era read. Sir Walter Scott was one of the most popular writers of the time. When Tom says "We are highwaymen," he is likely alluding to Scott's *The Heart of Midlothian* (1818), which featured a gang of highwaymen, or robbers, on horseback. Twain grew up reading Scott and acting out his adventure stories, much like Tom, but grew to loathe Scott's tales of romantic, feudal chivalry and to take potshots at Scott wherever he could (Levy 2014, 20; Railton 2004, 77–78).

"Yes, he's got a father, but you can't never find him, these days. He used to lay drunk with the hogs in the tanyard, but he hain't been seen in these parts for a year or more."[16]

They talked it over, and they was going to rule me out, because they said every boy must have a family or somebody to kill, or else it wouldn't be fair and square for the others. Well, nobody could think of anything to do—everybody was stumped, and set still. I was most ready to cry; but all at once I thought of a way, and so I offered them Miss Watson—they could kill her. Everybody said:

"Oh, she'll do, she'll do. That's all right. Huck can come in."

Then they all stuck a pin in their fingers to get blood to sign with, and I made my mark on the paper.

"Now," says Ben Rogers, "what's the line of business of this Gang?"

"Nothing only robbery and murder," Tom said.

"But who are we going to rob? houses—or cattle—or"[17]

"Stuff! stealing cattle and such things ain't robbery, it's burglary," says Tom Sawyer. "We ain't burglars. That ain't no sort of style. We are high-waymen. We stop stages and carriages on the road,[18] with masks on, and kill the people and take their watches and money."

---

16. A tanyard was part of a tannery. Tanning animal hides was one of the relatively few manufacturing industries in the antebellum South. Southern factories tended to be small and to use locally obtained materials, as with sawmills that had an ample local supply of trees. In the North, manufacturing had taken off soon after 1800 and had grown to include mammoth textile companies such as Francis Lowell's. Historians have long debated the 19th-century South's failure to industrialize. Leading explanations include the high profitability of growing cotton, the fear of using slaves in an industrial setting, and an aristocratic rural mind-set among southern plantation owners who considered gentleman farming a nobler calling than manufacturing. Twain understood that romantic southern mind-set well and frequently ridiculed it in his writing, including later in this book.

17. Stealing cattle is a staple of villains in movie Westerns, but it is a bit of an anachronism here. With the big exception of Texas, the antebellum slave states generally did not have cattle ranches large enough to pique the interest of ambitious thieves. After Texas, Missouri, with almost as many cows as people in 1860, raised the most cattle of the slave states (Hawk 1934, 269). Like the Widow Douglas, many farm families owned cattle, typically milk cows, for home consumption. While it was common to sell one's surplus milk, beef, and hides, these markets tended to be limited and local. With the exception of Kentucky and Tennessee, most slave states imported more meat than they exported (Sexton 1986–1987, 161). The rise of the railroads and refrigerated rail cars after the Civil War changed the cattle industry forever.

18. Horse-drawn stagecoaches and carriages were the leading means of land transportation in the antebellum United States, before the great age of railroad building. The early highways were turnpikes, usually dirt road clearings requiring much maintenance. This form of transportation was extremely expensive, so much so that Congressman Daniel Webster said in 1824 that "Stockholm . . . may be considered as within fifty miles of Phila-

"Must we always kill the people?"

"Oh, certainly. It's best. Some authorities think different, but mostly it's considered best to kill them. Except some that you bring to the cave here and keep them till they're ransomed."

"Ransomed? What's that?"

"I don't know. But that's what they do. I've seen it in books; and so of course that's what we've got to do."

"But how can we do it if we don't know what it is?"

"Why blame it all, we've *got* to do it. Don't I tell you it's in the books? Do you want to go to doing different from what's in the books, and get things all muddled up?"

"Oh, that's all very fine to *say,* Tom Sawyer, but how in the nation are these fellows going to be ransomed if we don't know how to do it to them? that's the thing I want to get at. Now, what do you *reckon* it is?"

"Well I don't know. But per'aps if we keep them till they're ransomed, it means that we keep them till they're dead."

"Now, that's something *like.* That'll answer. Why couldn't you said that before? We'll keep them till they're ransomed to death—and a bothersome lot they'll be, too, eating up everything and always trying to get loose."

"How you talk, Ben Rogers. How can they get loose when there's a guard over them, ready to shoot them down if they move a peg?"

"A guard! Well, that *is* good. So somebody's got to set up all night and never get any sleep, just so as to watch them. I think that's foolishness. Why can't a body take a club and ransom them as soon as they get here?"

"Because it ain't in the books so—that's why. Now, Ben Rogers, do you want to do things regular, or don't you?—that's the idea. Don't you reckon that the people that made the books knows what's the correct thing to do? Do you reckon *you* can learn 'em anything? Not by a good deal. No, sir, we'll just go on and ransom them in the regular way."

"All right. I don't mind; but I say it's a fool way, anyhow. Say, do we kill the women, too?"

---

delphia," because the cost of moving freight 50 miles inland was as high as shipping it across an ocean (Attack and Passell, 143). The need for cheaper transportation as America's landholdings expanded, notably with the Louisiana Purchase and victory in the Mexican-American War, sparked the 19th-century transportation revolution, first with steamboats and then with canals and railroads. Although America's first railroad, the Baltimore & Ohio, began operations in 1830, it would be decades before the railroads overtook the canals and steamboats. Early American cities and towns had been near navigable waters, and the pattern continued through the first half of the 19th century until the railroads opened up the rest of the country for settlement.

"Well, Ben Rogers, if I was as ignorant as you I wouldn't let on. Kill the women? No—nobody ever saw anything in the books like that. You fetch them to the cave, and you're always as polite as pie to them; and by and by they fall in love with you and never want to go home any more."

"Well, if that's the way, I'm agreed, but I don't take no stock in it. Mighty soon we'll have the cave so cluttered up with women, and fellows waiting to be ransomed, that there won't be no place for the robbers. But go ahead, I ain't got nothing to say."

Little Tommy Barnes was asleep, now, and when they waked him up he was scared, and cried, and said he wanted to go home to his ma, and didn't want to be a robber any more.

So they all made fun of him, and called him cry-baby, and that made him mad, and he said he would go straight and tell all the secrets. But Tom give him five cents to keep quiet,[19] and said we would all go home and meet next week, and rob somebody and kill some people.

Ben Rogers said he couldn't get out much, only Sundays, and so he wanted to begin next Sunday; but all the boys said it would be wicked to do it on Sunday, and that settled the thing. They agreed to get together and fix a day as soon as they could, and then we elected Tom Sawyer first captain and Jo Harper second captain of the Gang, and so started home.

I clumb up the shed and crept into my window just before day was breaking. My new clothes was all greased up and clayey, and I was dog-tired.

CHAPTER III.

WELL, I got a good going-over in the morning from old Miss Watson, on account of my clothes; but the widow she didn't scold, but only cleaned off the grease and clay and looked so sorry that I thought I would behave a while if I could. Then Miss Watson she took me in the closet and prayed, but nothing come of it. She told me to pray every day, and whatever I asked for I would get it. But it warn't so. I tried it. Once I got a fish-line, but no hooks. It warn't any good to me without hooks. I tried for the hooks three or four times, but somehow I couldn't make it work. By and by, one day, I asked Miss Watson to try for me, but she said I was a fool. She never told me why, and I couldn't make it out no way.

---

19. Five cents times 30 equals $1.50 in 2015 money.

I set down, one time back in the woods, and had a long think about it. I says to myself, if a body can get anything they pray for, why don't Deacon Winn get back the money he lost on pork?[20] Why can't the widow get back her silver snuff-box that was stole? Why can't Miss Watson fat up? No, says I to myself, there ain't nothing in it. I went and told the widow about it, and she said the thing a body could get by praying for it was "spiritual gifts." This was too many for me, but she told me what she meant—I must help other people, and do everything I could for other people, and look out for them all the time, and never think about myself. This was including Miss Watson, as I took it. I went out in the woods and turned it over in my mind a long time, but I couldn't see no advantage about it—except for the other people—so at last I reckoned I wouldn't worry about it any more, but just let it go. Sometimes the widow would take me one side and talk about Providence in a way to make a body's mouth water; but maybe next day Miss Watson would take hold and knock it all down again. I judged I could see that there was two Providences, and a poor chap would stand consider-able show with the widow's Providence, but if Miss Watson's got him there warn't no help for him any more. I thought it all out, and reckoned I would belong to the widow's if he wanted me, though I couldn't make out how he was agoing to be any better off then than what he was before, seeing I was so ignorant, and so kind of low-down and ornery.[21]

---

20. Deacon Winn apparently speculated on pork and made a bad bet. Speculation, roughly defined as buying something in order to sell it later at a profit, was perhaps more common in 19th-century America than anyplace else on Earth. "Every man is a speculator," wrote Jeremiah Church in an 1845 travelogue of the Midwest and the South, "from a wood-sawyer to a President, as far as his means will go, and credit also" (qtd. in Fraser 2006, vii). Economist John Kenneth Galbraith wrote that "the speculative imagination was in its most ardent form in the United States" (1994, 54). Several likely factors explain Americans' spec-ulative tendencies in the 19th century. The country was prosperous and growing fast, so investment opportunities were numerous (though not always easy to spot). Americans had long had a more entrepreneurial spirit than their European counterparts, dating back to colonial times (Perkins 1989, 169). "I do not know a country where the love of money holds a larger place in the heart of man," Alexis de Tocqueville wrote in 1835 (Tocqueville 2000, 50). "We have been primarily a business people," said historian Thomas C. Cochran, "and business has been most important in our lives" (Cochran and Miller 1961, 2).

21. "Ornery" is an American slang term derived from "ordinary" and dating back to 1816. It appears 14 times in this novel. The term has always had a negative connotation, origi-nally meaning commonplace, crude, or inferior. That usage had a whiff of snobbery to it, since by definition most people are ordinary. It seems rooted in American ambition; the notion that anyone can be rich and successful—the American Dream?—implies that the poor and even the middle class are failures. Huck in his ruminations seems to internalize that mind-set.

By 1860, well after Huck's time but well before Twain wrote *Huckleberry Finn,* the main definition of "ornery" had become the modern one: irritable, belligerent, unpleasant (Online Etymology Dictionary).

Pap he hadn't been seen for more than a year, and that was comfortable for me; I didn't want to see him no more. He used to always whale me when he was sober and could get his hands on me; though I used to take to the woods most of the time when he was around. Well, about this time he was found in the river drownded, about twelve mile above town, so people said. They judged it was him, anyway; said this drownded man was just his size, and was ragged, and had uncommon long hair—which was all like pap—but they couldn't make nothing out of the face, because it had been in the water so long it warn't much like a face at all. They said he was floating on his back in the water. They took him and buried him on the bank. But I warn't comfortable long, because I happened to think of something. I knowed mighty well that a drownded man don't float on his back, but on his face. So I knowed, then, that this warn't pap, but a woman dressed up in a man's clothes. So I was uncomfortable again. I judged the old man would turn up again by and by, though I wished he wouldn't.

We played robber now and then about a month, and then I resigned. All the boys did. We hadn't robbed nobody, we hadn't killed any people, but only just pretended. We used to hop out of the woods and go charging down on hog-drovers and women in carts taking garden stuff to market, but we never hived any of them. Tom Sawyer called the hogs "ingots," and he called the turnips and stuff "julery," and we would go to the cave and powwow over what we had done, and how many people we had killed and marked. But I couldn't see no profit in it. One time Tom sent a boy to run about town with a blazing stick, which he called a slogan (which was the sign for the Gang to get together), and then he said he had got secret news by his spies that next day a whole parcel of Spanish merchants and rich A-rabs was going to camp in Cave Hollow with two hundred elephants, and six hundred camels, and over a thousand "sumter" mules, all loaded down with di'monds, and they didn't have only a guard of four hundred soldiers, and so we would lay in ambuscade, as he called it, and kill the lot and scoop the things.[22] He said we must slick up our swords and

---

22. Tom's inspirations clearly involve other times and other places. The great age of Spanish exploration and extraction in the Americas was in the 1490s, beginning with Christopher Columbus's multiple voyages, and the 16th century. Spain was still a rich country in the 19th century, but by 1826 it had lost all of its American colonies except Cuba and Puerto Rico. Arabs did not immigrate to the United States in significant numbers until the 1880s, and the Arab world of the 19th century, ruled by a weakened Ottoman Empire, was not one that most people would associate with wealth. *The Arabian Nights* (1706) may be the inspiration here. Tom appropriately mentions *Don Quixote* (1605), the story of a delusional "knight-errant" led astray by reading too many chivalric novels.

guns, and get ready. He never could go after even a turnip-cart but he must have the swords and guns all scoured up for it; though they was only lath and broomsticks, and you might scour at them till you rotted and then they warn't worth a mouthful of ashes more than what they was before. I didn't believe we could lick such a crowd of Spaniards and A-rabs, but I wanted to see the camels and elephants, so I was on hand next day, Saturday, in the ambuscade; and when we got the word, we rushed out of the woods and down the hill. But there warn't no Spaniards and A-rabs, and there warn't no camels nor no elephants. It warn't anything but a Sunday-school picnic, and only a primer-class at that. We busted it up, and chased the children up the hollow; but we never got anything but some doughnuts and jam, though Ben Rogers got a rag doll, and Jo Harper got a hymn-book and a tract; and then the teacher charged in and made us drop everything and cut. I didn't see no di'monds, and I told Tom Sawyer so. He said there was loads of them there, anyway; and he said there was A-rabs there, too, and elephants and things. I said, why couldn't we see them, then? He said if I warn't so ignorant, but had read a book called "Don Quixote," I would know without asking. He said it was all done by enchantment. He said there was hundreds of soldiers there, and elephants and treasure, and so on, but we had enemies which he called magicians, and they had turned the whole thing into an infant Sunday school, just out of spite. I said, all right, then the thing for us to do was to go for the magicians. Tom Sawyer said I was a numskull.

"Why," says he, "a magician could call up a lot of genies, and they would hash you up like nothing before you could say Jack Robinson. They are as tall as a tree and as big around as a church."

"Well," I says, "s'pose we got some genies to help *us*—can't we lick the other crowd then?"

"How you going to get them?"

"I don't know. How do *they* get them?"

"Why, they rub an old tin lamp or an iron ring, and then the genies come tearing in, with the thunder and lightning a-ripping around and the smoke a-rolling, and everything they're told to do they up and do it. They don't think nothing of pulling a shot tower[23] up by the roots, and

---

23. A shot tower is used in making buckshot ammunition for shotguns. The production method is crude: molten lead is dropped into a tall cylindrical tower, and on the way down it congeals into little balls, which are cooled when they fall into a pool of water at the bottom. Despite the relative scarcity of manufacturing in the slave states, shotgun ammunition was always in high demand, and buckshot was easy enough to produce, so it is no surprise that Tom and his friends would be familiar with shot towers.

belting a Sunday-school superintendent over the head with it—or any other man."

"Who makes them tear around so?"

"Why, whoever rubs the lamp or the ring. They belong to whoever rubs the lamp or the ring, and they've got to do whatever he says. If he tells them to build a palace forty miles long out of di'monds, and fill it full of chewing gum, or whatever you want, and fetch an emperor's daughter from China for you to marry, they've got to do it—and they've got to do it before sun-up next morning, too. And more—they've got to waltz that palace around over the country wherever you want it, you understand."

"Well," says I, "I think they are a pack of flatheads for not keeping the palace themselves 'stead of fooling them away like that. And what's more—if I was one of them I would see a man in Jericho before I would drop my business and come to him for the rubbing of an old tin lamp."

"How you talk, Huck Finn. Why, you'd *have* to come when he rubbed it, whether you wanted to or not."

"What, and I as high as a tree and as big as a church? All right, then; I *would* come; but I lay I'd make that man climb the highest tree there was in the country."

"Shucks, it ain't no use to talk to you, Huck Finn. You don't seem to know anything, somehow—perfect sap-head."

I thought all this over for two or three days, and then I reckoned I would see if there was anything in it. I got an old tin lamp and an iron ring, and went out in the woods and rubbed and rubbed till I sweat like an Injun,[24] calculating to build a palace and sell it; but it warn't no use, none of the genies come. So then I judged that all that stuff was only just one of Tom Sawyer's lies. I reckoned he believed in the A-rabs and the elephants, but as for me I think different. It had all the marks of a Sunday-school.

---

24. "Sweat like an Injun" appears to refer to Native American purification ceremonies held in "sweat lodges," structures similar to saunas, with heated stones and water poured over them to make steam.

"Injun" was a 19th-century colloquial spelling and pronunciation of "Indian" (Online Etymology Dictionary). It appears 11 times in the novel. The term is widely considered to be offensive today, but it appears to have originated innocently as American dialect. A colonel in 1812 noted that people in Tennessee said "Injun." Twain himself is widely credited for popularizing "Injun" and "Honest Injun" in *Roughing It, Tom Sawyer,* and *Huckleberry Finn* and also widely blamed for turning "Injun" into a derogatory term, as his "Injuns" in *Roughing It* are squalid scoundrels, and his Injun Joe is an archvillain (Wolfram and Reaser 2014, 189).

CHAPTER IV.

WELL, three or four months run along, and it was well into the winter, now. I had been to school most all the time, and could spell, and read, and write just a little, and could say the multiplication table up to six times seven is thirty-five, and I don't reckon I could ever get any further than that if I was to live forever. I don't take no stock in mathematics, anyway.[25]

At first I hated the school, but by and by I got so I could stand it. Whenever I got uncommon tired I played hookey, and the hiding I got next day done me good and cheered me up. So the longer I went to school the easier it got to be. I was getting sort of used to the widow's ways, too, and they warn't so raspy on me. Living in a house and sleeping in a bed pulled on me pretty tight, mostly, but before the cold weather I used to slide out and sleep in the woods, sometimes, and so that was a rest to me. I liked the old ways best, but I was getting so I liked the new ones, too, a little bit. The widow said I was coming along slow but sure, and doing very satisfactory. She said she warn't ashamed of me.

One morning I happened to turn over the salt-cellar at breakfast. I reached for some of it as quick as I could to throw over my left shoulder and keep off the bad luck, but Miss Watson was in ahead of me, and crossed me off. She says, "Take your hands away, Huckleberry—what a mess you are always making." The widow put in a good word for me, but that warn't going to keep off the bad luck, I knowed that well enough. I started out, after breakfast, feeling worried and shaky, and wondering where it was going to fall on me, and what it was going to be. There is ways to keep off some kinds of bad luck, but this wasn't one of them kind; so I never tried to do anything, but just poked along low-spirited and on the watch-out.

I went down to the front garden and clumb over the stile, where you go through the high board fence. There was an inch of new snow on the ground, and I seen somebody's tracks. They had come up from the quarry

---

25. Huck, although about 14 years old (as we learn in Chapter 17), was not in school until the Widow Douglas enrolled him a few months earlier and, presumably, paid his tuition. Free and compulsory public education did not become the norm in the South, even for whites, until much later. Twain wrote with customary hyperbole: "There were no public schools in Missouri, but there were two private schools" (Twain 2010, 2:177). Public education came much earlier to northern states, with more diversified economies and more egalitarian traditions. The antebellum South's dependence on agriculture, and on cotton slavery in particular, tended to militate against investing in public education. The wealthiest families could afford private tutors or private schools, and agriculture was so entrenched that the return on investing in education was hard to see, especially when all but the youngest children could be productive in the fields.

and stood around the stile a while, and then went on around the garden fence. It was funny they hadn't come in, after standing around so. I couldn't make it out. It was very curious, somehow. I was going to follow around, but I stooped down to look at the tracks first. I didn't notice anything at first, but next I did. There was a cross in the left boot-heel made with big nails, to keep off the devil.

I was up in a second and shinning down the hill. I looked over my shoulder every now and then, but I didn't see nobody. I was at Judge Thatcher's as quick as I could get there. He said:

"Why, my boy, you are all out of breath. Did you come for your interest?"

"No, sir," I says; "is there some for me?"

"Oh, yes, a half-yearly is in, last night. Over a hundred and fifty dollars. Quite a fortune for you. You better let me invest it along with your six thousand, because if you take it you'll spend it."

"No, sir," I says, "I don't want to spend it.[26] I don't want it at all—nor the six thousand, nuther. I want you to take it; I want to give it to you—the six thousand and all."

He looked surprised. He couldn't seem to make it out. He says:

"Why, what can you mean, my boy?"

I says, "Don't you ask me no questions about it, please. You'll take it—won't you?"

He says:

"Well, I'm puzzled. Is something the matter?"

"Please take it," says I, "and don't ask me nothing—then I won't have to tell no lies."

He studied a while, and then he says:

"Oho-o. I think I see. You want to *sell* all your property to me—not give it. That's the correct idea."

Then *he* wrote something on a paper and read it over, and says:

"There—you see it says 'for a consideration.' That means I have bought it of you and paid you for it. Here's a dollar for you. Now you sign it."

So I signed it, and left.[27]

---

26. Huck might have had a hard time spending that much money even if he had wanted to. At a dollar a day, the "half-yearly" interest would be about $182, or roughly $5,460 in today's money. This is more than most 13- or 14-year-olds could imagine spending, especially in a small town and in a time when people were far more self-sufficient than today.

27. It looks like Judge Thatcher has just cheated Huck out of his fortune, just as Pap Finn sought to do, but we know from *The Adventures of Tom Sawyer* that Judge Thatcher is scrupulously honest. We cannot tell at this point whether Huck cares about the money, but clearly he cares enough to want to keep it from Pap. Judge Thatcher embodies the idea of fiduciary responsibility—that is, of putting the clients' interest ahead of his own. He has

Miss Watson's nigger, Jim, had a hair-ball as big as your fist, which had been took out of the fourth stomach of an ox, and he used to do magic with it. He said there was a spirit inside of it, and it knowed everything. So I went to him that night and told him pap was here again, for I found his tracks in the snow. What I wanted to know was, what he was going to do, and was he going to stay? Jim got out his hair-ball, and said something over it, and then he held it up and dropped it on the floor. It fell pretty solid, and only rolled about an inch. Jim tried it again, and then another time, and it acted just the same. Jim got down on his knees and put his ear against it and listened. But it warn't no use; he said it wouldn't talk. He said sometimes it wouldn't talk without money. I told him I had an old slick counterfeit quarter that warn't no good because the brass showed through the silver a little, and it wouldn't pass nohow, even if the brass didn't show, because it was so slick it felt greasy, and so that would tell on it every time. (I reckoned I wouldn't say nothing about the dollar I got from the judge.) I said it was pretty bad money, but maybe the hair-ball would take it, because maybe it wouldn't know the difference. Jim smelt it and bit it and rubbed it, and said he would manage so the hair-ball would think it was good. He said he would split open a raw Irish potato[28] and stick the quarter in between and keep it there all night, and next morning you couldn't see no brass, and it wouldn't feel greasy no more, and so anybody in town would take it in a minute, let alone a hair-ball. Well, I knowed a potato would do that, before, but I had forgot it.

Jim put the quarter under the hair-ball and got down and listened again. This time he said the hair-ball was all right. He said it would tell my whole fortune if I wanted it to. I says, go on. So the hair-ball talked to Jim, and Jim told it to me. He says:

"Yo' ole father doan' know yit what he's a-gwyne to do. Sometimes he spec he'll go 'way, en den agin he spec he'll stay. De bes' way is to res' easy en let de ole man take his own way. Dey's two angels hoverin' roun'

---

not really bought the gold coins from Huck for a dollar; instead, "for a consideration" is deliberately vague so as to humor Huck, and the judge is ready to return the gold to Huck at any time. Huck's trust in Judge Thatcher brings to mind a famous quotation from J. P. Morgan, who said at a congressional hearing that when it comes to commercial credit, "the first thing is character. . . . Before money or anything else. Money cannot buy it. . . . Because a man I do not trust could not get money from me on all the bonds in Christendom" (qtd. in Chernow 2010, 154).

28. Potatoes are associated with the Irish but originated in the New World and did not come to Europe until Spanish traders brought them from Peru. "Irish potatoes" refers to a class of potatoes that include the russet potatoes that are most common in the United States today. The term distinguishes them from the (biologically unrelated) sweet potatoes and yams that were cultivated by Indians in the warmer areas of the Americas.

'bout him. One uv 'em is white en shiny, en t'other one is black. De white one gits him to go right, a little while, den de black one sail in en bust it all up. A body can't tell, yit, which one gwyne to fetch him at de las'. But you is all right. You gwyne to have considable trouble in yo' life, en considable joy. Sometimes you gwyne to git hurt, en sometimes you gwyne to git sick; but every time you's gwyne to git well agin. Dey's two gals flyin' 'bout you in yo' life. One uv 'em's light en t'other one is dark. One is rich en t'other is po'. You's gwyne to marry de po' one fust en de rich one by en by. You wants to keep 'way fum de water as much as you kin, en don't run no resk, 'kase it's down in de bills dat you's gwyne to git hung."

When I lit my candle and went up to my room that night there set pap his own self![29]

CHAPTER V.

I had shut the door to. Then I turned around and there he was. I used to be scared of him all the time, he tanned me so much.[30] I reckoned I was

---

29. The segue from "Irish potato" to Pap Finn may be intentional. Finn is a common Irish surname, though also a common English surname, and Pap is a classic 19th-century Irish stereotype, drunken and shiftless. Especially after the first great wave of Irish immigration during the 1840s potato famine, the Irish were at the bottom of the economic pyramid in America, ahead of only blacks and Indians. Scurrilous images of "shanty Irish," often depicted with simian features, were common until late in the century. Twain said that Pap was a composite of Hannibal's two town drunkards, one of whom was named Jimmy Finn (Fischer et al. 2010, 380). Yet the book contains no references to Pap's Irishness, nor is there any trace of an Irish dialect in his speech. In fact, Twain complained that Huck looked too "Irishy" in Edward W. Kemble's initial illustrations for the book. Twain's complaint makes historical sense in that very few Irish immigrated to the Americas before 1830.

30. "Tanned," as in "tanned one's hide," means beat or whipped to the point where one's skin would be darker from the wounds. The usage dates back to the 1660s, the same decade in which "Spare the rod and spoil the child" first appeared in a poem by Samuel Butler ("tan," Online Etymology Dictionary). Several verses of the Old Testament call for "the rod" as well, notably Proverbs 22:15: "Foolishness is bound in the heart of a child; but the rod of correction shall drive it far from him." Corporal punishment of children was common throughout the 19th century—a post–Civil War study found that three-fourths of American children had been "hit with an instrument" as part of parental discipline (Mintz 2004, 169)—but Pap's excessive "tanning" was child abuse even by antebellum standards. And as early as the 1830s beatings had become less of a first resort for parents, especially as early industrialization allowed middle- and upper-class mothers to spend less time on household production of items such as cloth and soap and more time on child rearing. "Maternal tenderness, patience, and love," as seen in the Widow Douglas and Aunt Polly, called for a different approach than harsh physical punishment, as practiced by Pap (Mintz 2004, 81).

scared now, too; but in a minute I see I was mistaken. That is, after the first jolt, as you may say, when my breath sort of hitched, he being so unexpected; but right away after, I see I warn't scared of him worth bothering about.

He was most fifty, and he looked it.[31] His hair was long and tangled and greasy, and hung down, and you could see his eyes shining through like he was behind vines. It was all black, no gray; so was his long, mixed-up whiskers. There warn't no color in his face, where his face showed; it was white; not like another man's white, but a white to make a body sick, a white to make a body's flesh crawl—a tree-toad white, a fish-belly white. As for his clothes—just rags, that was all. He had one ankle resting on t'other knee; the boot on that foot was busted, and two of his toes stuck through, and he worked them now and then. His hat was laying on the floor; an old black slouch with the top caved in, like a lid.[32]

I stood a-looking at him; he set there a-looking at me, with his chair tilted back a little. I set the candle down. I noticed the window was up; so he had clumb in by the shed. He kept a-looking me all over. By and by he says:

"Starchy clothes—very. You think you're a good deal of a big-bug, *don't* you?"

"Maybe I am, maybe I ain't," I says.

"Don't you give me none o' your lip," says he. "You've put on considerble many frills since I been away. I'll take you down a peg before I get done with you. You're educated, too, they say; can read and

---

31. Fifty was old in the 19th century. The life expectancy for white males (not counting those who died before their 10th birthday) was about 50–55 and actually seems to have decreased in the first half of the century. The decreased life expectancy during this time of rapid economic growth is a famous puzzle of American economic history. Likely factors are poor public sanitation, unsafe water supplies, and easier transmission of diseases as people moved into cities and towns. Well-to-do urban dwellers such as Mark Twain, who himself was nearing 50 as he finished *Huckleberry Finn,* typically lived much longer (Atack and Passell 1994, 224–227).

32. Slouch hats were wide-brimmed hats that tilted to one side, hence the "slouch." The word "slouch" may be a pun on Pap's shiftlessness, and Twain was fond of using it, as in *Roughing It* where he describes a friend as "slouchily dressed" (437). Then again, slouch hats were common and would be regularly worn by both Union and Confederate troops in the Civil War. Virtually all men and women wore hats in the 19th century, partly as protection from the elements and partly due to the dictates of fashion. Hats were among the earliest manufacturing industries in America. As was true of manufactures in general, the vast majority of hats were made in the North, notably in Danbury, Connecticut.

write.[33] You think you're better'n your father, now, don't you, because he can't? *I'll* take it out of you. Who told you you might meddle with such hifalut'n foolishness, hey?—who told you you could?"

"The widow. She told me."

"The widow, hey?—and who told the widow she could put in her shovel about a thing that ain't none of her business?"

"Nobody never told her."

"Well, I'll learn her how to meddle. And looky here—you drop that school, you hear? I'll learn people to bring up a boy to put on airs over his own father and let on to be better'n what *he* is. You lemme catch you fooling around that school again, you hear? Your mother couldn't read, and she couldn't write, nuther, before she died. None of the family couldn't before *they* died. I can't; and here you're a-swelling yourself up like this. I ain't the man to stand it—you hear? Say, lemme hear you read."

I took up a book and begun something about General Washington and the wars. When I'd read about a half a minute, he fetched the book a whack with his hand and knocked it across the house. He says:

"It's so. You can do it. I had my doubts when you told me. Now looky here; you stop that putting on frills. I won't have it. I'll lay for you, my smarty; and if I catch you about that school I'll tan you good. First you know you'll get religion, too. I never see such a son."

He took up a little blue and yaller picture of some cows and a boy, and says:

"What's this?"

"It's something they give me for learning my lessons good."

He tore it up, and says—

"I'll give you something better—I'll give you a cowhide."[34]

---

33. Pap's equating of basic literacy with being educated may seem comical, as basic literacy is only the beginning of an education today, but in antebellum America schooling was minimal, and a large portion of even the white population was illiterate. On the eve of the Civil War 8.3 percent of white American adults were illiterate, as were 12.3 percent in Missouri (Lindert 2004, 126). As late as 1910, the overall high school graduation rate was only 10 percent in the United States and did not reach 50 percent until 1940, which actually was much sooner than for any other country in the world (Goldin 1998, 347–349). The state of schooling in the antebellum South was considerably more primitive than in the North, as noted earlier. Adult white male illiteracy rates were above the national average in 1860 in all of the slave states, ranging from 10 percent to 23 percent (Lindert 2004, 126). Pap's illiteracy is less exceptional than his chronic drunkenness and joblessness.

34. Cowhide whips were common at the time and are associated with the punishment of slaves (Twain 2001, 55n10). Pap's cowhiding of Huck, both threatened and actual, brings to mind another stereotype, namely of the cruel and ignorant slave overseer.

He set there a-mumbling and a-growling a minute, and then he says—

"*Ain't* you a sweet-scented dandy, though? A bed; and bedclothes; and a look'n-glass; and a piece of carpet on the floor[35]—and your own father got to sleep with the hogs in the tanyard. I never see such a son. I bet I'll take some o' these frills out o' you before I'm done with you. Why, there ain't no end to your airs—they say you're rich. Hey?—how's that?"

"They lie—that's how."

"Looky here—mind how you talk to me; I'm a-standing about all I can stand, now—so don't gimme no sass. I've been in town two days, and I hain't heard nothing but about you bein' rich. I heard about it away down the river, too. That's why I come. You git me that money to-morrow—I want it."

"I hain't got no money."

"It's a lie. Judge Thatcher's got it. You git it. I want it."

"I hain't got no money, I tell you. You ask Judge Thatcher; he'll tell you the same."

"All right. I'll ask him; and I'll make him pungle, too, or I'll know the reason why. Say, how much you got in your pocket? I want it."

"I hain't got only a dollar, and I want that to—"

"It don't make no difference what you want it for—you just shell it out."

He took it and bit it to see if it was good, and then he said he was going down town to get some whisky; said he hadn't had a drink all day.[36] When

---

35. These manufactured goods would have been all the more exotic to Pap because they almost surely would have been imported from the North or Europe. Finer textiles and garments generally came from Europe, whereas American textile factories tended to specialize in coarser, cheaper fabrics, a pattern that reflected Europe's industrial head start and U.S. tariff policies that protected cheap U.S. textiles (Irwin and Temin 2001, 778–779, 791–792).

36. Whiskey was by far the most popular alcoholic drink in antebellum America, way ahead of lager beer, which by midcentury had found a foothold in German-heavy cities such as St. Louis and Milwaukee but did not overtake whiskey and other spirits until about 1900 (Rorabaugh 1979, Table A1.2). Pap may once again be acting according to Irish stereotype, this time in his preference for whiskey. In *Life on the Mississippi,* Twain recalled meeting an Irishman who had lived in St. Louis for decades and said that his compatriots had no use for beer: "'They don't drink it, sir. They can't drink it, sir. Give an Irishman lager for a month, and he's a dead man. An Irishman is lined with copper, and the beer corrodes it. But whiskey polishes the copper and is the saving of him, sir'" (Twain 1963, 117).

A dollar would have been easily enough for a drunken binge back then. Whiskey price data from the 1840s are fragmentary, but a gallon of cheap whiskey seems to have cost no more than 25 to 50 cents.

he had got out on the shed he put his head in again, and cussed me for putting on frills and trying to be better than him; and when I reckoned he was gone he come back and put his head in again, and told me to mind about that school, because he was going to lay for me and lick me if I didn't drop that.

Next day he was drunk, and he went to Judge Thatcher's and bully-ragged him and tried to make him give up the money, but he couldn't, and then he swore he'd make the law force him.

The judge and the widow went to law to get the court to take me away from him and let one of them be my guardian; but it was a new judge that had just come, and he didn't know the old man; so he said courts mustn't interfere and separate families if they could help it; said he'd druther not take a child away from its father. So Judge Thatcher and the widow had to quit on the business.

That pleased the old man till he couldn't rest. He said he'd cowhide me till I was black and blue if I didn't raise some money for him. I borrowed three dollars from Judge Thatcher, and pap took it and got drunk, and went a-blowing around and cussing and whooping and carrying on; and he kept it up all over town, with a tin pan, till most midnight; then they jailed him, and next day they had him before court, and jailed him again for a week. But he said *he* was satisfied; said he was boss of his son, and he'd make it warm for *him*.

When he got out the new judge said he was agoing to make a man of him. So he took him to his own house, and dressed him up clean and nice, and had him to breakfast and dinner and supper with the family, and was just old pie to him, so to speak. And after supper he talked to him about temperance and such things till the old man cried, and said he'd been a fool, and fooled away his life; but now he was agoing to turn over a new leaf and be a man nobody wouldn't be ashamed of, and he hoped the judge would help him and not look down on him. The judge said he could hug him for them words; so he cried, and his wife she cried again; pap said he'd been a man that had always been misunderstood before, and the judge said he believed it. The old man said that what a man wanted that was down was sympathy, and the judge said it was so; so they cried again. And when it was bedtime, the old man rose up and held out his hand, and says:

"Look at it, gentlemen and ladies all; take a-hold of it; shake it. There's a hand that was the hand of a hog; but it ain't so no more; it's the hand of a man that's started in on a new life, and'll die before he'll go back. You mark them words—don't forget I said them. It's a clean hand now; shake it—don't be afeard."

So they shook it, one after the other, all around, and cried. The judge's wife she kissed it. Then the old man he signed a pledge—made his

(Illustration by Edward W. Kemble. From Mark Twain, *Adventures of Huckleberry Finn*. New York: C. L. Webster, 1885. Digitized by the University of Virginia Library.)

mark.[37] The judge said it was the holiest time on record, or something like that. Then they tucked the old man into a beautiful room, which was the spare room, and in the night some time he got powerful thirsty and clumb out on to the porch-roof and slid down a stanchion and traded his

---

37. Pap has signed a temperance pledge. The temperance movement began as a crusade against drunkenness, especially public drunkenness, and singled out hard liquor such as "demon" rum and "poison" whiskey while making an exception for softer beverages such as alcoholic cider, beer, and wine. It became more ambitious over time. By midcentury, the temperance pledge typically meant a pledge of abstinence from all alcoholic beverages. Temperance pledges, as opposed to later government prohibitions on the sale or consumption of alcohol, were voluntary and individual-based. They were also stunningly successful in reducing drinking, especially of spirits, the consumption of which fell 60 percent from 1825 to 1850 and 80 percent from 1825 to 1900 (Rorabaugh 1979, Table A1.2).

new coat for a jug of forty-rod,[38] and clumb back again and had a good old time; and towards daylight he crawled out again, drunk as a fiddler, and rolled off the porch and broke his left arm in two places and was most froze to death when somebody found him after sun-up. And when they come to look at that spare room they had to take soundings before they could navigate it.

The judge he felt kind of sore. He said he reckoned a body could reform the old man with a shot-gun, maybe, but he didn't know no other way.[39]

CHAPTER VI.

WELL, pretty soon the old man was up and around again, and then he went for Judge Thatcher in the courts to make him give up that money, and he went for me, too, for not stopping school. He catched me a couple of times and thrashed me, but I went to school just the same, and dodged him or out-run him most of the time. I didn't want to go to school much before, but I reckoned I'd go now to spite pap. That law trial was a slow business; appeared like they warn't ever going to get started on it; so every now and then I'd borrow two or three dollars off of the judge for him,[40] to keep from getting a cowhiding. Every time he got money he got drunk; and every time he got drunk he raised Cain around town; and every time he raised Cain he got jailed. He was just suited—this kind of thing was right in his line.

He got to hanging around the widow's too much, and so she told him at last, that if he didn't quit using around there she would make trouble for him. Well, *wasn't* he mad? He said he would show who was Huck Finn's boss. So he watched out for me one day in the spring, and catched me, and took me up the river about three mile in a skiff, and crossed over to the

---

38. Forty-rod was cheap but potent whiskey, which legend claimed could kill a man before he could walk 40 rods, equivalent to an eighth of a mile (Twain 2001, 58n20).

39. The word "reform" also appears in the chapter's long descriptive title ("Huck's Father.—The Fond Parent.—Reform.") and as the caption of Kemble's illustration ("Reforming the Drunkard"). Temperance, which later became prohibitionism, was one of the leading reform movements in 19th century. So was abolitionism (which of course was stronger in northern states). Both were tied to Christian churches and drew some of their fervor from the religious revivalism of the period, dubbed the Second Great Awakening and coinciding with the growth of evangelical Baptist and Methodist sects in 1790–1840.

40. Sixty to 90 dollars in today's money (converted by multiplying by 30). This is a substantial amount of money for a boy to be borrowing and lending.

Illinois shore where it was woody and there warn't no houses but an old log hut in a place where the timber was so thick you couldn't find it if you didn't know where it was.[41] He kept me with him all the time, and I never got a chance to run off. We lived in that old cabin, and he always locked the door and put the key under his head, nights. He had a gun which he had stole, I reckon, and we fished and hunted, and that was what we lived on. Every little while he locked me in and went down to the store, three miles, to the ferry, and traded fish and game for whisky and fetched it home and got drunk and had a good time, and licked me.[42] The widow she found out where I was, by and by, and she sent a man over to try to get hold of me; but pap drove him off with the gun, and it warn't long after that till I was used to being where I was, and liked it; all but the cowhide part.

It was kind of lazy and jolly, laying off comfortable all day, smoking and fishing, and no books nor study. Two months or more run along, and my clothes got to be all rags and dirt, and I didn't see how I'd ever

---

41. America's dense forests were among the abundant natural resources that were pivotal to American prosperity. Wood was cheap, and wood-based industries such as shipbuilding and furniture production were important early manufacturing sectors all the way back to colonial times. Even in the South, which severely lagged behind the North in industrial development, sawmills were numerous and essential to producing lumber for homes and other buildings. Even small villages often had sawmills, especially if it was cheaper to cut down nearby trees and have the wood cut into lumber than to purchase precut lumber from an out-of-town mill.

In the absence of access to a sawmill, houses were often built directly from felled trees. Log cabins were both a symbol and a reality of the American frontier. Trees were abundant and labor was scarce on the frontier, and one person with an ax could build a cabin in a couple of weeks. The first store built in Twain's hometown of Hannibal was in a log cabin (Holcombe 1884, 148). Log cabins tended to be temporary dwellings; people often moved up from log cabins to full-sized log houses (Weslager 1969). The vast majority of houses in almost every state were made of wood, reflecting the nation's abundance of timber. It is easier to imagine the shiftless Pap moving into an abandoned log cabin than building one himself.

42. Living off the land was a tantalizing alternative to trying to make a living in civilization not only to Huck and Pap but also to many white Americans. Here the fish and game are so plentiful that Pap has a surplus to trade in town. The abundance of land, especially as the American Indians were decimated by disease, war, and forced relocation, gave many American laborers in frontier areas a high standard of living. Workers had considerable bargaining power, because if they did not like the wage an employer offered them they could refuse it and live quite well on their own. As a result, wages were high. This had been the general case from the beginning, when the inland portions of the British colonies in America were thickly forested but thinly populated; as the population in the East grew denser, the frontier and its abundance shifted west.

got to like it so well at the widow's, where you had to wash, and eat on a plate, and comb up, and go to bed and get up regular, and be forever bothering over a book, and have old Miss Watson pecking at you all the time. I didn't want to go back no more. I had stopped cussing, because the widow didn't like it; but now I took to it again because pap hadn't no objections. It was pretty good times up in the woods there, take it all around.

But by and by pap got too handy with his hick'ry, and I couldn't stand it. I was all over welts. He got to going away so much, too, and locking me in. Once he locked me in and was gone three days. It was dreadful lonesome. I judged he had got drownded, and I wasn't ever going to get out any more. I was scared. I made up my mind I would fix up some way to leave there. I had tried to get out of that cabin many a time, but I couldn't find no way. There warn't a window to it big enough for a dog to get through. I couldn't get up the chimbly, it was too narrow. The door was thick, solid oak slabs. Pap was pretty careful not to leave a knife or anything in the cabin when he was away; I reckon I had hunted the place over as much as a hundred times; well, I was most all the time at it, because it was about the only way to put in the time. But this time I found something at last; I found an old rusty wood-saw without any handle; it was laid in between a rafter and the clapboards of the roof. I greased it up and went to work. There was an old horse-blanket nailed against the logs at the far end of the cabin behind the table, to keep the wind from blowing through the chinks and putting the candle out. I got under the table and raised the blanket and went to work to saw a section of the big bottom log out, big enough to let me through. Well, it was a good long job, but I was getting towards the end of it when I heard pap's gun in the woods. I got rid of the signs of my work, and dropped the blanket and hid my saw, and pretty soon pap come in.

Pap warn't in a good humor—so he was his natural self. He said he was down town, and everything was going wrong. His lawyer said he reckoned he would win his lawsuit and get the money, if they ever got started on the trial; but then there was ways to put it off a long time, and Judge Thatcher knowed how to do it. And he said people allowed there'd be another trial to get me away from him and give me to the widow for my guardian, and they guessed it would win this time. This shook me up considerable, because I didn't want to go back to the widow's any more and be so cramped up and sivilized, as they called it. Then the old man got to cussing, and cussed everything and everybody he could think of, and then cussed them all over again to make sure he hadn't skipped any, and after that he polished off with a kind of a general cuss all round, including a considerable parcel of people which he didn't know the names of, and so called them what's-his-name, when he got to them, and went right along with his cussing.

He said he would like to see the widow get me. He said he would watch out, and if they tried to come any such game on him he knowed of a place six or seven mile off to stow me in, where they might hunt till they dropped and they couldn't find me. That made me pretty uneasy again, but only for a minute; I reckoned I wouldn't stay on hand till he got that chance.

The old man made me go to the skiff and fetch the things he had got. There was a fifty-pound sack of corn meal, and a side of bacon, ammunition, and a four-gallon jug of whisky, and an old book and two newspapers for wadding,[43] besides some tow. I toted up a load, and went back and set down on the bow of the skiff to rest. I thought it all over, and I reckoned I would walk off with the gun and some lines, and take to the woods when I run away. I guessed I wouldn't stay in one place, but just tramp right across the country, mostly night times, and hunt and fish to keep alive, and so get so far away that the old man nor the widow couldn't ever find me any more. I judged I would saw out and leave that night if pap got drunk enough, and I reckoned he would. I got so full of it I didn't notice how long I was staying till the old man hollered and asked me whether I was asleep or drownded.

I got the things all up to the cabin, and then it was about dark. While I was cooking supper the old man took a swig or two and got sort of warmed up, and went to ripping again. He had been drunk over in town, and laid in the gutter all night, and he was a sight to look at. A body would a thought he was Adam, he was just all mud. Whenever his liquor begun to work, he most always went for the govment. This time he says:

"Call this a govment! why, just look at it and see what it's like. Here's the law a-standing ready to take a man's son away from him—a man's own son, which he has had all the trouble and all the anxiety and all the expense of raising. Yes, just as that man has got that son raised at last, and ready to go to work and begin to do suthin' for *him* and give him a rest, the law up and goes for him. And they call *that* govment! That ain't all, nuther.

---

43. Pap, proudly illiterate, has no use for newspapers other than as padding, but for most 19th-century Americans newspapers had become a vital and nearly universal commodity, their main contact with the world beyond their community. The spread of newspapers was one of the great manifestations of the 19th-century industrial and communications revolutions that included the steam-powered printing press and later the telegraph. The nation had under 100 newspapers in 1790 and more than 1,400 in 1840, and circulation per newspaper increased as larger papers extended their reach into small towns and rural areas (Blumin 2000, 828). St. Louis County had 6 daily newspapers in 1840. Even a small county such as Marion, where Hannibal was located and which had a free population of only about 7,400 people in 1840, had 3 weekly newspapers (United States Department of State 1841, 90, 319).

The law backs that old Judge Thatcher up and helps him to keep me out o' my property. Here's what the law does. The law takes a man worth six thousand dollars and up'ards, and jams him into an old trap of a cabin like this, and lets him go round in clothes that ain't fitten for a hog. They call that govment! A man can't get his rights in a govment like this. Sometimes I've a mighty notion to just leave the country for good and all. Yes, and I *told* 'em so; I told old Thatcher so to his face. Lots of 'em heard me, and can tell what I said. Says I, for two cents I'd leave the blamed country and never come a-near it agin. Them's the very words. I says look at my hat— if you call it a hat—but the lid raises up and the rest of it goes down till it's below my chin, and then it ain't rightly a hat at all, but more like my head was shoved up through a jint o' stove-pipe. Look at it, says I—such a hat for me to wear—one of the wealthiest men in this town, if I could git my rights.[44]

"Oh, yes, this is a wonderful govment, wonderful. Why, looky here. There was a free nigger there, from Ohio; a mulatter, most as white as a white man. He had the whitest shirt on you ever see, too, and the shiniest hat; and there ain't a man in that town that's got as fine clothes as what he

---

44. Pap's political rant, especially the revelation that he votes at all, is in keeping with the Jacksonian democracy of that era. Political participation soared during this time. The 1824 presidential election was the first in which ordinary voters in the vast majority of states cast ballots for president, with over 350,000 Americans voting. In 1828 well over 1 million Americans voted. Although the electoral college still made the final selection then as today, originally the members of the electoral college were generally chosen by state legislatures. States and localities also broadened the franchise significantly. Although most places still limited the franchise to white males, by 1840 all but three states had abolished property requirements for voters, people could vote directly for governors and county officials in most places, and voter turnout soared (Mintz and McNeil 2013).

Andrew Jackson, a Democrat best known for heroism in the War of 1812, won a plurality of the popular vote in 1824 but lost the electoral college vote to John Quincy Adams. Jackson ran again in 1828 as the people's choice, with broad populist appeals to the rights of ordinary Americans against privileged institutions such as the Bank of the United States, a forerunner of the Federal Reserve System, and won handily. His reelection in 1836 was a landslide as well. As president, Jackson made good on his promise to dismantle the Bank of the United States, which did not help the nation's economic stability but did endear him to millions of bank-hating Americans. Jackson also burnished his populist credentials by opening up the White House for a postinaugural party that drew unruly multitudes. "The reign of King Mob seemed triumphant," said U.S. Supreme Court justice Joseph Story at the time (Douglas 1999, 2). Jackson was perhaps the most popular of all of America's 19th-century presidents. His populist rhetoric was legendary. Even today Jackson remains one of our most iconic presidents, with his picture on the $20 bill (ironic, since he hated banknotes and preferred gold and silver coins), scores of cities and counties named after him, and an annual Jefferson-Jackson Dinner as a key Democratic Party fund-raising event.

had; and he had a gold watch and chain, and a silver-headed cane—the awfulest old gray-headed nabob in the State. And what do you think? they said he was a p'fessor in a college, and could talk all kinds of languages, and knowed everything.[45] And that ain't the wust. They said he could *vote*, when he was at home. Well, that let me out. Thinks I, what is the country a-coming to? It was 'lection day, and I was just about to go and vote, myself if I warn't too drunk to get there; but when they told me there was a State in this country where they'd let that nigger vote, I drawed out. I says I'll never vote agin. Them's the very words I said; they all heard me; and the country may rot for all me—I'll never vote agin as long as I live. And to see the cool way of that nigger—why, he wouldn't a give me the road if I hadn't shoved him out o' the way. I says to the people, why ain't this nigger put up at auction and sold?—that's what I want to know. And what do you reckon they said? Why, they said he couldn't be sold till he'd been in the State six months, and he hadn't been there that long yet. There, now— that's a specimen. They call that a govment that can't sell a free nigger till he's been in the State six months. Here's a govment that calls itself a govment, and lets on to be a govment, and thinks it is a govment, and yet's got to set stock-still for six whole months before it can take a hold of a prowling, thieving, infernal, white-shirted free nigger, and—"[46]

On the other hand, the content of Pap's political fulminations is reactionary, such as his insinuation that his supposed $6,000 in wealth entitles him to better treatment from the government. (This may be why Twain titled this chapter subsection "Political Economy.") And Jackson's presidency, as opposed to his rhetoric, was not so progressive, either, even by the standards of the time. The bank's destruction was a symbolic victory at best and did not benefit ordinary Americans, the nation's Indian removal policies were accelerated, and Jackson, himself a Tennessee slaveholder, strongly favored the expansion of slavery and the suppression of abolitionist mailings.

45. The "mulatter" professor bears an uncanny resemblance to the Reverend John G. Mitchell, a light-skinned African American who graduated from Oberlin College and became a professor at Wilberforce University in Ohio in 1863, where he taught Greek, Latin, and mathematics (Fischer et al. 2010, 392). He also resembles a tour guide whom Twain describes in the *The Innocents Abroad* (1869). The guide was born to slave parents in South Carolina and raised in Venice. "He is well educated. He reads, writes, and speaks English, Italian, Spanish, and French, with perfect facility; is a worshipper of art and thoroughly conversant with it; knows the history of Venice by heart and never tires of talking of her illustrious career. He dresses better than any of us, I think, and is daintily polite. Negroes are deemed as good as white people, in Venice, and so this man feels no desire to go back to his native land. His judgment is correct" (150–151).

46. Pap's rant about the "free nigger" brings to mind a quote from Lyndon B. Johnson, the president who helped pass the monumental civil rights legislation of the 1960s. Rising to power in Texas in the Jim Crow era, Johnson had seen all the tricks of segregationist politicians. He said in 1960 that "If you can convince the lowest white man he's better than the best colored man, he won't notice you're picking his pocket. Hell, give him somebody to

Pap was agoing on so, he never noticed where his old limber legs was taking him to, so he went head over heels over the tub of salt pork and barked both shins, and the rest of his speech was all the hottest kind of language—mostly hove at the nigger and the govment, though he give the tub some, too, all along, here and there. He hopped around the cabin considerable, first on one leg and then on the other, holding first one shin and then the other one, and at last he let out with his left foot all of a sudden and fetched the tub a rattling kick. But it warn't good judgment, because that was the boot that had a couple of his toes leaking out of the front end of it; so now he raised a howl that fairly made a body's hair raise, and down he went in the dirt, and rolled there, and held his toes; and the cussing he done then laid over anything he had ever done previous. He said so his own self, afterwards. He had heard old Sowberry Hagan in his best days, and he said it laid over him, too; but I reckon that was sort of piling it on, maybe.

After supper pap took the jug, and said he had enough whisky there for two drunks and one delirium tremens. That was always his word. I judged he would be blind drunk in about an hour, and then I would steal the key, or saw myself out, one or t'other. He drank and drank, and tumbled down on his blankets, by and by; but luck didn't run my way. He didn't go sound asleep, but was uneasy. He groaned and moaned and thrashed around this way and that for a long time. At last I got so sleepy I couldn't keep my eyes open, all I could do, and so before I knowed what I was about I was sound asleep, and the candle burning.

---

look down on, and he'll empty his pockets for you" (Dallek 1991, 584). Historians have long pondered how it was that nonslaveholding southern whites willingly served in compulsory slave patrols and especially in the Confederate military. Pap's rant is indicative of a frequent answer to that question: slaveholders successfully fanned the flames of antiblack racism, convincing other whites that free blacks posed a threat to society. Free blacks, even if not revolutionary like Denmark Vesey, who plotted a massive slave uprising in South Carolina in 1822, struck fear into the hearts of southern whites. A St. Louis police report said that "It is the saucy and insolent air of the *free* negroes which is most dangerous to the slave population" (Wade 1964, 228–241, 250–252).

Free blacks could not vote in Ohio at the time. In fact, by 1840 about 93 percent of northern free blacks lived in states that explicitly or effectively denied them the right to vote. Only Massachusetts, Maine, New Hampshire, and Vermont allowed blacks to vote on the same basis as whites. Three other eastern states—Connecticut, New Jersey, and Pennsylvania—had allowed blacks to vote at one time and then disenfranchised them (Litwack 1965, 74–75). Free blacks were generally regarded as a menace by northern and southern whites alike (Stampp 1956, 93). Northern antiblack racism boiled over in 1863 in the New York City Draft Riots, when working-class whites protested the "nigger war" with a week of rioting that included 11 lynchings, the destruction of the Coloured Orphan Asylum, and the exodus of hundreds of blacks from the city (Harris 2003, 280–285).

I don't know how long I was asleep, but all of a sudden there was an awful scream and I was up. There was pap, looking wild, and skipping around every which way and yelling about snakes. He said they was crawling up his legs; and then he would give a jump and scream, and say one had bit him on the cheek—but I couldn't see no snakes. He started and run round and round the cabin, hollering "Take him off! take him off! he's biting me on the neck!" I never see a man look so wild in the eyes. Pretty soon he was all fagged out, and fell down panting; then he rolled over and over, wonderful fast, kicking things every which way, and striking and grabbing at the air with his hands, and screaming, and saying there was devils ahold of him. He wore out, by and by, and laid still a while, moaning. Then he laid stiller, and didn't make a sound. I could hear the owls and the wolves, away off in the woods, and it seemed terrible still. He was laying over by the corner. By and by he raised up, part way, and listened, with his head to one side. He says, very low:

"Tramp—tramp—tramp; that's the dead; tramp—tramp—tramp; they're coming after me; but I won't go— Oh, they're here! don't touch me—don't! hands off—they're cold; let go— Oh, let a poor devil alone!"[47]

Then he went down on all fours and crawled off, begging them to let him alone, and he rolled himself up in his blanket and wallowed in under the old pine table, still a-begging; and then he went to crying. I could hear him through the blanket.

By and by he rolled out and jumped up on his feet looking wild, and he see me and went for me. He chased me round and round the place, with a clasp-knife, calling me the Angel of Death, and saying he would kill me, and then I couldn't come for him no more. I begged, and told him I was only Huck; but he laughed *such* a screechy laugh, and roared and cussed, and kept on chasing me up. Once when I turned short and dodged under his arm he made a grab and got me by the jacket between my shoulders, and I thought I was gone; but I slid out of the jacket quick as lightning, and saved myself. Pretty soon he was all tired out, and dropped down with his back against the door, and said he would rest a minute and then kill me. He put his knife under him, and said he would sleep and get strong, and then he would see who was who.

---

47. Though the judge's temperance lecture did not affect Pap's drinking, Pap appears to be haunted by a temperance song. "Tramp! Tramp! Tramp!" was a famous Civil War song written by George F. Root as an anthem of hope for Union soldiers. It was adapted into a temperance rallying song that included the lines "Tramp, tramp, tramp, in the drunkard's way / March the feet of a million men." Unless "Tramp, tramp, tramp" was already an old phrase when Root wrote his song, its use here is an anachronism, as the book is set least two decades before the song was written. See Fischer et al. 2010, 393n36.8; Hartsock 2014, 817.

So he dozed off, pretty soon. By and by I got the old split-bottom chair and clumb up, as easy as I could, not to make any noise, and got down the gun. I slipped the ramrod down it to make sure it was loaded, and then I laid it across the turnip barrel, pointing towards pap, and set down behind it to wait for him to stir. And how slow and still the time did drag along.

CHAPTER VII.

"GIT up! What you 'bout?"

I opened my eyes and looked around, trying to make out where I was. It was after sun-up, and I had been sound asleep. Pap was standing over me, looking sour and sick, too. He says—

"What you doin' with this gun?"

I judged he didn't know nothing about what he had been doing, so I says:

"Somebody tried to get in, so I was laying for him."

"Why didn't you roust me out?"

"Well, I tried to, but I couldn't; I couldn't budge you."

"Well, all right. Don't stand there palavering all day, but out with you and see if there's a fish on the lines for breakfast. I'll be along in a minute."

He unlocked the door and I cleared out, up the river bank. I noticed some pieces of limbs and such things floating down, and a sprinkling of bark; so I knowed the river had begun to rise. I reckoned I would have great times, now, if I was over at the town. The June rise used to be always luck for me; because as soon as that rise begins, here comes cord-wood floating down, and pieces of log rafts—sometimes a dozen logs together; so all you have to do is to catch them and sell them to the wood yards and the sawmill.[48]

---

48. The property losses from the annual "June rise" and from the current of the river itself—which devastated numerous buildings, farms, and even whole towns, as Twain details in *Life on the Mississippi*—point to the inefficiency of river transportation, even on powerful steamboats, relative to the railroads. By the 1850s, railroads were already beginning to overtake steamboats; by the time of *Huckleberry Finn*'s publication in the 1880s, railroads were dominant.

Log rafts were crude rafts made of logs rather than processed lumber. They were an ingenious way of shipping timber downriver, as the rafts could be cut up and used as logs once they reached their destination instead of being dragged back upriver at much higher cost. Even after steamboats came to dominate American transportation, floating a log raft downriver remained a cheap alternative to shipping timber as steamboat cargo. The raftsmen could deliver their raft and whatever freight it carried, and then they could ride a

I went along up the bank with one eye out for pap and t'other one out for what the rise might fetch along. Well, all at once, here comes a canoe; just a beauty, too, about thirteen or fourteen foot long, riding high like a duck. I shot head first off of the bank like a frog, clothes and all on, and struck out for the canoe. I just expected there'd be somebody laying down in it, because people often done that to fool folks, and when a chap had pulled a skiff out most to it they'd raise up and laugh at him. But it warn't so this time. It was a drift-canoe sure enough, and I clumb in and paddled her ashore. Thinks I, the old man will be glad when he sees this—she's worth ten dollars.[49] But when I got to shore pap wasn't in sight yet, and as I was running her into a little creek like a gully, all hung over with vines and willows, I struck another idea; I judged I'd hide her good, and then, stead of taking to the woods when I run off, I'd go down the river about fifty mile and camp in one place for good, and not have such a rough time tramping on foot.

It was pretty close to the shanty, and I thought I heard the old man coming, all the time; but I got her hid; and then I out and looked around a bunch of willows, and there was the old man down the path apiece just drawing a bead on a bird with his gun. So he hadn't seen anything.

When he got along, I was hard at it taking up a "trot" line. He abused me a little for being so slow, but I told him I fell in the river and that was what made me so long. I knowed he would see I was wet, and then he would be asking questions. We got five cat-fish off the lines and went home.

While we laid off, after breakfast, to sleep up, both of us being about wore out, I got to thinking that if I could fix up some way to keep pap and the widow from trying to follow me, it would be a certainer thing than trusting to luck to get far enough off before they missed me; you see, all kinds of things might happen. Well, I didn't see no way for a while, but by and by pap raised up a minute, to drink another barrel of water, and he says:

"Another time a man comes a-prowling round here, you roust me out, you hear? That man warn't here for no good. I'd a shot him. Next time you roust me out, you hear?"

---

steamboat back to where they had started. Log rafts could be huge—Huck implies that a dozen logs together is just a piece of log raft, and he is correct. Logs were customarily pushed together into "strings" 16 feet wide, which could be 12 logs. The length of a string would be 400 feet, as many logs would be laid end to end. Poles would be laid across each string to hold it together and tied on with small tree branches (Larson 1949, 93).

49. The lost canoe worth $10, or about $300 in today's money, provides another example of the financial risks associated with river commerce.

THE SHANTY.

(Illustration by Edward W. Kemble. From Mark Twain, *Adventures of Huckleberry Finn*. New York: C. L. Webster, 1885. Digitized by the University of Virginia Library.)

Then he dropped down and went to sleep again—but what he had been saying give me the very idea I wanted. I says to myself, I can fix it now so nobody won't think of following me.

About twelve o'clock we turned out and went along up the bank. The river was coming up pretty fast, and lots of drift-wood going by on the rise. By and by, along comes part of a log raft—nine logs fast together. We went out with the skiff and towed it ashore. Then we had dinner. Anybody but pap would a waited and seen the day through, so as to catch more stuff; but that warn't pap's style. Nine logs was enough for one time; he must shove right over to town and sell. So he locked me in and took the skiff, and started off towing the raft about half-past three. I judged he wouldn't come back that night. I waited till I reckoned he had got a good start, then I out with my saw and went to work on that log again. Before he was t'other side of the river I was out of the hole; him and his raft was just a speck on the water away off yonder.

I took the sack of corn meal and took it to where the canoe was hid, and shoved the vines and branches apart and put it in; then I done the same with the side of bacon; then the whisky jug. I took all the coffee and sugar there was, and all the ammunition; I took the wadding; I took the bucket and gourd; I took a dipper and a tin cup, and my old saw and two blankets, and the skillet and the coffee-pot. I took fish-lines and matches and other things—everything that was worth a cent. I cleaned out the place. I wanted an axe, but there wasn't any, only the one out at the wood pile, and I knowed why I was going to leave that. I fetched out the gun, and now I was done.

I had wore the ground a good deal crawling out of the hole and dragging out so many things. So I fixed that as good as I could from the outside by scattering dust on the place, which covered up the smoothness and the sawdust. Then I fixed the piece of log back into its place, and put two rocks under it and one against it to hold it there,—for it was bent up at that place, and didn't quite touch ground. If you stood four or five foot away and didn't know it was sawed, you wouldn't ever notice it; and besides, this was the back of the cabin, and it warn't likely anybody would go fooling around there.

It was all grass clear to the canoe, so I hadn't left a track. I followed around to see. I stood on the bank and looked out over the river. All safe. So I took the gun and went up a piece into the woods and was hunting around for some birds, when I see a wild pig; hogs soon went wild in them bottoms after they had got away from the prairie farms. I shot this fellow and took him into camp.[50]

I took the axe and smashed in the door—I beat it and hacked it considerable, a-doing it. I fetched the pig in and took him back nearly to the table and hacked into his throat with the axe, and laid him down on the ground to bleed; I say ground because it *was* ground—hard packed, and no boards. Well, next I took an old sack and put a lot of big rocks in it,—all I could drag—and I started it from the pig and dragged it to the door and through the woods down to the river and dumped it in, and down it sunk, out of sight. You could easy see that something had been dragged over the ground. I did wish Tom Sawyer was there, I knowed he would take an

---

50. Pork was the main source of meat in southern diets. It was not uncommon, especially in the winter, for southern hogs to run wild in the woods, where they could eat acorns and other nuts that had fallen to the ground. Some of these pigs became feral, and most were scrawny in comparison with corn-fed pigs. Note that Huck mentions no difficulty in carrying the pig, so it seems to be a particularly meager specimen; hogs in the Chicago and Cincinnati markets typically weighed over 200 pounds. A top historian of slavery says that southern livestock was meager in general for several reasons, including poor transportation and slaves' lack of incentive to properly maintain the livestock (Genovese 1967, 113, 115, 117).

interest in this kind of business, and throw in the fancy touches. Nobody could spread himself like Tom Sawyer in such a thing as that.

Well, last I pulled out some of my hair, and blooded the axe good, and stuck it on the back side, and slung the axe in the corner. Then I took up the pig and held him to my breast with my jacket (so he couldn't drip) till I got a good piece below the house and then dumped him into the river. Now I thought of something else. So I went and got the bag of meal and my old saw out of the canoe and fetched them to the house. I took the bag to where it used to stand, and ripped a hole in the bottom of it with the saw, for there warn't no knives and forks on the place—pap done eve-rything with his clasp-knife, about the cooking. Then I carried the sack about a hundred yards across the grass and through the willows east of the house, to a shallow lake that was five mile wide and full of rushes—and ducks too, you might say, in the season. There was a slough or a creek leading out of it on the other side, that went miles away, I don't know where, but it didn't go to the river. The meal sifted out and made a little track all the way to the lake. I dropped pap's whetstone there too, so as to look like it had been done by accident. Then I tied up the rip in the meal sack with a string, so it wouldn't leak no more, and took it and my saw to the canoe again.

It was about dark now; so I dropped the canoe down the river under some willows that hung over the bank, and waited for the moon to rise. I made fast to a willow; then I took a bite to eat, and by and by laid down in the canoe to smoke a pipe and lay out a plan. I says to myself, they'll fol-low the track of that sackful of rocks to the shore and then drag the river for me. And they'll follow that meal track to the lake and go browsing down the creek that leads out of it to find the robbers that killed me and took the things. They won't ever hunt the river for anything but my dead carcass. They'll soon get tired of that, and won't bother no more about me. All right; I can stop anywhere I want to. Jackson's Island is good enough for me; I know that island pretty well, and nobody ever comes there. And then I can paddle over to town, nights, and slink around and pick up things I want. Jackson's Island's the place.

I was pretty tired, and the first thing I knowed, I was asleep. When I woke up I didn't know where I was, for a minute. I set up and looked around, a little scared. Then I remembered. The river looked miles and miles across. The moon was so bright I could a counted the drift logs that went a-slipping along, black and still, hundreds of yards out from shore. Everything was dead quiet, and it looked late, and *smelt* late. You know what I mean—I don't know the words to put it in.

I took a good gap and a stretch, and was just going to unhitch and start when I heard a sound away over the water. I listened. Pretty soon I made it out. It was that dull kind of a regular sound that comes from oars working in rowlocks when it's a still night. I peeped out through the willow branches, and there it was—a skiff, away across the water. I couldn't tell how many was in it. It kept a-coming, and when it was abreast of me I see there warn't but one man in it. Think's I, maybe it's pap, though I warn't expecting him. He dropped below me with the current, and by and by he come a-swinging up shore in the easy water, and he went by so close I could a reached out the gun and touched him. Well, it *was* pap, sure enough—and sober, too, by the way he laid to his oars.

I didn't lose no time. The next minute I was a-spinning down stream soft but quick in the shade of the bank. I made two mile and a half, and then struck out a quarter of a mile or more towards the middle of the river, because pretty soon I would be passing the ferry landing and people might see me and hail me. I got out amongst the drift-wood and then laid down in the bottom of the canoe and let her float. I laid there and had a good rest and a smoke out of my pipe, looking away into the sky, not a cloud in it. The sky looks ever so deep when you lay down on your back in the moonshine; I never knowed it before. And how far a body can hear on the water such nights! I heard people talking at the ferry landing. I heard what they said, too, every word of it. One man said it was getting towards the long days and the short nights now. T'other one said *this* warn't one of the short ones, he reckoned—and then they laughed, and he said it over again, and they laughed again; then they waked up another fellow and told him, and laughed, but he didn't laugh; he ripped out something brisk and said let him alone. The first fellow said he 'lowed to tell it to his old woman—she would think it was pretty good; but he said that warn't nothing to some things he had said in his time. I heard one man say it was nearly three o'clock, and he hoped day-light wouldn't wait more than about a week longer. After that the talk got further and further away, and I couldn't make out the words any more; but I could hear the mumble; and now and then a laugh, too, but it seemed a long ways off.

I was away below the ferry now. I rose up and there was Jackson's Island, about two mile and a half down stream, heavy-timbered and stand-ing up out of the middle of the river, big and dark and solid, like a steam-boat without any lights. There warn't any signs of the bar at the head—it was all under water now.

It didn't take me long to get there. I shot past the head at a ripping rate, the current was so swift, and then I got into the dead water and landed on the side towards the Illinois shore. I run the canoe into a deep dent in the bank that I knowed about; I had to part the willow branches to get in; and when I made fast nobody could a seen the canoe from the outside.

I went up and set down on a log at the head of the island and looked out on the big river and the black driftwood and away over to the town, three mile away, where there was three or four lights twinkling. A mon-strous big lumber-raft was about a mile up stream, coming along down,

This engraving by Alfred Rudolph Waud shows the massive size of log rafts. A typical log raft was longer than a football field; lumber rafts, consisting of sawn boards or beams, were even longer. Lumber and log rafts were a common means of shipping wood downriver, where the raft would be cut up. (Wood engraving by Alfred Rudolph Waud, circa 1871. Digitally repaired and toned by Finn for Steamboat Times, http://steamboattimes.com.)

with a lantern in the middle of it. I watched it come creeping down, and when it was most abreast of where I stood I heard a man say, "Stern oars, there! heave her head to stabboard!" I heard that just as plain as if the man was by my side.

There was a little gray in the sky, now; so I stepped into the woods, and laid down for a nap before breakfast.

CHAPTER VIII.

THE sun was up so high when I waked, that I judged it was after eight o'clock. I laid there in the grass and the cool shade, thinking about things, and feeling rested and ruther comfortable and satisfied. I could see the sun out at one or two holes, but mostly it was big trees all about, and gloomy in there amongst them. There was freckled places on the ground where the light sifted down through the leaves, and the freckled places swapped about a little, showing there was a little breeze up there. A couple of squirrels set on a limb and jabbered at me very friendly.

I was powerful lazy and comfortable—didn't want to get up and cook breakfast. Well, I was dozing off again when I thinks I hears a deep sound of "boom!" away up the river. I rouses up and rests on my elbow and listens; pretty soon I hears it again. I hopped up and went and looked out at a hole in the leaves, and I see a bunch of smoke laying on the water a long ways up—about abreast the ferry. And there was the ferry-boat full of people, floating along down. I knowed what was the matter, now. "Boom!" I see the white smoke squirt out of the ferry-boat's side. You see, they was firing cannon over the water, trying to make my carcass come to the top.

I was pretty hungry, but it warn't going to do for me to start a fire, because they might see the smoke. So I set there and watched the cannon-smoke and listened to the boom. The river was a mile wide, there, and it always looks pretty on a summer morning—so I was having a good enough time seeing them hunt for my remainders, if I only had a bite to eat. Well, then I happened to think how they always put quicksilver in loaves of bread and float them off because they always go right to the drownded carcass and stop there. So says I, I'll keep a lookout, and if any of them's floating around after me, I'll give them a show. I changed to the Illinois edge of the island to see what luck I could have, and I warn't disappointed. A big double loaf come along, and I most got it, with a long stick, but my foot slipped and she floated out further. Of course I was where the current set in the closest to the shore—I knowed enough for that. But by and by along comes another one, and this time I won. I took out the plug and shook out the little dab of quicksilver, and set my teeth in. It was "baker's bread"—what the quality eat—none of your low-down corn-pone.[51]

---

51. Corn pone, or corn bread, is still famous today as a staple of southern cooking. "Bakers' bread," likely made from wheat flour imported from northern farms, was a luxury. Corn pone was typically made from corn grown on one's own farm, as self-sufficiency was still the norm in the slave states. Many poorer whites could not afford store-bought food on a regular basis, and even plantations tended to be risk-averse, producing their own food, notably pork and corn, so as to avoid getting squeezed by fluctuations in crop and food prices. The relative self-sufficiency of the slave states is evident from census data on the number of stores in each state. In 1840 the slave states had one store for every 401 people, and the nonslave states had one for every 248 people. Missouri's comparatively high number of stores per person (one store per 347 people) may be a function of its comparatively low number of slaves (15 percent of the population versus 34 percent in the slave states as a whole) and the presence of a major trading center, St. Louis. Except for Louisiana and Maryland, which contained the great port emporiums of New Orleans and Baltimore, respectively, all of the states with higher slave concentrations than Missouri ranked near the bottom in terms of stores per person (United States Department of State 1841, 360, 368).

Corn pone also figures into an immortal Twain line, which he said he got from a slave he knew in Missouri: "You tell me whar a man gits his corn pone, en I'll tell you what his 'pinions is" (Twain 1994, 282).

I got a good place amongst the leaves, and set there on a log, munching the bread and watching the ferry-boat, and very well satisfied. And then something struck me. I says, now I reckon the widow or the parson or somebody prayed that this bread would find me, and here it has gone and done it. So there ain't no doubt but there is something in that thing—that is, there's something in it when a body like the widow or the parson prays, but it don't work for me, and I reckon it don't work for only just the right kind.

I lit a pipe and had a good long smoke and went on watching. The ferry-boat was floating with the current, and I allowed I'd have a chance to see who was aboard when she come along, because she would come in close, where the bread did. When she'd got pretty well along down towards me, I put out my pipe and went to where I fished out the bread, and laid down behind a log on the bank in a little open place. Where the log forked I could peep through.

By and by she come along, and she drifted in so close that they could a run out a plank and walked ashore. Most everybody was on the boat. Pap, and Judge Thatcher, and Bessie Thatcher, and Jo Harper, and Tom Sawyer, and his old Aunt Polly, and Sid and Mary, and plenty more. Everybody was talking about the murder, but the captain broke in and says:

"Look sharp, now; the current sets in the closest here, and maybe he's washed ashore and got tangled amongst the brush at the water's edge. I hope so, anyway."

I didn't hope so. They all crowded up and leaned over the rails, nearly in my face, and kept still, watching with all their might. I could see them first-rate, but they couldn't see me. Then the captain sung out:

"Stand away!" and the cannon let off such a blast right before me that it made me deef with the noise and pretty near blind with the smoke, and I judged I was gone. If they'd a had some bullets in, I reckon they'd a got the corpse they was after. Well, I see I warn't hurt, thanks to goodness. The boat floated on and went out of sight around the shoulder of the island. I could hear the booming, now and then, further and further off, and by and by after an hour, I didn't hear it no more. The island was three mile long. I judged they had got to the foot, and was giving it up. But they didn't yet a while. They turned around the foot of the island and started up the channel on the Missouri side, under steam, and booming once in a while as they went. I crossed over to that side and watched them. When they got abreast the head of the island they quit shooting and dropped over to the Missouri shore and went home to the town.

I knowed I was all right now. Nobody else would come a-hunting after me. I got my traps out of the canoe and made me a nice camp in the thick woods. I made a kind of a tent out of my blankets to put my things under so the rain couldn't get at them. I catched a catfish and haggled him open with my saw, and towards sundown I started my camp fire and had supper. Then I set out a line to catch some fish for breakfast.

When it was dark I set by my camp fire smoking, and feeling pretty satisfied; but by and by it got sort of lonesome, and so I went and set on the bank and listened to the currents washing along, and counted the stars and drift-logs and rafts that come down, and then went to bed; there ain't no better way to put in time when you are lonesome; you can't stay so, you soon get over it.

And so for three days and nights. No difference—just the same thing. But the next day I went exploring around down through the island. I was boss of it; it all belonged to me, so to say, and I wanted to know all about it; but mainly I wanted to put in the time. I found plenty strawberries, ripe and prime; and green summer-grapes, and green razberries; and the green blackberries was just beginning to show. They would all come handy by and by, I judged.

Well, I went fooling along in the deep woods till I judged I warn't far from the foot of the island. I had my gun along, but I hadn't shot nothing; it was for protection; thought I would kill some game nigh home. About this time I mighty near stepped on a good-sized snake, and it went sliding off through the grass and flowers, and I after it, trying to get a shot at it. I clipped along, and all of a sudden I bounded right on to the ashes of a camp fire that was still smoking.

My heart jumped up amongst my lungs. I never waited for to look further, but uncocked my gun and went sneaking back on my tip-toes as fast as ever I could. Every now and then I stopped a second, amongst the thick leaves and listened; but my breath come so hard I couldn't hear nothing else. I slunk along another piece further, then listened again; and so on, and so on; if I see a stump, I took it for a man; if I trod on a stick and broke it, it made me feel like a person had cut one of my breaths in two and I only got half, and the short half, too.

When I got to camp I warn't feeling very brash, there warn't much sand in my craw; but I says, this ain't no time to be fooling around. So I got all my traps into my canoe again so as to have them out of sight, and I put out the fire and scattered the ashes around to look like an old last year's camp, and then clumb a tree.

I reckon I was up in the tree two hours; but I didn't see nothing, I didn't hear nothing—I only *thought* I heard and seen as much as a thousand things. Well, I couldn't stay up there forever; so at last I got down, but I kept in the thick woods and on the lookout all the time. All I could get to eat was berries and what was left over from breakfast.

By the time it was night I was pretty hungry. So when it was good and dark I slid out from shore before moonrise and paddled over to the Illinois bank—about a quarter of a mile. I went out in the woods and cooked a supper, and I had about made up my mind I would stay there all night, when I hear a *plunkety-plunk, plunkety-plunk,* and says to myself, horses coming; and next I hear people's voices. I got everything into the canoe as quick as I could, and then went creeping through the woods to see what I could find out. I hadn't got far when I hear a man say:

"We better camp here, if we can find a good place; the horses is about beat out. Let's look around."

I didn't wait, but shoved out and paddled away easy. I tied up in the old place, and reckoned I would sleep in the canoe.

I didn't sleep much. I couldn't, somehow, for thinking. And every time I waked up I thought somebody had me by the neck. So the sleep didn't do me no good. By and by I says to myself, I can't live this way; I'm agoing to find out who it is that's here on the island with me; I'll find it out or bust. Well, I felt better, right off.

So I took my paddle and slid out from shore just a step or two, and then let the canoe drop along down amongst the shadows. The moon was shining, and outside of the shadows it made it most as light as day. I poked along well onto an hour, everything still as rocks and sound asleep. Well, by this time I was most down to the foot of the island. A little ripply, cool breeze begun to blow, and that was as good as saying the night was about done. I give her a turn with the paddle and brung her nose to shore; then I got my gun and slipped out and into the edge of the woods. I sat down there on a log and looked out through the leaves. I see the moon go off watch and the darkness begin to blanket the river. But in a little while I see a pale streak over the tree tops, and knowed the day was coming. So I took my gun and slipped off towards where I had run across that camp fire, stopping every minute or two to listen. But I hadn't no luck, somehow; I couldn't seem to find the place. But by and by, sure enough, I catched a glimpse of fire, away through the trees. I went for it, cautious and slow. By and by I was close enough to have a look, and there laid a man on the ground. It most give me the fan-tods. He had a blanket around his head, and his head was nearly in the fire. I set there behind a clump of bushes, in about six foot of him, and kept my eyes on him steady. It was getting gray daylight, now. Pretty soon he gapped, and stretched himself, and hove off the blanket, and it was Miss Watson's Jim![52] I bet I was glad to see him. I says:

---

52. Jackson's Island was modeled after Glasscock Island, located about three miles downstream from Hannibal. Glasscock Island was an alluvial soil island, created by the river's soil deposits and by now long since destroyed by the river. A boyhood friend of Twain's said that the densely forested, uninhabited island was a haven for escaped slaves (Twain 2001, 76n18). But it was sufficiently close by that they could not stay long without being caught. Where they would go from the island is unclear.

The name Jackson's Island goes with the 19th-century pattern of naming places after Andrew Jackson.

"Hello, Jim!" and skipped out.

He bounced up and stared at me wild. Then he drops down on his knees, and puts his hands together and says:

"Doan' hurt me—don't! I hain't ever done no harm to a ghos'. I alwuz liked dead people, en done all I could for 'em. You go en git in de river agin, whah you b'longs, en doan' do nuffn to Ole Jim, 'at 'uz awluz yo' fren'."

Well, I warn't long making him understand I warn't dead. I was ever so glad to see Jim. I warn't lonesome, now. I told him I warn't afraid of *him* telling the people where I was. I talked along, but he only set there and looked at me; never said nothing. Then I says:

"It's good daylight. Le's get breakfast. Make up your camp fire good."

"What's de use er makin' up de camp fire to cook strawbries en sich truck?[53] But you got a gun, hain't you? Den we kin git sumfn better den strawbries."

"Strawberries and such truck," I says. "Is that what you live on?"

"I couldn' git nuffn else," he says.

"Why, how long you been on the island, Jim?"

"I come heah de night arter you's killed."

"What, all that time?"

"Yes-indeedy."

"And ain't you had nothing but that kind of rubbage to eat?"[54]

"No, sah—nuffn else."

"Well, you must be most starved, ain't you?"

"I reck'n I could eat a hoss. I think I could. How long you ben on de islan'?"

"Since the night I got killed."

"No! W'y, what has you lived on? But you got a gun. Oh, yes, you got a gun. Dat's good. Now you kill sumfn en I'll make up de fire."

---

53. In early America, "truck" meant surplus garden produce brought, often carted ("trucked"), to market. Many farmers, including poorer southern whites on marginal land, produced mainly for their own subsistence (Taylor 1964, 441), but when they had surplus crops they were eager to sell them. Over the course of the 19th century "truck" came to mean "stuff in general," including edibles that grew wild (Online Etymology Dictionary).

54. Adult slaves were typically on a high-protein, high-calorie diet that was heavy on pork and corn, both of which tended to be raised on the plantations, and Jim seems to miss it. The hearty slave diets were not necessarily benevolence on the part of the slaveholders, nor were they rich in vitamins, but they did provide fuel for the arduous work. Meat was a notably large component of American diets in general, partly on account of the availability of fish and wildlife. It is notable that even a poor boy like Huck and a slave like Jim are so accustomed to meat that they scorn strawberries as "rubbage" (an apparent combination of "rubbish" and "garbage").

So we went over to where the canoe was, and while he built a fire in a grassy open place amongst the trees, I fetched meal and bacon and coffee, and coffee-pot and frying-pan, and sugar and tin cups, and the nigger was set back considerable, because he reckoned it was all done with witchcraft. I catched a good big catfish, too, and Jim cleaned him with his knife, and fried him.

When breakfast was ready, we lolled on the grass and eat it smoking hot. Jim laid it in with all his might, for he was most about starved. Then when we had got pretty well stuffed, we laid off and lazied.

By and by Jim says:

"But looky here, Huck, who wuz it dat 'uz killed in dat shanty, ef it warn't you?"

Then I told him the whole thing, and he said it was smart. He said Tom Sawyer couldn't get up no better plan than what I had. Then I says:

"How do you come to be here, Jim, and how'd you get here?"

He looked pretty uneasy, and didn't say nothing for a minute. Then he says:

"Maybe I better not tell."

"Why, Jim?"

"Well, dey's reasons. But you wouldn' tell on me ef I uz to tell you, would you, Huck?"

"Blamed if I would, Jim."

"Well, I b'lieve you, Huck. I—I *run off*."

"Jim!"

"But mind, you said you wouldn' tell—you know you said you wouldn' tell, Huck."

"Well, I did. I said I wouldn't, and I'll stick to it. Honest *injun,* I will. People would call me a low-down Ablitionist and despise me for keeping mum—but that don't make no difference.[55] I ain't agoing to tell, and I ain't agoing back there, anyways. So now, le's know all about it."

---

55. Abolitionists were still rather new and rare at the time when this book is set. The organized abolitionist movement is often thought to begin with the publication of David Walker's *An Appeal to the Coloured Citizens of the World* (1829), the first issue of William Lloyd Garrison's *The Liberator* (1831), and especially the formation of the American Anti-Slavery Society, which Garrison cofounded. The society engulfed the nation in controversy in 1835 when it launched a campaign to flood the South with abolitionist newspapers and other literature. Many southern postmasters destroyed this incoming mail, an interference with the national mail service that won the blessing of President Andrew Jackson and his postmaster general. The abolitionist cause was a lonely one even in the North, where there were "mobs that terrorized abolitionists, sacked newspaper offices, and destroyed anti-slavery presses." The postmaster of New York City made common cause with his southern brethren by refusing to mail abolitionist literature (Richards 1979, 108–109).

"Well, you see, it 'uz dis way. Ole missus—dat's Miss Watson—she pecks on me all de time, en treats me pooty rough, but she awluz said she wouldn' sell me down to Orleans. But I noticed dey wuz a nigger trader roun' de place considable, lately, en I begin to git oneasy. Well, one night I creeps to de do', pooty late, en de do' warn't quite shet, en I hear old missus tell de widder she gwyne to sell me down to Orleans, but she didn' want to, but she could git eight hund'd dollars for me, en it 'uz sich a big stack o' money she couldn' resis'.[56] De widder she try to git her to say she wouldn' do it, but I never waited to hear de res'. I lit out mighty quick, I tell you.[57]

"I tuck out en shin down de hill en 'spec to steal a skift 'long de sho' som'ers 'bove de town, but dey wuz people a-stirrin' yit, so I hid in de ole tumble-down cooper shop on de bank to wait for everybody to go 'way. Well, I wuz dah all night. Dey wuz somebody roun' all de time. 'Long 'bout six in de mawnin' skifts begin to go by, en 'bout eight er nine every skift dat went 'long wuz talkin' 'bout how yo' pap come over to de town en say you's killed. Dese las' skifts wuz full o' ladies en genlmen agoin' over for to see de place. Sometimes dey'd pull up at de sho' en take a res' b'fo' dey started acrost, so by de talk I got to know all 'bout de killin'. I 'uz powerful sorry you's killed, Huck, but I ain't no mo', now.

"I laid dah under de shavin's all day. I 'uz hungry, but I warn't afeard; bekase I knowed ole missus en de widder wuz goin' to start to de campmeetn' right arter breakfas' en be gone all day, en dey knows I goes off wid de cattle 'bout daylight, so dey wouldn' 'spec to see me roun' de place,

---

56. Eight hundred dollars is roughly what a prime-age male field hand would have sold for at a New Orleans slave auction in 1840. The market price for any slave varied considerably by year, but the general trend was upward, from about $600 in the early 1820s to over $1,000 in the late 1850s. Slave prices fluctuated so much—jumping to almost $1,200 in 1837, at the peak of that decade's credit bubble, before plunging to about $550 in 1843, following the collapse of 1839—that it seems fair to conclude that people speculated on slaves just like they did on stocks, land, and commodities (Kotlikoff 1979, 498). Historian Michael Tadman finds that speculation was central to the business of slaveholding and that the vast majority of slave sales were for profit (1989, 211).

57. As we see from Jim's account of the discussion between Miss Watson and the Widow Douglas, some slave owners tried to avoid selling their slaves "down the river," whereas others were more inclined to coldly regard them as moneymaking assets that could be sold whenever the price was right. Many owners encouraged stable slave families for labor discipline, procreation, and other reasons (Fogel and Engerman 1974, 52, 127). But slave sales that broke up families were still common, especially as slavery moved into the rich cotton-growing country of the Southwest in the 1840s and 1850s. In the Upper South, including Missouri, one out of every five married slave couples were separated by a sale, and one in three children (under age 14) were separated from their parents (Tadman 1989, 211–212).

en so dey wouldn' miss me tell arter dark in de evenin'. De yuther servants wouldn' miss me, kase dey'd shin out en take holiday, soon as de ole folks 'uz out'n de way.

"Well, when it come dark I tuck out up de river road, en went 'bout two mile er more to whah dey warn't no houses. I'd made up my mine 'bout what I's agwyne to do. You see, ef I kep' on tryin' to git away afoot, de dogs 'ud track me; ef I stole a skift to cross over, dey'd miss dat skift, you see, en dey'd know 'bout whah I'd lan' on de yuther side en whah to pick up my track. So I says, a raff is what I's arter; it doan' *make* no track.

"I see a light a-comin' roun' de p'int bymeby, so I wade' in en shove' a log ahead o' me en swum more'n half-way acrost de river, en got in 'mongst de drift-wood, en kep' my head down low, en kinder swum agin de current tell de raff come along. Den I swum to de stern uv it en tuck a-holt. It clouded up en 'uz pooty dark for a little while. So I clumb up en laid down on de planks. De men 'uz all 'way yonder in de middle, whah de lantern wuz. De river wuz a-risin' en dey wuz a good current; so I reck'n'd 'at by fo' in de mawnin' I'd be twenty-five mile down de river, en den I'd slip in, jis b'fo' daylight en swim asho' en take to de woods on de Illinoi side.[58]

"But I didn' have no luck. When we 'uz mos' down to de head er de islan' a man begin to come aft wid de lantern. I see it warn't no use fer to wait, so I slid overboard, en struck out fer de islan'. Well, I had a notion I could lan' mos' anywhers, but I couldn't—bank too bluff. I 'uz mos' to de foot er de islan' b'fo' I found' a good place. I went into de woods en jedged I wouldn' fool wid raffs no mo', long as dey move de lantern roun' so.[59]

---

58. The Mississippi River was all that separated the slave state of Missouri and the free state of Illinois. Slave escapes from border states—slave states that bordered at least one free state—were relatively common in view of the proximity to free land. According to the 1850 census, nearly half of the nation's fugitive slaves were from the four border states of Missouri, Maryland, Delaware, and Kentucky, with more than half of border state fugitives escaping from Maryland (United States Senate 1854, 64). Although Missouri's number of fugitives was unexceptional, it was the ultimate border state, as it was bordered on three sides—west, north, and east—by free states or territories. The Missouri Compromise (1820), an early milestone in the long-running dispute over the expansion of slavery into new states, admitted Missouri to the union as a slave state but established the dividing line between slave and free states at the 36° 30' latitude, Missouri's southern border. At this point it looks like Jim's easiest path to freedom is to swim or paddle to Illinois.

59. The man with the lantern provides an indication of why successful slave escapes into Illinois, and in general, were rare. Runaway slaves were typically pursued into free states, often with the help of local law enforcement or free-state citizens seeking the reward money. The infamous fugitive slave clause of the U.S. Constitution required that slaves who had escaped into another state "shall be delivered up on claim of the party to whom such service or labor may be due," and the Fugitive Slave Act of 1793 made it unlawful to

I had my pipe en a plug er dog-leg, en some matches in my cap, en dey warn't wet, so I 'uz all right."

"And so you ain't had no meat nor bread to eat all this time? Why didn't you get mud-turkles?"

"How you gwyne to git 'm? You can't slip up on um en grab um; en how's a body gwyne to hit um wid a rock? How could a body do it in de night? En I warn't gwyne to show mysef on de bank in de daytime."

"Well, that's so. You've had to keep in the woods all the time, of course. Did you hear 'em shooting the cannon?"

"Oh, yes. I knowed dey was arter you. I see um go by heah; watched um thoo de bushes."

Some young birds come along, flying a yard or two at a time and lighting. Jim said it was a sign it was going to rain. He said it was a sign when young chickens flew that way, and so he reckoned it was the same way when young birds done it. I was going to catch some of them, but Jim wouldn't let me. He said it was death. He said his father laid mighty sick once, and some of them catched a bird, and his old granny said his father would die, and he did.

And Jim said you mustn't count the things you are going to cook for dinner, because that would bring bad luck. The same if you shook the table-cloth after sundown. And he said if a man owned a bee-hive, and that man died, the bees must be told about it before sun-up next morning, or else the bees would all weaken down and quit work and die. Jim said bees wouldn't sting idiots; but I didn't believe that, because I had tried them lots of times myself, and they wouldn't sting me.

---

obstruct the recapture of an escaped slave. Some northern states passed personal liberty laws that guaranteed a fair trial to accused runaway slaves or in some cases declared all inhabitants of their states to be free, but Illinois was not one of them. In fact, Illinois and several other free states denied basic citizenship rights to free blacks and voted to bar any further immigration of free blacks (Litwack 1965, 70–71). By contrast, the state went out of its way to assist slave catchers (Davis 1998, 258).

Compare Jim's situation with Pap's. In Chapter 6 Pap rows across to the Illinois side, finds an abandoned log cabin in the woods, and is able to live off the fat of the land. For Jim to find freedom in Illinois, he would have to elude slave catchers and locals who had heard about whatever reward was being offered for him. He would have to find sympathetic people to harbor him, such as Dr. Richard Eells, a prominent abolitionist who lived from 1835 to 1848 in the town of Quincy, 20 miles north of Hannibal ("Dr. Richard Eells House," n.d.). Unless Jim knew specifically of someone like Dr. Eells, he would have been on his own, pursued by slave catchers in a state with draconian restrictions on free blacks. While some whites were sympathetic to runaway slaves and would not turn them in, there were many others who valued the reward money more. Not until the polarizing Fugitive Slave Act of 1850 and Harriet Beecher Stowe's gripping novel *Uncle Tom's Cabin* (1852) did substantial majorities of northern whites appear willing to forgo that reward money.

I had heard about some of these things before, but not all of them. Jim knowed all kinds of signs. He said he knowed most everything. I said it looked to me like all the signs was about bad luck, and so I asked him if there warn't any good-luck signs. He says:

"Mighty few—an' *dey* ain't no use to a body. What you want to know when good luck's a-comin' for? Want to keep it off?" And he said: "Ef you's got hairy arms en a hairy breas', it's a sign dat you's agwyne to be rich. Well, dey's some use in a sign like dat, 'kase it's so fur ahead. You see, maybe you's got to be po' a long time fust, en so you might git discourage' en kill yo'sef 'f you didn' know by de sign dat you gwyne to be rich bymeby."

"Have you got hairy arms and a hairy breast, Jim?"

"What's de use to ax dat question? Don't you see I has?"

"Well, are you rich?"

"No, but I ben rich wunst, and gwyne to be rich agin. Wunst I had foteen dollars, but I tuck to specalat'n', en got busted out."

"What did you speculate in, Jim?"

"Well, fust I tackled stock."

"What kind of stock?"

"Why, live stock. Cattle, you know. I put ten dollars in a cow. But I ain' gwyne to resk no mo' money in stock. De cow up 'n' died on my han's."[60]

"So you lost the ten dollars."

"No, I didn't lose it all. I on'y los' 'bout nine of it. I sole de hide en taller for a dollar en ten cents."

"You had five dollars and ten cents left. Did you speculate any more?"

"Yes. You know that one-laigged nigger dat b'longs to old Misto Bradish? Well, he sot up a bank, en say anybody dat put in a dollar would git fo' dollars mo' at de en' er de year. Well, all de niggers went in, but dey didn't have much. I wuz de on'y one dat had much. So I stuck out for mo'

---

60. Twain reminds us again of what a speculative age it was. While Jim's example is obviously fictional and comical, speculative investments were common even among the vast majority of Americans who had no contact with the stock market. Get-rich-quick schemes abounded in 19th-century America. Ironically, livestock was actually a reasonable, though not riskless, investment for small farmers back to colonial times (Perkins 1989). A cow's daily milk, and later its beef and hide, were fairly predictable benefits. Economists often distinguish between *investing* in something that you reasonably expect to provide a stream of money or services over time and *speculating,* in which the commodity is extremely risky or perhaps even intrinsically worthless but might be resellable later at a higher price to some "greater fool." Jim was either an unlucky investor or took a chance on a sick cow. Or perhaps any investment was risky for a slave, since slaves had no more rights to their property than to their own persons.

dan fo' dollars, en I said 'f I didn' git it I'd start a bank mysef. Well, o' course dat nigger want' to keep me out er de business, bekase he says dey warn't business 'nough for two banks, so he say I could put in my five dollars en he pay me thirty-five at de en' er de year.

"So I done it. Den I reck'n'd I'd inves' de thirty-five dollars right off en keep things a-movin'. Dey wuz a nigger name' Bob, dat had ketched a wood-flat, en his marster didn' know it; en I bought it off'n him en told him to take de thirty-five dollars when de en' er de year come; but somebody stole de wood-flat dat night, en nex day de one-laigged nigger say de bank's busted. So dey didn' none uv us git no money."[61]

"What did you do with the ten cents, Jim?"

"Well, I 'uz gwyne to spen' it, but I had a dream, en de dream tole me to give it to a nigger name' Balum—Balum's Ass dey call him for short; he's one er dem chuckleheads, you know. But he's lucky, dey say, en I see I warn't lucky. De dream say let Balum inves' de ten cents en he'd make a raise for me. Well, Balum he tuck de money, en when he wuz in church he hear de preacher say dat whoever give to de po' len' to de Lord, en boun' to git his money back a hund'd times. So Balum he tuck en give de ten cents to de po', en laid low to see what wuz gwyne to come of it."

"Well, what did come of it, Jim?"

"Nuffn' never come of it. I couldn' manage to k'leck dat money no way; en Balum he couldn'. I ain' gwyne to len' no mo' money 'dout I see de security. Boun' to git yo' money back a hund'd times, de preacher says! Ef I could git de ten *cents* back, I'd call it squah, en be glad er de chanst."

"Well, it's all right anyway, Jim, long as you're going to be rich again some time or other."

"Yes—en I's rich now, come to look at it. I owns mysef, en I's wuth eight hund'd dollars. I wisht I had de money, I wouldn' want no mo'."[62]

---

61. Jim uses the word "nigger" almost as freely as Huck. The nuances of the word's use by blacks are an old and enduring topic. See, for example, Randall Kennedy's book *Nigger: The Strange Career of a Troublesome Word* (2002). After emancipation blacks hated its use by whites, but many blacks used it themselves to mean everything from "a description of slavish personalities to an expression of endearment" (Litwack 1979, 254). Others used it with resignation to indicate their skepticism that white attitudes toward them had changed at all: an elderly black woman in Savannah told a Quaker missionary: "We *are* niggers. We always was niggers, and we always shall be; nigger here, and nigger there, nigger do this, and nigger do that. We've got no souls, we are animals" (qtd. in Litwack 1979, 255).

62. What Jim describes brings to mind the situation of the 4 million African Americans who were emancipated during and after the Civil War. Their emancipation represented a massive transfer of wealth, roughly $3 billion, from the slaveholders to the former slaves. The average market value of a slave, $750, was determined by the money that slave could generate for his or her master over the rest of the slave's life, and at least in theory the average freedman could generate the same amount over time and get paid for it. But as Jim

CHAPTER IX.

I wanted to go and look at a place right about the middle of the island, that I'd found when I was exploring; so we started, and soon got to it, because the island was only three miles long and a quarter of a mile wide.

This place was a tolerable long, steep hill or ridge, about forty foot high. We had a rough time getting to the top, the sides was so steep and the bushes so thick. We tramped and clumb around all over it, and by and by found a good big cavern in the rock, most up to the top on the side towards Illinois. The cavern was as big as two or three rooms bunched together, and Jim could stand up straight in it. It was cool in there. Jim was for putting our traps in there, right away, but I said we didn't want to be climbing up and down there all the time.

Jim said if we had the canoe hid in a good place, and had all the traps in the cavern, we could rush there if anybody was to come to the island, and they would never find us without dogs. And besides, he said them little birds had said it was going to rain, and did I want the things to get wet?

So we went back and got the canoe and paddled up abreast the cavern, and lugged all the traps up there. Then we hunted up a place close by to hide the canoe in, amongst the thick willows. We took some fish off of the lines and set them again, and begun to get ready for dinner.

The door of the cavern was big enough to roll a hogshead in, and on one side of the door the floor stuck out a little bit and was flat and a good place to build a fire on. So we built it there and cooked dinner.

We spread the blankets inside for a carpet, and eat our dinner in there. We put all the other things handy at the back of the cavern. Pretty soon it darkened up and begun to thunder and lighten; so the birds was right about it. Directly it begun to rain, and it rained like all fury, too, and I never see

---

notes, it would be a lot easier to have the money, just as a slave owner could have sold the average slave for $750 and collected all of that money. Slaves were liquid assets; free laborers are not. Except for their own persons, the new freedmen had "nothing but freedom" (Foner 1983).

"Forty acres and a mule" was what many African Americans had been hoping for upon emancipation. Such hopes had first been raised by General William T. Sherman's famous march to the sea in which he had confiscated Confederate-owned plantations and temporarily turned over 40-acre parcels to individual slaves. Some freedmen received mules from soldiers. The chief of the Freedmen's Bureau and some Radical Republicans in Congress had favored giving 40 acres of land to every male ex-slave, but those plans were unable to overcome the opposition of President Andrew Johnson and others who favored a more lenient policy toward the ex-slaveholders. In the interest of unity between southern elites and the North, the ex-slaveholders retained their land, and the former slaves received no compensation at all.

the wind blow so. It was one of these regular summer storms. It would get so dark that it looked all blue-black outside, and lovely; and the rain would thrash along by so thick that the trees off a little ways looked dim and spider-webby; and here would come a blast of wind that would bend the trees down and turn up the pale underside of the leaves; and then a perfect ripper of a gust would follow along and set the branches to tossing their arms as if they was just wild; and next, when it was just about the bluest and blackest—*fst*! it was as bright as glory, and you'd have a little glimpse of tree-tops a-plunging about, away off yonder in the storm, hundreds of yards further than you could see before; dark as sin again in a second, and now you'd hear the thunder let go with an awful crash and then go rumbling, grumbling, tumbling, down the sky towards the under side of the world, like rolling empty barrels down stairs, where it's long stairs and they bounce a good deal, you know.

"Jim, this is nice," I says. "I wouldn't want to be nowhere else but here. Pass me along another hunk of fish and some hot corn-bread."

"Well, you wouldn't a ben here, 'f it hadn't a ben for Jim. You'd a ben down dah in de woods widout any dinner, en gittn' mos' drownded, too; dat you would, honey. Chickens knows when it's gwyne to rain, en so do de birds, chile."

The river went on raising and raising for ten or twelve days, till at last it was over the banks. The water was three or four foot deep on the island in the low places and on the Illinois bottom. On that side it was a good many miles wide, but on the Missouri side it was the same old distance across—a half a mile—because the Missouri shore was just a wall of high bluffs.

Daytimes we paddled all over the island in the canoe. It was mighty cool and shady in the deep woods even if the sun was blazing outside. We went winding in and out amongst the trees; and sometimes the vines hung so thick we had to back away and go some other way. Well, on every old broken-down tree you could see rabbits, and snakes, and such things; and when the island had been overflowed a day or two, they got so tame, on account of being hungry, that you could paddle right up and put your hand on them if you wanted to; but not the snakes and turtles—they would slide off in the water. The ridge our cavern was in, was full of them. We could a had pets enough if we'd wanted them.

One night we catched a little section of a lumber raft—nice pine planks. It was twelve foot wide and about fifteen or sixteen foot long, and the top stood above water six or seven inches—a solid level floor. We could see saw-logs go by in the daylight, sometimes, but we let them go; we didn't show ourselves in daylight.

Another night when we was up at the head of the island, just before daylight, here comes a frame house down, on the west side. She was a two-story, and tilted over, considerable. We paddled out and got aboard—clumb in at an up-stairs window. But it was too dark to see yet, so we made the canoe fast and set in her to wait for daylight.

The light begun to come before we got to the foot of the island. Then we looked in at the window. We could make out a bed, and a table, and two old chairs, and lots of things around about on the floor; and there was clothes hanging against the wall. There was something laying on the floor in the far corner that looked like a man. So Jim says:

"Hello, you!"

But it didn't budge. So I hollered again, and then Jim says:

"De man ain't asleep—he's dead. You hold still—I'll go en see."

He went, and bent down and looked, and says:

"It's a dead man. Yes, indeedy; naked, too. He's ben shot in de back. I reck'n he's ben dead two er three days. Come in, Huck, but doan' look at his face—it's too gashly."

I didn't look at him at all. Jim throwed some old rags over him, but he needn't done it; I didn't want to see him. There was heaps of old greasy cards scattered around over the floor, and old whisky bottles, and a

JIM SEES A DEAD MAN.

(Illustration by Edward W. Kemble. From Mark Twain, *Adventures of Huckleberry Finn*. New York: C. L. Webster, 1885. Digitized by the University of Virginia Library.)

couple of masks made out of black cloth; and all over the walls was the ignorantest kind of words and pictures, made with charcoal. There was two old dirty calico dresses, and a sun-bonnet, and some women's under-clothes hanging against the wall, and some men's clothing, too. We put the lot into the canoe; it might come good. There was a boy's old speckled straw hat on the floor; I took that, too. And there was a bottle that had had milk in it; and it had a rag stopper for a baby to suck. We would a took the bottle, but it was broke. There was a seedy old chest, and an old hair trunk with the hinges broke. They stood open, but there warn't nothing left in them that was any account. The way things was scattered about, we reck-oned the people left in a hurry, and warn't fixed so as to carry off most of their stuff.

We got an old tin lantern, and a butcher-knife without any handle, and a bran-new Barlow knife worth two bits in any store,[63] and a lot of tallow candles, and a tin candlestick, and a gourd, and a tin cup, and a ratty old bed-quilt off the bed, and a reticule with needles and pins and beeswax and buttons and thread and all such truck in it, and a hatchet and some nails, and a fish-line as thick as my little finger, with some monstrous hooks on it, and a roll of buckskin, and a leather dog-collar, and a horseshoe, and some vials of medicine that didn't have no label on them; and just as we was leaving I found a tolerable good curry-comb, and Jim he found a ratty old fiddle-bow, and a wooden leg. The straps was broke off of it, but, bar-ring that, it was a good enough leg, though it was too long for me and not long enough for Jim, and we couldn't find the other one, though we hunted all around.[64]

And so, take it all around, we made a good haul. When we was ready to shove off we was a quarter of a mile below the island, and it was pretty broad day; so I made Jim lay down in the canoe and cover up with the quilt, because if he set up, people could tell he was a nigger a good ways off. I paddled over to the Illinois shore, and drifted down most a half a mile

63. "Two bits" is 25 cents. This slang term comes from the U.S. dollar's derivation from the Spanish dollar (which itself derives from a medieval Germain coin called the taler), which commonly circulated in the colonies. One Spanish dollar was worth eight pesos, which sounded like "eight pieces" to British American ears. So, a quarter of a dollar was two pieces, or two bits.

64. Could the floating house be a brothel, as British author V. S. Pritchett has sug-gested (cited in Twain 2001, 101n12)? The details seem to fit, from the women's undergar-ments on the wall to "the ignorantest kind of words and pictures on the walls." The whiskey bottles, the (playing?) cards, and the fiddle bow all sound like standard bordello accesso-ries. Even the dog collar was a common sadomasochistic prop in some 19th-century broth-els (Perrottet 2011, 81). Prostitution was common in the mostly male world of the frontier and the riverboat trades, and the antebellum Mississippi River was home to many "floating brothels" (Sandlin 2010).

doing it. I crept up the dead water under the bank, and hadn't no accidents and didn't see nobody. We got home all safe.

CHAPTER X.

AFTER breakfast I wanted to talk about the dead man and guess out how he come to be killed, but Jim didn't want to. He said it would fetch bad luck; and besides, he said, he might come and ha'nt us; he said a man that warn't buried was more likely to go a-ha'nting around than one that was planted and comfortable. That sounded pretty reasonable, so I didn't say no more; but I couldn't keep from studying over it and wishing I knowed who shot the man, and what they done it for.

We rummaged the clothes we'd got, and found eight dollars in silver sewed up in the lining of an old blanket overcoat.[65] Jim said he reckoned the people in that house stole the coat, because if they'd a knowed the money was there they wouldn't a left it. I said I reckoned they killed him, too; but Jim didn't want to talk about that. I says:

"Now you think it's bad luck; but what did you say when I fetched in the snake-skin that I found on the top of the ridge day before yesterday? You said it was the worst bad luck in the world to touch a snake-skin with my hands. Well, here's your bad luck! We've raked in all this truck and eight dollars besides. I wish we could have some bad luck like this every day, Jim."

"Never you mind, honey, never you mind. Don't you git too peart. It's a-comin'. Mind I tell you, it's a-comin'."

It did come, too. It was a Tuesday that we had that talk. Well, after dinner Friday we was laying around in the grass at the upper end of the ridge, and got out of tobacco. I went to the cavern to get some, and found a rattlesnake in there. I killed him, and curled him up on the foot of Jim's blanket, ever so natural, thinking there'd be some fun when Jim found him there. Well, by night I forgot all about the snake, and when Jim flung himself down on the blanket while I struck a light, the snake's mate was there, and bit him.

---

65. Eight dollars equates to about $240 in today's money, so a silver dollar was worth about $30. This is too large for many transactions, so silver coins, like gold coins, tended to be stored away, typically in a bank. The dead man, by contrast, may have been on the run and carrying all his savings in a secret compartment. Either way, people usually conducted their smaller transactions with paper banknotes (issued by the banks to people who deposited silver and gold coins with them, much like banks give out checkbooks and debit cards today) or smaller-denomination coins made out of base metals such as copper and nickel.

He jumped up yelling, and the first thing the light showed was the varmint curled up and ready for another spring. I laid him out in a second with a stick, and Jim grabbed pap's whisky jug and begun to pour it down.

He was barefooted, and the snake bit him right on the heel. That all comes of my being such a fool as to not remember that wherever you leave a dead snake its mate always comes there and curls around it. Jim told me to chop off the snake's head and throw it away, and then skin the body and roast a piece of it. I done it, and he eat it and said it would help cure him. He made me take off the rattles and tie them around his wrist, too. He said that that would help. Then I slid out quiet and throwed the snakes clear away amongst the bushes; for I warn't going to let Jim find out it was all my fault, not if I could help it.

Jim sucked and sucked at the jug, and now and then he got out of his head and pitched around and yelled; but every time he come to himself he went to sucking at the jug again. His foot swelled up pretty big, and so did his leg; but by and by the drunk begun to come, and so I judged he was all right; but I'd druther been bit with a snake than pap's whisky.

Jim was laid up for four days and nights. Then the swelling was all gone and he was around again. I made up my mind I wouldn't ever take aholt of a snake-skin again with my hands, now that I see what had come of it. Jim said he reckoned I would believe him next time. And he said that handling a snake-skin was such awful bad luck that maybe we hadn't got to the end of it yet. He said he druther see the new moon over his left shoulder as much as a thousand times than take up a snake-skin in his hand. Well, I was getting to feel that way myself, though I've always reckoned that looking at the new moon over your left shoulder is one of the carelessest and foolishest things a body can do. Old Hank Bunker done it once, and bragged about it; and in less than two years he got drunk and fell off of the shot-tower, and spread himself out so that he was just a kind of a layer, as you may say; and they slid him edgeways between two barn doors for a coffin, and buried him so, so they say, but I didn't see it. Pap told me. But anyway it all come of looking at the moon that way, like a fool.

Well, the days went along, and the river went down between its banks again; and about the first thing we done was to bait one of the big hooks with a skinned rabbit and set it and catch a catfish that was as big as a man, being six foot two inches long, and weighed over two hundred pounds. We couldn't handle him, of course; he would a flung us into Illinois. We just set there and watched him rip and tear around till he drownded. We found a brass button in his stomach, and a round ball, and lots of rubbage. We split the ball open with the hatchet, and there was a spool in it. Jim said he'd had it there a long time, to coat it over so and make a ball of it. It was as big a fish as was ever catched in the Mississippi, I reckon. Jim said he hadn't ever seen a bigger one. He would a been worth a good deal over at the village. They peddle out such a fish as that by the pound in the market house there; everybody buys some of him; his meat's as white as snow and makes a good fry.

Next morning I said it was getting slow and dull, and I wanted to get a stirring up, some way. I said I reckoned I would slip over the river and find out what was going on. Jim liked that notion; but he said I must go in the dark and look sharp. Then he studied it over and said, couldn't I put on some of them old things and dress up like a girl? That was a good notion, too. So we shortened up one of the calico gowns and I turned up my trowser-legs to my knees and got into it. Jim hitched it behind with the hooks, and it was a fair fit. I put on the sun-bonnet and tied it under my chin, and then for a body to look in and see my face was like looking down a joint of stove-pipe. Jim said nobody would know me, even in the daytime, hardly. I practiced around all day to get the hang of the things, and by and by I could do pretty well in them, only Jim said I didn't walk like a girl; and he said I must quit pulling up my gown to get at my britches pocket. I took notice, and done better.

I started up the Illinois shore in the canoe just after dark.

I started across to the town from a little below the ferry-landing, and the drift of the current fetched me in at the bottom of the town. I tied up and started along the bank. There was a light burning in a little shanty that hadn't been lived in for a long time, and I wondered who had took up quarters there. I slipped up and peeped in at the window. There was a woman about forty year old in there, knitting by a candle that was on a pine table. I didn't know her face; she was a stranger, for you couldn't start a face in that town that I didn't know. Now this was lucky, because I was weakening; I was getting afraid I had come; people might know my voice and find me out. But if this woman had been in such a little town two days she could tell me all I wanted to know; so I knocked at the door, and made up my mind I wouldn't forget I was a girl.

CHAPTER XI.

"Come in," says the woman, and I did. She says:

"Take a cheer."

I done it. She looked me all over with her little shiny eyes, and says:

"What might your name be?"

"Sarah Williams."

"Where 'bouts do you live? In this neighborhood?'

"No'm. In Hookerville, seven mile below. I've walked all the way and I'm all tired out."

"Hungry, too, I reckon. I'll find you something."

"No'm, I ain't hungry. I was so hungry I had to stop two mile below here at a farm; so I ain't hungry no more. It's what makes me so late. My mother's down sick, and out of money and everything, and I come to tell my uncle Abner Moore. He lives at the upper end of the town, she says. I hain't ever been here before. Do you know him?"

"No; but I don't know everybody yet. I haven't lived here quite two weeks. It's a considerable ways to the upper end of the town. You better stay here all night. Take off your bonnet."

"No," I says; "I'll rest a while, I reckon, and go on. I ain't afeard of the dark."

She said she wouldn't let me go by myself, but her husband would be in by and by, maybe in a hour and a half, and she'd send him along with me. Then she got to talking about her husband, and about her relations up the river, and her relations down the river, and about how much better off they used to was, and how they didn't know but they'd made a mistake coming to our town, instead of letting well alone—and so on and so on, till I was afeard *I* had made a mistake coming to her to find out what was going on in the town; but by and by she dropped onto pap and the murder, and then I was pretty willing to let her clatter right along. She told about me and Tom Sawyer finding the six thousand dollars (only she got it ten) and all about pap and what a hard lot he was, and what a hard lot I was, and at last she got down to where I was murdered. I says:

"Who done it? We've heard considerable about these goings on, down in Hookerville, but we don't know who 'twas that killed Huck Finn."

"Well, I reckon there's a right smart chance of people *here* that'd like to know who killed him. Some think old Finn done it himself."

"No—is that so?"

"Most everybody thought it at first. He'll never know how nigh he come to getting lynched.[66] But before night they changed around and judged it was done by a runaway nigger named Jim."

"Why *he*—"

I stopped. I reckoned I better keep still. She run on, and never noticed I had put in at all.

---

66. Lynchings are most often associated with African Americans, but the first lynching in this novel is of a white man. This is historically appropriate, as prior to the Civil War African Americans were almost never lynched or put to death except in rare cases such as Nat Turner's slave rebellion of 1831 in Virginia, in which slaves killed some 60 whites. The state executed Turner and 55 other rebels, and white mobs killed perhaps 150 more blacks, many of whom were not involved with the rebellion. Otherwise, slaves were simply too valuable to their owners as property. After emancipation in 1865 and especially with the end of Reconstruction in 1877, African Americans no longer had the protection of their masters or of the federal government, and lynching became a common means of keeping free blacks in a subordinate place.

"The nigger run off the very night Huck Finn was killed. So there's a reward out for him—three hundred dollars. And there's a reward out for old Finn, too—two hundred dollars.[67] You see, he come to town the morning after the murder, and told about it, and was out with 'em on the ferryboat hunt, and right away after he up and left. Before night they wanted to lynch him, but he was gone, you see. Well, next day they found out the nigger was gone; they found out he hadn't ben seen sence ten o'clock the night the murder was done. So then they put it on him, you see, and while they was full of it, next day back comes old Finn, and went boo-hooing to Judge Thatcher to get money to hunt for the nigger all over Illinois with. The judge gave him some, and that evening he got drunk and was around till after midnight with a couple of mighty hard-looking strangers, and then went off with them. Well, he hain't come back sence, and they ain't looking for him back till this thing blows over a little, for people thinks now that he killed his boy and fixed things so folks would think robbers done it, and then he'd get Huck's money without having to bother a long time with a lawsuit. People do say he warn't any too good to do it. Oh, he's sly, I reckon. If he don't come back for a year, he'll be all right. You can't prove anything on him, you know; everything will be quieted down then, and he'll walk in Huck's money as easy as nothing."

"Yes, I reckon so, 'm. I don't see nothing in the way of it. Has everybody quit thinking the nigger done it?"

"Oh, no, not everybody. A good many thinks he done it. But they'll get the nigger pretty soon now, and maybe they can scare it out of him."

"Why, are they after him yet?"

"Well, you're innocent, ain't you! Does three hundred dollars lay around every day for people to pick up?[68] Some folks think the nigger ain't far from here. I'm one of them—but I hain't talked it around. A few days ago I was talking with an old couple that lives next door in the log shanty, and they happened to say hardly anybody ever goes to that island over yonder that they call Jackson's Island. Don't anybody live there? says I. No, nobody, says they. I didn't say any more, but I done some thinking. I was pretty near certain I'd seen smoke over there, about the head of the

---

67. Strikingly, the reward for Jim is $100 more than the reward for Pap. Jim's extra value as a slave, at least if he is not found guilty of a child's murder, accounts for the difference. Indeed, if the reward for Jim is that high, then the woman is surely correct that most people no longer suspect that Jim is the murderer.

68. Here we see another way in which slavery was able to survive—other whites in the community, including nonslaveholders, were motivated by the reward money. Even those who were uncomfortable with slavery might be swayed by the $300 (equivalent to $9,000 in today's money). For something like the underground railroad to work, many if not most people have to be willing to forgo that reward money.

island, a day or two before that, so I says to myself, like as not that nigger's hiding over there; anyway, says I, it's worth the trouble to give the place a hunt. I hain't seen any smoke sence, so I reckon maybe he's gone, if it was him; but husband's going over to see—him and another man. He was gone up the river; but he got back to-day, and I told him as soon as he got here two hours ago."

I had got so uneasy I couldn't set still. I had to do something with my hands; so I took up a needle off of the table and went to threading it. My hands shook, and I was making a bad job of it. When the woman stopped talking, I looked up, and she was looking at me pretty curious, and smiling a little. I put down the needle and thread, and let on to be interested—and I was, too—and says:

"Three hundred dollars is a power of money. I wish my mother could get it. Is your husband going over there to-night?"

"Oh, yes. He went up town with the man I was telling you of, to get a boat and see if they could borrow another gun. They'll go over after midnight."

"Couldn't they see better if they was to wait till daytime?"

"Yes. And couldn't the nigger see better, too? After midnight he'll likely be asleep, and they can slip around through the woods and hunt up his camp fire all the better for the dark, if he's got one."

"I didn't think of that."

The woman kept looking at me pretty curious, and I didn't feel a bit comfortable. Pretty soon she says,

"What did you say your name was, honey?"

"M—Mary Williams."

Somehow it didn't seem to me that I said it was Mary before, so I didn't look up—seemed to me I said it was Sarah; so I felt sort of cornered, and was afeared maybe I was looking it, too. I wished the woman would say something more; the longer she set still, the uneasier I was. But now she says:

"Honey, I thought you said it was Sarah when you first come in?"

"Oh, yes'm, I did. Sarah Mary Williams. Sarah's my first name. Some calls me Sarah, some calls me Mary."

"Oh, that's the way of it?"

"Yes'm."

I was feeling better then, but I wished I was out of there, anyway. I couldn't look up yet.

Well, the woman fell to talking about how hard times was, and how poor they had to live, and how the rats was as free as if they owned the place, and so forth and so on, and then I got easy again. She was right about the rats. You'd see one stick his nose out of a hole in the corner every little while. She said she had to have things handy to throw at them when she was alone, or they wouldn't give her no peace. She showed me a bar of lead, twisted up into a knot, and said she was a good shot with it generly, but she'd wrenched her arm a day or two ago, and didn't know whether she could throw true, now. But she watched for a chance, and directly banged away at a rat, but she missed him wide, and said "Ouch!" it hurt her arm so. Then she told me to try for the next one. I wanted to be getting away before the old man got back, but of course I didn't let on. I got the thing, and the first rat that showed his nose I let drive, and if he'd a stayed where he was he'd a been a tolerable sick rat. She said that was first-rate, and she reckoned I would hive the next one. She went and got the lump of lead and fetched it back, and brought along a hank of yarn which she wanted me to help her with. I held up my two hands and she put the hank over them, and went on talking about her and her husband's matters. But she broke off to say:

"Keep your eye on the rats. You better have the lead in your lap, handy."

So she dropped the lump into my lap, just at that moment, and I clapped my legs together on it and she went on talking. But only about a minute. Then she took off the hank and looked me straight in the face, and very pleasant, and says:

"Come, now—what's your real name?"

"Wh-what, mum?"

"What's your real name? Is it Bill, or Tom, or Bob?—or what is it?"

I reckon I shook like a leaf, and I didn't know hardly what to do. But I says:

"Please to don't poke fun at a poor girl like me, mum. If I'm in the way, here, I'll—"

"No, you won't. Set down and stay where you are. I ain't going to hurt you, and I ain't going to tell on you, nuther. You just tell me your secret, and trust me. I'll keep it; and, what's more, I'll help you. So'll my old man if you want him to. You see, you're a runaway 'prentice, that's all. It ain't anything. There ain't no harm in it. You've been treated bad, and you made up your mind to cut. Bless you, child, I wouldn't tell on you. Tell me all about it, now—that's a good boy."[69]

---

69. Apprenticeships were common in early America, just as they had been in England for centuries. Ideally, an apprenticeship provides the young apprentice with education and training to prepare him to be an independent tradesman, but cases of abuse were frequent. A famous case was that of future president Andrew Johnson, who became a tailor's apprentice at age 10 after the death of his father. In that role "he labored for five years at the whim of his master, an experience not all that different from slavery. At age 15, the rebellious apprentice ran away with his brother, fleeing into South Carolina for almost two years before returning and resolving matters with his former master" (Stewart 2009, 14–15). Note that the woman is sympathetic to a runaway white apprentice but not to a runaway slave.

So I said it wouldn't be no use to try to play it any longer, and I would just make a clean breast and tell her everything, but she musn't go back on her promise. Then I told her my father and mother was dead, and the law had bound me out to a mean old farmer in the country thirty mile back from the river, and he treated me so bad I couldn't stand it no longer;[70] he went away to be gone a couple of days, and so I took my chance and stole some of his daughter's old clothes and cleared out, and I had been three nights coming the thirty miles; I traveled nights, and hid daytimes and slept, and the bag of bread and meat I carried from home lasted me all the way, and I had aplenty. I said I believed my uncle Abner Moore would take care of me, and so that was why I struck out for this town of Goshen.

"Goshen, child? This ain't Goshen. This is St. Petersburg. Goshen's ten mile further up the river. Who told you this was Goshen?"

"Why, a man I met at daybreak this morning, just as I was going to turn into the woods for my regular sleep. He told me when the roads forked I must take the right hand, and five mile would fetch me to Goshen."

"He was drunk, I reckon. He told you just exactly wrong."

"Well, he did act like he was drunk, but it ain't no matter now. I got to be moving along. I'll fetch Goshen before daylight."

"Hold on a minute. I'll put you up a snack to eat. You might want it."

So she put me up a snack, and says:

"Say, when a cow's laying down, which end of her gets up first? Answer up prompt now—don't stop to study over it. Which end gets up first?"

"The hind end, mum."

"Well, then, a horse?"

"The for'rard end, mum."

"Which side of a tree does the most moss grow on?"

"North side."

---

70. Huck describes a forced apprenticeship, which "the law" has imposed on him as an orphan. Such "pauper apprenticeships" were common in early America and rooted in English tradition (Herndon and Murray 2009). An apprenticeship was often imposed on a boy after his father died, as in the case of Sam Clemens and his father before him. Since a forced apprentice had no bargaining power, the pay and treatment were likely to be poor. What Huck describes sounds more like indentured servitude, as he gives no indication that the "mean old farmer" is teaching him a trade. The line between apprenticeship and indentureship or even slavery was sometimes murky, especially before the Thirteenth Amendment outlawed slavery and involuntary servitude. In some states, including antebellum New Jersey, some emancipated blacks were reclassified as apprentices for life (McManus 1973, 181). More typically, apprentices were bound until age 21. Runaways appear to have been common, partly because they could usually earn more on the outside, and their success rate appears to have been high. By the end of the 19th century, the American apprenticeship system was on its last legs (Elbaum 1989, 346–348).

"If fifteen cows is browsing on a hillside, how many of them eats with their heads pointed the same direction?"

"The whole fifteen, mum."

"Well, I reckon you *have* lived in the country. I thought maybe you was trying to hocus me again. What's your real name, now?"

"George Peters, mum."

"Well, try to remember it, George. Don't forget and tell me it's Elexander before you go, and then get out by saying it's George Elexander when I catch you. And don't go about women in that old calico. You do a girl tolerable poor, but you might fool men, maybe. Bless you, child, when you set out to thread a needle, don't hold the thread still and fetch the needle up to it; hold the needle still and poke the thread at it—that's the way a woman most always does; but a man always does t'other way. And when you throw at a rat or anything, hitch yourself up a tip-toe and fetch your hand up over your head as awkard as you can, and miss your rat about six or seven foot. Throw stiff-armed from the shoulder, like there was a pivot there for it to turn on—like a girl; not from the wrist and elbow, with your arm out to one side, like a boy. And mind you, when a girl tries to catch anything in her lap, she throws her knees apart; she don't clap them together, the way you did when you catched the lump of lead. Why, I spotted you for a boy when you was threading the needle; and I contrived the other things just to make certain. Now trot along to your uncle, Sarah Mary Williams George Elexander Peters, and if you get into trouble you send word to Mrs. Judith Loftus, which is me, and I'll do what I can to get you out of it. Keep the river road, all the way, and next time you tramp take shoes and socks with you. The river road's a rocky one, and your feet'll be in a condition when you get to Goshen, I reckon."

I went up the bank about fifty yards, and then I doubled on my tracks and slipped back to where my canoe was, a good piece below the house. I jumped in and was off in a hurry. I went up stream far enough to make the head of the island, and then started across. I took off the sun-bonnet, for I didn't want no blinders on, then. When I was about the middle, I heard the clock begin to strike; so I stops and listens; the sound come faint over the water, but clear—eleven. When I struck the head of the island I never waited to blow, though I was most winded, but I shoved right into the timber where my old camp used to be, and started a good fire there on a high-and-dry spot.

Then I jumped in the canoe and dug out for our place, a mile and a half below, as hard as I could go. I landed, and slopped through the timber and up the ridge and into the cavern. There Jim laid, sound asleep on the ground. I roused him out and says:

"Git up and hump yourself, Jim! There ain't a minute to lose. They're after us!"

Jim never asked no questions, he never said a word; but the way he worked for the next half an hour showed about how he was scared. By that time everything we had in the world was on our raft and she was ready to be shoved out from the willow cove where she was hid. We put out the camp fire at the cavern the first thing, and didn't show a candle outside after that.

I took the canoe out from shore a little piece and took a look, but if there was a boat around I couldn't see it, for stars and shadows ain't good to see by. Then we got out the raft and slipped along down in the shade, past the foot of the island dead still, never saying a word.[71]

CHAPTER XII.

IT must a been close onto one o'clock when we got below the island at last, and the raft did seem to go mighty slow. If a boat was to come along we was going to take to the canoe and break for the Illinois shore; and it was well a boat didn't come, for we hadn't ever thought to put the gun into the canoe, or a fishing-line, or anything to eat. We was in ruther too much of a sweat to think of so many things. It warn't good judgment to put *everything* on the raft.

If the men went to the island, I just expect they found the camp fire I built, and watched it all night for Jim to come. Anyways, they stayed away from us, and if my building the fire never fooled them it warn't no fault of mine. I played it as low-down on them as I could.

When the first streak of day begun to show, we tied up to a tow-head in a big bend on the Illinois side, and hacked off cottonwood branches with the hatchet and covered up the raft with them so she looked like there had been a cave-in in the bank there. A tow-head is a sandbar that has cotton-woods on it as thick as harrow-teeth.

---

71. The raft is going downstream, or south, which is paradoxical. Accounts from the underground railroad usually involve slaves going north into free territory, and by all accounts slavery was harsher in the Deep South than in the border states, partly because it was harder to escape into free states. At this point we don't know why they're going south, other than the obvious point that they would not get far paddling a raft upstream against the powerful Mississippi River. But we should note that many fugitive slaves successfully escaped to free black communities in the South, notably in larger cities such as Louisville and New Orleans. Once in those communities, some escaped slaves managed to conceal themselves with relative ease. Not surprisingly, many slave-state legislatures passed laws to restrict the liberties of free blacks or even banish them from their states. Efforts to banish free blacks had little success, however. In the three decades before the Civil War, the free black population increased in at least 10 of the largest cities in slave states (Wade 1964, 325–327).

ON THE RAFT.

(Illustration by Edward W. Kemble. From Mark Twain, *Adventures of Huckleberry Finn*. New York: C. L. Webster, 1885. Digitized by the University of Virginia Library.)

We had mountains on the Missouri shore and heavy timber on the Illinois side, and the channel was down the Missouri shore at that place, so we warn't afraid of anybody running across us. We laid there all day and watched the rafts and steamboats spin down the Missouri shore, and up-bound steamboats fight the big river in the middle. I told Jim all about the time I had jabbering with that woman; and Jim said she was a smart one, and if she was to start after us herself *she* wouldn't set down and watch a camp fire—no, sir, she'd fetch a dog.[72] Well, then, I said, why couldn't she tell her husband to fetch a dog? Jim said he bet she did think of it by the time the men was ready to start, and he believed they must a gone up town to get a dog and so they lost all that time, or else we wouldn't be here on a tow-head sixteen or seventeen mile below the village—no, indeedy, we would be in that same old town again. So I said I didn't care what was the reason they didn't get us, as long as they didn't.

When it was beginning to come on dark we poked our heads out of the cottonwood thicket, and looked up, and down, and across; nothing in sight; so Jim took up some of the top planks of the raft and built a snug wigwam to get under in blazing weather and rainy, and to keep the things dry. Jim made a floor for the wigwam, and raised it a foot or more above the level of the raft, so now the blankets and all the traps was out of reach of steamboat waves. Right in the middle of the wigwam we made a layer of dirt about five or six inches deep with a frame around it for to hold it to its place; this was to build a fire on in sloppy weather or chilly; the wigwam would keep it from being seen. We made an extra steering oar, too, because one of the others might get broke, on a snag or something. We fixed up a short forked stick to hang the old lantern on; because we must always light the lantern whenever we see a steamboat coming down stream, to keep from getting run over; but we wouldn't have to light it for up-stream boats unless we see we was in what they call a "crossing"; for the river was pretty high yet, very low banks being still a little under water; so up-bound boats didn't always run the channel, but hunted easy water.

---

72. Judith Loftus is indeed one of the shrewdest characters that Huck meets. We get the sense that she, unlike the men in her midst, is clever enough to find an escaped slave. Yet she appears to be a housewife who has not been consulted by her husband and the other men in the search party. This is in keeping with the "domestic code" of the 19th century, under which women were expected to leave the paid workforce upon getting married, at least if they could afford to do so, and become full-time mothers and homemakers (Kessler-Harris 1982, 49–52). Twain appears to be making a feminist statement here, as befits a man who married a woman with a college degree and whose father-in-law cofounded a women's college, Elmira College in upstate New York.

This second night we run between seven and eight hours, with a current that was making over four mile an hour. We catched fish, and talked, and we took a swim now and then to keep off sleepiness. It was kind of solemn, drifting down the big still river, laying on our backs looking up at the stars, and we didn't ever feel like talking loud, and it warn't often that we laughed, only a little kind of a low chuckle. We had mighty good weather, as a general thing, and nothing ever happened to us at all, that night, nor the next, nor the next.

Every night we passed towns, some of them away up on black hillsides, nothing but just a shiny bed of lights, not a house could you see. The fifth night we passed St. Louis, and it was like the whole world lit up. In St. Petersburg they used to say there was twenty or thirty thousand people in St. Louis, but I never believed it till I see that wonderful spread of lights at two o'clock that still night.[73] There warn't a sound there; everybody was asleep.

This panoramic print from the 1850s depicts a bustling St. Louis, on the banks of the Mississippi River, with numerous steamboats. Other than New Orleans, St. Louis was by far the biggest city on the Mississippi at mid-century. Its location at the junction of the Mississippi and Missouri Rivers made it a natural trading port and "gateway" to the western frontier. (Library of Congress)

---

73. Huck is in the right ballpark. St. Louis had a population of 16,469 in 1840, making it the largest American city west of the Mississippi River. By 1850 its population had more than quadrupled to 77,860, which made it the eighth-largest city in America (United States Census 1998; United States Senate 1854, 380).

Every night, now, I used to slip ashore towards ten o'clock at some little village, and buy ten or fifteen cents' worth of meal or bacon or other stuff to eat; and sometimes I lifted a chicken that warn't roosting comfortable, and took him along. Pap always said, take a chicken when you get a chance, because if you don't want him yourself you can easy find somebody that does, and a good deed ain't ever forgot. I never see pap when he didn't want the chicken himself, but that is what he used to say, anyway.

Mornings before daylight I slipped into cornfields and borrowed a watermelon, or a mushmelon, or a punkin, or some new corn, or things of that kind. Pap always said it warn't no harm to borrow things, if you was meaning to pay them back some time; but the widow said it warn't anything but a soft name for stealing, and no decent body would do it. Jim said he reckoned the widow was partly right and pap was partly right; so the best way would be for us to pick out two or three things from the list and say we wouldn't borrow them any more—then he reckoned it wouldn't be no harm to borrow the others. So we talked it over all one night, drifting along down the river, trying to make up our minds whether to drop the watermelons, or the cantelopes, or the mushmelons, or what. But towards daylight we got it all settled satisfactory, and concluded to drop crabapples and p'simmons. We warn't feeling just right before that, but it was all comfortable now. I was glad the way it come out, too, because crabapples ain't ever good, and the p'simmons wouldn't be ripe for two or three months yet.

We shot a water-fowl, now and then, that got up too early in the morning or didn't go to bed early enough in the evening. Take it all round, we lived pretty high.

The fifth night below St. Louis we had a big storm after midnight, with a power of thunder and lightning, and the rain poured down in a solid sheet. We stayed in the wigwam and let the raft take care of itself. When the lightning glared out we could see a big straight river ahead, and high rocky bluffs on both sides. By and by says I, "Hel-lo, Jim, looky yonder!" It was a steamboat that had killed herself on a rock.[74] We was drifting straight down for her. The lightning showed her

---

74. Steamboat accidents were very common during the antebellum era, especially on the Mississippi, Ohio, and Missouri Rivers. In fact, the first steamboat ever to successfully navigate the Ohio and Mississippi Rivers, in 1812, ended up sinking near Baton Rouge just two years later. "Snags," or submerged trees, took many a ship down. At the time federal spending on internal transportation improvements was slight and widely viewed as unconstitutional, but starting in 1821 the government saw no choice but to commit money to improving river safety. The funds were not always adequate, especially in the face of increased steamboat traffic, and steamboat accidents remained high. At midcentury, about 45 steamboats were lost to natural hazards each year (Paskoff 2007, 1, 36, 39).

EXPLOSION OF THE MOSELLE.

This woodcut print from the popular *Lloyd's Steamboat Directory, and Disasters on the Western Waters* shows one of the most famous industrial accidents ever. Some 135 people died in the *Moselle* explosion. The tragedy prompted government safety laws in the form of the 1838 Steamboat Act, said to be the first step toward the modern regulatory state. (James T. Lloyd, *Lloyd's Steamboat Directory and Disasters on the Western Waters*. Cincinnati: J. T. Lloyd & Co., 1856)

Other steamboat disasters took the form of explosions, usually on account of boiler problems. Steamboat disasters were the first major industrial accidents in antebellum America, which was still mostly rural. The volume of steamboat traffic continued to increase, however, and the disasters, however gruesome, became part of American folklore. *Lloyd's Steamboat Directory, and Disasters on the Western Waters,* a book published in 1856, cataloged the many deadly steamboat sinkings, burnings, and explosions with the aid of dozens of woodcut prints of selected disasters. Lloyd cautioned that it was not his intention "to gratify a morbid taste for the horrific" but rather to call attention to the "gross and criminal mismanagement of steam power which has made the navigation of the Western waters so eminently perilous and destructive to human life" (Lloyd 1856, iii). Twain experienced the devastation firsthand in 1858, when his younger brother Henry died as the result of a steamboat explosion. The deadliest maritime accident in American history occurred near the end of the Civil War on an overloaded Mississippi River steamboat carrying Union soldiers. Three boilers exploded, and some 1,800 people died (Klein 2015).

very distinct. She was leaning over, with part of her upper deck above water, and you could see every little chimbly-guy clean and clear, and a chair by the big bell, with an old slouch hat hanging on the back of it when the flashes come.

Well, it being away in the night, and stormy, and all so mysterious-like, I felt just the way any other boy would a felt when I see that wreck laying there so mournful and lonesome in the middle of the river. I wanted to get aboard of her and slink around a little, and see what there was there. So I says:

"Le's land on her, Jim."

But Jim was dead against it, at first. He says:

"I doan' want to go fool'n 'long er no wrack. We's doin' blame' well, en we better let blame' well alone, as de good book says. Like as not dey's a watchman on dat wrack."

"Watchman your grandmother," I says; "there ain't nothing to watch but the texas and the pilot-house; and do you reckon anybody's going to resk his life for a texas and a pilot-house such a night as this, when it's likely to break up and wash off down the river any minute?"[75] Jim couldn't say nothing to that, so he didn't try. "And besides," I says, "we might borrow something worth having, out of the captain's stateroom. Seegars, *I* bet you—and cost five cents apiece, solid cash. Steamboat captains is always rich, and get sixty dollars a month, and *they* don't care a cent what a thing costs, you know, long as they want it. Stick a candle in your pocket; I can't rest, Jim, till we give her a rummaging. Do you reckon Tom Sawyer would ever go by this thing? Not for pie, he wouldn't. He'd call it an adventure—that's what he'd call it; and he'd land on that wreck if it was his last act. And wouldn't he throw style into it?—wouldn't he spread himself, nor nothing? Why, you'd think it was Christopher C'lumbus discovering Kingdom-Come. I wish Tom Sawyer *was* here."

---

75. The "texas" of a steamboat was the largest of the boat's private compartments and included the pilothouse and the crew's quarters. The "staterooms" of a steamboat were typically named for states, and the texas was the largest, upon the state's admission to the union in 1845. For the previous nine years it had been the independent Republic of Texas, formed after a group of American settlers, largely slaveholders, had moved into the Mexican state of Texas and overrun the native population. This usage may indicate that the novel is set in 1845 or later. Setting the novel *after* 1845, however, would have complicated its historical setting, as the annexation of Texas led to the Mexican-American War of 1846–1848. The war transformed the nation forever, with the addition of California and the rest of the Southwest to the United States and the fateful heightening of North-South tensions over the issue of the expansion of slavery. The war is not mentioned at all in the novel, which suggests it is set before 1846 or Twain was simply not meticulous about dates.

Jim he grumbled a little, but give in. He said we mustn't talk any more than we could help, and then talk mighty low. The lightning showed us the wreck again, just in time, and we fetched the stabboard derrick, and made fast there.

The deck was high out, here. We went sneaking down the slope of it to labboard, in the dark, towards the texas, feeling our way slow with our feet, and spreading our hands out to fend off the guys, for it was so dark we couldn't see no sign of them. Pretty soon we struck the forward end of the skylight, and clumb on to it; and the next step fetched us in front of the captain's door, which was open, and by Jimminy, away down through the texas-hall we see a light! and all in the same second we seem to hear low voices in yonder!

Jim whispered and said he was feeling powerful sick, and told me to come along. I says, all right; and was going to start for the raft; but just then I heard a voice wail out and say:

"Oh, please don't, boys; I swear I won't ever tell!"

Another voice said, pretty loud:

"It's a lie, Jim Turner. You've acted this way before. You always want more'n your share of the truck, and you've always got it, too, because you've swore 't if you didn't you'd tell. But this time you've said it jest one time too many. You're the meanest, treacherousest hound in this country."

By this time Jim was gone for the raft. I was just a-biling with curiosity; and I says to myself, Tom Sawyer wouldn't back out now, and so I won't either; I'm agoing to see what's going on here. So I dropped on my hands and knees, in the little passage, and crept aft in the dark, till there warn't but one stateroom betwixt me and the cross-hall of the texas. Then, in there I see a man stretched on the floor and tied hand and foot, and two men standing over him, and one of them had a dim lantern in his hand, and the other one had a pistol. This one kept pointing the pistol at the man's head on the floor and saying—

"I'd *like* to! And I orter, too, a mean skunk!"

The man on the floor would shrivel up and say, "Oh, please don't, Bill—I hain't ever goin' to tell."

And every time he said that, the man with the lantern would laugh and say:

"'Deed you *ain't*! You never said no truer thing 'n that, you bet you." And once he said: "Hear him beg! and yit if we hadn't got the best of him and tied him, he'd a killed us both. And what *for*? Jist for noth'n. Jist because we stood on our *rights*—that's what for. But I lay you ain't agoin' to threaten nobody any more, Jim Turner. Put *up* that pistol, Bill."

Bill says:

"I don't want to, Jake Packard. I'm for killin' him—and didn't he kill old Hatfield jist the same way—and don't he deserve it?"

"But I don't *want* him killed, and I've got my reasons for it."

"Bless yo' heart for them words, Jake Packard! I'll never forgit you long's I live!" says the man on the floor, sort of blubbering.

Packard didn't take no notice of that, but hung up his lantern on a nail, and started towards where I was, there in the dark, and motioned Bill to come. I crawfished as fast as I could, about two yards, but the boat slanted so that I couldn't make very good time; so to keep from getting run over and catched I crawled into a stateroom on the upper side. The man come a-pawing along in the dark, and when Packard got to my stateroom, he says:

"Here—come in here."

And in he come, and Bill after him. But before they got in, I was up in the upper berth, cornered, and sorry I come. Then they stood there, with their hands on the ledge of the berth, and talked. I couldn't see them, but I could tell where they was, by the whisky they'd been having. I was glad I didn't drink whisky; but it wouldn't made much difference, anyway, because most of the time they couldn't a treed me because I didn't breathe. I was too scared. And, besides, a body *couldn't* breathe, and hear such talk. They talked low and earnest. Bill wanted to kill Turner. He says:

"He's said he'll tell, and he will. If we was to give both our shares to him *now*, it wouldn't make no difference after the row, and the way we've served him. Shore's you're born, he'll turn State's evidence; now you hear *me*. I'm for putting him out of his troubles."

"So'm I," says Packard, very quiet.

"Blame it, I'd sorter begun to think you wasn't. Well, then, that's all right. Le's go and do it."

"Hold on a minute; I hain't had my say yit. You listen to me. Shooting's good, but there's quieter ways if the thing's *got* to be done. But what *I* say, is this: it ain't good sense to go court'n around after a halter if you can git at what you're up to in some way that's jist as good and at the same time don't bring you into no resks. Ain't that so?"

"You bet it is. But how you goin' to manage it this time?"

"Well, my idea is this: we'll rustle around and gether up whatever pickins we've overlooked in the staterooms, and shove for shore and hide the truck. Then we'll wait. Now I say it ain't agoin' to be more'n two hours befo' this wrack breaks up and washes off down the river. See? He'll be drownded, and won't have nobody to blame for it but his own self. I reckon that's a considerble sight better 'n killin' of him. I'm unfavorable to killin' a man as long as you can git around it; it ain't good sense, it ain't good morals. Ain't I right?"

"Yes—I reck'n you are. But s'pose she *don't* break up and wash off?"

"Well, we can wait the two hours, anyway, and see, can't we?"

"All right, then; come along."

So they started, and I lit out, all in a cold sweat, and scrambled forward. It was dark as pitch there; but I said, in a kind of a coarse whisper, "Jim!" and he answered up, right at my elbow, with a sort of a moan, and I says:

"Quick, Jim, it ain't no time for fooling around and moaning; there's a gang of murderers in yonder, and if we don't hunt up their boat and set her drifting down the river so these fellows can't get away from the wreck, there's one of 'em going to be in a bad fix. But if we find their boat we can put *all* of 'em in a bad fix—for the Sheriff 'll get 'em. Quick—hurry! I'll hunt the labboard side, you hunt the stabboard. You start at the raft, and—"

"Oh, my lordy, lordy! *Raf'*? Dey ain' no raf' no mo'; she done broke loose en gone!—en here we is!"

CHAPTER XIII.

WELL, I catched my breath and most fainted. Shut up on a wreck with such a gang as that! But it warn't no time to be sentimentering. We'd *got* to find that boat now—had to have it for ourselves. So we went a-quaking and shaking down the stabboard side, and slow work it was, too—seemed a week before we got to the stern. No sign of a boat. Jim said he didn't believe he could go any further—so scared he hadn't hardly any strength left, he said. But I said come on, if we get left on this wreck we are in a fix, sure. So on we prowled, again. We struck for the stern of the texas, and found it, and then scrabbled along forwards on the skylight, hanging on from shutter to shutter, for the edge of the skylight was in the water. When we got pretty close to the cross-hall door, there was the skiff, sure enough! I could just barely see her. I felt ever so thankful. In another second I would a been aboard of her, but just then the door opened. One of the men stuck his head out, only about a couple of foot from me, and I thought I was gone; but he jerked it in again, and says:

"Heave that blame lantern out o' sight, Bill!"

He flung a bag of something into the boat, and then got in himself, and set down. It was Packard. Then Bill *he* come out and got in. Packard says, in a low voice:

"All ready—shove off!"

I couldn't hardly hang on to the shutters, I was so weak. But Bill says:

"Hold on—'d you go through him?"

"No. Didn't you?"

"No. So he's got his share o' the cash yet."

"Well, then, come along—no use to take truck and leave money."

"Say—won't he suspicion what we're up to?"

"Maybe he won't. But we got to have it anyway. Come along."

So they got out and went in.

The door slammed to, because it was on the careened side; and in a half second I was in the boat, and Jim come a tumbling after me. I out with my knife and cut the rope, and away we went!

We didn't touch an oar, and we didn't speak nor whisper, nor hardly even breathe. We went gliding swift along, dead silent, past the tip of the paddle-box, and past the stern; then in a second or two more we was a hundred yards below the wreck, and the darkness soaked her up, every last sign of her, and we was safe, and knowed it.

When we was three or four hundred yards down stream, we see the lantern show like a little spark at the texas door, for a second, and we knowed by that that the rascals had missed their boat, and was beginning to understand that they was in just as much trouble, now, as Jim Turner was.

Then Jim manned the oars, and we took out after our raft. Now was the first time that I begun to worry about the men—I reckon I hadn't had time to before. I begun to think how dreadful it was, even for murderers, to be in such a fix. I says to myself, there ain't no telling but I might come to be a murderer myself, yet, and then how would *I* like it? So says I to Jim:

"The first light we see, we'll land a hundred yards below it or above it, in a place where it's a good hiding-place for you and the skiff, and then I'll go and fix up some kind of a yarn, and get somebody to go for that gang and get them out of their scrape, so they can be hung when their time comes."

But that idea was a failure; for pretty soon it begun to storm again, and this time worse than ever. The rain poured down, and never a light showed; everybody in bed, I reckon. We boomed along down the river, watching for lights and watching for our raft. After a long time the rain let up, but the clouds staid, and the lightning kept whimpering, and by and by a flash showed us a black thing ahead, floating, and we made for it.

It was the raft, and mighty glad was we to get aboard of it again. We seen a light, now, away down to the right, on shore. So I said I would go for it. The skiff was half full of plunder which that gang had stole, there on the wreck. We hustled it onto the raft in a pile, and I told Jim to float along down, and show a light when he judged he had gone about two mile, and keep it burning till I come; then I manned my oars and shoved for the light. As I got down towards it, three or four more showed—up on a hillside. It was a village. I closed in above the shore-light, and laid on my oars and floated. As I went by, I see it was a lantern hanging on the jackstaff of a double-hull ferry-boat. I skimmed around for the watchman, a-wondering whereabouts he slept; and by and by I found him roosting on the bitts, forward, with his head down between his knees. I gave his shoulder two or three little shoves, and begun to cry.

He stirred up, in a kind of a startlish way; but when he see it was only me he took a good gap and stretch, and then he says:

"Hello, what's up? Don't cry, bub. What's the trouble?"

I says:

"Pap, and mam, and sis, and—"

Then I broke down. He says:

"Oh, dang it now, *don't* take on so, we all has to have our troubles, and this 'n 'll come out all right. What's the matter with 'em?"

"They're—they're—are you the watchman of the boat?"

"Yes," he says, kind of pretty-well-satisfied like. "I'm the captain and the owner, and the mate, and the pilot, and watchman and head deck-hand; and sometimes I'm the freight and passengers. I ain't as rich as old Jim Hornback, and I can't be so blame' generous and good to Tom, Dick and Harry as what he is, and slam around money the way he does; but I've told him a many a time 't I wouldn't trade places with him; for, says I, a sailor's life's the life for me, and I'm derned if *I'd* live two mile out o' town, where there ain't nothing ever goin' on, not for all his spondulicks and as much more on top of it. Says I—"

I broke in and says:

"They're in an awful peck of trouble, and—"

"*Who* is?"

"Why, pap, and mam, and sis, and Miss Hooker; and if you'd take your ferry-boat and go up there—"

"Up where? Where are they?"

"On the wreck."

"What wreck?"

"Why, there ain't but one."

"What, you don't mean the *Walter Scott*?"[76]

"Yes."

"Good land! what are they doin' *there,* for gracious sakes?"

"Well, they didn't go there a-purpose."

"I bet they didn't! Why, great goodness, there ain't no chance for 'em if they don't git off mighty quick! Why, how in the nation did they ever git into such a scrape?"

---

76. Sir Walter Scott was one of the most popular writers of the time. His historical novels of chivalric romance in Scotland and England captivated the attention of many readers on both sides of the Atlantic, including a young Samuel Clemens. As Clemens grew older, he found himself detesting Scott's influence on America, especially on the South. In *Life on the Mississippi* (1883) Twain lambasted Scott at length for glorifying barbaric relics such as duels, family feuds, and other ritualized violence. Naming the shipwreck the *Walter Scott* seems to be one of many swipes Twain took at Scott. It could also be Twain's way of saying that death is the inevitable outcome of blood feuds, duels, and the like.

"Easy enough. Miss Hooker was a-visiting, up there to the town—"

"Yes, Booth's Landing—go on."

"She was a-visiting, there at Booth's Landing, and just in the edge of the evening she started over with her nigger woman in the horse-ferry, to stay all night at her friend's house, Miss What-you-may-call-her, I disremember her name, and they lost their steering-oar, and swung around and went a-floating down, stern first, about two mile, and saddle-baggsed on the wreck, and the ferry man and the nigger woman and the horses was all lost, but Miss Hooker she made a grab and got aboard the wreck. Well, about an hour after dark, we come along down in our trading-scow,[77] and it was so dark we didn't notice the wreck till we was right on it; and so *we* saddle-baggsed; but all of us was saved but Bill Whipple—and oh, he *was* the best cretur!—I most wish't it had been me, I do."

"My George! It's the beatenest thing I ever struck. And *then* what did you all do?"

"Well, we hollered and took on, but it's so wide there we couldn't make nobody hear. So pap said somebody got to get ashore and get help somehow. I was the only one that could swim, so I made a dash for it, and Miss Hooker she said if I didn't strike help sooner, come here and hunt up her uncle, and he'd fix the thing. I made the land about a mile below, and been fooling along ever since, trying to get people to do something, but they said, 'What, in such a night and such a current? there ain't no sense in it; go for the steam-ferry.' Now if you'll go, and—"

"By Jackson,[78] I'd *like* to, and blame it I don't know but I will; but who in the dingnation's agoing' to *pay* for it? Do you reckon your pap—"

"Why *that's* all right. Miss Hooker she told me, *particular*, that her uncle Hornback—"

---

77. Scows were flat-bottomed boats, or flatboats, that lacked steam power and generally only traveled downstream. Upon reaching their destination they were typically cut up for their lumber, much like log rafts. Small trading scows, like the one mentioned here, might carry local crops, livestock, or crafts for sale at a downstream market (Sandlin 2010, 7, 18–19). Larger trading scows often traveled long distances, sometimes all the way from northern cities such as Pittsburgh and St. Paul to New Orleans. A notable trading-scow worker was Abraham Lincoln, who worked on flatboat crews as a young man. By his own account, his antislavery convictions developed in New Orleans, where the close exposure to slave trading horrified him (Campanella 2010).

78. "By Jackson" seems to be yet another invocation of Andrew Jackson, the most commanding president and public persona of the time. The original expression was "By Jove," after the Roman god Jove (or Jupiter). Long before Jackson was a president he was a folk hero as a victorious general and Indian fighter in the War of 1812, where his valor earned him the nickname "Old Hickory."

"Great guns! is *he* her uncle? Looky here, you break for that light over yonder-way, and turn out west when you git there, and about a quarter of a mile out you'll come to the tavern; tell 'em to dart you out to Jim Horn-back's and he'll foot the bill. And don't you fool around any, because he'll want to know the news. Tell him I'll have his niece all safe before he can get to town. Hump yourself, now; I'm agoing up around the corner here, to roust out my engineer."

I struck for the light, but as soon as he turned the corner I went back and got into my skiff and bailed her out and then pulled up shore in the easy water about six hundred yards, and tucked myself in among some woodboats; for I couldn't rest easy till I could see the ferryboat start. But take it all around, I was feeling ruther comfortable on accounts of taking all this trouble for that gang, for not many would a done it. I wished the widow knowed about it. I judged she would be proud of me for helping these rapscallions, because rapscallions and dead beats is the kind the widow and good people takes the most interest in.

Well, before long here comes the wreck, dim and dusky, sliding along down! A kind of cold shiver went through me, and then I struck out for her. She was very deep, and I see in a minute there warn't much chance for

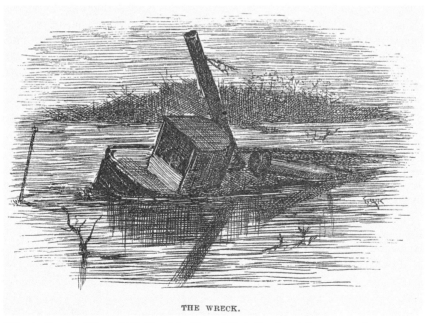

THE WRECK.

(Illustration by Edward W. Kemble. From Mark Twain, *Adventures of Huckleberry Finn*. New York: C. L. Webster, 1885. Digitized by the University of Virginia Library.)

anybody being alive in her. I pulled all around her and hollered a little, but there wasn't any answer; all dead still. I felt a little bit heavy-hearted about the gang, but not much, for I reckoned if they could stand it, I could.

Then here comes the ferryboat; so I shoved for the middle of the river on a long down-stream slant; and when I judged I was out of eye-reach I laid on my oars, and looked back and see her go and smell around the wreck for Miss Hooker's remainders, because the captain would know her uncle Hornback would want them; and then pretty soon the ferryboat give it up and went for the shore, and I laid into my work and went a-booming down the river.

It did seem a powerful long time before Jim's light showed up; and when it did show, it looked like it was a thousand mile off. By the time I got there the sky was beginning to get a little gray in the east; so we struck for an island, and hid the raft, and sunk the skiff, and turned in and slept like dead people.

CHAPTER XIV.

By and by, when we got up, we turned over the truck the gang had stole off of the wreck, and found boots, and blankets, and clothes, and all sorts of other things, and a lot of books, and a spyglass, and three boxes of seegars. We hadn't ever been this rich before, in neither of our lives. The seegars was prime. We laid off all the afternoon in the woods talking, and me reading the books, and having a general good time. I told Jim all about what happened inside the wreck and at the ferryboat, and I said these kinds of things was adventures; but he said he didn't want no more adventures. He said that when I went in the texas and he crawled back to get on the raft and found her gone, he nearly died, because he judged it was all up with *him*, anyway it could be fixed; for if he didn't get saved he would get drownded; and if he did get saved, whoever saved him would send him back home so as to get the reward, and then Miss Watson would sell him South, sure. Well, he was right; he was most always right; he had an uncommon level head, for a nigger.

I read considerable to Jim about kings, and dukes, and earls and such, and how gaudy they dressed, and how much style they put on, and called each other your majesty, and your grace, and your lordship, and so on, 'stead of mister; and Jim's eyes bugged out, and he was interested.[79] He says:

---

79. Although Huck is poorly educated and only semiliterate, as we shall see, he still has some ability to read and is entertained by the books they have found on the shipwreck.

"I didn' know dey was so many un um. I hain't hearn 'bout none un um, skasely, but ole King Sollermun, onless you counts dem kings dat's in a pack er k'yards. How much do a king git?"

"Get?" I says; "why, they get a thousand dollars a month if they want it; they can have just as much as they want; everything belongs to them."

"*Ain'* dat gay? En what dey got to do, Huck?"

"*They* don't do nothing! Why, how you talk. They just set around."

"No—is dat so?"

"Of course it is. They just set around. Except maybe when there's a war; then they go to the war. But other times they just lazy around; or go hawking—just hawking and sp— Sh!—d' you hear a noise?"

We skipped out and looked; but it warn't nothing but the flutter of a steamboat's wheel, away down coming around the point; so we come back.

"Yes," says I, "and other times, when things is dull, they fuss with the parlyment; and if everybody don't go just so he whacks their heads off. But mostly they hang round the harem."

"Roun' de which?"

"Harem."

"What's de harem?"

"The place where he keeps his wives. Don't you know about the harem? Solomon had one; he had about a million wives."

"Why, yes, dat's so; I—I'd done forgot it. A harem's a bo'd'n-house, I reck'n. Mos' likely dey has rackety times in de nussery. En I reck'n de wives quarrels considable; en dat 'crease de racket. Yit dey say Sollermun de wises' man dat ever live'. I doan' take no stock in dat. Bekase why: would a wise man want to live in de mids' er sich a blimblammin' all de time? No—'deed he wouldn't. A wise man 'ud take en buil' a biler-factry; en den he could shet *down* de biler-factry when he want to res'."

"Well, but he *was* the wisest man, anyway; because the widow she told me so, her own self."

Popular books, such as the "pirate books and robber books" from the early scenes with Tom Sawyer, generally had to be easy to read, extensively illustrated, or both, because advanced readers were rare. Leaving school at age 14 or earlier was the norm at the time; the modern American high school did not exist until the 20th century, and even at the turn of the century barely 1 in 10 Americans aged 14 to 19 was still enrolled in school (Goldin 1998, 348–349).

Jim is completely illiterate, which was the norm for slaves. Frederick Douglass called literacy "the pathway from slavery to freedom" (1982, 78), and slaveholders seemed to agree. Almost all the slave states, including Missouri by 1847, made it a crime to teach a slave to read. After the bloody slave uprising in 1831 led by Nat Turner, a highly literate slave, the southern states tightened these restrictions further. W. E. B. Du Bois estimated that only about 5 percent of slaves in 1860 had learned to read (Genovese 1974, 563).

"I doan k'yer what de widder say, he *warn't* no wise man, nuther. He had some er de dad-fetchedes' ways I ever see. Does you know 'bout dat chile dat he 'uz gwyne to chop in two?"

"Yes, the widow told me all about it."

"*Well,* den! Warn' dat de beatenes' notion in de worl'? You jes' take en look at it a minute. Dah's de stump, dah—dat's one er de women; heah's you—dat's de yuther one; I's Sollermun; en dish-yer dollar bill's de chile. Bofe un you claims it. What does I do? Does I shin aroun' mongs' de neighbors en fine out which un you de bill *do* b'long to, en han' it over to de right one, all safe en soun', de way dat anybody dat had any gumption would? No—I take en whack de bill in *two,* en give half un it to you, en de yuther half to de yuther woman. Dat's de way Sollermun was gwyne to do wid de chile. Now I want to ast you: what's de use er dat half a bill?—can't buy noth'n wid it. En what use is a half a chile? I wouldn' give a dern for a million un um."

"But hang it, Jim, you've clean missed the point—blame it, you've missed it a thousand mile."

"Who? Me? Go 'long. Doan' talk to *me* 'bout yo' pints. I reck'n I knows sense when I sees it; en dey ain' no sense in sich doin's as dat. De 'spute warn't 'bout a half a chile, de 'spute was 'bout a whole chile; en de man dat think he kin settle a 'spute 'bout a whole chile wid a half a chile, doan' know enough to come in out'n de rain. Doan' talk to me 'bout Sollermun, Huck, I knows him by de back."

"But I tell you you don't get the point."

"Blame de pint! I reck'n I knows what I knows. En mine you, de *real* pint is down furder—it's down deeper. It lays in de way Sollermun was raised. You take a man dat's got on'y one or two chillen; is dat man gwyne to be waseful o' chillen? No, he ain't; he can't 'ford it. *He* know how to value 'em. But you take a man dat's got 'bout five million chillen runnin' roun' de house, en it's diffunt. *He* as soon chop a chile in two as a cat. Dey's plenty mo'. A chile er two, mo' er less, warn't no consekens to Sollermun, dad fetch him!"

I never see such a nigger. If he got a notion in his head once, there warn't no getting it out again. He was the most down on Solomon of any nigger I ever see. So I went to talking about other kings, and let Solomon slide. I told about Louis Sixteenth that got his head cut off in France long time ago; and about his little boy the dolphin, that would a been a king, but they took and shut him up in jail, and some say he died there.

"Po' little chap."

"But some says he got out and got away, and come to America."[80]

---

80. Huck's account of Louis XVI and his son is surprisingly accurate. Louis XVI was guillotined in 1793 during the French Revolution. Even Huck's use of "dolphin" to describe

"Dat's good! But he'll be pooty lonesome—dey ain' no kings here, is dey, Huck?"

"No."

"Den he cain't git no situation. What he gwyne to do?"

"Well, I don't know. Some of them gets on the police, and some of them learns people how to talk French."

"Why, Huck, doan' de French people talk de same way we does?"

"*No,* Jim; you couldn't understand a word they said—not a single word."

"Well, now, I be ding-busted! How do dat come?"

"I don't know; but it's so. I got some of their jabber out of a book. Spose a man was to come to you and say *Polly-voo-franzy*—what would you think?"

"I wouldn' think nuff'n; I'd take en bust him over de head. Dat is, if he warn't white. I wouldn't 'low no nigger to call me dat."

"Shucks, it ain't calling you anything. It's only saying, do you know how to talk French?"

"Well, den, why couldn't he *say* it?"

"Why, he *is* a-saying it. That's a Frenchman's *way* of saying it."

"Well, it's a blame ridicklous way, en I doan' want to hear no mo' 'bout it. Dey ain' no sense in it."

"Looky here, Jim; does a cat talk like we do?"

"No, a cat don't."

"Well, does a cow?"

"No, a cow don't, nuther."

"Does a cat talk like a cow, or a cow talk like a cat?"

"No, dey don't."

"It's natural and right for 'em to talk different from each other, ain't it?"

"Course."

"And ain't it natural and right for a cat and a cow to talk different from *us*?"

"Why, mos' sholy it is."

"Well, then, why ain't it natural and right for a *Frenchman* to talk different from us? You answer me that."

"Is a cat a man, Huck?"

"No."

Louis's young son is correct in a sense: "dauphin" is French for "dolphin," and the coat of arms for the heir apparent prominently featured two dolphins. Although the dauphin died in prison in 1795 at age 10, many people believed that he was still alive. The controversy was not completely settled until the year 2000, when his remains were subjected to DNA testing (Daley 2000, A1).

"Well, den, dey ain't no sense in a cat talkin' like a man. Is a cow a man?—er is a cow a cat?"

"No, she ain't either of them."

"Well, den, she ain' got no business to talk like either one er the yuther of 'em. Is a Frenchman a man?"

"Yes."

"*Well,* den! Dad blame it, why doan' he *talk* like a man? You answer me *dat*!"

I see it warn't no use wasting words—you can't learn a nigger to argue. So I quit.[81]

CHAPTER XV.

WE judged that three nights more would fetch us to Cairo, at the bottom of Illinois, where the Ohio River comes in, and that was what we was after. We would sell the raft and get on a steamboat and go way up the Ohio amongst the free States, and then be out of trouble.[82]

---

81. The "King Sollerman" scene was one of Twain's favorites to perform before audiences, and it is also a favorite of Twain scholars. It is a deeply revealing passage. Huck's and Jim's disagreement over King Solomon's split-the-baby decree says much about each one's place in the world. Huck has no family except a shiftless father he is escaping. Jim has a wife and two daughters, and he fears that he is about to be "sold down the river" and separated from them forever. Jim takes Solomon's decree literally and is horrified by it. Huck does not bother to explain that the king's real intention was to find out which woman was the true mother, so he too seems to take it literally and unquestioningly, perhaps because it is in a book (à la his friend Tom Sawyer). If one takes the story of Solomon literally, Jim is clearly right. But Huck, exasperated, falls back on the customary racism of his time and place and cuts the argument short, rationalizing that "you can't learn a nigger to argue." Huck's befriending of Jim has its limits, at least at this point, and he is a long way from regarding Jim as an equal.

82. The Ohio River, like the Mississippi north of Cairo, had slave states on one side and free states on the other. Going upstream on the Ohio, a steamboat traveling the full length of the river to Pittsburgh would go by Illinois, Indiana, and Ohio as well as Kentucky and Virginia. As noted before, Illinois was much friendlier to slave catchers than to escaped slaves, so the Ohio River plan may have been more promising. Abolitionist Levi Coffin, famously dubbed the "president" of the underground railroad, claimed to have assisted more than 3,000 Canada-bound slaves in Indiana and Ohio (Coffin 1880, 671). Historian Wilbur H. Siebert claimed that the Ohio River was itself an underground railroad route, with access to a vast network of escape routes that crisscrossed the state of Ohio. Modern historians tend to downplay the notion of such a vast network, but it does appear that many successful slave escapes to the North involved the Ohio River. Among the slave owners who fretted about the possibility of slave escapes via Mississippi and Ohio River steamboats was future Confederate president Jefferson Davis, who had a plantation by the Mississippi River.

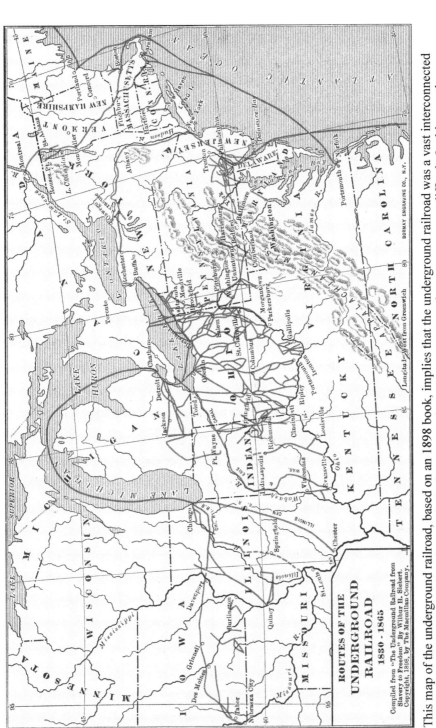

This map of the underground railroad, based on an 1898 book, implies that the underground railroad was a vast interconnected network like the modern railroad network. In fact, connections were tenuous and escape was very difficult. In this map the escape routes are most numerous in the state of Ohio, down to its southern border, the Ohio River, consistent with Jim's plan to travel up the Ohio River to freedom. (Dixon Ryan Fox. *Harper's Atlas of American History*. New York: Harper & Brothers, 1920, 41.)

Well, the second night a fog begun to come on, and we made for a tow-head to tie to, for it wouldn't do to try to run in a fog; but when I paddled ahead in the canoe, with the line, to make fast, there warn't anything but little saplings to tie to. I passed the line around one of them right on the edge of the cut bank, but there was a stiff current, and the raft come booming down so lively she tore it out by the roots and away she went. I see the fog closing down, and it made me so sick and scared I couldn't budge for most a half a minute it seemed to me—and then there warn't no raft in sight; you couldn't see twenty yards. I jumped into the canoe and run back to the stern and grabbed the paddle and set her back a stroke. But she didn't come. I was in such a hurry I hadn't untied her. I got up and tried to untie her, but I was so excited my hands shook so I couldn't hardly do anything with them.

As soon as I got started I took out after the raft, hot and heavy, right down the tow-head. That was all right as far as it went, but the tow-head warn't sixty yards long, and the minute I flew by the foot of it I shot out into the solid white fog, and hadn't no more idea which way I was going than a dead man.

Thinks I, it won't do to paddle; first I know I'll run into the bank or a tow-head or something; I got to set still and float, and yet it's mighty fidgety business to have to hold your hands still at such a time. I whooped and listened. Away down there, somewheres I hears a small whoop, and up comes my spirits. I went tearing after it, listening sharp to hear it again. The next time it come, I see I warn't heading for it, but heading away to the right of it. And the next time, I was heading away to the left of it—and not gaining on it much, either, for I was flying around, this way and that and t'other, but it was going straight ahead all the time.

I did wish the fool would think to beat a tin pan, and beat it all the time, but he never did, and it was the still places between the whoops that was making the trouble for me. Well, I fought along, and directly I hears the whoop *behind* me. I was tangled good now. That was somebody else's whoop, or else I was turned around.

Davis said in Congress in 1850 that "the boats constantly passing by our long line of river frontier furnish great facility to get into Ohio; and when they do escape it is with great difficulty that they are recovered; indeed, it seldom occurs that they are restored" (qtd. in Siebert 2000, 312–313). Cincinnati in particular was a gateway to freedom for runaway slaves, and several other ports on the Ohio River were frequent jumping-off points as well (Buchanan 2004, 119–120).

There is still the question of how easy it would be to conceal Jim's runaway status on a steamboat. Nearly one in five members of steamboat crews were black (12 percent slaves, 6 percent free blacks), and black crewmen often assisted fugitive slaves, but Huck and Jim would need a good ruse or Jim would have to stow away. Either way, escaping via steamboat was difficult and often unsuccessful (Buchanan 2004, 109–118).

I throwed the paddle down. I heard the whoop again; it was behind me yet, but in a different place; it kept coming, and kept changing its place, and I kept answering, till by and by it was in front of me again and I knowed the current had swung the canoe's head down stream, and I was all right, if that was Jim and not some other raftsman hollering. I couldn't tell nothing about voices in a fog, for nothing don't look natural nor sound natural in a fog.

The whooping went on, and in about a minute I come a booming down on a cut bank with smoky ghosts of big trees on it, and the current throwed me off to the left and shot by, amongst a lot of snags that fairly roared, the currrent was tearing by them so swift.

In another second or two it was solid white and still again. I set perfectly still, then, listening to my heart thump, and I reckon I didn't draw a breath while it thumped a hundred.

I just give up then. I knowed what the matter was. That cut bank was an island, and Jim had gone down t'other side of it. It warn't no tow-head, that you could float by in ten minutes. It had the big timber of a regular island; it might be five or six mile long and more than a half a mile wide.

I kept quiet, with my ears cocked, about fifteen minutes, I reckon. I was floating along, of course, four or five mile an hour; but you don't ever think of that. No, you *feel* like you are laying dead still on the water; and if a little glimpse of a snag slips by, you don't think to yourself how fast *you're* going, but you catch your breath and think, my! how that snag's tearing along. If you think it ain't dismal and lonesome out in a fog that way, by yourself, in the night, you try it once—you'll see.

Next, for about a half an hour, I whoops now and then; at last I hears the answer a long ways off, and tries to follow it, but I couldn't do it, and directly I judged I'd got into a nest of tow-heads, for I had little dim glimpses of them on both sides of me, sometimes just a narrow channel between; and some that I couldn't see, I knowed was there because I'd hear the wash of the current against the old dead brush and trash that hung over the banks. Well, I warn't long loosing the whoops down amongst the tow-heads; and I only tried to chase them a little while, anyway, because it was worse than chasing a Jack-o'-lantern. You never knowed a sound dodge around so, and swap places so quick and so much.

I had to claw away from the bank pretty lively, four or five times, to keep from knocking the islands out of the river; and so I judged the raft must be butting into the bank every now and then, or else it would get further ahead and clear out of hearing—it was floating a little faster than what I was.

Well, I seemed to be in the open river again, by and by, but I couldn't hear no sign of a whoop nowheres. I reckoned Jim had fetched up on a snag, maybe, and it was all up with him. I was good and tired, so I laid down in the canoe and said I wouldn't bother no more. I didn't want to go to sleep, of course; but I was so sleepy I couldn't help it; so I thought I would take just one little cat-nap.

But I reckon it was more than a cat-nap, for when I waked up the stars was shining bright, the fog was all gone, and I was spinning down a big bend stern first. First I didn't know where I was; I thought I was dreaming; and when things began to come back to me, they seemed to come up dim out of last week.

It was a monstrous big river here, with the tallest and the thickest kind of timber on both banks; just a solid wall, as well as I could see, by the stars. I looked away down stream, and seen a black speck on the water. I took out after it; but when I got to it it warn't nothing but a couple of saw-logs made fast together. Then I see another speck, and chased that; then another, and this time I was right. It was the raft.

When I got to it Jim was setting there with his head down between his knees, asleep, with his right arm hanging over the steering-oar. The other oar was smashed off, and the raft was littered up with leaves and branches and dirt. So she'd had a rough time.

I made fast and laid down under Jim's nose on the raft, and began to gap, and stretch my fists out against Jim, and says:

"Hello, Jim, have I been asleep? Why didn't you stir me up?"

"Goodness gracious, is dat you, Huck? En you ain' dead—you ain' drownded—you's back agin? It's too good for true, honey, it's too good for true. Lemme look at you chile, lemme feel o' you. No, you ain' dead! you's back agin, 'live en soun', jis de same ole Huck—de same ole Huck, thanks to goodness!"

"What's the matter with you, Jim? You been a drinking?"

"Drinkin'? Has I ben a drinkin'? Has I had a chance to be a drinkin'?"

"Well, then, what makes you talk so wild?"

"How does I talk wild?"

"*How*? Why, hain't you been talking about my coming back, and all that stuff, as if I'd been gone away?"

"Huck—Huck Finn, you look me in de eye; look me in de eye. *Hain't* you ben gone away?"

"Gone away? Why, what in the nation do you mean? *I* hain't been gone anywheres. Where would I go to?"

"Well, looky here, boss, dey's sumf'n wrong, dey is. Is I *me,* or who *is* I? Is I heah, or whah *is* I? Now dat's what I wants to know."

"Well, I think you're here, plain enough, but I think you're a tangle-headed old fool, Jim."

"I is, is I? Well, you answer me dis: Didn't you tote out de line in de canoe, fer to make fas' to de tow-head?"

"No, I didn't. What tow-head? I hain't see no tow-head."

"You hain't seen no tow-head? Looky here—didn't de line pull loose en de raf' go a hummin' down de river, en leave you en de canoe behine in de fog?"

"What fog?"

"Why, *de* fog. De fog dat's been aroun' all night. En didn't you whoop, en didn't I whoop, tell we got mix' up in de islands en one un us got los' en t'other one was jis' as good as los', 'kase he didn' know whah he wuz? En didn't I bust up agin a lot er dem islands en have a turrible time en mos' git drownded? Now ain' dat so, boss—ain't it so? You answer me dat."

"Well, this is too many for me, Jim. I hain't seen no fog, nor no islands, nor no troubles, nor nothing. I been setting here talking with you all night till you went to sleep about ten minutes ago, and I reckon I done the same. You couldn't a got drunk in that time, so of course you've been dreaming."

"Dad fetch it, how is I gwyne to dream all dat in ten minutes?"

"Well, hang it all, you did dream it, because there didn't any of it happen."

"But, Huck, it's all jis' as plain to me as—"

"It don't make no difference how plain it is; there ain't nothing in it. I know, because I've been here all the time."

Jim didn't say nothing for about five minutes, but set there studying over it. Then he says:

"Well, den, I reck'n I did dream it, Huck; but dog my cats ef it ain't de powerfullest dream I ever see. En I hain't ever had no dream b'fo' dat's tired me like dis one."

"Oh, well, that's all right, because a dream does tire a body like everything sometimes. But this one was a staving dream; tell me all about it, Jim."

So Jim went to work and told me the whole thing right through, just as it happened, only he painted it up considerable. Then he said he must start in and "'terpret" it, because it was sent for a warning. He said the first tow-head stood for a man that would try to do us some good, but the current was another man that would get us away from him. The whoops was warnings that would come to us every now and then, and if we didn't try hard to make out to understand them they'd just take us into bad luck, 'stead of keeping us out of it. The lot of tow-heads was troubles we was going to get into with quarrelsome people and all kinds of mean folks, but if we minded our business and didn't talk back and aggravate them, we would pull through and get out of the fog and into the big clear river, which was the free States, and wouldn't have no more trouble.

It had clouded up pretty dark just after I got on to the raft, but it was clearing up again, now.

"Oh, well, that's all interpreted well enough, as far as it goes, Jim," I says; "but what does *these* things stand for?"

It was the leaves and rubbish on the raft, and the smashed oar. You could see them first-rate, now.

Jim looked at the trash, and then looked at me, and back at the trash again. He had got the dream fixed so strong in his head that he couldn't seem to shake it loose and get the facts back into its place again, right away. But when he did get the thing straightened around he looked at me steady, without ever smiling, and says:

"What do dey stan' for? I'se gwyne to tell you. When I got all wore out wid work, en wid de callin' for you, en went to sleep, my heart wuz mos' broke bekase you wuz los', en I didn' k'yer no' mo' what become er me en de raf'. En when I wake up en fine you back agin, all safe en soun', de tears come, en I could a got down on my knees en kiss yo' foot I's so thankful. En all you wuz thinkin' 'bout wuz how you could make a fool uv ole Jim wid a lie. Dat truck dah is *trash;* en trash is what people is dat puts dirt on de head er dey fren's en makes 'em ashamed."

Then he got up slow, and walked to the wigwam, and went in there without saying anything but that. But that was enough. It made me feel so mean I could almost kissed *his* foot to get him to take it back.

It was fifteen minutes before I could work myself up to go and humble myself to a nigger—but I done it, and I warn't ever sorry for it afterwards, neither. I didn't do him no more mean tricks, and I wouldn't done that one if I'd a knowed it would make him feel that way.

CHAPTER XVI.

WE slept most all day, and started out at night, a little ways behind a monstrous long raft that was as long going by as a procession. She had four long sweeps at each end, so we judged she carried as many as thirty men, likely. She had five big wigwams aboard, wide apart, and an open camp fire in the middle, and a tall flag-pole at each end. There was a power of style about her. It *amounted* to something being a raftsman on such a craft as that.[83]

---

83. "Monstrous long" sounds about right. As noted earlier, each "string" of a log raft was about 400 feet, or longer than a football field. Lumber rafts, made from planks and beams, were even longer (Larson 1949, 91). The mammoth size of this raft provides a sense of the importance of rafts in antebellum commerce. The astounding bulk of the nation's timber and lumber output—lumber production increased fourteenfold between 1819 and 1859—militated for a cheap and easy way to get it to market (Taylor 1951, 387–388). Most likely this raft is made of logs or lumber to be disassembled at their destination. Despite the preeminence of steamboats, the old method of shipping logs and lumber by bundling them together as rafts and floating them downstream remained cost-effective.

We went drifting down into a big bend, and the night clouded up and got hot. The river was very wide, and was walled with solid timber on both sides; you couldn't see a break in it hardly ever, or a light. We talked about Cairo, and wondered whether we would know it when we got to it. I said likely we wouldn't, because I had heard say there warn't but about a dozen houses there, and if they didn't happen to have them lit up, how was we going to know we was passing a town?[84] Jim said if the two big rivers

---

In noting the elevated status of these raftsmen, Twain touches on a point that he made at length in Chapter 3 of *Life on the Mississippi.* In that chapter he sketched out a scene for *Huckleberry Finn,* in which Huck swims over to a huge raft and eavesdrops on a group of raftsmen who used to be keelboatmen. Many raftsmen in the steamboat era were displaced keelboat workers who had suffered a sharp loss in status. Keelboats were large flat-bottomed boats or barges that had once dominated river commerce. The greatest disadvantage of keelboats, which was not a problem for steamboats, was the return trip. On the long upstream trip the crew would variously sail, pole, and row the boat, and sometimes they would have to loop a rope around a tree on the bank and pull on it or bushwhack by pulling on trees or bushes near the bank (Taylor 1951, 57). This was arduous work, and the slow-moving keelboats were also tempting targets for river pirates and hostile Indians (Work Projects Administration 1998, 96). All of this made the keelboatman a legendary frontier figure, much more so than the raftsman. Twain described keelboatmen as "rough and hardy men; rude, uneducated, brave, suffering terrific hardships with sailor-like stoicism; heavy drinkers, coarse frolickers in moral sties like the Natchez-under-the-hill of that day, heavy fighters, reckless fellows, every one, elephantinely jolly, foul-witted, profane; prodigal of their money, bankrupt at the end of the trip, fond of barbaric finery, prodigious braggarts; yet, in the main, honest, trustworthy, faithful to promises and duty, and often picturesquely magnanimous" (Twain 1963, 10).

84. Cairo was a small struggling city, despite its strategic position at the junction of the Mississippi and Ohio Rivers. The city was chartered in 1818 by a group of investors who failed to fully pay for it, so ownership reverted to the government, which had little incentive or means to improve the city. As of the mid-1830s Cairo was barely populated, little more than a stopping point for steamboats in need of firewood. As the transportation revolution intensified, Cairo got a new lease on life. The original tracts were repurchased in 1835 and were chartered to the Cairo City and Canal Company. The town's population grew rapidly, soon reaching 2,000. In 1841 a member of the state legislature pleaded for "the building of a large commercial city at Cairo," adding that "Cairo presents as many flattering prospects of future greatness as any other place in the state" (Lansden 2009, 40, 42, 47).

The claim may have been true at the time, but of course a different city would soon emerge as the great commercial city of Illinois and the epitome of America's extraordinary growth in the 19th century. Chicago's rise was by no means inevitable. It was low-lying and flood-prone (as was Cairo) and hampered by a giant swamp to the west. For Chicago to get the crucial canal and railroad charters that made it a great water *and* rail nexus took enormous entrepreneurial effort and ability and not a little luck (Licht 1995, 124). Cairo, by contrast, was plagued by a faulty institutional setup, bad decisions, and no luck. It was a "company town," chartered to companies and run by their agents, with no local government, until 1857. In the crucial early years of 1839–1846, land could be leased but not purchased from the Cairo City and Canal Company, so individuals had virtually no incentive to

joined together there, that would show. But I said maybe we might think we was passing the foot of an island and coming into the same old river again. That disturbed Jim—and me too. So the question was, what to do? I said, paddle ashore the first time a light showed, and tell them pap was behind, coming along with a trading-scow, and was a green hand at the business, and wanted to know how far it was to Cairo. Jim thought it was a good idea, so we took a smoke on it and waited.

There warn't nothing to do now but to look out sharp for the town, and not pass it without seeing it. He said he'd be mighty sure to see it, because he'd be a free man the minute he seen it,[85] but if he missed it he'd be in a slave[86] country again and no more show for freedom. Every little while he jumps up and says:

"Dah she is?"

But it warn't. It was Jack-o'-lanterns, or lightning bugs; so he set down again, and went to watching, same as before. Jim said it made him all over trembly and feverish to be so close to freedom. Well, I can tell you it made me all over trembly and feverish, too, to hear him, because I begun to get it through my head that he *was* most free—and who was to blame for it? Why, *me*. I couldn't get that out of my conscience, no how nor no way. It got to troubling me so I couldn't rest; I couldn't stay still in

develop it. The company was supposed to develop it but repeatedly came up short. The company did manage to get a railroad stop in Cairo as part of the state's big internal improvements bill of 1837, but other cities got much bigger parts of the large eight-railroad network. Unlike Chicago, which benefited enormously from its new canal, Cairo's investment in a canal was questionable, both because of the competition from the railroads and because the rivers' enormous rises and drops made it extremely difficult to maintain the water level of a Cairo-based canal. In 1858 the Mississippi River's "June rise" broke through a defective levee and caused flooding of the entire city (Lansden 2009, 42–44, 49–54, 177).

85. Jim is either naive or exaggerating—just as swimming across the Mississippi to the western shore of Illinois did not automatically confer freedom on a runaway slave, neither did arriving at Cairo, on the southern tip of Illinois, or any other free state for that matter. Cairo in particular typically teemed with slave catchers (Buchanan 2004, 118). As noted before, the U.S. Constitution required that escaped slaves be returned to their owners, federal law made it unlawful to assist a runaway slave, and reward money from the slaves' owners provided a strong incentive to hunt down runaway slaves. It is small wonder, then, that many runaway slaves set their sights on Canada.

86. Remarkably, this is the first occurrence of the word "slave" in this novel. It appears 11 times in all, compared with 214 occurrences of "nigger." The contrast tells us something about the racial attitudes of Huck's time, including the dehumanization of African Americans that was necessary for whites to view their enslavement as acceptable and not inherently cruel. As the French intellectual Montesquieu wrote in 1748, "It is impossible for us to suppose these creatures to be men, because, allowing them to be men, a suspicion would follow that we ourselves are not Christians" (Montesquieu 1873, 275).

one place. It hadn't ever come home to me before, what this thing was that I was doing. But now it did; and it stayed with me, and scorched me more and more. I tried to make out to myself that *I* warn't to blame, because *I* didn't run Jim off from his rightful owner; but it warn't no use, conscience up and says, every time, "But you knowed he was running for his freedom, and you could a paddled ashore and told somebody." That was so—I couldn't get around that, noway. That was where it pinched. Conscience says to me, "What had poor Miss Watson done to you that you could see her nigger go off right under your eyes and never say one single word?[87] What did that poor old woman do to you, that you could treat her so mean? Why, she tried to learn you your book, she tried to learn you your manners, she tried to be good to you every way she knowed how. *That's* what she done."

I got to feeling so mean and so miserable I most wished I was dead. I fidgeted up and down the raft, abusing myself to myself, and Jim was fidgeting up and down past me. We neither of us could keep still. Every time he danced around and says, "Dah's Cairo!" it went through me like a shot, and I thought if it *was* Cairo I reckoned I would die of miserableness.

Jim talked out loud all the time while I was talking to myself. He was saying how the first thing he would do when he got to a free State he would

---

87. Here we have the classic collision between human rights and property rights that was slavery. Huck feels guilty about depriving Miss Watson of $800 worth of property, but he has already been abetting Jim's escape from slavery. In the nation as a whole the value of all that slave property, some $3 billion in 1860, was arguably the biggest reason why a peaceful resolution of the North-South conflict was unlikely.

Rasmussen (2014, 343) raises a compelling question: Why doesn't Huck use some of his $6,000 in gold coins to free Jim and his family? This would be an instance of compensated emancipation, the means by which many countries abolished slavery in the 19th century. The United States was not one of them except for the District of Columbia. In 1862 Congress abolished slavery in the District of Columbia, with payments to slaveholders of up to $300 per slave. But President Abraham Lincoln's proposal of compensated emancipation for the slave states still in the Union, including Missouri, went nowhere (Rodriguez 2007, 239, 689). Compensated emancipation at market prices would have been far cheaper than civil war, but nobody expected the war to be so costly and bloody, and compensated emancipation had almost no political support. Southern slaveholders had come to defend slavery as a "positive good" and might well have refused to sell their slaves, and far too few northerners cared enough about slavery to be willing to spend $3 billion to end it. Huck may have been similarly constrained, given how bizarre the act of paying thousands of dollars to free slaves would have been viewed in his community. Would Judge Thatcher have allowed him to use the money for that purpose? Huck, though an outsider and a rebel, is not immune to his community's racial norms and has not yet fully committed himself to Jim's freedom.

go to saving up money and never spend a single cent, and when he got enough he would buy his wife, which was owned on a farm close to where Miss Watson lived; and then they would both work to buy the two children,[88] and if their master wouldn't sell them, they'd get an Ab'litionist to go and steal them.

It most froze me to hear such talk.[89] He wouldn't ever dared to talk such talk in his life before. Just see what a difference it made in him the minute he judged he was about free. It was according to the old saying,

---

88. Here we learn that Jim is not merely escaping to avoid being "sold down the river" but is trying to keep his family intact. While they did not all live on the same plantation, his wife lived close by, and presumably the two children live with their mother. This is a big reason why slave sales were uncommon: the involuntary separation of families was so traumatic that the affected slaves were likely to run off or find ways, such as slacking and sabotage, to get back at their master. Many slave sales, though perhaps not most, were of entire families so as to keep them together. Sales that broke up slave families were one of the cruelest aspects of slavery. The frequency of such breakups has been a controversial issue among historians. The 1974 book *Time on the Cross: The Economics of American Negro Slavery*, by economic historians Robert W. Fogel and Stanley L. Engerman, examined mountains of plantation and other data and concluded that slave sales were rare and tended to be of whole families. Herbert Gutman (1988) and Paul A. David et al. (1976) refute those claims with additional data.

A tiny number of slaves, mostly skilled workers in the Upper South, were able to purchase their own freedom or that of other slaves (Stampp 1956, 96–97). Missouri was among those states where some slaves did so (Trexler 1914, 222). One of the most famous American slaves, Denmark Vesey, bought his freedom thanks to a winning lottery ticket. Raising the money was obviously difficult for most slaves, considering that they were not normally paid in cash. To do so, a slave had to be allowed to hire himself out on evenings and Sundays and collect and store the payments, in addition to any cash bonuses he might receive for his regular work. Not all southern states allowed self-purchase, and most clamped down on it in the decades before the Civil War, first requiring freed blacks to leave the state immediately and eventually barring slaves from hiring out their own labor (Cimprich 1988, 662–663).

89. The numbers of abolitionists and successful slave escapes were much lower in reality than in legend. A proposition to abolish slavery everywhere in the United States was not on the ballot in November 1860, when Abraham Lincoln was elected president, but a top historian estimated that had there been such a referendum in the North, it would have fetched no more than 2–5 percent of the vote (Benson 1972, 246). Likewise, the total number of successful slave escapes in the three decades before the Civil War is estimated at no more than 1,000–5,000 (Foner 2015, 4). The 1850 census reported a total of 1,011 fugitive slaves (United States Senate 1854, 64). Yet as Huck's reaction suggests, the principle and prospect of slave escapes, especially assisted escapes, was horrifying to white southerners. It became a matter of honor as well as profits; even nonslaveholding southern whites tended to regard slaves more as property than people and were aghast at the notion of white people who sought to abet the "theft" of their region's most valuable property. Many historians believe that the fugitive slave issue was central to the secession of the 11 states that formed the Confederacy.

"give a nigger an inch and he'll take an ell." Thinks I, this is what comes of my not thinking. Here was this nigger, which I had as good as helped to run away, coming right out flat-footed and saying he would steal his children—children that belonged to a man I didn't even know; a man that hadn't ever done me no harm.

I was sorry to hear Jim say that, it was such a lowering of him. My conscience got to stirring me up hotter than ever, until at last I says to it, "Let up on me—it ain't too late, yet—I'll paddle ashore at the first light, and tell." I felt easy, and happy, and light as a feather, right off. All my troubles was gone. I went to looking out sharp for a light, and sort of singing to myself. By and by one showed. Jim sings out:

"We's safe, Huck, we's safe! Jump up and crack yo' heels, dat's de good ole Cairo at las', I jis knows it!"

I says:

"I'll take the canoe and go and see, Jim. It mightn't be, you know."

He jumped and got the canoe ready, and put his old coat in the bottom for me to set on, and give me the paddle; and as I shoved off, he says:

"Pooty soon I'll be a-shout'n' for joy, en I'll say, it's all on accounts o' Huck; I's a free man, en I couldn't ever ben free ef it hadn' ben for Huck; Huck done it. Jim won't ever forgit you, Huck; you's de bes' fren' Jim's ever had; en you's de *only* fren' ole Jim's got now."

I was paddling off, all in a sweat to tell on him; but when he says this, it seemed to kind of take the tuck all out of me. I went along slow then, and I warn't right down certain whether I was glad I started or whether I warn't. When I was fifty yards off, Jim says:

"Dah you goes, de ole true Huck; de on'y white genlman dat ever kep' his promise to ole Jim."

Well, I just felt sick. But I says, I *got* to do it—I can't get *out* of it. Right then along comes a skiff with two men in it, with guns, and they stopped and I stopped. One of them says:

"What's that yonder?"

"A piece of a raft," I says.

"Do you belong on it?"

"Yes, sir."

"Any men on it?"

"Only one, sir."

"Well, there's five niggers run off to-night, up yonder above the head of the bend. Is your man white or black?"

I didn't answer up prompt. I tried to, but the words wouldn't come. I tried, for a second or two, to brace up and out with it, but I warn't man enough—hadn't the spunk of a rabbit. I see I was weakening; so I just give up trying, and up and says—

"He's white."

"I reckon we'll go and see for ourselves."

"I wish you would," says I, "because it's pap that's there, and maybe you'd help me tow the raft ashore where the light is. He's sick—and so is mam and Mary Ann."

"Oh, the devil! we're in a hurry, boy. But I s'pose we've got to. Come, buckle to your paddle, and let's get along."

I buckled to my paddle and they laid to their oars. When we had made a stroke or two, I says:

"Pap'll be mighty much obleeged to you, I can tell you. Everybody goes away when I want them to help me tow the raft ashore, and I can't do it by myself."

"Well, that's infernal mean. Odd, too. Say, boy, what's the matter with your father?"

"It's the—a—the—well, it ain't anything, much."

They stopped pulling. It warn't but a mighty little ways to the raft, now. One says:

"Boy, that's a lie. What *is* the matter with your pap? Answer up square, now, and it'll be the better for you."

"I will, sir, I will, honest—but don't leave us, please. It's the—the—gentlemen, if you'll only pull ahead, and let me heave you the head-line, you won't have to come a-near the raft—please do."

"Set her back, John, set her back!" says one. They backed water. "Keep away, boy—keep to looard. Confound it, I just expect the wind has blowed it to us. Your pap's got the small-pox, and you know it precious well. Why didn't you come out and say so? Do you want to spread it all over?"

"Well," says I, a-blubbering, "I've told everybody before, and then they just went away and left us."

"Poor devil, there's something in that. We are right down sorry for you, but we—well, hang it, we don't want the small-pox, you see. Look here, I'll tell you what to do. Don't you try to land by yourself, or you'll smash everything to pieces. You float along down about twenty miles and you'll come to a town on the left-hand side of the river. It will be long after sun-up, then, and when you ask for help, you tell them your folks are all down with chills and fever. Don't be a fool again, and let people guess what is the matter. Now we're trying to do you a kindness; so you just put twenty miles between us, that's a good boy. It wouldn't do any good to land yonder where the light is—it's only a wood-yard. Say—I reckon your father's poor, and I'm bound to say he's in pretty hard luck. Here—I'll put a twenty-dollar gold piece on this board, and you get it when it floats by. I feel mighty mean to leave you, but my kingdom! it won't do to fool with small-pox, don't you see?"

"Hold on, Parker," says the other man, "here's a twenty to put on the board for me. Good-bye, boy, you do as Mr. Parker told you, and you'll be all right."[90]

"That's so, my boy—good-bye, good-bye. If you see any runaway niggers, you get help and nab them, and you can make some money by it."

"Good-bye, sir," says I, "I won't let no runaway niggers get by me if I can help it."

They went off, and I got aboard the raft, feeling bad and low, because I knowed very well I had done wrong, and I see it warn't no use for me to try to learn to do right; a body that don't get *started* right when he's little ain't got no show—when the pinch comes there ain't nothing to back him up and keep him to his work, and so he gets beat. Then I thought a minute, and says to myself, hold on; s'pose you'd a done right and give Jim up; would you felt better than what you do now? No, says I, I'd feel bad—I'd feel just the same way I do now. Well, then, says I, what's the use you learning to do right, when it's troublesome to do right and ain't no trouble to do wrong, and the wages is just the same? I was stuck. I couldn't answer that. So I reckoned I wouldn't bother no more about it, but after this always do whichever come handiest at the time.

I went into the wigwam; Jim warn't there. I looked all around; he warn't anywhere. I says:

"Jim!"

"Here I is, Huck. Is dey out o' sight yit? Don't talk loud."

He was in the river under the stern oar, with just his nose out. I told him they were out of sight, so he come aboard. He says:

"I was a-listenin' to all de talk, en I slips into de river en was gwyne to shove for sho' if dey come aboard. Den I was gwyne to swim to de raf' agin when dey was gone. But lawsy, how you did fool 'em, Huck! Dat *wuz* de smartes' dodge! I tell you, chile, I 'speck it save' ole Jim—ole Jim ain't gwyne to forget you for dat, honey."

---

90. The slave catchers' gift initially seems astonishingly generous—two $25 gold pieces, worth a total of $1,200 in today's money—but ulterior motives may be present. They understandably want Huck to follow the "floating currency" so that his "pap's" smallpox does not infect their town, and perhaps they want to ease their consciences for not helping the boy and his family by buying them off.

Smallpox, or variola, is one of the most devastating and contagious viruses in human history. In North America, smallpox and other diseases killed off much, perhaps most, of the Native American population both before and after European settlers arrived. European Americans were also afflicted by recurring epidemics, including one during the American Revolution and a particularly deadly outbreak in 1837. In 19th-century America an early vaccine existed but was risky and not widely used, so outbreaks of smallpox were not uncommon (Hopkins 2002, 255–290).

Then we talked about the money. It was a pretty good raise, twenty dollars apiece. Jim said we could take deck passage on a steamboat now, and the money would last us as far as we wanted to go in the free States. He said twenty mile more warn't far for the raft to go, but he wished we was already there.

Towards daybreak we tied up, and Jim was mighty particular about hiding the raft good. Then he worked all day fixing things in bundles, and getting all ready to quit rafting.

That night about ten we hove in sight of the lights of a town away down in a left-hand bend.

I went off in the canoe, to ask about it. Pretty soon I found a man out in the river with a skiff, setting a trot-line. I ranged up and says:

"Mister, is that town Cairo?"

"Cairo? no. You must be a blame' fool."

"What town is it, mister?"

"If you want to know, go and find out. If you stay here botherin' around me for about a half a minute longer, you'll get something you won't want."

I paddled to the raft. Jim was awful disappointed, but I said never mind, Cairo would be the next place, I reckoned.

We passed another town before daylight, and I was going out again; but it was high ground, so I didn't go. No high ground about Cairo, Jim said. I had forgot it. We laid up for the day on a tow-head tolerable close to the left-hand bank. I begun to suspicion something. So did Jim. I says:

"Maybe we went by Cairo in the fog that night."

He says:

"Doan' less' talk about it, Huck. Po' niggers can't have no luck. I awluz 'spected dat rattle-snake skin warn't done wid its work."

"I wish I'd never seen that snake-skin, Jim—I do wish I'd never laid eyes on it."

"It ain't yo' fault, Huck; you didn' know. Don't you blame yo'self 'bout it."

When it was daylight, here was the clear Ohio water in shore, sure enough, and outside was the old regular Muddy! So it was all up with Cairo.[91]

---

91. As mentioned earlier in the chapter, Cairo was easy to miss. Cairo's sad state was world famous, thanks to a travelogue by Charles Dickens titled *American Notes* (1842). Dickens's descriptions of Cairo were devastating, perhaps all the more so given Cairo's reputation as a sinkhole for English investors. Foreign investors helped finance much of American economic development, notably canals and railroads, but not all of those investments were successful. Cairo, Dickens wrote, was "vaunted in England as a mine of Golden Hope, and speculated in, on the faith of monstrous representations, to many people's ruin." After a steamboat ride down the Ohio River to the Mississippi, Dickens had this to say about

We talked it all over. It wouldn't do to take to the shore; we couldn't take the raft up the stream, of course. There warn't no way but to wait for dark, and start back in the canoe and take the chances. So we slept all day amongst the cottonwood thicket, so as to be fresh for the work, and when we went back to the raft about dark the canoe was gone!

We didn't say a word for a good while. There warn't anything to say. We both knowed well enough it was some more work of the rattlesnake skin; so what was the use to talk about it? It would only look like we was finding fault, and that would be bound to fetch more bad luck—and keep on fetching it, too, till we knowed enough to keep still.

By and by we talked about what we better do, and found there warn't no way but just to go along down with the raft till we got a chance to buy a canoe to go back in. We warn't going to borrow it when there warn't anybody around, the way pap would do, for that might set people after us.

So we shoved out, after dark, on the raft.

Anybody that don't believe yet, that it's foolishness to handle a snake-skin, after all that that snake-skin done for us, will believe it now if they read on and see what more it done for us.

The place to buy canoes is off of rafts laying up at shore. But we didn't see no rafts laying up; so we went along during three hours and more. Well, the night got gray and ruther thick, which is the next meanest thing to fog. You can't tell the shape of the river, and you can't see no distance. It got to be very late and still, and then along comes a steamboat up the river. We lit the lantern, and judged she would see it. Up-stream boats

---

the town at their junction: "A dismal swamp, on which the half-built houses rot away: cleared here and there for the space of a few yards; and teeming, then, with rank unwholesome vegetation, in whose baleful shade the wretched wanderers who are tempted hither, droop, and die, and lay their bones; the hateful Mississippi circling and eddying before it, and turning off upon its southern course a slimy monster hideous to behold; a hotbed of disease, an ugly sepulchre, a grave uncheered by any gleam of promise: a place without one single quality, in earth or air or water, to commend it: such is this dismal Cairo." Later in the book he called it a "detestable morass," "that ill-fated Cairo" (Dickens 1997, 171, 187, 246).

Cairo's fate brightened considerably after the Civil War, as it became an important regional railroad hub and handled a great deal of ferry traffic, but its heyday was modest and followed by decades of desolation. The city's population rose to a peak of about 15,000 in 1920, making it the 28th-largest city in Illinois, a far cry from the great metropolis that some had prophesied in antebellum times (Ridgeley 1921, 360). Cairo's decline since then, to a population of under 3,000 in 2010, is shocking even by the standards of the Rust Belt and the Mississippi Delta region, the two hard-hit regions in which it is situated. New railroad bridges and highways made Cairo increasingly superfluous as a transportation and shipping center. Racial violence in the 1960s accelerated Cairo's decline. For multiple perspectives on Cairo's woes, the award-winning documentary film *Between Two Rivers* (2012) is highly recommended.

didn't generly come close to us; they go out and follow the bars and hunt for easy water under the reefs; but nights like this they bull right up the channel against the whole river.

We could hear her pounding along, but we didn't see her good till she was close. She aimed right for us. Often they do that and try to see how close they can come without touching; sometimes the wheel bites off a sweep, and then the pilot sticks his head out and laughs, and thinks he's mighty smart. Well, here she comes, and we said she was going to try and shave us; but she didn't seem to be sheering off a bit. She was a big one, and she was coming in a hurry, too, looking like a black cloud with rows of glow-worms around it; but all of a sudden she bulged out, big and scary, with a long row of wide-open furnace doors shining like red-hot teeth, and her monstrous bows and guards hanging right over us. There was a yell at us, and a jingling of bells to stop the engines, a pow-wow of cussing, and whistling of steam—and as Jim went overboard on one side and I on the other, she come smashing straight through the raft.

I dived—and I aimed to find the bottom, too, for a thirty-foot wheel had got to go over me, and I wanted it to have plenty of room. I could always stay under water a minute; this time I reckon I stayed under a minute and a half. Then I bounced for the top in a hurry, for I was nearly busting. I popped out to my arm-pits and blowed the water out of my nose, and puffed a bit. Of course there was a booming current; and of course that boat started her engines again ten seconds after she stopped them, for they never cared much for raftsmen; so now she was churning along up the river, out of sight in the thick weather, though I could hear her.

I sung out for Jim about a dozen times, but I didn't get any answer; so I grabbed a plank that touched me while I was "treading water," and struck out for shore, shoving it ahead of me. But I made out to see that the drift of the current was towards the left-hand shore, which meant that I was in a crossing; so I changed off and went that way.

It was one of these long, slanting, two-mile crossings; so I was a good long time in getting over. I made a safe landing, and clumb up the bank. I couldn't see but a little ways, but I went poking along over rough ground for a quarter of a mile or more, and then I run across a big old-fashioned double log house before I noticed it.[92] I was going to rush by and get away, but a lot of dogs jumped out and went to howling and barking at me, and I knowed better than to move another peg.

---

92. It is nighttime, and the streets do not seem to be lit. Coal-powered gaslights originated in late 18th-century Britain and had become standard in the principal streets of American cities by the 1830s (Gordon 2004, 163), so Huck seems to have landed in the country or in a small town.

CHAPTER XVII.

IN about a minute somebody spoke out of a window without putting his head out, and says:

"Be done, boys! Who's there?"

I says:

"It's me."

"Who's me?"

"George Jackson, sir."

"What do you want?"

"I don't want nothing, sir. I only want to go along by, but the dogs won't let me."

"What are you prowling around here this time of night for—hey?"

"I warn't prowling around, sir; I fell overboard off of the steamboat."

"Oh, you did, did you? Strike a light there, somebody. What did you say your name was?"

"George Jackson, sir. I'm only a boy."

"Look here; if you're telling the truth, you needn't be afraid—nobody'll hurt you. But don't try to budge; stand right where you are. Rouse out Bob and Tom, some of you, and fetch the guns. George Jackson, is there anybody with you?"

"No, sir, nobody."

I heard the people stirring around in the house, now, and see a light. The man sung out:

"Snatch that light away, Betsy, you old fool—ain't you got any sense? Put it on the floor behind the front door. Bob, if you and Tom are ready, take your places."

"All ready."

"Now, George Jackson, do you know the Shepherdsons?"

"No, sir—I never heard of them."

"Well, that may be so, and it mayn't. Now, all ready. Step forward, George Jackson. And mind, don't you hurry—come mighty slow. If there's anybody with you, let him keep back—if he shows himself he'll be shot. Come along now. Come slow; push the door open yourself—just enough to squeeze in, d' you hear?"

I didn't hurry; I couldn't if I'd a wanted to. I took one slow step at a time, and there warn't a sound, only I thought I could hear my heart. The dogs were as still as the humans, but they followed a little behind me. When I got to the three log door-steps, I heard them unlocking and unbarring and unbolting. I put my hand on the door and pushed it a little and a little more, till somebody said, "There, that's enough—put your head in." I done it, but I judged they would take it off.

The candle was on the floor, and there they all was, looking at me, and me at them, for about a quarter of a minute. Three big men with guns pointed at me,[93] which made me wince, I tell you; the oldest, gray and about sixty, the other two thirty or more—all of them fine and handsome— and the sweetest old gray-headed lady, and back of her two young women which I couldn't see right well. The old gentleman says:

"There—I reckon it's all right. Come in."

As soon as I was in, the old gentleman he locked the door and barred it and bolted it, and told the young men to come in with their guns, and they all went in a big parlor that had a new rag carpet on the floor, and got together in a corner that was out of the range of the front windows—there warn't none on the side. They held the candle,[94] and took a good look at me, and all said, "Why, *he* ain't a Shepherdson—no, there ain't any Shepherdson about him." Then the old man said he hoped I wouldn't mind being searched for arms, because he didn't mean no harm by it—it was only to make sure. So he didn't pry into my pockets, but only felt outside with his hands, and said it was all right. He told me to make myself easy and at home, and tell all about myself; but the old lady says:

"Why, bless you, Saul, the poor thing's as wet as he can be; and don't you reckon it may be he's hungry?"

"True for you, Rachel—I forgot."

So the old lady says:

"Betsy" (this was a nigger woman), "you fly around and get him something to eat, as quick as you can, poor thing; and one of you girls go and wake up Buck and tell him—Oh, here he is himself. Buck, take this

---

93. American gun culture has long been a hot topic. This scene is set on the frontier and in the South, two places where guns were especially prominent historically. The guns' practical uses, aside from hunting, would have included self-defense, as frontier areas tended to have little police protection, and enforcement of slavery. Firearms helped maintain slave discipline and prevent insurrections and were also used in pursuing runaways. We don't know yet if this household has slaves of its own, but even nonslaveholding males were expected to take part in slave patrols. These patrols were compulsory and have been likened to military conscription, but nonslaveholders often required little coercion, as the slaveholders had long ago convinced them that slavery was the cornerstone of their society and that escaped slaves were a menace to it. As Ta-Nehisi Coates (2015) has argued, although they did not own slaves, they wanted to. The reward money was obviously a motivator as well.

Beyond those practical uses, gun ownership was simply the cultural norm in the old South. As we shall soon see, this family had another use for guns that was socially sanctioned back then but is not now.

94. Candles were still the main source of indoor light as late as 1850. Although the technology for interior gas lighting was available, many Americans regarded it as unsafe. Interior lighting was yet another innovation that reached the big cities, especially in the North, before it reached the South. An 1851 article in a New York newspaper noted that "scarcely a respectable dwelling-house is now built without gas fixtures" (Gordon 2004, 163).

little stranger and get the wet clothes off from him and dress him up in some of yours that's dry."

Buck looked about as old as me—thirteen or fourteen or along there, though he was a little bigger than me. He hadn't on anything but a shirt, and he was very frowzy-headed. He came in gaping and digging one fist into his eyes, and he was dragging a gun along with the other one. He says:

"Ain't they no Shepherdsons around?"

They said, no, 'twas a false alarm.

"Well," he says, "if they'd a ben some, I reckon I'd a got one."

They all laughed, and Bob says:

"Why, Buck, they might have scalped us all, you've been so slow in coming."

"Well, nobody come after me, and it ain't right. I'm always kep' down; I don't get no show."

"Never mind, Buck, my boy," says the old man, "you'll have show enough, all in good time, don't you fret about that. Go 'long with you now, and do as your mother told you."

When we got up stairs to his room, he got me a coarse shirt and a roundabout and pants of his, and I put them on. While I was at it he asked me what my name was, but before I could tell him he started to tell me about a blue jay and a young rabbit he had catched in the woods day before yesterday, and he asked me where Moses was when the candle went out. I said I didn't know; I hadn't heard about it before, no way.

"Well, guess," he says.

"How'm I going to guess," says I, "when I never heard tell of it before?"

"But you can guess, can't you? It's just as easy."

"*Which* candle?" I says.

"Why, any candle," he says.

"I don't know where he was," says I; "where was he?"

"Why, he was in the *dark!* That's where he was!"

"Well, if you knowed where he was, what did you ask me for?"

"Why, blame it, it's a riddle, don't you see? Say, how long are you going to stay here? You got to stay always. We can just have booming times—they don't have no school now. Do you own a dog? I've got a dog—and he'll go in the river and bring out chips that you throw in. Do you like to comb up Sundays, and all that kind of foolishness? You bet I don't, but ma she makes me. Confound these ole britches, I reckon I'd better put 'em on, but I'd ruther not, it's so warm. Are you all ready? All right—come along, old hoss."

Cold corn-pone, cold corn-beef, butter and buttermilk—that is what they had for me down there, and there ain't nothing better that ever I've come across yet. Buck and his ma and all of them smoked cob pipes, except the nigger woman,[95] which was gone, and the two young women. They all smoked and talked, and I eat and talked. The young women had quilts around them, and their hair down their backs. They all asked me questions, and I told them how pap and me and all the family was living on a little farm down at the bottom of Arkansaw, and my sister Mary Ann run off and got married and never was heard of no more, and Bill went to hunt them and he warn't heard of no more, and Tom and Mort died, and then there warn't nobody but just me and pap left, and he was just trimmed down to nothing, on account of his troubles; so when he died I took what there was left, because the farm didn't belong to us, and started up the river, deck passage, and fell overboard; and that was how I come to be here.[96] So they said I could have a home there as long as I wanted it. Then it was most daylight, and everybody went to bed, and I went to bed with Buck, and when I waked up in the morning, drat it all, I had forgot what my name was. So I laid there about an hour trying to think, and when Buck waked up, I says:

"Can you spell, Buck?"

"Yes," he says.

"I bet you can't spell my name," says I.

"I bet you what you dare I can," says he.

"All right," says I, "go ahead."

"G-o-r-g-e J-a-x-o-n—there now," he says.[97]

"Well," says I, "you done it, but I didn't think you could. It ain't no slouch of a name to spell—right off without studying."

---

95. Here we note several signs that this family may be wealthy. First, they have at least one slave. The corn pone and corned beef are both cold in the summertime, which suggests that this family may have an icehouse. The meat is beef instead of pork, which was cheaper and far more common in the South. Note also that the beef is corned beef, which, being salt-cured and nonperishable, could have been imported from anywhere. Twain mentions this food again in a description of the "sumptuous" meals at the farm owned by his well-to-do uncle in Florida, Missouri, whom he visited as a child (Twain 2010, 1:210).

96. Huck's story, though made up, accurately conveys that most white southerners were not wealthy slaveholders. The bulk of white southerners were middle-class yeoman farmers who produced enough for self-sufficiency and sometimes had a modest surplus to take to market. At the bottom of the economic ladder were poor farmers who did not own their own land—"the farm didn't belong to us"—but worked as tenants or laborers on someone else's land (Owsley 1949, 7–8). This phenomenon was far more common after the Civil War, when the bulk of the African American population and many poor whites worked as sharecroppers or fixed-rent tenant farmers for wealthy landlords, including many ex-slaveholders.

97. Buck's spelling error might be an indictment of the Old South's inadequate invest-ment in education, as Buck is a teenager, attends school, and still can't spell "George" or "Jackson," both of which were common names. But there may be more to it, as we will see in the next few pages.

I set it down, private, because somebody might want *me* to spell it, next, and so I wanted to be handy with it and rattle it off like I was used to it.

It was a mighty nice family, and a mighty nice house, too. I hadn't seen no house out in the country before that was so nice and had so much style. It didn't have an iron latch on the front door, nor a wooden one with a buckskin string, but a brass knob to turn, the same as houses in town. There warn't no bed in the parlor, nor a sign of a bed; but heaps of parlors in towns has beds in them. There was a big fireplace that was bricked on the bottom, and the bricks was kept clean and red by pouring water on them and scrubbing them with another brick; sometimes they washed them over with red water-paint that they call Spanish-brown, same as they do in town. They had big brass dog-irons that could hold up a saw-log. There was a clock on the middle of the mantel-piece, with a picture of a town painted on the bottom half of the glass front, and a round place in the middle of it for the sun, and you could see the pendulum swinging behind it. It was beautiful to hear that clock tick; and sometimes when one of these peddlers had been along and scoured her up and got her in good shape, she would start in and strike a hundred and fifty before she got tuckered out. They wouldn't took any money for her.

Well, there was a big outlandish parrot on each side of the clock, made out of something like chalk, and painted up gaudy.[98] By one of the parrots was a cat made of crockery, and a crockery dog by the other; and when you pressed down on them they squeaked, but didn't open their mouths nor look different nor interested. They squeaked through underneath. There was a couple of big wild-turkey-wing fans spread out behind those things. On the table in the middle of the room was a kind of a lovely crockery basket that had apples and oranges and peaches and grapes piled up in it which was much redder and yellower and prettier than real ones is, but they warn't real because you could see where pieces had got chipped off and showed the white chalk or whatever it was, underneath.

---

98. The word "gaudy" appears seven times in Twain's book. The word has meant "flashy" or "showy" for centuries—Shakespeare's Hamlet was advised to dress as well "as thy purse can buy / But not expressed in fancy—rich, not gaudy"—but Huck uses it in a complimentary way, which is unusual. It may be a malapropism, or it may be that Huck's lack of sophistication makes him unable to distinguish between the gaudy and the good. Huck's use of it befits his fawning description of the Grangerfords' decor, which by upper-class standards was kitschy and was something that Twain mercilessly mocked in Chapter 38 of *Life on the Mississippi*. "Every town and village along that stretch of double river-frontage had a best dwelling . . .—the home of the wealthiest and most conspicuous citizen" (Twain 2001, 170–171). Twain may have also been getting in a dig at Americans' conspicuous consumption, which had become more pronounced in the boom decades after the Civil War. Twain said in 1899, "We are the lavishest and showiest and most luxury-loving people on the earth," with even "the gaudiest flag the world has ever seen" (Twain 1992, 45).

This table had a cover made out of beautiful oil-cloth, with a red and blue spread-eagle painted on it, and a painted border all around. It come all the way from Philadelphia, they said. There was some books, too, piled up perfectly exact, on each corner of the table. One was a big family Bible, full of pictures. One was "Pilgrim's Progress," about a man that left his family, it didn't say why. I read considerable in it now and then. The statements was interesting, but tough. Another was "Friendship's Offering," full of beautiful stuff and poetry; but I didn't read the poetry. Another was Henry Clay's Speeches,[99] and another was Dr. Gunn's Family Medicine, which told you all about what to do if a body was sick or dead. There was a hymn book, and a lot of other books. And there was nice split-bottom chairs, and perfectly sound, too—not bagged down in the middle and busted, like an old basket.

They had pictures hung on the walls—mainly Washingtons and Lafayettes, and battles, and Highland Marys, and one called "Signing the Declaration." There was some that they called crayons, which one of the daughters which was dead made her own self when she was only fifteen years old. They was different from any pictures I ever see before; blacker, mostly, than is common. One was a woman in a slim black dress, belted small under the arm-pits, with bulges like a cabbage in the middle of the sleeves, and a

---

99. Henry Clay of Kentucky was another dominant political force of the time, having served as Speaker of the House of Representatives and U.S. senator for almost 40 years. Clay was known as the "Great Compromiser" for his roles in the Missouri Compromise of 1820 and the Compromise of 1850. The Missouri Compromise admitted Missouri into the union as a slave state and admitted Maine as a free state while decreeing that all other states above the 36'30" parallel would be free states. This kept the peace between the North and South for almost 30 years, until the acquisition of the vast new territories in the West from the Mexican-American War and a treaty with Britain. Years of tense debate over the fate of those lands were supposed to be settled by the Compromise of 1850, which opened most of the Southwest to slavery under "popular sovereignty," by which the white male settlers of each state could decide the issue, and imposed a tough new fugitive slave law. Unlike the 1820 measure, the 1850 compromise was unpopular and touched off a decade of rising North-South tensions over slavery and its expansion and enforcement.

The violence that Clay's last compromise touched off is appropriate to this chapter, which is dominated by the Grangersons' feud with the Shepherdsons. Their feud also parallels the political enmity between Clay, the leader of the Whig Party, and Democrat Andrew Jackson, the Whigs' archrival, who defeated Clay in presidential elections in 1824 and 1832. Fischer et al. (2010) have appropriately placed this scene in the town of Compromise, Kentucky, where Twain recalled nearly "being an eye-witness" to a violent feud and that also happened to be on the border of Jackson's home state of Tennessee (369, 415, 423). The Clay-Jackson rivalry was so intense that Jackson allegedly said on his deathbed that he had only two regrets, one of which was that he did not shoot Henry Clay. (The other was that he did not hang John C. Calhoun, another political opponent.) This would make it fitting that Buck is unable to spell "Jackson."

large black scoop-shovel bonnet with a black veil, and white slim ankles crossed about with black tape, and very wee black slippers, like a chisel, and she was leaning pensive on a tombstone on her right elbow, under a weeping willow, and her other hand hanging down her side holding a white handkerchief and a reticule, and underneath the picture it said "Shall I Never See Thee More Alas." Another one was a young lady with her hair all combed up straight to the top of her head, and knotted there in front of a comb like a chair-back, and she was crying into a handkerchief and had a dead bird laying on its back in her other hand with its heels up, and underneath the picture it said "I Shall Never Hear Thy Sweet Chirrup More Alas." There was one where a young lady was at a window looking up at the moon, and tears running down her cheeks; and she had an open letter in one hand with black sealing-wax showing on one edge of it, and she was mashing a locket with a chain to it against her mouth, and underneath the picture it said "And Art Thou Gone Yes Thou Art Gone Alas." These was all nice pictures, I reckon, but I didn't somehow seem to take to them, because if ever I was down a little, they always give me the fan-tods. Everybody was sorry she died, because she had laid out a lot more of these pictures to do, and a body could see by what she had done what they had lost. But I reckoned, that with her disposition, she was having a better time in the graveyard. She was at work on what they said was her greatest picture when she took sick, and every day and every night it was her prayer to be allowed to live till she got it done, but she never got the chance. It was a picture of a young woman in a long white gown, standing on the rail of a bridge all ready to jump off, with her hair all down her back, and looking up to the moon, with the tears running down her face, and she had two arms folded across her breast, and two arms stretched out in front, and two more reaching up towards the moon—and the idea was to see which pair would look best and then scratch out all the other arms; but, as I was saying, she died before she got her mind made up, and now they kept this picture over the head of the bed in her room, and every time her birthday come they hung flowers on it. Other times it was hid with a little curtain. The young woman in the picture had a kind of a nice sweet face, but there was so many arms it made her look too spidery, seemed to me.

This young girl kept a scrap-book when she was alive, and used to paste obituaries and accidents and cases of patient suffering in it out of the *Presbyterian Observer*,[100] and write poetry after them out of her own head.

---

100. The *Presbyterian Observer* reveals something about the family's class status as well as its religion. The frontier South, unlike the Bible Belt of today, was not particularly religious on account of such factors as the sparse population, the heavily male population (lack of families), and the lack of clergy and churches. This chapter appears to be set near the Kentucky-Tennessee border. Scholars estimate that only about 35–42 percent of Kentuckians and 30–35 percent of Tennesseans in 1850 were religious adherents. The vast majority of those southerners that

It was very good poetry. This is what she wrote about a boy by the name of Stephen Dowling Bots that fell down a well and was drownded:

ODE TO STEPHEN DOWLING BOTS, DEC'D

And did young Stephen sicken,
    And did young Stephen die?
And did the sad hearts thicken,
    And did the mourners cry?

No; such was not the fate of
    Young Stephen Dowling Bots;
Though sad hearts round him thickened,
    'Twas not from sickness' shots.

No whooping-cough did rack his frame,
    Nor measles drear, with spots;
Not these impaired the sacred name
    Of Stephen Dowling Bots.

Despised love struck not with woe
    That head of curly knots,
Nor stomach troubles laid him low,
    Young Stephen Dowling Bots.

O no. Then list with tearful eye,
    Whilst I his fate do tell.
His soul did from this cold world fly
    By falling down a well.

They got him out and emptied him;
    Alas it was too late;
His spirit was gone for to sport aloft
    In the realms of the good and great.

---

were religious belonged to the "upstart sects," who relied less on formally educated ministers and more on charismatic amateur "circuit riders." By 1850 the Baptists and Methodists had overtaken the traditional Protestant churches (Congregationalist, Episcopal, Presbyterian) in every state but Connecticut, but they were most dominant in the South. A southern family that belonged to a Presbyterian church, as Twain's did, would likely have been relatively affluent, educated, and tradition-minded (Finke and Stark 1994, 66–69, 82–83, 282–288).

If Emmeline Grangerford could make poetry like that before she was four-teen, there ain't no telling what she could a done by and by. Buck said she could rattle off poetry like nothing. She didn't ever have to stop to think. He said she would slap down a line, and if she couldn't find anything to rhyme with it would just scratch it out and slap down another one, and go ahead. She warn't particular; she could write about anything you choose to give her to write about, just so it was sadful. Every time a man died, or a woman died, or a child died, she would be on hand with her "tribute" be-fore he was cold. She called them tributes. The neighbors said it was the doctor first, then Emmeline, then the undertaker—the undertaker never got in ahead of Emmeline but once, and then she hung fire on a rhyme for the dead person's name, which was Whistler. She warn't ever the same after that; she never complained, but she kinder pined away and did not live long. Poor thing, many's the time I made myself go up to the little room that used to be hers and get out her poor old scrap-book and read in it when her pictures had been aggravating me and I had soured on her a little. I liked all that family, dead ones and all, and warn't going to let any-thing come between us. Poor Emmeline made poetry about all the dead people when she was alive, and it didn't seem right that there warn't no-body to make some about her now she was gone; so I tried to sweat out a verse or two myself, but I couldn't seem to make it go, somehow. They kept Emmeline's room trim and nice, and all the things fixed in it just the way she liked to have them when she was alive, and nobody ever slept there.[101] The old lady took care of the room herself, though there was plenty of niggers,[102] and she sewed there a good deal and read her Bible there, mostly.

Well, as I was saying about the parlor, there was beautiful curtains on the windows: white, with pictures painted on them, of castles with vines all down the walls, and cattle coming down to drink. There was a little old piano, too, that had tin pans in it, I reckon, and nothing was ever so lovely as to hear the young ladies sing "The Last Link is Broken" and play "The Battle of Prague" on it. The walls of all the rooms was plastered, and most

---

101. Infant and child mortality rates were extremely high at this time, even among wealthy families. The state of medicine and public health was primitive. The leading causes of death for children included many that are preventable or easily treatable today: diphthe-ria, dysentery, infant diarrhea, lobar pneumonia, tuberculosis, and scarlet and typhoid fe-vers (Shulman 2004).

102. Here we get confirmation that this is indeed a wealthy family, living on a planta-tion with "plenty of" slaves. On the eve of the Civil War, most white southern families owned either no slaves or fewer than 10. Only about 4 percent of southern whites owned 10 or more slaves (Miller and Sexton 2005, 124).

had carpets on the floors, and the whole house was whitewashed on the outside.

It was a double house, and the big open place betwixt them was roofed and floored, and sometimes the table was set there in the middle of the day, and it was a cool, comfortable place. Nothing couldn't be better. And warn't the cooking good, and just bushels of it too!

CHAPTER XVIII.

COL. Grangerford was a gentleman, you see. He was a gentleman all over; and so was his family. He was well born, as the saying is, and that's worth as much in a man as it is in a horse, so the Widow Douglas said, and nobody ever denied that she was of the first aristocracy in our town; and pap he always said it, too, though he warn't no more quality than a mud-cat himself.[103] Col. Grangerford was very tall and very slim, and had a darkish-paly complexion, not a sign of red in it anywheres; he was clean-shaved every morning, all over his thin face, and he had the thinnest kind of lips, and the thinnest kind of nostrils, and a high nose, and heavy eyebrows, and the blackest kind of eyes, sunk so deep back that they seemed like they was looking out of caverns at you, as you may say. His forehead was high, and his hair was black and straight and hung to his shoulders. His hands was long and thin, and every day of his life he put on a clean shirt and a full suit from head to foot made out of linen so white it hurt your eyes to look at it; and on Sundays he wore a blue tail-coat with brass buttons on it. He carried a mahogany cane with a silver head to it. There warn't no frivolishness about him, not a bit, and he warn't ever loud. He

103. Huck's remarks are a reminder that wealth inequality and hereditary privilege have been around for a long time. The inequality was obviously felt most sharply by slaves, who were born into that condition and numbered almost four million in 1860. Among whites, however, America in Huck's time actually had considerably less inequality than Western Europe (J. Williamson 2015). Despite the existence of wealthy capitalists in the North and planters in the South, America's elite were less wealthy and less influential than their European counterparts, and opportunity was far greater in America (Piketty 2014, 152). Even the slave states boasted a sizable white middle class, as noted earlier. In fact, in 1860 the top 1 percent of free adult males owned the same share of wealth (27 percent) in each region, and the top 10 percent owned slightly less in the South (68 percent) than in the North (75 percent) (Williamson and Lindert 1980, 38). That is still a considerable amount of inequality, however, and inequality rose in America during the 19th century, reaching European levels and roughly the same level as today by the eve of the Civil War. Inequality rose with urbanization and as the wealthiest planters and industrialists grew wealthier still (J. Williamson 2015).

was as kind as he could be—you could feel that, you know, and so you had confidence. Sometimes he smiled, and it was good to see; but when he straightened himself up like a liberty-pole, and the lightning begun to flicker out from under his eyebrows, you wanted to climb a tree first, and find out what the matter was afterwards. He didn't ever have to tell anybody to mind their manners—everybody was always good mannered where he was. Everybody loved to have him around, too; he was sunshine most always—I mean he made it seem like good weather. When he turned into a cloud-bank it was awful dark for half a minute, and that was enough; there wouldn't nothing go wrong again for a week.

When him and the old lady come down in the morning, all the family got up out of their chairs and give them good-day, and didn't set down again till they had set down. Then Tom and Bob went to the sideboard where the decanter was, and mixed a glass of bitters and handed it to him, and he held it in his hand and waited till Tom's and Bob's was mixed, and then they bowed and said, "Our duty to you, sir, and madam;" and *they* bowed the least bit in the world and said thank you, and so they drank, all three, and Bob and Tom poured a spoonful of water on the sugar and the mite of whisky or apple brandy in the bottom of their tumblers, and give it to me and Buck, and we drank to the old people too.[104]

Bob was the oldest and Tom next. Tall, beautiful men with very broad shoulders and brown faces, and long black hair and black eyes. They dressed in white linen from head to foot, like the old gentleman, and wore broad Panama hats.

Then there was Miss Charlotte, she was twenty-five, and tall and proud and grand, but as good as she could be, when she warn't stirred up;

---

104. Such heavy drinking was surprisingly normal in early 19th-century America; one historical study calls it "the alcoholic republic" (Rorabaugh 1979). "It was common to down a glass of whiskey or other spirits before breakfast, 'and so conducive to health was this nostrum esteemed,' noted a journalist in 1830, 'that no sex, and scarcely any age, were deemed exempt from its application'" (Lender and Martin 1982, 47). Former slave William Wells Brown recalled a pitcher of mint julep at his master's house every morning, "of which they all partook freely, not excepting little master William," the family's young nephew (Brown 2003, 13). British travelers reported that southerners drank more than northerners but said that Americans held their liquor well and rarely appeared drunk (Berger 1964, 65). Whiskey was the closest thing to a national drink at the time and was especially popular in states such as Kentucky and Tennessee (where this section of the book takes place), which continue to be major producers of whiskey. The distilling of brandy and other fruit-based liquors went back to early colonial days (Lender and Martin 1982, 6). Apple brandy in particular was easy to distill because apples grew easily in much of the nation, including the Upper South. Distilled spirits were more popular than beer and wine, in part because they were easier to ship and store.

but when she was, she had a look that would make you wilt in your tracks, like her father. She was beautiful.

So was her sister, Miss Sophia, but it was a different kind. She was gentle and sweet, like a dove, and she was only twenty.

Each person had their own nigger to wait on them—Buck, too. My nigger had a monstrous easy time, because I warn't used to having anybody do anything for me, but Buck's was on the jump most of the time.

This was all there was of the family, now, but there used to be more—three sons; they got killed; and Emmeline that died.

The old gentleman owned a lot of farms and over a hundred niggers. Sometimes a stack of people would come there, horseback, from ten or fifteen mile around, and stay five or six days, and have such junketings round about and on the river, and dances and picnics in the woods, daytimes, and balls at the house, nights. These people was mostly kinfolks of the family. The men brought their guns with them. It was a handsome lot of quality, I tell you.

There was another clan of aristocracy around there—five or six families—mostly of the name of Shepherdson. They was as high-toned and well born, and rich and grand as the tribe of Grangerfords. The Shepherdsons and Grangerfords used the same steamboat landing, which was about two mile above our house; so sometimes when I went up there with a lot of our folks I used to see a lot of the Shepherdsons there, on their fine horses.[105]

One day Buck and me was away out in the woods hunting, and heard a horse coming. We was crossing the road. Buck says:

"Quick! Jump for the woods!"

We done it, and then peeped down the woods through the leaves. Pretty soon a splendid young man come galloping down the road, setting his horse easy and looking like a soldier. He had his gun across his pommel. I had seen him before. It was young Harney Shepherdson. I heard Buck's gun go off at my ear, and Harney's hat tumbled off from his head. He grabbed his gun and rode straight to the place where we was hid. But we didn't wait. We started through the woods on a run. The woods warn't thick, so I looked over my shoulder, to dodge the bullet, and twice I seen Harney cover Buck with his gun; and then he rode away the way he

---

105. Even wealthy families such as the Grangerfords and Shepherdsons relied on horses and horse-drawn wagons for land transportation. Horses had Old World grandeur and were exhilarating to ride, but they were an inefficient and expensive means of transportation, especially for cargo. Much of American economic history in the 19th century is about overcoming prohibitively high transport costs so the nation could settle the vast territory that it claimed and establish the world's largest domestic market. Steamboats, canals, and finally railroads constituted the century's transportation revolution.

come—to get his hat, I reckon, but I couldn't see. We never stopped running till we got home. The old gentleman's eyes blazed a minute—'twas pleasure, mainly, I judged—then his face sort of smoothed down, and he says, kind of gentle:

"I don't like that shooting from behind a bush. Why didn't you step into the road, my boy?"

"The Shepherdsons don't, father. They always take advantage."

Miss Charlotte she held her head up like a queen while Buck was telling his tale, and her nostrils spread and her eyes snapped. The two young men looked dark, but never said nothing. Miss Sophia she turned pale, but the color come back when she found the man warn't hurt.

Soon as I could get Buck down by the corn-cribs under the trees by ourselves, I says:

"Did you want to kill him, Buck?"

"Well, I bet I did."

"What did he do to you?"

"Him? He never done nothing to me."

"Well, then, what did you want to kill him for?"

"Why, nothing—only it's on account of the feud."

"What's a feud?"

"Why, where was you raised? Don't you know what a feud is?"

"Never heard of it before—tell me about it."

"Well," says Buck, "a feud is this way. A man has a quarrel with another man, and kills him; then that other man's brother kills *him;* then the other brothers, on both sides, goes for one another; then the *cousins* chip in—and by and by everybody's killed off, and there ain't no more feud. But it's kind of slow, and takes a long time."

"Has this one been going on long, Buck?"

"Well, I should *reckon!* It started thirty year ago, or som'ers along there. There was trouble 'bout something, and then a lawsuit to settle it; and the suit went agin one of the men, and so he up and shot the man that won the suit—which he would naturally do, of course. Anybody would."

"What was the trouble about, Buck?—land?"

"I reckon maybe—I don't know."

"Well, who done the shooting?—was it a Grangerford or a Shepherdson?"

"Laws, how do *I* know? It was so long ago."

"Don't anybody know?"

"Oh, yes, pa knows, I reckon, and some of the other old people; but they don't know, now, what the row was about in the first place."

"Has there been many killed, Buck?"

"Yes—right smart chance of funerals. But they don't always kill. Pa's got a few buck-shot in him; but he don't mind it 'cuz he don't weigh much anyway. Bob's been carved up some with a bowie, and Tom's been hurt once or twice."

"Has anybody been killed this year, Buck?"

"Yes, we got one and they got one. 'Bout three months ago, my cousin Bud, fourteen year old, was riding through the woods, on t'other side of the river, and didn't have no weapon with him, which was blame' foolishness, and in a lonesome place he hears a horse a-coming behind him, and sees old Baldy Shepherdson a-linkin' after him with his gun in his hand and his white hair a-flying in the wind; and 'stead of jumping off and taking to the brush, Bud 'lowed he could out run him; so they had it, nip and tuck, for five mile or more, the old man a-gaining all the time; so at last Bud seen it warn't any use, so he stopped and faced around so as to have the bullet holes in front, you know, and the old man he rode up and shot him down. But he didn't git much chance to enjoy his luck, for inside of a week our folks laid *him* out."

"I reckon that old man was a coward, Buck."

"I reckon he *warn't* a coward. Not by a blame' sight. There ain't a coward amongst them Shepherdsons—not a one. And there ain't no cowards amongst the Grangerfords, either. Why, that old man kep' up his end in a fight one day, for half an hour, against three Grangerfords, and come out winner. They was all a-horseback; he lit off of his horse and got behind a little woodpile, and kep' his horse before him to stop the bullets; but the Grangerfords staid on their horses and capered around the old man, and peppered away at him, and he peppered away at them. Him and his horse both went home pretty leaky and crippled, but the Grangerfords had to be *fetched* home—and one of 'em was dead, and another died the next day. No, sir, if a body's out hunting for cowards, he don't want to fool away any time amongst them Shepherdsons, becuz they don't breed any of that *kind.*"[106]

---

106. Family feuds were indeed common in the Old South. The most famous of them, the Hatfield-McCoy feud (1863–1891) near the Kentucky–West Virginia border, has long been enshrined in American popular culture and continues to appear in novels, movies, television shows, and even cartoons. Legendary southern author William Faulkner's great-grandfather was involved in a family feud in Mississippi in the 1850s. Some historians suggest that feuds between families, much like fear and loathing of Native American tribes, grew out of competition for land between southern frontier settlers (Wyatt-Brown 1986, 143–144). On the frontier, as we see at many points in *Huckleberry Finn,* police and legal protection were often inadequate, so people involved in disputes resorted to violence, which often begat more violence. Why did the violence come to involve entire families? Historian Grady McWhiney suggests that "Southern families, like those of their Celtic ancestors, were extended and clannish, and family feuds in the Old South were as easy to start and as difficult to stop as they were in premodern Scotland and Ireland" (1988, 160–162).

Next Sunday we all went to church, about three mile, everybody a-horseback. The men took their guns along, so did Buck, and kept them between their knees or stood them handy against the wall. The Shepherdsons done the same. It was pretty ornery preaching—all about brotherly love, and such-like tiresomeness; but everybody said it was a good sermon, and they all talked it over going home, and had such a powerful lot to say about faith, and good works, and free grace, and preforeordestination, and I don't know what all, that it did seem to me to be one of the roughest Sundays I had run across yet.

About an hour after dinner everybody was dozing around, some in their chairs and some in their rooms, and it got to be pretty dull. Buck and a dog was stretched out on the grass in the sun, sound asleep. I went up to our room, and judged I would take a nap myself. I found that sweet Miss Sophia standing in her door, which was next to ours, and she took me in her room and shut the door very soft, and asked me if I liked her, and I said I did; and she asked me if I would do something for her and not tell anybody, and I said I would. Then she said she'd forgot her Testament, and left it in the seat at church, between two other books, and would I slip out quiet and go there and fetch it to her, and not say nothing to nobody. I said I would. So I slid out and slipped off up the road, and there warn't anybody at the church, except maybe a hog or two, for there warn't any lock on the door, and hogs likes a puncheon floor in summer-time because it's cool. If you notice, most folks don't go to church only when they've got to; but a hog is different.

Says I to myself, something's up—it ain't natural for a girl to be in such a sweat about a Testament; so I give it a shake, and out drops a little piece of paper with "*Half-past two*" wrote on it with a pencil. I ransacked it, but couldn't find anything else. I couldn't make anything out of that, so I put the paper in the book again, and when I got home and up stairs, there was Miss Sophia in her door waiting for me. She pulled me in and shut the door; then she looked in the Testament till she found the paper, and as soon as she read it she looked glad; and before a body could think, she grabbed me and give me a squeeze, and said I was the best boy in the world, and not to tell anybody. She was mighty red in the face, for a minute, and her eyes lighted up, and it made her powerful pretty. I was a good deal astonished, but when I got my breath I asked her what the paper was about, and she asked me if I had read it, and I said no, and she asked me if I could read writing, and I told her "no, only coarse-hand," and then she said the paper warn't anything but a book-mark to keep her place, and I might go and play now.

I went off down to the river, studying over this thing, and pretty soon I noticed that my nigger was following along behind. When we was out of sight of the house he looked back and around a second, and then comes a-running, and says:

"Mars Jawge, if you'll come down into de swamp, I'll show you a whole stack o' water-moccasins."[107]

Thinks I, that's mighty curious; he said that yesterday. He oughter know a body don't love water-moccasins enough to go around hunting for them. What is he up to, anyway? So I says:

"All right; trot ahead."

I followed a half a mile, then he struck out over the swamp and waded ankle deep as much as another half-mile. We come to a little flat piece of land which was dry and very thick with trees and bushes and vines, and he says—

"You shove right in dah, jist a few steps, Mars Jawge, dah's whah dey is. I's seed 'm befo', I don't k'yer to see 'em no mo'."

Then he slopped right along and went away, and pretty soon the trees hid him. I poked into the place a-ways, and come to a little open patch as big as a bedroom, all hung around with vines, and found a man laying there asleep—and by jings it was my old Jim!

I waked him up, and I reckoned it was going to be a grand surprise to him to see me again, but it warn't. He nearly cried, he was so glad, but he warn't surprised. Said he swum along behind me, that night, and heard me yell every time, but dasn't answer, because he didn't want nobody to pick *him* up, and take him into slavery again. Says he—

"I got hurt a little, en couldn't swim fas', so I wuz a considable ways behine you, towards de las'; when you landed I reck'ned I could ketch up wid you on de lan' 'dout havin' to shout at you, but when I see dat house I begin to go slow. I 'uz off too fur to hear what dey say to you—I wuz 'fraid o' de dogs—but when it 'uz all quiet agin, I knowed you's in de house, so I struck out for de woods to wait for day. Early in de mawnin' some er de niggers come along, gwyne to de fields, en dey tuck me en showed me dis place, whah de dogs can't track me on accounts o' de water, en dey brings me truck to eat every night, en tells me how you's a gitt'n along."[108]

---

107. "Mars" as in "master." Note that Jim calls Huck "Huck," not "Mars Huck," whereas later in the book Tom and Sid Sawyer are "Mars Tom" and "Mars Sid" to him, even though they are not part of his master's family. The southern class and racial caste system was clear even to slaves. Jim is not being disrespectful to Huck but knows him as a relative equal, and Huck mostly treats Jim as such. The young slave Jack in this scene knows Huck not as a member of the white underclass of St. Petersburg but as a guest of his master's family, with an assumed name and a backstory that is sad but not squalid.

108. Jim would have had good reason to fear the dogs for the sake of both detection and injury. "Slaves consistently noted the importance of dogs to the repressive regime of slavery," says historian David Doddington. The dogs were noted for their savagery. Louisiana planter Bennett H. Barrow offered this account of his dogs and a runaway: "hunting Ruffins Boy Henry, came across Williams runaway caught him dogs nearly et his legs off,

"Why didn't you tell my Jack to fetch me here sooner, Jim?"

"Well, 'twarn't no use to 'sturb you, Huck, tell we could do sumfn—but we's all right now. I ben a-buyin' pots en pans en vittles, as I got a chanst, en a-patchin' up de raf' nights when—"

"*What* raft, Jim?"

"Our ole raf'."

"You mean to say our old raft warn't smashed all to flinders?"

"No, she warn't. She was tore up a good deal—one en' of her was—but dey warn't no great harm done, on'y our traps was mos' all los'. Ef we hadn' dive' so deep en swum so fur under water, en de night hadn' ben so dark, en we warn't so sk'yerd, en ben sich punkin-heads, as de sayin' is, we'd a seed de raf'. But it's jis' as well we didn't, 'kase now she's all fixed up agin mos' as good as new, en we's got a new lot o' stuff, too, in de place o' what 'uz los'."

"Why, how did you get hold of the raft again, Jim—did you catch her?"

"How I gwyne to ketch her, en I out in de woods? No, some er de niggers foun' her ketched on a snag along heah in de ben', en dey hid her in a crick, 'mongst de willows, en dey wuz so much jawin' 'bout which un 'um she b'long to de mos', dat I come to heah 'bout it pooty soon, so I ups en settles de trouble by tellin' 'um she don't b'long to none uv um, but to you en me; en I ast 'm if dey gwyne to grab a young white genlman's propaty, en git a hid'n for it? Den I gin 'm ten cents apiece, en dey 'uz mighty well satisfied, en wisht some mo' raf's 'ud come along en make 'm rich agin. Dey's mighty good to me, dese niggers is, en whatever I wants 'm to do fur me I doan' have to ast 'm twice, honey. Dat Jack's a good nigger, en pooty smart."

"Yes, he is. He ain't ever told me you was here; told me to come, and he'd show me a lot of water-moccasins. If anything happens, *he* ain't mixed up in it. He can say he never seen us together, and it'll be the truth."

I don't want to talk much about the next day. I reckon I'll cut it pretty short. I waked up about dawn, and was agoing to turn over and go to sleep again, when I noticed how still it was—didn't seem to be anybody stirring. That warn't usual. Next I noticed that Buck was up and gone. Well, I gets up, a-wondering, and goes down stairs—nobody around; everything as

---

near killing him." An ex-slave noted another reason for the ferocity of plantation dogs: "if the colored folks had started an uprising the white folks would have set the hounds on us and killed us" (Doddington 2012). The most horrific documented episodes, which may have inspired a scene in Quentin Tarantino's 2012 movie *Django Unchained,* occurred not on U.S. soil but slightly to the south during the Haitian Revolution of 1791–1804, when Napoleon's army, attempting to suppress the revolution, used dogs to hunt down rebelling slaves and eat them (Gates 2013).

still as a mouse. Just the same outside; thinks I, what does it mean? Down by the wood-pile I comes across my Jack, and says:

"What's it all about?"

Says he:

"Don't you know, Mars Jawge?"

"No," says I, "I don't."

"Well, den, Miss Sophia's run off! 'deed she has. She run off in de night, some time—nobody don't know jis' when—run off to get married to dat young Harney Shepherdson, you know—leastways, so dey 'spec. De fambly foun' it out, 'bout half an hour ago—maybe a little mo'—en' I *tell* you dey warn't no time los'. Sich another hurryin' up guns en hosses *you* never see! De women folks has gone for to stir up de relations, en ole Mars Saul en de boys tuck dey guns en rode up de river road for to try to ketch dat young man en kill him 'fo' he kin git acrost de river wid Miss Sophia. I reck'n dey's gwyne to be mighty rough times."

"Buck went off 'thout waking me up."

"Well, I reck'n he *did!* Dey warn't gwyne to mix you up in it. Mars Buck he loaded up his gun en 'lowed he's gwyne to fetch home a Shepherdson or bust. Well, dey'll be plenty un 'm dah, I reck'n, en you bet you he'll fetch one ef he gits a chanst."

I took up the river road as hard as I could put. By and by I begin to hear guns a good ways off. When I come in sight of the log store and the wood-pile where the steamboats lands, I worked along under the trees and brush till I got to a good place, and then I clumb up into the forks of a cotton-wood that was out of reach, and watched. There was a wood-rank four foot high, a little ways in front of the tree, and first I was going to hide behind that; but maybe it was luckier I didn't.

There was four or five men cavorting around on their horses in the open place before the log store, cussing and yelling, and trying to get at a couple of young chaps that was behind the wood-rank alongside of the steamboat landing—but they couldn't come it. Every time one of them showed himself on the river side of the wood-pile he got shot at. The two boys was squatting back to back behind the pile, so they could watch both ways.

By and by the men stopped cavorting around and yelling. They started riding towards the store; then up gets one of the boys, draws a steady bead over the wood-rank, and drops one of them out of his saddle. All the men jumped off of their horses and grabbed the hurt one and started to carry him to the store; and that minute the two boys started on the run. They got half-way to the tree I was in before the men noticed. Then the men see them, and jumped on their horses and took out after them. They gained on the boys, but it didn't do no good, the boys had too good a start; they got to the wood-pile that was in front of my tree, and slipped in behind it, and so they had the bulge on the men again. One of the boys was Buck, and the other was a slim young chap about nineteen years old.

The men ripped around awhile, and then rode away. As soon as they was out of sight, I sung out to Buck and told him. He didn't know what to make of my voice coming out of the tree, at first. He was awful surprised. He told me to watch out sharp and let him know when the men come in sight again; said they was up to some devilment or other—wouldn't be gone long. I wished I was out of that tree, but I dasn't come down. Buck begun to cry and rip, and 'lowed that him and his cousin Joe (that was the other young chap) would make up for this day, yet. He said his father and his two brothers was killed, and two or three of the enemy. Said the Shepherdsons laid for them, in ambush. Buck said his father and brothers ought to waited for their relations—the Shepherdsons was too strong for them. I asked him what was become of young Harney and Miss Sophia. He said they'd got across the river and was safe. I was glad of that; but the way Buck did take on because he didn't manage to kill Harney that day he shot at him—I hain't ever heard anything like it.

All of a sudden, bang! bang! bang! goes three or four guns—the men had slipped around through the woods and come in from behind without their horses! The boys jumped for the river—both of them hurt—and as they swum down the current the men run along the bank shooting at them and singing out, "Kill them, kill them!" It made me so sick I most fell out of the tree. I ain't agoing to tell *all* that happened—it would make me sick again if I was to do that. I wished I hadn't ever come ashore that night, to see such things. I ain't ever going to get shut of them—lots of times I dream about them.

I stayed in the tree till it begun to get dark, afraid to come down. Sometimes I heard guns away off in the woods; and twice I seen little gangs of men gallop past the log store with guns; so I reckoned the trouble was still agoing on. I was mighty down-hearted; so I made up my mind I wouldn't ever go anear that house again, because I reckoned I was to blame, somehow. I judged that that piece of paper meant that Miss Sophia was to meet Harney somewheres at half-past two and run off; and I judged I ought to told her father about that paper and the curious way she acted, and then maybe he would a locked her up and this awful mess wouldn't ever happened.

When I got down out of the tree I crept along down the river bank a piece, and found the two bodies laying in the edge of the water, and tugged at them till I got them ashore; then I covered up their faces, and got away as quick as I could. I cried a little when I was covering up Buck's face, for he was mighty good to me.

It was just dark, now. I never went near the house, but struck through the woods and made for the swamp. Jim warn't on his island, so I tramped off in a hurry for the crick, and crowded through the willows, red-hot to jump aboard and get out of that awful country—the raft was gone! My souls, but I was scared! I couldn't get my breath for most a minute. Then I raised a yell. A voice not twenty-five foot from me says—

"Good lan'! is dat you, honey? Doan' make no noise."

It was Jim's voice—nothing ever sounded so good before. I run along the bank a piece and got aboard, and Jim he grabbed me and hugged me, he was so glad to see me. He says—

"Laws bless you, chile, I 'uz right down sho' you's dead agin. Jack's been heah, he say he reck'n you's ben shot, kase you didn' come home no mo'; so I's jes' dis minute a startin' de raf' down towards de mouf er de crick, so's to be all ready for to shove out en leave soon as Jack comes agin en tells me for certain you *is* dead. Lawsy, I's mighty glad to git you back again, honey."

I says—

"All right—that's mighty good; they won't find me, and they'll think I've been killed, and floated down the river—there's something up there that'll help them think so—so don't you lose no time, Jim, but just shove off for the big water as fast as ever you can."

I never felt easy till the raft was two mile below there and out in the middle of the Mississippi. Then we hung up our signal lantern, and judged that we was free and safe once more. I hadn't had a bite to eat since yesterday; so Jim he got out some corn-dodgers and butter-milk, and pork and cabbage, and greens—there ain't nothing in the world so good when it's cooked right—and whilst I eat my supper we talked, and had a good time. I was powerful glad to get away from the feuds, and so was Jim to get away from the swamp. We said there warn't no home like a raft, after all. Other places do seem so cramped up and smothery, but a raft don't. You feel mighty free and easy and comfortable on a raft.

CHAPTER XIX.

Two or three days and nights went by; I reckon I might say they swum by, they slid along so quiet and smooth and lovely. Here is the way we put in the time. It was a monstrous big river down there—sometimes a mile and a half wide; we run nights, and laid up and hid daytimes; soon as night was most gone, we stopped navigating and tied up—nearly always in the dead water under a tow-head; and then cut young cottonwoods and willows and hid the raft with them. Then we set out the lines. Next we slid into the river and had a swim, so as to freshen up and cool off; then we set down on the sandy bottom where the water was about knee deep, and watched the daylight come. Not a sound, anywheres—perfectly still—just like the whole world was asleep, only sometimes the bull-frogs a-cluttering, maybe. The first thing to see, looking away over the water, was a kind of dull line—that was the woods on t'other side—you couldn't make nothing else out; then a pale place in the sky; then more paleness, spreading around; then the river softened up, away off, and warn't black any more, but gray; you could see little dark spots drifting along, ever so far away—trading scows, and such things; and long black streaks—rafts; sometimes you could hear a sweep screaking; or jumbled up voices, it was so still, and sounds come so far; and by and by you could see a streak on the water which you know by the look of the streak that there's a snag there in a swift current which breaks on it and makes that streak look that way; and you see the mist curl up off of the water, and the east reddens up, and the river, and you make out a log cabin in the edge of the woods, away on the bank on t'other side of the river, being a wood-yard, likely, and piled by them cheats so you can throw a dog through it anywheres; then the nice breeze springs up, and comes fanning you from over there, so cool and fresh, and sweet to smell, on account of the woods and the flowers; but sometimes not that way, because they've left dead fish laying around, gars, and such, and they do get pretty rank; and next you've got the full day, and everything smiling in the sun, and the song-birds just going it!

A little smoke couldn't be noticed, now, so we would take some fish off of the lines, and cook up a hot breakfast. And afterwards we would watch the lonesomeness of the river, and kind of lazy along, and by and by lazy off to sleep. Wake up, by and by, and look to see what done it, and maybe see a steamboat, coughing along up stream, so far off towards the other side you couldn't tell nothing about her only whether she was a stern-wheel or side-wheel; then for about an hour there wouldn't be nothing to hear nor nothing to see—just solid lonesomeness. Next you'd see a raft sliding by, away off yonder, and maybe a galoot on it chopping, because they're most always doing it on a raft; you'd see the axe flash and come down—you don't hear nothing; you see that axe go up again, and by the time it's above the man's head, then you hear the *k'chunk!*—it had took all that time to come over the water. So we would put in the day, lazying around, listening to the stillness. Once there was a thick fog, and the rafts and things that went by was beating tin pans so the steamboats wouldn't run over them. A scow or a raft went by so close we could hear them talking and cussing and laughing—heard them plain; but we couldn't see no sign of them; it made you feel crawly, it was like spirits carrying on that way in the air. Jim said he believed it was spirits; but I says:

"No, spirits wouldn't say, 'Dern the dern fog.'"

Soon as it was night, out we shoved; when we got her out to about the middle, we let her alone, and let her float wherever the current wanted her to; then we lit the pipes, and dangled our legs in the water and talked about all kinds of things—we was always naked, day and night, whenever the mosquitoes would let us—the new clothes Buck's folks made for me[109] was too good to be comfortable, and besides I didn't go much on clothes, nohow.

Sometimes we'd have that whole river all to ourselves for the longest time. Yonder was the banks and the islands, across the water; and maybe a spark—which was a candle in a cabin window—and sometimes on the water you could see a spark or two—on a raft or a scow, you know; and maybe you could hear a fiddle or a song coming over from one of them crafts. It's lovely to live on a raft. We had the sky, up there, all speckled with stars, and we used to lay on our backs and look up at them, and discuss about whether they was made, or only just happened—Jim he allowed they was made, but I allowed they happened; I judged it would have took too long to *make* so many. Jim said the moon could a *laid* them; well, that looked kind of reasonable, so I didn't say nothing against it, because I've seen a frog lay most as many, so of course it could be done. We used to watch the stars that fell, too, and see them streak down. Jim allowed they'd got spoiled and was hove out of the nest.

Once or twice of a night we would see a steamboat slipping along in the dark, and now and then she would belch a whole world of sparks up out of her chimbleys, and they would rain down in the river and look awful pretty; then she would turn a corner and her lights would wink out and her pow-wow shut off and leave the river still again; and by and by her waves would get to us, a long time after she was gone, and joggle the raft a bit, and after that you wouldn't hear nothing for you couldn't tell how long, except maybe frogs or something.

After midnight the people on shore went to bed, and then for two or three hours the shores was black—no more sparks in the cabin windows. These sparks was our clock—the first one that showed again meant morning was coming, so we hunted a place to hide and tie up, right away.

One morning about daybreak, I found a canoe and crossed over a chute to the main shore—it was only two hundred yards—and paddled about a

---

109. At the turn of the 19th century, homemade clothes were the norm. Technological developments in textile manufacturing as well as the invention of the cotton gin made clothing a good deal more affordable, as did steamboats and canals, which also made clothing and other goods more available. By midcentury home production of goods had shrunk considerably but not completely, partly because cheaper textiles also meant cheaper fabrics for home sewing. The frontier states and slave states—including Kentucky, Tennessee, Arkansas, and Missouri, the states in which this book is set—had particularly high rates of home production relative to the rest of the country (Tyron 1966, 308–310, 370–375). Farmers, including plantation owners, typically strove for self-sufficiency in clothing as well as food, because specializing in cash crops such as cotton or tobacco, although more profitable on average, would have left them exposed to the risk of poor crop yields and falling market prices (Wright 1978, 57–74).

mile up a crick amongst the cypress woods, to see if I couldn't get some berries. Just as I was passing a place where a kind of a cowpath crossed the crick, here comes a couple of men tearing up the path as tight as they could foot it. I thought I was a goner, for whenever anybody was after anybody I judged it was *me*—or maybe Jim. I was about to dig out from there in a hurry, but they was pretty close to me then, and sung out and begged me to save their lives—said they hadn't been doing nothing, and was being chased for it—said there was men and dogs a-coming. They wanted to jump right in, but I says—

"Don't you do it. I don't hear the dogs and horses yet; you've got time to crowd through the brush and get up the crick a little ways; then you take to the water and wade down to me and get in—that'll throw the dogs off the scent."

They done it, and soon as they was aboard I lit out for our tow-head, and in about five or ten minutes we heard the dogs and the men away off, shouting. We heard them come along towards the crick, but couldn't see them; they seemed to stop and fool around a while; then, as we got further and further away all the time, we couldn't hardly hear them at all; by the time we had left a mile of woods behind us and struck the river, everything was quiet, and we paddled over to the tow-head and hid in the cotton-woods and was safe.

One of these fellows was about seventy, or upwards, and had a bald head and very gray whiskers. He had an old battered-up slouch hat on, and a greasy blue woollen shirt, and ragged old blue jeans britches stuffed into his boot tops, and home-knit galluses—no, he only had one. He had an old long-tailed blue jeans coat with slick brass buttons, flung over his arm, and both of them had big, fat ratty-looking carpet-bags.[110]

---

110. Carpetbags will forever be associated with the southern stereotype of carpet-baggers who moved from the North to the South during Reconstruction (1865–1877), when the federal government sent army troops to the former Confederate states to help build a new society without slavery and enforce new constitutional amendments and civil rights laws guaranteeing equal protection to African Americans. Reconstruction saw remarkable gains for southern blacks and earned the support of some southern whites, but by and large it was extremely unpopular with the former Confederates. Neo-Confederate accounts of Reconstruction depict it as a period of unrelenting corruption, humiliation of white southern elites, and Negro rule, abetted by northern carpetbaggers and southern scalawags (a synonym for scoundrels, applied to white southerners who cooperated with the Reconstruction authorities). Margaret Mitchell's best-selling novel *Gone with the Wind,* and to a lesser extent the Academy Award–winning movie adaptation, epitomizes this conception of trashy Yankees who came to the South carrying their carpetbags and went on to exploit the South through corrupt political and business practices. As a title sequence in the movie version put it: "And with [the army] came another invader . . . more cruel and vicious than any they had fought . . . the carpetbaggers."

The other fellow was about thirty and dressed about as ornery. After breakfast we all laid off and talked, and the first thing that come out was that these chaps didn't know one another.

"What got you into trouble?" says the baldhead to t'other chap.

"Well, I'd been selling an article to take the tartar off the teeth—and it does take it off, too, and generly the enamel along with it—but I staid about one night longer than I ought to, and was just in the act of sliding out when I ran across you on the trail this side of town, and you told me they were coming, and begged me to help you to get off. So I told you I was expecting trouble myself and would scatter out *with* you. That's the whole yarn—what's yourn?

"Well, I'd ben a-running' a little temperance revival thar, 'bout a week, and was the pet of the women-folks, big and little, for I was makin' it mighty warm for the rummies, I *tell* you, and takin' as much as five or six dollars a night—ten cents a head, children and niggers free—and business a growin' all the time; when somehow or another a little report got around, last night, that I had a way of puttin' in my time with a private jug, on the sly.[111] A nigger rousted me out this mornin', and told me the people was

---

Although Twain was certainly aware of this negative connotation when he wrote *Huckleberry Finn* and uses it to establish the low character of these two newcomers, carpetbags were perfectly acceptable travel bags at the time. Carpet fabric was easy to fashion into sturdy bags, and suitcases would not begin to replace them until the 1890s. Traveling with carpetbags meant that you were traveling light. For longer trips or relocations, people would use heavy trunks of wood, metal, and leather (such as one might find in an elderly relative's attic). In Jules Verne's 1873 novel *Around the World in 80 Days,* for example, the wealthy and sympathetic protagonist Phileas Fogg, before embarking on his journey, tells his servant, "We'll have no trunks, only a carpet bag, with two shirts and three pairs of stockings for me, and the same for you. We'll buy our clothes on the way" (Gross 2014). "Carpetbagger" was a derogatory term not because of the type of bag carried but because of the implication that all of the person's possessions fit into that bag; that is, the carpetbaggers were lower-class people who sought to get rich through corrupt schemes. It could also mean that rather than putting down roots in the South, they were on a short-term mission of plunder.

111. The temperance movement was deeply rooted in religious revivalism, and temperance pledges to abstain from drinking were common among Baptists and Methodists in particular. Many frontier areas did not yet have churches and were served instead by traveling ministers who held camp meetings. Unlike more established denominations such as the Presbyterian Church, the upstart Baptists and Methodists placed less stress on formal credentials for their ministers, which opened the door to frauds such as these two characters, as did the frontier setting (Finke and Stark 1994, 39, 75–79, 92–96, 101–104).

Note that the old man mentions his temperance revivals without reference to preaching, which he mentions later. In the early 1840s a new temperance movement, unaffiliated with religion, took the nation by storm. The new society, called the Washington Movement, began in a Baltimore tavern when six drinkers pledged to abstain from liquor and help each

getherin' on the quiet, with their dogs and horses, and they'd be along pretty soon and give me 'bout half an hour's start, and then run me down, if they could; and if they got me they'd tar and feather me and ride me on a rail, sure. I didn't wait for no breakfast—I warn't hungry."

"Old man," said the young one, "I reckon we might double-team it together; what do you think?"

"I ain't undisposed. What's your line—mainly?"

"Jour printer, by trade;[112] do a little in patent medicines; theater-actor—tragedy, you know; take a turn to mesmerism and phrenology when there's a chance; teach singing-geography school for a change; sling a lecture, sometimes—oh, I do lots of things—most anything that comes handy, so it ain't work. What's your lay?"

"I've done considerble in the doctoring way in my time. Layin' on o' hands is my best holt—for cancer, and paralysis, and sich things; and I k'n tell a fortune pretty good, when I've got somebody along to find out the facts for me. Preachin's my line, too; and workin' camp-meetin's, and missionaryin' around."[113]

---

other stay sober. The movement grew even faster than any temperance movement before it and attracted a wide variety of people: alcoholics and teetotalers, evangelicals and the less religious, and people of all classes. Yet it was at heart a populist movement with a working-class orientation. Historian James Morone's description of their revivals offers a sense of why temperance lectures might have been right up this "ornery" old fraud's alley: "Workers flocked to the rowdy rallies. They shared ribald confessions, sang lusty nondrinking songs, and pledged abstinence. The Washingtonians sponsored revivals without the religion, bashes without the beer" (Morone 2003, 284; Pegram 1998, 19–29; Tyrrell 2000, 159–161).

112. "Jour" is short for "journeyman," the intermediate step between apprentice and master in a trade. Journeyman printers appear to have journeyed farther than their counterparts in other trades. The large number of print shops and miscellaneous publications as well as a fraternal spirit among printers made their skills exceptionally portable. A "jour" printer "might work his passage all around the continent and see life in all its phases, as no man of any other trade or profession could" (Vedder 1894, 126). Twain himself worked as a journeyman printer, more precisely as a typesetter, in a variety of cities including St. Louis, New York, and Philadelphia.

113. Here the two men establish themselves once and for all as professional frauds. Confidence men were a visible part of the economic landscape by this time; the term "confidence man" entered the lexicon in 1849. Practically every occupation these men list involves something one can fake (teaching, preaching, acting), bogus science of the time (phrenology was about inferring people's mental capacities and personalities from the shape of their skulls), or fraudulent medical techniques (laying on of hands to cure cancer).

The primitive state of medicine in the 19th century left much scope for dubious remedies such as patent medicines. Although a few may have been effective, the vast majority appear to have been pure swindles, with snake oil being the classic example. (The Pure Food and Drug Act of 1906, by requiring that medicines be demonstrably safe and

Nobody never said anything for a while; then the young man hove a sigh and says—

"Alas!"

"What 're you alassin' about?" says the bald-head.

"To think I should have lived to be leading such a life, and be degraded down into such company." And he begun to wipe the corner of his eye with a rag.

"Dern your skin, ain't the company good enough for you?" says the baldhead, pretty pert and uppish.

"Yes, it *is* good enough for me; it's as good as I deserve; for who fetched me so low, when I was so high? *I* did myself. I don't blame *you,* gentlemen—far from it; I don't blame anybody. I deserve it all. Let the cold world do its worst; one thing I know—there's a grave somewhere for me. The world may go on just as it's always done, and take everything from me—loved ones, property, everything—but it can't take that. Some day I'll lie down in it and forget it all, and my poor broken heart will be at rest." He went on a-wiping.

"Drot your pore broken heart," says the baldhead; "what are you heaving your pore broken heart at *us* f'r? *we* hain't done nothing."

"No, I know you haven't. I ain't blaming you, gentlemen. I brought myself down—yes, I did it myself. It's right I should suffer—perfectly right—I don't make any moan."

"Brought you down from whar? Whar was you brought down from?"

"Ah, you would not believe me; the world never believes—let it pass—'tis no matter. The secret of my birth—"

"The secret of your birth? Do you mean to say—"

"Gentlemen," says the young man, very solemn, "I will reveal it to you, for I feel I may have confidence in you. By rights I am a duke!"

Jim's eyes bugged out when he heard that; and I reckon mine did, too. Then the baldhead says: "No! you can't mean it?"

"Yes. My great-grandfather, eldest son of the Duke of Bridgewater, fled to this country about the end of the last century, to breathe the pure air of freedom; married here, and died, leaving a son, his own father dying about the same time. The second son of the late duke seized the titles and estates—the infant real duke was ignored. I am the lineal descendant of

---

effective, put an end to the profusion of fake patent medicines.) Yet orthodox medicine was not much better. Oliver Wendell Holmes, sounding a bit like Twain, said that if most medicines "could be sunk to the bottom of the sea, it would be all the better for mankind,—and all the worse for the fishes" (1861, 39). Similarly, for most of the century professional doctors had little more to offer than did quacks; visiting a doctor often did more harm than good (Miller and Sexton 2005, 154).

that infant—I am the rightful Duke of Bridgewater; and here am I, forlorn, torn from my high estate, hunted of men, despised by the cold world, ragged, worn, heart-broken, and degraded to the companionship of felons on a raft!"

Jim pitied him ever so much, and so did I. We tried to comfort him, but he said it warn't much use, he couldn't be much comforted; said if we was a mind to acknowledge him, that would do him more good than most anything else; so we said we would, if he would tell us how. He said we ought to bow, when we spoke to him, and say "Your Grace," or "My Lord," or "Your Lordship"—and he wouldn't mind it if we called him plain "Bridgewater," which, he said, was a title, anyway, and not a name; and one of us ought to wait on him at dinner, and do any little thing for him he wanted done.

Well, that was all easy, so we done it. All through dinner Jim stood around and waited on him, and says, "Will yo' Grace have some o' dis or some o' dat?" and so on, and a body could see it was mighty pleasing to him.

But the old man got pretty silent, by and by—didn't have much to say, and didn't look pretty comfortable over all that petting that was going on around that duke. He seemed to have something on his mind. So, along in the afternoon, he says:

"Looky here, Bilgewater," he says, "I'm nation sorry for you, but you ain't the only person that's had troubles like that."

"No?"

"No, you ain't. You ain't the only person that's ben snaked down wrongfully out'n a high place."

"Alas!"

"No, you ain't the only person that's had a secret of his birth." And by jings, *he* begins to cry.

"Hold! What do you mean?"

"Bilgewater, kin I trust you?" says the old man, still sort of sobbing.

"To the bitter death!" He took the old man by the hand and squeezed it, and says, "That secret of your being: speak!"

"Bilgewater, I am the late Dauphin!"

You bet you Jim and me stared, this time. Then the duke says:

"You are what?"

"Yes, my friend, it is too true—your eyes is lookin' at this very moment on the pore disappeared Dauphin, Looy the Seventeen, son of Looy the Sixteen and Marry Antonette."[114]

---

114. France's monarchy was abolished in 1792 during the French Revolution, and King Louis XVI and Queen Marie Antoinette were executed on the guillotine the next year. They did have a son, Louis XVII, who was only seven years old when his father was executed.

"I AM THE LATE DAUPHIN."

(Illustration by Edward W. Kemble. From Mark Twain, *Adventures of Huckleberry Finn*. New York: C. L. Webster, 1885. Digitized by the University of Virginia Library.)

France's royalist faction regarded Louis XVII, the dauphin, or heir apparent, as the rightful king, but the dauphin died in prison of an illness at age 10. The old man either is unaware of the dauphin's death or hopes that his audience is.

   A modern-day equivalent of the old man's scheme might be the profusion of fraudulent e-mails from close relatives of Nigerian princes or other monarchs or deposed dictators asking for assistance with the transfer of large sums of money.

"You! At your age! No! You mean you're the late Charlemagne; you must be six or seven hundred years old, at the very least."

"Trouble has done it, Bilgewater, trouble has done it; trouble has brung these gray hairs and this premature balditude. Yes, gentlemen, you see before you, in blue jeans and misery, the wanderin', exiled, trampled-on and sufferin' rightful King of France."[115]

Well, he cried and took on so, that me and Jim didn't know hardly what to do, we was so sorry—and so glad and proud we'd got him with us, too. So we set in, like we done before with the duke, and tried to comfort *him.* But he said it warn't no use, nothing but to be dead and done with it all could do him any good; though he said it often made him feel easier and better for a while if people treated him according to his rights, and got down on one knee to speak to him, and always called him "Your Majesty," and waited on him first at meals, and didn't set down in his presence till he asked them. So Jim and me set to majestying him, and doing this and that and t'other for him, and standing up till he told us we might set down. This done him heaps of good, and so he got cheerful and comfortable. But the duke kind of soured on him, and didn't look a bit satisfied with the way things was going; still, the king acted real friendly towards him, and said the duke's great-grandfather and all the other Dukes of Bilgewater was a good deal thought of by *his* father and was allowed to come to the palace considerable; but the duke stayed huffy a good while, till by and by the king says:

"Like as not we got to be together a blamed long time, on this h-yer raft, Bilgewater, and so what's the use o' your bein' sour? It'll only make things oncomfortable. It ain't my fault I warn't born a duke, it ain't your fault you warn't born a king—so what's the use to worry? Make the best o' things the way you find 'em, says I—that's my motto. This ain't no bad thing that we've struck here—plenty grub and an easy life—come, give us your hand, duke, and less all be friends."

The duke done it, and Jim and me was pretty glad to see it. It took away all the uncomfortableness, and we felt mighty good over it, because it would a been a miserable business to have any unfriendliness on the raft;

---

115. Americans' fascination with monarchs remained long after the American Revolution, thus the choice of "king" and "duke" for these impostors' identities. Twain himself despised monarchy—much of *A Connecticut Yankee in King Arthur's Court* is an expression of that disgust—but noted of his countrymen that "We adore titles and heredities in our hearts, and ridicule them with our mouths" (Twain 2010, 2:37). Americans' somewhat conflicted view of monarchy dates back to the Revolution itself: in 1776 Thomas Paine's influential pamphlet *Common Sense* compellingly denounced monarchy, but the Declaration of Independence denounced only the current abuses of power by King George III.

for what you want, above all things, on a raft, is for everybody to be satisfied, and feel right and kind towards the others.

It didn't take me long to make up my mind that these liars warn't no
kings nor dukes, at all, but just low-down humbugs and frauds. But I never
said nothing, never let on; kept it to myself; it's the best way; then you
don't have no quarrels, and don't get into no trouble. If they wanted us to
call them kings and dukes, I hadn't no objections, 'long as it would keep
peace in the family; and it warn't no use to tell Jim, so I didn't tell him. If
I never learnt nothing else out of pap, I learnt that the best way to get along
with his kind of people is to let them have their own way.

CHAPTER XX.

THEY asked us considerable many questions; wanted to know what we
covered up the raft that way for, and laid by in the day-time instead of running—was Jim a runaway nigger? Says I:

"Goodness sakes! would a runaway nigger run *south?*"[116]

No, they allowed he wouldn't. I had to account for things some way,
so I says:

"My folks was living in Pike County, in Missouri, where I was born,[117]
and they all died off but me and pa and my brother Ike. Pa, he 'lowed he'd

---

116. Traveling downriver on the Mississippi appears insane for a slave, since the journey took him deeper and deeper into slave country. The conditions of slavery tended to be
harsher the farther south one went, partly because escape was presumably more difficult
and slaveholders had less reason to worry that discontented slaves would escape and
partly because the work on sugar plantations was particularly arduous. Yet as noted earlier,
the traditional underground railroad story of slaves trekking north into Canada or into sympathetic northern communities omits an important reality: several of the greatest havens
for runaway slaves were the big cities of the South such as New Orleans, which had large
free black communities that harbored runaways.

117. The story that Huck tells here is mostly false, of course, but we do not know if the
Pike County part is false. As noted at the beginning, Pike County was one of two counties
south of the Missouri county that contained Hannibal, Twain's hometown and the inspiration for Huck's hometown of St. Petersburg, but Twain may have used artistic license to put
St. Petersburg in Pike County. Pike County was more rural than Marion County, and Huck's
last alibi involved a family farm, so maybe he is lying but trying to keep his stories straight.
Twain may also have been making a literary allusion: Pike County was the home of some
memorable characters in antebellum stories and songs, such as "Sweet Betsy from Pike"
and "Joe Bowers" (Fischer et al. 2010, 430). Those two songs are about Pike County citizens
who travel a long way—namely to California as part of the gold rush—so the ruse is a fitting
one for Huck. It could also be that Twain simply liked the sound of the word "Pike," as he
also introduces towns called "Pikesville" and "Pokeville."

break up and go down and live with Uncle Ben, who's got a little one-horse place on the river, forty-four mile below Orleans. Pa was pretty poor, and had some debts; so when he'd squared up there warn't nothing left but sixteen dollars and our nigger, Jim.[118] That warn't enough to take us fourteen hundred mile, deck passage nor no other way. Well, when the river rose, pa had a streak of luck one day; he ketched this piece of a raft; so we reckoned we'd go down to Orleans on it. Pa's luck didn't hold out; a steamboat run over the forrard corner of the raft, one night, and we all went overboard and dove under the wheel; Jim and me come up, all right, but pa was drunk, and Ike was only four years old, so they never come up no more. Well, for the next day or two we had considerable trouble, because people was always coming out in skiffs and trying to take Jim away from me, saying they believed he was a runaway nigger. We don't run day-times no more, now; nights they don't bother us."

The duke says—

"Leave me alone to cipher out a way so we can run in the day-time if we want to. I'll think the thing over—I'll invent a plan that'll fix it. We'll let it alone for to-day, because of course we don't want to go by that town yonder in daylight—it mightn't be healthy."

Towards night it begun to darken up and look like rain; the heat lightning was squirting around, low down in the sky, and the leaves was beginning to shiver—it was going to be pretty ugly, it was easy to see that. So the duke and the king went to overhauling our wigwam, to see what the beds was like. My bed was a straw tick—better than Jim's, which was a corn-shuck tick; there's always cobs around about in a shuck tick, and they poke into you and hurt; and when you roll over, the dry shucks sound like you was rolling over in a pile of dead leaves; it makes such a rustling that you wake up. Well, the duke allowed he would take my bed; but the king allowed he wouldn't. He says—

"I should a reckoned the difference in rank would a sejested to you that a corn-shuck bed warn't just fitten for me to sleep on. Your Grace'll take the shuck bed yourself."

Jim and me was in a sweat again, for a minute, being afraid there was going to be some more trouble amongst them; so we was pretty glad when the duke says—

"'Tis my fate to be always ground into the mire under the iron heel of oppression. Misfortune has broken my once haughty spirit; I

---

118. Unlike his previous hard-luck story about his family, this time Huck says that they own a slave, which would have been unusual for a "pretty poor" family. After settling up, they still have $16 (about $480 in today's money) and a prime-age slave, who could fetch about $800 (or $24,000 in today's money) at auction. Huck's made-up family is cash-poor but has a fair bit of illiquid wealth, at least enough to keep the duke and the king interested.

yield, I submit; 'tis my fate. I am alone in the world—let me suffer; I can bear it."

We got away as soon as it was good and dark. The king told us to stand well out towards the middle of the river, and not show a light till we got a long ways below the town. We come in sight of the little bunch of lights by and by—that was the town, you know—and slid by, about a half a mile out, all right. When we was three-quarters of a mile below, we hoisted up our signal lantern; and about ten o'clock it come on to rain and blow and thunder and lighten like everything; so the king told us to both stay on watch till the weather got better; then him and the duke crawled into the wigwam and turned in for the night. It was my watch below, till twelve, but I wouldn't a turned in, anyway, if I'd had a bed; because a body don't see such a storm as that every day in the week, not by a long sight. My souls, how the wind did scream along! And every second or two there'd come a glare that lit up the white-caps for a half a mile around, and you'd see the islands looking dusty through the rain, and the trees thrashing around in the wind; then comes a *h-wack!*—bum! bum! bumble-umble-um-bum-bum-bum-bum— and the thunder would go rumbling and grumbling away, and quit—and then *rip* comes another flash and another sockdolager. The waves most washed me off the raft, sometimes, but I hadn't any clothes on, and didn't mind. We didn't have no trouble about snags; the lightning was glaring and flittering around so constant that we could see them plenty soon enough to throw her head this way or that and miss them.

I had the middle watch, you know, but I was pretty sleepy by that time, so Jim he said he would stand the first half of it for me; he was always mighty good, that way, Jim was. I crawled into the wigwam, but the king and the duke had their legs sprawled around so there warn't no show for me; so I laid outside—I didn't mind the rain, because it was warm, and the waves warn't running so high, now. About two they come up again, though, and Jim was going to call me, but he changed his mind because he reckoned they warn't high enough yet to do any harm; but he was mistaken about that, for pretty soon all of a sudden along comes a regular ripper, and washed me overboard. It most killed Jim a-laughing. He was the easiest nigger to laugh that ever was, anyway.

I took the watch, and Jim he laid down and snored away; and by and by the storm let up for good and all; and the first cabin-light that showed, I rousted him out and we slid the raft into hiding-quarters for the day.

The king got out an old ratty deck of cards, after breakfast, and him and the duke played seven-up a while, five cents a game. Then they got tired of it, and allowed they would "lay out a campaign," as they called it. The duke went down into his carpet-bag, and fetched up a lot of little printed bills and read them out loud. One bill said, "The celebrated Dr. Armand de Montalban, of Paris," would "lecture on the Science of Phrenology" at such and such a place, on the blank day of blank, at ten cents admission, and "furnish charts of character at twenty-five cents apiece."[119] The duke said that was *him*. In another bill he was the "world-renowned Shakespearian tragedian, Garrick the Younger, of Drury Lane, London." In other bills he had a lot of other names and done other wonderful things, like finding water and gold with a "divining rod,"[120] "dissipating witch-spells," and so on. By and by he says:

"But the histrionic muse is the darling. Have you ever trod the boards, Royalty?"

"No," says the king.

"You shall, then, before you're three days older, Fallen Grandeur," says the duke. "The first good town we come to, we'll hire a hall and do the sword-fight in Richard III. and the balcony scene in Romeo and Juliet. How does that strike you?"

"I'm in, up to the hub, for anything that will pay, Bilgewater, but, you see, I don't know nothing about play-actin', and hain't ever seen much of it. I was too small when pap used to have 'em at the palace. Do you reckon you can learn me?"

"Easy!"

"All right. I'm jist a-freezn' for something fresh, anyway. Less commence, right away."

So the duke he told him all about who Romeo was, and who Juliet was, and said he was used to being Romeo, so the king could be Juliet.

"But if Juliet's such a young gal, Duke, my peeled head and my white whiskers is goin' to look oncommon odd on her, maybe."

"No, don't you worry—these country jakes won't ever think of that. Besides, you know, you'll be in costume, and that makes all the difference in the world; Juliet's in a balcony, enjoying the moonlight before she goes to bed, and she's got on her night-gown and her ruffled night-cap. Here are the costumes for the parts."[121]

He got out two or three curtain-calico suits, which he said was meedy-evil armor for Richard III. and t'other chap, and a long white cotton

---

119. Converting into today's money by multiplying by 30, we see that admission to the phrenology lecture is $3.00, and a "chart of character" costs $7.50. With enough participants, this scam could be lucrative.

120. Dowsing, or the use of forked sticks or rods to try to find water or precious minerals, was yet another pseudoscience of the day. Modern scientific studies in the 20th century have consistently debunked dowsing (Daempfle 2013, 115), and Twain's inclusion of it here suggests that it was dubious in his time as well.

121. The rural frontier offered almost nothing in the way of organized entertainment, so a traveling theater troupe had the potential to draw well. Theaters did exist in bigger cities along the Mississippi, such as New Orleans and St. Louis, but the countryside lacked the population to sustain such a venture.

night-shirt and a ruffled night-cap to match. The king was satisfied; so the duke got out his book and read the parts over in the most splendid spread-eagle way, prancing around and acting at the same time, to show how it had got to be done; then he give the book to the king and told him to get his part by heart.

There was a little one-horse town about three mile down the bend, and after dinner the duke said he had ciphered out his idea about how to run in daylight without it being dangersome for Jim; so he allowed he would go down to the town and fix that thing. The king allowed he would go, too, and see if he couldn't strike something. We was out of coffee, so Jim said I better go along with them in the canoe and get some.[122]

When we got there, there warn't nobody stirring; streets empty, and perfectly dead and still, like Sunday. We found a sick nigger sunning himself in a back yard, and he said everybody that warn't too young or too sick or too old, was gone to camp-meeting, about two mile back in the woods. The king got the directions, and allowed he'd go and work that camp-meeting for all it was worth, and I might go, too.

The duke said what he was after was a printing office. We found it; a little bit of a concern, up over a carpenter shop—carpenters and printers all gone to the meeting, and no doors locked. It was a dirty, littered-up place, and had ink marks, and handbills with pictures of horses and runaway niggers on them, all over the walls. The duke shed his coat and said he was all right, now. So me and the king lit out for the camp-meeting.[123]

---

122. In this novel coffee is repeatedly implied to be a staple of the American diet, even for slaves and children of the underclass. It is often imagined that Americans switched from tea to coffee because of the Boston Tea Party and the American Revolution, but in fact the tea boycotts were temporary. Americans went back to drinking tea after the Revolution. Tea became cheaper because it no longer had to pass through English ports and because of improvements in shipping technology, and tea sales rose until the Civil War. But coffee overtook tea in the 1830s thanks to newly available, cheap, and highly caffeinated coffee from South America (Smith 2013, 900–903).

123. Even this "one-horse town" has a print shop, which is reasonably accurate, historically speaking. Although the rural South had little industry, print shops and newspapers were seen as indispensable to civilized living. The town appears to be in Arkansas, about halfway between Memphis and where the Arkansas River empties into the Mississippi (Fischer et al. 2010, 430–431). This would be Phillips County. In 1840 the county had two print shops and two newspapers, both of them tiny one- or two-man operations (United States Department of State 1841, 331). Twain himself worked in print shops for several years.

We learn immediately what a southern print shop's primary business included. Handbills, now called flyers, were commonly used for a multitude of purposes, including giving notice of lost property, namely horses and slaves. This, of course, was an inefficient means of communication. The telegraph allowed for instantaneous communication and the railroad allowed for rapid delivery of newspapers and images, but both were still too new to

We got there in about a half an hour, fairly dripping, for it was a most awful hot day. There was as much as a thousand people there, from twenty mile around. The woods was full of teams and wagons, hitched every-wheres, feeding out of the wagon troughs and stomping to keep off the flies. There was sheds made out of poles and roofed over with branches, where they had lemonade and gingerbread to sell, and piles of watermel-ons and green corn and such-like truck.

The preaching was going on under the same kinds of sheds, only they was bigger and held crowds of people. The benches was made out of out-side slabs of logs, with holes bored in the round side to drive sticks into for legs. They didn't have no backs. The preachers had high platforms to stand on, at one end of the sheds. The women had on sun-bonnets; and some had linsey-woolsey frocks, some gingham ones, and a few of the young ones had on calico. Some of the young men was barefooted, and some of the children didn't have on any clothes but just a tow-linen shirt. Some of the old women was knitting, and some of the young folks was courting on the sly.[124]

The first shed we come to, the preacher was lining out a hymn. He lined out two lines, everybody sung it, and it was kind of grand to hear it, there was so many of them and they done it in such a rousing way; then he lined out two more for them to sing—and so on. The people woke up more and more, and sung louder and louder; and towards the end, some begun to groan, and some begun to shout. Then the preacher begun to preach; and begun in earnest, too; and went weaving first to one side of the platform and then the other, and then a-leaning down over the front of it, with his arms and his body going all the time, and shouting his words out with all his might; and every now and then he would hold up his Bible and spread it open, and kind of pass it around this way and that, shouting, "It's the brazen serpent in the wilderness! Look upon it and live!" And people would shout out, "Glory!—A-a-*men!*" And so he went on, and the people groaning and crying and saying amen:

---

have penetrated deep into the country. In the case of fugitive slaves, the transportation and communication revolutions were a double-edged sword, making it easier for slave catch-ers to learn about and locate their quarry but also easier for abolitionists and underground railroad operators to assist escaping slaves.

124. Camp meetings, as "mammoth picnics," were among the biggest social events that visited these rural areas. So, they naturally attracted many people whose interests were more physical than spiritual. As Roger Finke and Rodney Stark put it: "Camp meetings not only satisfied the soul, they were fun. It was widely said along the frontier that during camp meetings as many souls were conceived as were saved" (1992, 96).

This 1830 lithograph by Hugh Bridport captures the social aspect of religious revival meetings on the frontier. Rural folk at the time had few entertainment options, and traveling evangelical preachers tended to be good showmen, so camp meetings usually were big draws. The many tents in the background suggest that people traveled great distances to be there. (Library of Congress)

"Oh, come to the mourners' bench! come, black with sin! (*Amen!*) come, sick and sore! (*Amen!*) come, lame and halt, and blind! (*Amen!*) come, pore and needy, sunk in shame! (*A-a-men!*) come all that's worn, and soiled, and suffering!—come with a broken spirit! come with a contrite heart! come in your rags and sin and dirt! the waters that cleanse is free, the door of heaven stands open—oh, enter in and be at rest!" (*A-a-men! Glory, glory hallelujah!*)

And so on. You couldn't make out what the preacher said, any more, on account of the shouting and crying. Folks got up, everywheres in the crowd, and worked their way, just by main strength, to the mourners' bench, with the tears running down their faces; and when all the mourners had got up there to the front benches in a crowd, they sung, and shouted, and flung themselves down on the straw, just crazy and wild.

Well, the first I knowed, the king got agoing, and you could hear him over everybody; and next he went a-charging up on to the platform and the preacher he begged him to speak to the people, and he done it. He told them he was a pirate—been a pirate for thirty years, out in the Indian Ocean,[125] and his crew was thinned out considerable, last spring in a fight, and he was home now, to take out some fresh men, and thanks to goodness he'd been robbed last night, and put ashore off of a steamboat without a cent, and he was glad of it, it was the blessedest thing that ever happened to him, because he was a changed man now, and happy for the first time in his life; and, poor as he was, he was going to start right off and work his way back to the Indian Ocean and put in the rest of his life trying to turn the pirates into the true path; for he could do it better than anybody else, being acquainted with all pirate crews in that ocean; and though it would take him a long time to get there, without money, he would get there anyway, and every time he convinced a pirate he would say to him, "Don't you thank me, don't you give me no credit, it all belongs to them dear people in Pokeville[126] camp-meeting, natural brothers and benefactors of the race—and that dear preacher there, the truest friend a pirate ever had!"

And then he busted into tears, and so did everybody. Then somebody sings out, "Take up a collection for him, take up a collection!" Well, a half a dozen made a jump to do it, but somebody sings out, "Let *him* pass the hat around!" Then everybody said it, the preacher too.

So the king went all through the crowd with his hat, swabbing his eyes, and blessing the people and praising them and thanking them for being so good to the poor pirates away off there; and every little while the prettiest kind of girls, with the tears running down their cheeks, would up and ask him would he let them kiss him, for to remember him by; and he always done it; and some of them he hugged and kissed as many as five or six

---

125. Piracy has been around for centuries and has not completely disappeared, as Somalian pirates demonstrated with a rash of attacks and hijackings off the northeast coast of Africa beginning in 2005. Piracy was a tremendous concern in colonial times, when trade was mostly conducted by ocean ships. Hijacking those ships and stealing their cargo could be a lucrative business. Piracy had been minimized on the Atlantic Ocean and European seas almost a century before this novel's setting, thanks to concerted military action by governments and Britain's East India Company. Indian Ocean piracy was in decline in Huck's time, but it remained enough of a news item for the king's lie to be a good one (Walton and Rockoff 2014, 81–86; Pitney and Levin 2013, 7–14).

Piracy still existed in antebellum America's waters. As late as 1850 there were some 400–500 "river pirates," drawn from local gangs, operating on New York City's waterfront (Sante 1991, 204).

126. Pokeville appears to be in Arkansas, a state that has never been particularly prosperous and was very new, rural, and thinly populated at the time, having just been admitted to the union in 1836, so it lent itself to stereotypes of ignorant and gullible "country jakes."

times—and he was invited to stay a week; and everybody wanted him to live in their houses, and said they'd think it was an honor; but he said as this was the last day of the camp-meeting he couldn't do no good, and besides he was in a sweat to get to the Indian Ocean right off and go to work on the pirates.

When we got back to the raft and he come to count up, he found he had collected eighty-seven dollars and seventy-five cents.[127] And then he had fetched away a three-gallon jug of whisky, too, that he found under a wagon when he was starting home through the woods. The king said, take it all around, it laid over any day he'd ever put in in the missionarying line. He said it warn't no use talking, heathens don't amount to shucks, alongside of pirates, to work a camp-meeting with.

The duke was thinking *he'd* been doing pretty well, till the king come to show up, but after that he didn't think so so much. He had set up and printed off two little jobs for farmers, in that printing office—horse bills—and took the money, four dollars. And he had got in ten dollars worth of advertisements for the paper, which he said he would put in for four dollars if they would pay in advance—so they done it. The price of the paper was two dollars a year, but he took in three subscriptions for half a dollar apiece on condition of them paying him in advance; they were going to pay in cord-wood and onions, as usual, but he said he had just bought the concern and knocked down the price as low as he could afford it, and was going to run it for cash.[128] He set up a little piece of poetry which he made, himself, out of his own head—three verses—kind of sweet and saddish—the name of it was, "Yes, crush, cold world, this breaking heart"—and he left that all set up and ready to print in the paper, and didn't charge nothing for it. Well, he took in nine dollars and a half and said he'd done a pretty square day's work for it.[129]

Then he showed us another little job he'd printed and hadn't charged for, because it was for us. It had a picture of a runaway nigger, with

---

127. This is a huge haul—$87.75 then is equivalent to more than $2,600 today.

128. Barter was common on the antebellum frontier. It was hard to avoid, as silver and gold coins were scarce, banks were often nonexistent on the frontier, and the banknotes from other banks were often unreliable and regarded with suspicion (see, e.g., Hahn 1983, 73, 181, and Byrne 2006, 48). Credit was common as well, as farmers received most of their income at harvest time (Ransom and Sutch 2001, 123). The duke's insistence on being paid in cash is right in line with negative portrayals of rural merchants in southern literature, such as the merchant in William Faulkner's *The Hamlet,* and also reflected the duke's plans to get out of town as fast as possible.

129. Approximately $285 in today's money.

a bundle on a stick, over his shoulder, and "$200 reward" under it. The reading was all about Jim, and just described him to a dot. It said he run away from St. Jacques' plantation, forty mile below New Orleans,[130] last winter, and likely went north, and whoever would catch him and send him back, he could have the reward and expenses.

"Now," says the duke, "after to-night we can run in the daytime if we want to. Whenever we see anybody coming, we can tie Jim hand and foot with a rope, and lay him in the wigwam and show this handbill and say we captured him up the river, and were too poor to travel on a steamboat, so we got this little raft on credit from our friends and are going down to get the reward. Handcuffs and chains would look still better on Jim, but it wouldn't go well with the story of us being so poor. Too much like jewelry. Ropes are the correct thing—we must preserve the unities, as we say on the boards."

We all said the duke was pretty smart, and there couldn't be no trouble about running daytimes. We judged we could make miles enough that night to get out of the reach of the pow-wow we reckoned the duke's work in the printing office was going to make in that little town—then we could boom right along if we wanted to.

We laid low and kept still, and never shoved out till nearly ten o'clock; then we slid by, pretty wide away from the town, and didn't hoist our lantern till we was clear out of sight of it.

When Jim called me to take the watch at four in the morning, he says—

"Huck, does you reck'n we gwyne to run acrost any mo' kings on dis trip?"

"No," I says, "I reckon not."

"Well," says he, "dat's all right, den. I doan' mine one er two kings, but dat's enough. Dis one's powerful drunk, en de duke ain' much better."

I found Jim had been trying to get him to talk French, so he could hear what it was like; but he said he had been in this country so long, and had so much trouble, he'd forgot it.

---

130. There actually were plantations 40 miles south of New Orleans, in the Mississippi Delta, producing rice and sugar. (The duke's handbill could have been inspired by Huck's lie about his uncle who lived 44 miles south of New Orleans.) Slave escapes from that far south to the North were virtually unheard of. The few slaves who did escape the grueling work on those plantations generally found refuge in the free black community of New Orleans or another Deep South city.

ANOTHER LITTLE JOB.

(Illustration by Edward W. Kemble. From Mark Twain, *Adventures of Huckleberry Finn.* New York: C. L. Webster, 1885. Digitized by the University of Virginia Library.)

$500, REWARD.

Ran away from the undersigned, on Sunday the 9th inst., a negro boy named

AARON OR APE.

He is about **20** years old, six feet high, with rather unusually large legs and arms; walks bent forward with one foot turned out more than the other. I will give **$150,00** reward for him if taken in the county; **$100,00** reward if taken in the counties south of this and **$200,00** if taken in any of the Mississippi counties or **$500** if taken out of the State.

O. M. HARRIS,

Three miles south of Midddle Grove Monroe Coounty, Missouri.

REGISTER PRINT—MACON CITY, MO.

This poster offers a reward for a slave who has escaped from his master in Monroe County, Missouri, next to Twain's home county of Marion. The large reward, equivalent to $15,000 in today's money, indicates that slave labor was highly profitable. Rural southern counties often had several print shops, in part to meet the demand for posters and handbills concerning runaway slaves. (Duke University Library, Broadsides and Ephemera Collection, Folder MO1.)

CHAPTER XXI.

IT was after sun-up now, but we went right on and didn't tie up. The king and the duke turned out by and by looking pretty rusty; but after they'd jumped overboard and took a swim it chippered them up a good deal. After breakfast the king he took a seat on the corner of the raft, and pulled off his boots and rolled up his britches, and let his legs dangle in the water, so as to be comfortable, and lit his pipe, and went to getting his Romeo and Juliet by heart. When he had got it pretty good him and the duke begun to practice it together. The duke had to learn him over and over again how to say every speech; and he made him sigh, and put his hand on his heart, and after a while he said he done it pretty well; "only," he says, "you mustn't bellow out *Romeo*! that way, like a bull—you must say it soft and sick, and languishy, so—R-o-o-meo! that is the idea; for Juliet's a dear sweet mere child of a girl, you know, and she doesn't bray like a jackass."

Well, next they got out a couple of long swords that the duke made out of oak laths, and begun to practice the sword-fight—the duke called himself Richard III.; and the way they laid on and pranced around the raft was grand to see. But by and by the king tripped and fell overboard, and after that they took a rest, and had a talk about all kinds of adventures they'd had in other times along the river.

After dinner the duke says:

"Well, Capet,[131] we'll want to make this a first-class show, you know, so I guess we'll add a little more to it. We want a little something to answer encores with, anyway."

"What's onkores, Bilgewater?"

The duke told him, and then says:

"I'll answer by doing the Highland fling or the sailor's hornpipe; and you—well, let me see—oh, I've got it—you can do Hamlet's soliloquy."

"Hamlet's which?"

"Hamlet's soliloquy, you know; the most celebrated thing in Shakespeare. Ah, it's sublime, sublime! Always fetches the house. I haven't got it in the book—I've only got one volume—but I reckon I can piece it out from memory. I'll just walk up and down a minute, and see if I can call it back from recollection's vaults."

So he went to marching up and down, thinking, and frowning horrible every now and then; then he would hoist up his eyebrows; next he would squeeze his hand on his forehead and stagger back and kind of moan; next he would sigh, and next he'd let on to drop a tear. It was beautiful to see him. By and by he got it. He told us to give attention. Then he strikes a most noble attitude, with one leg shoved forwards, and his arms stretched away up, and his head tilted back, looking up at the sky; and then he begins to rip and rave and grit his teeth; and after that, all through his speech he howled, and spread around, and swelled up his chest, and just knocked the spots out of any acting ever *I* see before. This is the speech—I learned it, easy enough, while he was learning it to the king:

To be, or not to be; that is the bare bodkin
That makes calamity of so long life;

---

131. Louis Capet is what the French revolutionaries renamed Louis XVI after dethroning him, to establish that he was just another civilian, "Citizen Capet." The Capet dynasty had ruled France for several centuries during the Middle Ages, but Louis was not related to them. Calling the old man "Capet" seems to be the duke's way of mocking his scam.

For who would fardels bear, till Birnam Wood do come to
Dunsinane,
But that the fear of something after death
Murders the innocent sleep,
Great nature's second course,
And makes us rather sling the arrows of outrageous fortune
Than fly to others that we know not of.
There's the respect must give us pause:
Wake Duncan with thy knocking! I would thou couldst;
For who would bear the whips and scorns of time,
The oppressor's wrong, the proud man's contumely,
The law's delay, and the quietus which his pangs might take,
In the dead waste and middle of the night, when churchyards
yawn
In customary suits of solemn black,
But that the undiscovered country from whose bourne no traveler
returns,
Breathes forth contagion on the world,
And thus the native hue of resolution, like the poor cat i' the adage,
Is sicklied o'er with care,
And all the clouds that lowered o'er our housetops,
With this regard their currents turn awry,
And lose the name of action.
'Tis a consummation devoutly to be wished. But soft you, the fair
Ophelia:
Ope not thy ponderous and marble jaws,
But get thee to a nunnery—go!

Well, the old man he liked that speech, and he mighty soon got it so he
could do it first rate. It seemed like he was just born for it; and when he had
his hand in and was excited, it was perfectly lovely the way he would rip
and tear and rair up behind when he was getting it off.

The first chance we got, the duke he had some show bills printed; and
after that, for two or three days as we floated along, the raft was a most
uncommon lively place, for there warn't nothing but sword-fighting and
rehearsing—as the duke called it—going on all the time. One morning,
when we was pretty well down the State of Arkansaw, we come in sight of
a little one-horse town in a big bend; so we tied up about three-quarters of
a mile above it, in the mouth of a crick which was shut in like a tunnel by
the cypress trees, and all of us but Jim took the canoe and went down there
to see if there was any chance in that place for our show.

We struck it mighty lucky; there was going to be a circus there that
afternoon, and the country people was already beginning to come in, in all
kinds of old shackly wagons, and on horses. The circus would leave before

night, so our show would have a pretty good chance. The duke he hired the court house, and we went around and stuck up our bills.[132] They read like this:

> Shaksperean Revival!!!
> Wonderful Attraction!
> For One Night Only!
> The world renowned tragedians,
> David Garrick the younger, of Drury Lane Theatre, London,
> and
> Edmund Kean the elder, of the Royal Haymarket Theatre,
> Whitechapel, Pudding Lane, Piccadilly, London,
> and the Royal Continental Theatres, in their
> sublime Shaksperean Spectacle entitled
> The Balcony Scene
> in
> Romeo and Juliet!!!
> Romeo.. Mr. Garrick.
> Juliet... Mr. Kean.
> Assisted by the whole strength of the company!
> New costumes, new scenery, new appointments!
>
> Also:
>
> The thrilling, masterly, and blood-curdling
> Broad-sword conflict
> In Richard III.!!!
> Richard III.. Mr. Garrick.
> Richmond.. Mr. Kean.
>
> Also:
>
> (by special request,)
> Hamlet's Immortal Soliloquy!!

---

132. The demand in river towns for entertainment of all kinds was high. Circuses often took place on circus boats, a notable one of which seated 3,000 people. Showboats brought a whole range of theatrical entertainment, including top actors such as the tragedian Junius Brutus Booth (father of John Wilkes Booth), who died on a touring steamship in Louisville apparently from drinking contaminated river water (Fisher 2015, 10). Minstrel shows were the most popular, and classics were regularly reworked or burlesqued to appeal to the crowd (Sandlin 2010, 173–177).

By the Illustrious Kean!
Done by him 300 consecutive nights in Paris!
For One Night Only,
On account of imperative European engagements!

Admission 25 cents; children and servants, 10 cents.

Then we went loafing around the town. The stores and houses was most all old shackly dried-up frame concerns that hadn't ever been painted; they was set up three or four foot above ground on stilts, so as to be out of reach of the water when the river was overflowed. The houses had little gardens around them, but they didn't seem to raise hardly anything in them but jimpson weeds, and sunflowers, and ash-piles, and old curled-up boots and shoes, and pieces of bottles, and rags, and played-out tin-ware. The fences was made of different kinds of boards, nailed on at different times; and they leaned every which-way, and had gates that didn't generly have but one hinge—a leather one. Some of the fences had been white-washed, some time or another, but the duke said it was in Clumbus's time, like enough. There was generly hogs in the garden, and people driving them out.

All the stores was along one street. They had white domestic awnings in front, and the country people hitched their horses to the awning-posts. There was empty dry-goods boxes under the awnings, and loafers roosting on them all day long, whittling them with their Barlow knives; and chawing tobacco, and gaping and yawning and stretching—a mighty ornery lot. They generly had on yellow straw hats most as wide as an umbrella, but didn't wear no coats nor waistcoats, they called one another Bill, and Buck, and Hank, and Joe, and Andy, and talked lazy and drawly, and used considerable many cuss words. There was as many as one loafer leaning up against every awning-post, and he most always had his hands in his britches pockets, except when he fetched them out to lend a chaw of tobacco or scratch. What a body was hearing amongst them all the time was—

"Gimme a chaw 'v tobacker, Hank."

"Cain't—I hain't got but one chaw left. Ask Bill."

Maybe Bill he gives him a chaw; maybe he lies and says he ain't got none. Some of them kinds of loafers never has a cent in the world, nor a chaw of tobacco of their own. They get all their chawing by borrowing—they say to a fellow, "I wisht you'd len' me a chaw, Jack, I jist this minute give Ben Thompson the last chaw I had"—which is a lie, pretty much every time; it don't fool nobody but a stranger; but Jack ain't no stranger, so he says—

"*You* give him a chaw, did you? so did your sister's cat's grandmother. You pay me back the chaws you've awready borry'd off'n me, Lafe Buckner, then I'll loan you one or two ton of it, and won't charge you no back intrust, nuther."

"Well, I *did* pay you back some of it wunst."

"Yes, you did—'bout six chaws. You borry'd store tobacker and paid back nigger-head."

Store tobacco is flat black plug, but these fellows mostly chaws the natural leaf twisted. When they borrow a chaw, they don't generly cut it off with a knife, but they set the plug in between their teeth, and gnaw with their teeth and tug at the plug with their hands till they get it in two—then sometimes the one that owns the tobacco looks mournful at it when it's handed back, and says, sarcastic—

"Here, gimme the *chaw,* and you take the *plug.*"

All the streets and lanes was just mud, they warn't nothing else *but* mud—mud as black as tar, and nigh about a foot deep in some places; and two or three inches deep in *all* the places. The hogs loafed and grunted around everywheres. You'd see a muddy sow and a litter of pigs come lazying along the street and whollop herself right down in the way, where folks had to walk around her, and she'd stretch out and shut her eyes, and wave her ears, whilst the pigs was milking her, and look as happy as if she was on salary. And pretty soon you'd hear a loafer sing out, "Hi! *so* boy! sick him, Tige!" and away the sow would go, squealing most horrible, with a dog or two swinging to each ear, and three or four dozen more a-coming; and then you would see all the loafers get up and watch the thing out of sight, and laugh at the fun and look grateful for the noise. Then they'd settle back again till there was a dog-fight. There couldn't anything wake them up all over, and make them happy all over, like a dog-fight—unless it might be putting turpentine on a stray dog and setting fire to him, or tying a tin pan to his tail and see him run himself to death.

On the river front some of the houses was sticking out over the bank, and they was bowed and bent, and about ready to tumble in. The people had moved out of them. The bank was caved away under one corner of some others, and that corner was hanging over. People lived in them yet, but it was dangersome, because sometimes a strip of land as wide as a house caves in at a time. Sometimes a belt of land a quarter of a mile deep will start in and cave along and cave along till it all caves into the river in one summer. Such a town as that has to be always moving back, and back, and back, because the river's always gnawing at it.

The nearer it got to noon that day, the thicker and thicker was the wagons and horses in the streets, and more coming all the time. Families fetched their dinners with them, from the country, and eat them in the wagons. There was considerable whisky drinking going on, and I seen three fights. By and by somebody sings out—

"Here comes old Boggs!—in from the country for his little old monthly drunk—here he comes, boys!"

All the loafers looked glad—I reckoned they was used to having fun out of Boggs. One of them says—

"Wonder who he's a gwyne to chaw up this time. If he'd a-chawed up all the men he's ben a gwyne to chaw up in the last twenty year he'd have considerable ruputation, now."

Another one says, "I wisht old Boggs 'd threaten me, 'cuz then I'd know I warn't gwyne to die for a thousan' year."

Boggs comes a-tearing along on his horse, whooping and yelling like an Injun, and singing out—

"Cler the track, thar. I'm on the waw-path, and the price uv coffins is a gwyne to raise."

He was drunk, and weaving about in his saddle; he was over fifty year old, and had a very red face. Everybody yelled at him, and laughed at him, and sassed him, and he sassed back, and said he'd attend to them and lay them out in their regular turns, but he couldn't wait now because he'd come to town to kill old Colonel Sherburn, and his motto was, "meat first, and spoon vittles to top off on."

He see me, and rode up and says—

"Whar'd you come f'm, boy? You prepared to die?"

Then he rode on. I was scared, but a man says—

"He don't mean nothing; he's always a carryin' on like that when he's drunk. He's the best-naturedest old fool in Arkansaw—never hurt nobody, drunk nor sober."

Boggs rode up before the biggest store in town and bent his head down so he could see under the curtain of the awning and yells—

"Come out here, Sherburn! Come out and meet the man you've swindled. You're the houn' I'm after, and I'm a gwyne to have you, too!"

And so he went on, calling Sherburn everything he could lay his tongue to, and the whole street packed with people listening and laughing and going on. By and by a proud-looking man about fifty-five—and he was a heap the best dressed man in that town, too—steps out of the store, and the crowd drops back on each side to let him come. He says to Boggs, mighty ca'm and slow—he says:

"I'm tired of this; but I'll endure it till one o'clock. Till one o'clock, mind—no longer. If you open your mouth against me only once, after that time, you can't travel so far but I will find you."

Then he turns and goes in. The crowd looked mighty sober; nobody stirred, and there warn't no more laughing. Boggs rode off blackguarding Sherburn as loud as he could yell, all down the street; and pretty soon back he comes and stops before the store, still keeping it up. Some men crowded around him and tried to get him to shut up, but he wouldn't; they told him it would be one o'clock in about fifteen minutes, and so he *must* go home—he must go right away. But it didn't do no good. He cussed away, with all his might, and threw his hat down in the mud and rode over it, and pretty soon away he went a-raging down the street again, with his gray hair a-flying. Everybody that could get a chance at him tried their best to coax him off of his horse so they could lock him up and get him sober; but it warn't no use—up the street he would tear again, and give Sherburn another cussing. By and by somebody says:

"Go for his daughter!—quick, go for his daughter; sometimes he'll listen to her. If anybody can persuade him, she can."

So somebody started on a run. I walked down street a ways and stopped. In about five or ten minutes, here comes Boggs again—but not on his horse. He was a-reeling across the street towards me, bare-headed, with a friend on both sides of him a-holt of his arms and hurrying him along. He was quiet, and looked uneasy; and he warn't hanging back any, but was doing some of the hurrying himself. Somebody sings out—

"Boggs!"

I looked over there to see who said it, and it was that Colonel Sherburn. He was standing perfectly still, in the street, and had a pistol raised in his right hand—not aiming it, but holding it out with the barrel tilted up towards the sky. The same second I see a young girl coming on the run, and two men with her. Boggs and the men turned round, to see who called him, and when they see the pistol the men jumped to one side, and the pistol barrel come down slow and steady to a level—both barrels cocked. Boggs throws up both of his hands and says, "O Lord, don't shoot!" Bang! goes the first shot, and he staggers back, clawing at the air—bang! goes the second one, and he tumbles backwards onto the ground, heavy and solid, with his arms spread out. That young girl screamed out, and comes rushing, and down she throws herself on her father, crying, and saying, "Oh, he's killed him, he's killed him!" The crowd closed up around them, and shouldered and jammed one another, with their necks stretched, trying to see, and people on the inside trying to shove them back and shouting, "Back, back! give him air, give him air!"

Colonel Sherburn he tossed his pistol onto the ground, and turned around on his heels and walked off.[133]

---

133. Sherburn is not necessarily a real colonel, despite his facility with a gun. Americans at the time, especially in the South, were fond of titles. British authors of American travelogues in the mid-19th century noted with amusement that in this most egalitarian of countries, whose founding document proclaimed that "All men are created equal," honorific but meaningless titles abounded. One traveler said that "in the South all tall men were generals, all stout men judges, and all men of medium proportions captains and colonels"

They took Boggs to a little drug store, the crowd pressing around, just the same, and the whole town following, and I rushed and got a good place at the window, where I was close to him and could see in. They laid him on the floor, and put one large Bible under his head, and opened another one and spread it on his breast—but they tore open his shirt first, and I seen where one of the bullets went in. He made about a dozen long gasps, his breast lifting the Bible up when he drawed in his breath, and letting it down again when he breathed it out—and after that he laid still; he was dead. Then they pulled his daughter away from him, screaming and crying, and took her off. She was about sixteen, and very sweet and gentle-looking, but awful pale and scared.

Well, pretty soon the whole town was there, squirming and scrouging and pushing and shoving to get at the window and have a look, but people that had the places wouldn't give them up, and folks behind them was saying all the time, "Say, now, you've looked enough, you fellows; 'tain't right and 'tain't fair, for you to stay thar all the time, and never give nobody a chance; other folks has their rights as well as you."

There was considerable jawing back, so I slid out, thinking maybe there was going to be trouble. The streets was full, and everybody was excited. Everybody that seen the shooting was telling how it happened, and there was a big crowd packed around each one of these fellows, stretching their necks and listening. One long lanky man, with long hair and a big white fur stove-pipe hat on the back of his head, and a crooked-handled cane, marked out the places on the ground where Boggs stood, and where Sherburn stood, and the people following him around from one place to t'other and watching everything he done, and bobbing their heads to show they understood, and stooping a little and resting their hands on their thighs to watch him mark the places on the ground with his cane; and then he stood up straight and stiff where Sherburn had stood, frowning and having his hat-brim down over his eyes, and sung out, "Boggs!" and then fetched his cane down slow to a level, and says "Bang!" staggered backwards, says "Bang!" again, and fell down flat on his back. The people that had seen the thing said he done it perfect; said it was just exactly the way it all happened. Then as much as a dozen people got out their bottles and treated him.

(Berger 1964, 60–61). In Twain's first novel, *The Gilded Age: A Tale of Today,* one of the main characters is introduced as "Colonel" Sellers, despite his apparent lack of military experience at the outset. Another, "Squire" Hawkins, is so-named in honor of his job as postmaster of a small town, and "as his wealth and popularity augmented, that title, by imperceptible stages, grew up into 'Judge'; indeed it based fair to swell into 'General' bye and bye" (Twain and Warner 1994, 55).

Well, by and by somebody said Sherburn ought to be lynched. In about a minute everybody was saying it; so away they went, mad and yelling, and snatching down every clothes-line they come to, to do the hanging with.

CHAPTER XXII.

THEY swarmed up towards Sherburn's house, a-whooping and yelling and raging like Injuns, and everything had to clear the way or get run over and tromped to mush, and it was awful to see. Children was heeling it ahead of the mob, screaming and trying to get out of the way; and every window along the road was full of women's heads, and there was nigger boys in every tree, and bucks and wenches looking over every fence; and as soon as the mob would get nearly to them they would break and skaddle back out of reach. Lots of the women and girls was crying and taking on, scared most to death.

They swarmed up in front of Sherburn's palings as thick as they could jam together, and you couldn't hear yourself think for the noise. It was a little twenty-foot yard. Some sung out "Tear down the fence! tear down the fence!" Then there was a racket of ripping and tearing and smashing, and down she goes, and the front wall of the crowd begins to roll in like a wave.

Just then Sherburn steps out on to the roof of his little front porch, with a double-barrel gun in his hand, and takes his stand, perfectly ca'm and deliberate, not saying a word. The racket stopped, and the wave sucked back.

Sherburn never said a word—just stood there, looking down. The stillness was awful creepy and uncomfortable. Sherburn run his eye slow along the crowd; and wherever it struck, the people tried a little to outgaze him, but they couldn't; they dropped their eyes and looked sneaky. Then pretty soon Sherburn sort of laughed; not the pleasant kind, but the kind that makes you feel like when you are eating bread that's got sand in it.

Then he says, slow and scornful:

"The idea of *you* lynching anybody! It's amusing. The idea of you thinking you had pluck enough to lynch a *man*! Because you're brave enough to tar and feather poor friendless cast-out women that come along here, did that make you think you had grit enough to lay your hands on a *man*? Why, a *man's* safe in the hands of ten thousand of your kind—as long as it's daytime and you're not behind him.

"Do I know you? I know you clear through. I was born and raised in the South, and I've lived in the North; so I know the average all around. The average man's a coward. In the North he lets anybody walk over him that wants to, and goes home and prays for a humble spirit to bear it. In the South one man, all by himself, has stopped a stage full of men, in the daytime, and robbed the lot. Your newspapers call you a brave people so much that you think you *are* braver than any other people—whereas you're just *as* brave, and no braver. Why don't your juries hang murderers? Because they're afraid the man's friends will shoot them in the back, in the dark—and it's just what they *would* do.[134]

"So they always acquit; and then a *man* goes in the night, with a hundred masked cowards at his back, and lynches the rascal. Your mistake is, that you didn't bring a man with you; that's one mistake, and the other is that you didn't come in the dark, and fetch your masks. You brought *part* of a man—Buck Harkness, there—and if you hadn't had him to start you, you'd a taken it out in blowing.

"You didn't want to come. The average man don't like trouble and danger. *You* don't like trouble and danger. But if only *half* a man—like Buck Harkness, there—shouts 'Lynch him! lynch him!' you're afraid to back down—afraid you'll be found out to be what you are—*cowards*—and so you raise a yell, and hang yourselves onto that half-a-man's coattail, and come raging up here, swearing what big things you're going to do. The pitifulest thing out is a mob; that's what an army is—a mob; they don't fight with courage that's born in them, but with courage that's borrowed from their mass, and from their officers. But a mob without any *man* at the head of it, is *beneath* pitifulness. Now the thing for *you* to do, is to droop your tails and go home and crawl in a hole. If any real lynching's going to be done, it will be done in the dark, Southern fashion; and when they come they'll bring their masks, and fetch a *man* along. Now *leave*—and take your half-a-man with you"—tossing his gun up across his left arm and cocking it, when he says this.[135]

---

134. A similar shooting and acquittal occurred in Hannibal when Clemens was nine or ten years old. A wealthy merchant killed an abusive, drunk farmer in broad daylight in front of several witnesses. He was acquitted, though it brought "a cloud on him—a social chill—and he moved away" (Twain 2010, 1:158, 514).

135. Lynchings were an all too common means of frontier justice. Most famously, lynchings reflected racial terrorism or "mob justice" in the sense of impatience with the legal process. In some cases lynch mobs took a prisoner away and executed him out of suspicion that the sheriff, judge, and jury would be too fearful of the prisoner and his allies. Members of a masked mob operating at nighttime might be just as cowardly but would at least have safety in numbers and anonymity. Sherburn's disdain for lynchers reflects Twain's own. In Twain's "A Double-Barreled Detective Story," a sheriff condemns lynch mobs as cowardly and says that a "sheriff that lets a mob take a prisoner away from him is the lowest-down coward there is." He adds, "By the statistics there was a hundred and eighty-two of them drawing sneak pay in America last year" (2012, 497).

The crowd washed back sudden, and then broke all apart, and went tearing off every which way, and Buck Harkness he heeled it after them, looking tolerable cheap. I could a staid, if I'd a wanted to, but I didn't want to.

I went to the circus, and loafed around the back side till the watchman went by, and then dived in under the tent. I had my twenty-dollar gold piece and some other money, but I reckoned I better save it, because there ain't no telling how soon you are going to need it, away from home and amongst strangers, that way. You can't be too careful. I ain't opposed to spending money on circuses, when there ain't no other way, but there ain't no use in *wasting* it on them.

It was a real bully circus. It was the splendidest sight that ever was, when they all come riding in, two and two, a gentleman and lady, side by side, the men just in their drawers and undershirts, and no shoes nor stirrups, and resting their hands on their thighs, easy and comfortable— there must a been twenty of them—and every lady with a lovely complexion, and perfectly beautiful, and looking just like a gang of real sure-enough queens, and dressed in clothes that cost millions of dollars, and just littered with diamonds. It was a powerful fine sight; I never see anything so lovely. And then one by one they got up and stood, and went a-weaving around the ring so gentle and wavy and graceful, the men looking ever so tall and airy and straight, with their heads bobbing and skimming along, away up there under the tent-roof, and every lady's rose-leafy dress flapping soft and silky around her hips, and she looking like the most loveliest parasol.

And then faster and faster they went, all of them dancing, first one foot stuck out in the air and then the other, the horses leaning more and more, and the ring-master going round and round the centre-pole, cracking his whip and shouting "hi!—hi!" and the clown cracking jokes behind him; and by and by all hands dropped the reins, and every lady put her knuckles

---

In an acerbic essay, "The United States of Lyncherdom," Twain harshly decried the lynching of three blacks in Missouri and the practice of lynching in general as well as the spinelessness of people who went along with them. Although he noted that lynchings had occurred in western states and pessimistically predicted that the practice would spread to the Northeast, he quoted a report that said that Alabama, Mississippi, Louisiana, and Georgia were "the worst offenders" (Twain 1979, 183). Twain was so horrified by the lynching of black Americans that he had begun collecting news reports of lynchings for the purpose of writing a book that he talked of about lynching. His publisher protested that the book would be career suicide in the South (Pettit 1974, 135–136). Twain eventually agreed: "I shouldn't have even half a friend left, after it issued from the press." The "Lyncherdom" essay was not published until after his death (Mensh and Mensh 2001, 76).

on her hips and every gentleman folded his arms, and then how the horses did lean over and hump themselves! And so, one after the other they all skipped off into the ring, and made the sweetest bow I ever see, and then scampered out, and everybody clapped their hands and went just about wild.

Well, all through the circus they done the most astonishing things; and all the time that clown carried on so it most killed the people. The ring-master couldn't ever say a word to him but he was back at him quick as a wink with the funniest things a body ever said; and how he ever *could* think of so many of them, and so sudden and so pat, was what I couldn't noway understand. Why, I couldn't a thought of them in a year. And by and by a drunk man tried to get into the ring—said he wanted to ride; said he could ride as well as anybody that ever was. They argued and tried to keep him out, but he wouldn't listen, and the whole show come to a standstill. Then the people begun to holler at him and make fun of him, and that made him mad, and he begun to rip and tear; so that stirred up the people, and a lot of men begun to pile down off of the benches and swarm towards the ring, saying, "Knock him down! throw him out!" and one or two women begun to scream. So, then, the ring-master he made a little speech, and said he hoped there wouldn't be no disturbance, and if the man would promise he wouldn't make no more trouble, he would let him ride, if he thought he could stay on the horse. So everybody laughed and said all right, and the man got on. The minute he was on, the horse begun to rip and tear and jump and cavort around, with two circus men hanging on to his bridle trying to hold him, and the drunk man hanging on to his neck, and his heels flying in the air every jump, and the whole crowd of people standing up shouting and laughing till tears rolled down. And at last, sure enough, all the circus men could do, the horse broke loose, and away he went like the very nation, round and round the ring, with that sot laying down on him and hanging to his neck, with first one leg hanging most to the ground on one side, and then t'other one on t'other side, and the people just crazy. It warn't funny to me, though; I was all of a tremble to see his danger. But pretty soon he struggled up astraddle and grabbed the bridle, a-reeling this way and that; and the next minute he sprung up and dropped the bridle and stood! and the horse a-going like a house afire too. He just stood up there, a-sailing around as easy and comfortable as if he warn't ever drunk in his life—and then he begun to pull off his clothes and sling them. He shed them so thick they kind of clogged up the air, and altogether he shed seventeen suits. And then, there he was, slim and handsome, and dressed the gaudiest and prettiest you ever saw, and he lit into that horse with his whip and made him fairly hum—and finally skipped off, and made his bow and danced off to the dressing-room, and everybody just a-howling with pleasure and astonishment.

Then the ring-master he see how he had been fooled, and he *was* the sickest ring-master you ever see, I reckon. Why, it was one of his own men! He had got up that joke all out of his own head, and never let on to nobody. Well, I felt sheepish enough, to be took in so, but I wouldn't a been in that ring-master's place, not for a thousand dollars. I don't know; there may be bullier circuses than what that one was, but I never struck them yet. Anyways, it was plenty good enough for *me;* and wherever I run across it, it can have all of *my* custom, every time.

Well, that night we had *our* show; but there warn't only about twelve people there; just enough to pay expenses. And they laughed all the time, and that made the duke mad; and everybody left, anyway, before the show was over, but one boy which was asleep. So the duke said these Arkansaw lunkheads couldn't come up to Shakespeare; what they wanted was low comedy—and maybe something ruther worse than low comedy, he reckoned. He said he could size their style. So next morning he got some big sheets of wrapping paper and some black paint, and drawed off some handbills, and stuck them up all over the village. The bills said:

AT THE COURT HOUSE!
FOR 3 NIGHTS ONLY!
The World-Renowned Tragedians
DAVID GARRICK THE YOUNGER!
AND
EDMUND KEAN THE ELDER!
*Of the London and Continental
Theatres,*
In their Thrilling Tragedy of
THE KING'S CAMELOPARD
OR
THE ROYAL NONESUCH!!!
Admission 50 *cents.*

Then at the bottom was the biggest line of all—which said:

LADIES AND CHILDREN NOT ADMITTED.

"There," says he, "if that line don't fetch them, I dont know Arkansaw!"[136]

---

136. The spelling "Arkansaw" is classic Twain dialect, but ironically enough it is the original spelling of the Arkansas Territory, back when it was carved out of the Missouri

CHAPTER XXIII.

WELL, all day him and the king was hard at it, rigging up a stage, and a curtain and a row of candles for footlights; and that night the house was jam full of men in no time. When the place couldn't hold no more, the duke he quit tending door and went around the back way and come on to the stage and stood up before the curtain, and made a little speech, and praised up this tragedy, and said it was the most thrillingest one that ever was; and so he went on a-bragging about the tragedy, and about Edmund Kean the Elder, which was to play the main principal part in it; and at last when he'd got everybody's expectations up high enough, he rolled up the curtain, and the next minute the king come a-prancing out on all fours, naked; and he was painted all over, ring-streaked-and-striped, all sorts of colors, as splendid as a rainbow. And—but never mind the rest of his out-fit; it was just wild, but it was awful funny. The people most killed themselves laughing; and when the king got done capering, and capered off behind the scenes, they roared and clapped and stormed and haw-hawed till he come back and done it over again; and after that, they made him do it another time. Well, it would make a cow laugh to see the shines that old idiot cut.

Then the duke he lets the curtain down, and bows to the people, and says the great tragedy will be performed only two nights more, on ac-counts of pressing London engagements, where the seats is all sold already for it in Drury Lane; and then he makes them another bow, and says if he has succeeded in pleasing them and instructing them, he will be deeply obleeged if they will mention it to their friends and get them to come and see it.

Twenty people sings out:

"What, is it over? Is that *all*?"

The duke says yes. Then there was a fine time. Everybody sings out, "Sold!" and rose up mad, and was agoing for that stage and them tragedi-ans. But a big, fine looking man jumps up on a bench and shouts:

Territory (the rest of the Louisiana Territory after Louisiana was admitted to statehood in 1812). The spelling came from explorer Zebulon Pike, for whom Pike County, Missouri, is named, so perhaps it is appropriate that Huck pretends to be from Pike County while they are in Arkansas. The 1819 act of Congress that created the territory stuck with Pike's spell-ing. The biggest push for the "Arkansas" spelling came from the publisher of the *Arkansas Gazette,* who emphatically believed that it was the superior spelling and always used it, even changing "Arkansaw" to "Arkansas" when he reprinted the congressional bill that created the territory. The matter was not officially resolved until 1881, when the state legis-lature passed a bill establishing "Arkansas" as the correct spelling and "Arkansaw" as the correct pronunciation ("ARKan-SAW or Ar-KANSAS" n.d.; Shinn 1908, 20–22).

"Hold on! Just a word, gentlemen." They stopped to listen. "We are sold—mighty badly sold. But we don't want to be the laughing-stock of this whole town, I reckon, and never hear the last of this thing as long as we live. *No.* What we want, is to go out of here quiet, and talk this show up, and sell the *rest* of the town! Then we'll all be in the same boat. Ain't that sensible?" ("You bet it is!—the jedge is right!" everybody sings out.) "All right, then—not a word about any sell. Go along home, and advise everybody to come and see the tragedy."

Next day you couldn't hear nothing around that town but how splendid that show was. House was jammed again, that night, and we sold this crowd the same way. When me and the king and the duke got home to the raft, we all had a supper; and by and by, about midnight, they made Jim and me back her out and float her down the middle of the river and fetch her in and hide her about two mile below town.

The third night the house was crammed again—and they warn't newcomers this time, but people that was at the show the other two nights. I stood by the duke at the door, and I see that every man that went in had his pockets bulging, or something muffled up under his coat—and I see it warn't no perfumery, neither, not by a long sight. I smelt sickly eggs by the barrel, and rotten cabbages, and such things; and if I know the signs of a dead cat being around, and I bet I do, there was sixty-four of them went in. I shoved in there for a minute, but it was too various for me; I couldn't stand it. Well, when the place couldn't hold no more people, the duke he give a fellow a quarter and told him to tend door for him a minute, and then he started around for the stage door, I after him; but the minute we turned the corner and was in the dark, he says:

"Walk fast, now, till you get away from the houses, and then shin for the raft like the dickens was after you!"

I done it, and he done the same. We struck the raft at the same time, and in less than two seconds we was gliding down stream, all dark and still, and edging towards the middle of the river, nobody saying a word. I reckoned the poor king was in for a gaudy time of it with the audience; but nothing of the sort; pretty soon he crawls out from under the wigwam, and says:

"Well, how'd the old thing pan out this time, duke?".

He hadn't been up town at all.

We never showed a light till we was about ten mile below the village. Then we lit up and had a supper, and the king and the duke fairly laughed their bones loose over the way they'd served them people. The duke says:

"Greenhorns, flatheads! *I* knew the first house would keep mum and let the rest of the town get roped in; and I knew they'd lay for us the third night, and consider it was *their* turn now. Well, it *is* their turn, and I'd give something to know how much they'd take for it. I *would* just like to know how they're putting in their opportunity. They can turn it into a picnic, if they want to—they brought plenty provisions."

Them rapscallions took in four hundred and sixty-five dollars in that three nights. I never see money hauled in by the wagon-load like that, before.

By and by, when they was asleep and snoring, Jim says:

"Don't it 'sprise you, de way dem kings carries on, Huck?"

"No," I says, "it don't."

"Why don't it, Huck?"

"Well, it don't, because it's in the breed. I reckon they're all alike."

"But, Huck, dese kings o' ourn is reglar rapscallions; dat's jist what dey is; dey's reglar rapscallions."

"Well, that's what I'm a-saying; all kings is mostly rapscallions, as fur as I can make out."

"Is dat so?"

"You read about them once—you'll see. Look at Henry the Eight; this 'n 's a Sunday-School Superintendent to *him.* And look at Charles Second, and Louis Fourteen, and Louis Fifteen, and James Second, and Edward Second, and Richard Third, and forty more; besides all them Saxon heptarchies that used to rip around so in old times and raise Cain. My, you ought to seen old Henry the Eight when he was in bloom. He *was* a blossom. He used to marry a new wife every day, and chop off her head next morning. And he would do it just as indifferent as if he was ordering up eggs. 'Fetch up Nell Gwynn,' he says. They fetch her up. Next morning, 'Chop off her head!' And they chop it off. 'Fetch up Jane Shore,' he says; and up she comes, Next morning, 'Chop off her head'—and they chop it off. 'Ring up Fair Rosamun.' Fair Rosamun answers the bell. Next morning, 'Chop off her head.' And he made every one of them tell him a tale every night; and he kept that up till he had hogged a thousand and one tales that way, and then he put them all in a book, and called it Domesday Book— which was a good name and stated the case. You don't know kings, Jim, but I know them; and this old rip[137] of ourn is one of the cleanest I've struck in history. Well, Henry he takes a notion he wants to get up some trouble with this country. How does he go at it—give notice?—give the country a show? No. All of a sudden he heaves all the tea in Boston Harbor overboard, and whacks out a declaration of independence, and dares them to come on. That was *his* style—he never give anybody a chance. He had suspicions of his

---

137. "Rip" apparently comes from "reprobate," that is, a "man of loose character; vicious, reckless and worthless person," and its usage dates back to about 1815 (Online Etymlogy Dictionary). "Rip" is rarely used today to describe a person, but its current slang usage similarly denotes something worthless, as in "I don't give a rip" (*Webster's Ninth New Collegiate Dictionary* 1991, 1017).

father, the Duke of Wellington. Well, what did he do?—ask him to show up? No—drownded him in a butt of mamsey, like a cat. Spose people left money laying around where he was—what did he do? He collared it. Spose he contracted to do a thing; and you paid him, and didn't set down there and see that he done it—what did he do? He always done the other thing. Spose he opened his mouth—what then? If he didn't shut it up powerful quick, he'd lose a lie, every time. That's the kind of a bug Henry was; and if we'd a had him along 'stead of our kings, he'd a fooled that town a heap worse than ourn done. I don't say that ourn is lambs, because they ain't, when you come right down to the cold facts; but they ain't nothing to *that* old ram, anyway. All I say is, kings is kings, and you got to make allowances. Take them all around, they're a mighty ornery lot. It's the way they're raised."

"But dis one do *smell* so like de nation, Huck."

"Well, they all do, Jim. *We* can't help the way a king smells; history don't tell no way."

"Now de duke, he's a tolerble likely man, in some ways."

"Yes, a duke's different. But not very different. This one's a middling hard lot, for a duke. When he's drunk, there ain't no near-sighted man could tell him from a king."

"Well, anyways, I doan' hanker for no mo' un um, Huck. Dese is all I kin stan'."

"It's the way I feel, too, Jim. But we've got them on our hands, and we got to remember what they are, and make allowances. Sometimes I wish we could hear of a country that's out of kings."

What was the use to tell Jim these warn't real kings and dukes? It wouldn't a done no good; and besides, it was just as I said: you couldn't tell them from the real kind.

I went to sleep, and Jim didn't call me when it was my turn. He often done that. When I waked up, just at daybreak, he was sitting there with his head down betwixt his knees, moaning and mourning to himself. I didn't take notice, nor let on. I knowed what it was about. He was thinking about his wife and his children, away up yonder, and he was low and homesick; because he hadn't ever been away from home before in his life; and I do believe he cared just as much for his people as white folks does for their'n. It don't seem natural, but I reckon it's so. He was often moaning and mourning that way, nights, when he judged I was asleep, and saying, "Po' little 'Lizabeth! po' little Johnny! it mighty hard; I spec' I ain't ever gwyne to see you no mo', no mo'!" He was a mighty good nigger, Jim was.

But this time I somehow got to talking to him about his wife and young ones; and by and by he says:

"What makes me feel so bad dis time 'uz bekase I hear sumpn over yonder on de bank like a whack, er a slam, while ago, en it mine me er de time I treat my little 'Lizabeth so ornery. She warn't on'y 'bout fo' year ole, en she tuck de sk'yarlet fever, en had a powful rough spell; but she got well, en one day she was a-stannin' aroun', en I says to her, I says:

"'Shet de do'.'

"She never done it; jis' stood dah, kiner smilin' up at me. It make me mad; en I says agin, mighty loud, I says:

"'Doan' you hear me?—shet de do'!'

"She jis stood de same way, kiner smilin' up. I was a-bilin'! I says:

"'I lay I *make* you mine!'

"En wid dat I fetch' her a slap side de head dat sont her a-sprawlin'. Den I went into de yuther room, en 'uz gone 'bout ten minutes; en when I come back, dah was dat do' a-stannin' open *yit,* en dat chile stannin' mos' right in it, a-lookin' down and mournin', en de tears runnin' down. My, but I *wuz* mad! I was agwyne for de chile, but jis' den—it was a do' dat open innerds—jis' den, 'long come de wind en slam it to, behine de chile, ker-*blam!*—en my lan', de chile never move'! My breff mos' hop outer me; en I feel so—so—I doan' know *how* I feel. I crope out, all a-tremblin', en crope aroun' en open de do' easy en slow, en poke my head in behine de chile, sof' en still, en all uv a sudden I says *pow!* jis' as loud as I could yell. *She never budge!* Oh, Huck, I bust out a-cryin' en grab her up in my arms, en say, 'Oh, de po' little thing! de Lord God Amighty fogive po' ole Jim, kaze he never gwyne to fogive hisself as long's he live!' Oh, she was plumb deef en dumb, Huck, plumb deef en dumb—en I'd ben a-treat'n her so!"

CHAPTER XXIV.

NEXT day, towards night, we laid up under a little willow tow-head out in the middle, where there was a village on each side of the river, and the duke and the king begun to lay out a plan for working them towns. Jim he spoke to the duke, and said he hoped it wouldn't take but a few hours, because it got mighty heavy and tiresome to him when he had to lay all day in the wigwam tied with the rope. You see, when we left him all alone we had to tie him, because if anybody happened on to him all by himself and not tied, it wouldn't look much like he was a runaway nigger, you know. So the duke said it *was* kind of hard to have to lay roped all day, and he'd cipher out some way to get around it.

He was uncommon bright, the duke was, and he soon struck it. He dressed Jim up in King Lear's outfit—it was a long curtain-calico gown, and a white horse-hair wig and whiskers; and then he took his theatre-paint and painted Jim's face and hands and ears and neck all over a dead dull solid blue, like a man that's been drownded nine days. Blamed if he warn't the horriblest looking outrage I ever see. Then the duke took and wrote out a sign on a shingle so—

Sick Arab—but harmless when not out of his head.

And he nailed that shingle to a lath, and stood the lath up four or five foot in front of the wigwam. Jim was satisfied. He said it was a sight better than laying tied a couple of years every day and trembling all over every time there was a sound. The duke told him to make himself free and easy, and if anybody ever come meddling around, he must hop out of the wigwam, and carry on a little, and fetch a howl or two like a wild beast, and he reckoned they would light out and leave him alone. Which was sound enough judgment; but you take the average man, and he wouldn't wait for him to howl. Why, he didn't only look like he was dead, he looked considerable more than that.

These rapscallions wanted to try the Nonesuch again, because there was so much money in it, but they judged it wouldn't be safe, because maybe the news might a worked along down by this time. They couldn't hit no project that suited, exactly; so at last the duke said he reckoned he'd lay off and work his brains an hour or two and see if he couldn't put up something on the Arkansaw village; and the king he allowed he would drop over to t'other village, without any plan, but just trust in Providence to lead him the profitable way—meaning the devil, I reckon. We had all bought store clothes where we stopped last; and now the king put his'n on, and he told me to put mine on. I done it, of course. The king's duds was all black, and he did look real swell and starchy. I never knowed how clothes could change a body before.[138] Why, before, he looked like the orneriest old rip that ever was; but now, when he'd take off his new white beaver and make a bow and do a smile, he looked that grand and good and pious that you'd say he had walked right out of the ark, and maybe was old Leviticus himself. Jim cleaned up the canoe, and I got my paddle ready. There was a big steamboat laying at the shore away up under the point, about three mile above the town—been there a couple of hours, taking on freight. Says the king:

"Seein' how I'm dressed, I reckon maybe I better arrive down from St. Louis or Cincinnati, or some other big place.[139] Go for the steamboat, Huckleberry; we'll come down to the village on her."

---

138. Notably, even the small town where they had stopped earlier has a store that sells clothes. Early in colonial life it had been customary for families to make their own clothes, and some still did, but factory-made store-bought clothes had become the norm, at least for men. Frontier stores tended to be general stores, selling a little of everything. They also tended to sprout up soon after settlement, such as in Twain's home county of Marion County, Missouri, where the first two general stores were established during the first big year of settlement, 1820 (Holcombe 1884, 148). Arkansas in 1840 was still small, with only 97,574 residents, and had only been a state for a few years, but it already had 263 retail stores (United States Department of State 1841, 360).

139. Aside from New Orleans, the river cities of Cincinnati and St. Louis were the largest American cities west of the original colonies. Both rose to great heights on account of

I didn't have to be ordered twice, to go and take a steamboat ride. I fetched the shore a half a mile above the village, and then went scooting along the bluff bank in the easy water. Pretty soon we come to a nice inno-cent-looking young country jake setting on a log swabbing the sweat off of his face, for it was powerful warm weather; and he had a couple of big carpet-bags by him.

"Run her nose in shore," says the king. I done it. "Wher' you bound for, young man?"

"For the steamboat; going to Orleans."

"Git aboard," says the king. "Hold on a minute, my servant 'll he'p you with them bags. Jump out and he'p the gentleman, Adolphus"—meaning me, I see.

I done so, and then we all three started on again. The young chap was mighty thankful; said it was tough work toting his baggage such weather. He asked the king where he was going, and the king told him he'd come down the river and landed at the other village this morning, and now he was going up a few mile to see an old friend on a farm up there. The young fellow says:

"When I first see you I says to myself, 'It's Mr. Wilks, sure, and he come mighty near getting here in time.' But then I says again, 'No, I reckon it ain't him, or else he wouldn't be paddling up the river.' You *ain't* him, are you?"

"No, my name's Blodgett—Elexander Blodgett—*Reverend* Elexander Blodgett, I s'pose I must say, as I'm one o' the Lord's poor servants. But still I'm jist as able to be sorry for Mr. Wilks for not arriving in time, all the same, if he's missed anything by it—which I hope he hasn't."

---

the 19th-century transportation revolution. St. Louis was well situated on a bluff high atop the Mississippi River and near the mouth of the Missouri River, which offered a "gateway to the west." It was originally settled centuries ago by Native American tribes. French ex-plorers colonized it in the late 17th century and established one of their larger North Ameri-can settlements. By the time of the Louisiana Purchase, St. Louis was well developed by frontier standards. When the invention of the steamboat slashed upriver transportation costs, St. Louis was one of the prime beneficiaries.

Cincinnati was well situated on the Ohio River, another of the largest tributaries of the Mississippi River. It benefited from all three key phases of the transportation revolution: steamboats; canals, notably the Miami and Erie Canal that connected it to the Great Lakes; and railroads, notably the railroad lines in the Pennsylvania Main Line, a network of canals and railroads that ultimately connected the Ohio River to the East Coast by connecting Pittsburgh, the source of the river, to Philadelphia. Aided also by rich coal and iron deposits and an already large population of farmers, Ohio became one of the nation's key industrial states by midcentury. In 1860, on the eve of the Civil War, Cincinnati produced more manu-facturing output than any U.S. city besides New York and Philadelphia (Licht 1995, 112–114).

"Well, he don't miss any property by it, because he'll get that all right; but he's missed seeing his brother Peter die—which he mayn't mind, nobody can tell as to that—but his brother would a give anything in this world to see *him* before he died; never talked about nothing else all these three weeks; hadn't seen him since they was boys together—and hadn't ever seen his brother William at all—that's the deef and dumb one—William ain't more than thirty or thirty-five. Peter and George were the only ones that come out here; George was the married brother; him and his wife both died last year. Harvey and William's the only ones that's left now; and, as I was saying, they haven't got here in time."

"Did anybody send 'em word?"

"Oh, yes; a month or two ago, when Peter was first took; because Peter said then that he sorter felt like he warn't going to get well this time. You see, he was pretty old, and George's g'yirls was too young to be much company for him, except Mary Jane the red-headed one; and so he was kinder lonesome after George and his wife died, and didn't seem to care much to live. He most desperately wanted to see Harvey—and William too, for that matter—because he was one of them kind that can't bear to make a will. He left a letter behind for Harvey, and said he'd told in it where his money was hid, and how he wanted the rest of the property divided up so George's g'yirls would be all right—for George didn't leave nothing. And that letter was all they could get him to put a pen to."

"Why do you reckon Harvey don't come? Wher' does he live?"

"Oh, he lives in England—Sheffield—preaches there—hasn't ever been in this country. He hasn't had any too much time—and besides he mightn't a got the letter at all, you know."

"Too bad, too bad he couldn't a lived to see his brothers, poor soul. You going to Orleans, you say?"

"Yes, but that ain't only a part of it. I'm going in a ship, next Wednesday, for Ryo Janeero, where my uncle lives."

"It's a pretty long journey. But it'll be lovely; I wisht I was agoing. Is Mary Jane the oldest? How old is the others?"

"Mary Jane's nineteen, Susan's fifteen, and Joanna's about fourteen—that's the one that gives herself to good works and has a hare-lip."

"Poor things! to be left alone in the cold world so."

"Well, they could be worse off. Old Peter had friends, and they ain't going to let them come to no harm. There's Hobson, the Babtis' preacher; and Deacon Lot Hovey, and Ben Rucker, and Abner Shackleford, and Levi Bell, the lawyer; and Dr. Robinson, and their wives, and the widow Bartley, and—well, there's a lot of them; but these are the ones that Peter was thickest with, and used to write about sometimes, when he wrote home; so Harvey 'll know where to look for friends when he gets here."

Well, the old man went on asking questions till he just fairly emptied that young fellow. Blamed if he didn't inquire about everybody and everything in that blessed town, and all about the Wilkses; and about Peter's business—which was a tanner; and about George's—which was a carpenter; and about Harvey's—which was a dissentering minister; and so on, and so on. Then he says:

"What did you want to walk all the way up to the steamboat for?"

"Because she's a big Orleans boat, and I was afeard she mightn't stop there. When they're deep they won't stop for a hail. A Cincinnati boat will, but this is a St. Louis one."

"Was Peter Wilks well off?"

"Oh, yes, pretty well off. He had houses and land, and it's reckoned he left three or four thousand in cash hid up som'ers."

"When did you say he died?"

"I didn't say, but it was last night."

"Funeral to-morrow, likely?"

"Yes, 'bout the middle of the day."

"Well, it's all terrible sad; but we've all got to go, one time or another. So what we want to do is to be prepared; then we're all right."

"Yes, sir, it's the best way. Ma used to always say that."

When we struck the boat, she was about done loading, and pretty soon she got off. The king never said nothing about going aboard, so I lost my ride, after all. When the boat was gone the king made me paddle up another mile to a lonesome place, and then he got ashore and says:

"Now hustle back, right off, and fetch the duke up here, and the new carpet-bags. And if he's gone over to t'other side, go over there and git him. And tell him to git himself up regardless. Shove along, now."

I see what *he* was up to; but I never said nothing, of course. When I got back with the duke, we hid the canoe, and then they set down on a log, and the king told him everything, just like the young fellow had said it—every last word of it. And all the time he was a doing it, he tried to talk like an Englishman; and he done it pretty well, too, for a slouch. I can't imitate him, and so I ain't agoing to try to; but he really done it pretty good. Then he says:

"How are you on the deef and dumb, Bilgewater?"

The duke said, leave him alone for that; said he had played a deef and dumb person on the histrionic boards. So then they waited for a steamboat.

About the middle of the afternoon a couple of little boats come along, but they didn't come from high enough up the river; but at last there was a big one, and they hailed her. She sent out her yawl, and we went aboard, and she was from Cincinnati; and when they found we only wanted to go four or five mile they was booming mad, and gave us a cussing, and said they wouldn't land us. But the king was ca'm. He says:

"If gentlemen kin afford to pay a dollar a mile apiece, to be took on and put off in a yawl, a steamboat kin afford to carry 'em, can't it?"

So they softened down and said it was all right; and when we got to the village they yawled us ashore. About two dozen men flocked down, when they see the yawl a coming; and when the king says—

"Kin any of you gentlemen tell me wher' Mr. Peter Wilks lives?" they give a glance at one another, and nodded their heads, as much as to say, "What d' I tell you?" Then one of them says, kind of soft and gentle:

"I'm sorry sir, but the best we can do is to tell you where he *did* live yesterday evening."

Sudden as winking, the ornery old cretur went all to smash, and fell up against the man, and put his chin on his shoulder, and cried down his back, and says:

"Alas, alas, our poor brother—gone, and we never got to see him; oh, it's *too*, too hard!"

Then he turns around, blubbering, and makes a lot of idiotic signs to the duke on his hands, and blamed if *he* didn't drop a carpet-bag and bust out a-crying. If they warn't the beatenest lot, them two frauds, that ever I struck.

Well, the men gethered around, and sympathized with them, and said all sorts of kind things to them, and carried their carpet-bags up the hill for them, and let them lean on them and cry, and told the king all about his brother's last moments, and the king he told it all over again on his hands to the duke, and both of them took on about that dead tanner like they'd lost the twelve disciples. Well, if ever I struck anything like it, I'm a nigger. It was enough to make a body ashamed of the human race.[140]

CHAPTER XXV.

THE news was all over town in two minutes, and you could see the people tearing down on the run, from every which way, some of them putting on their coats as they come. Pretty soon we was in the middle of a crowd, and the noise of the tramping was like a soldier-march. The

---

140. Of the many uses of "nigger" in *Adventures of Huckleberry Finn,* this one might be the most arresting. Twain appears to have been going for shock value and irony at the same time here. Huck and Jim are well into their journey together, have to come to depend on each other, and have forged a tight friendship, yet Huck still says "nigger" almost reflexively and without shame, using it to describe something both inferior and that he could never be.

windows and door-yards was full; and every minute somebody would say, over a fence:

"Is it *them*?"

And somebody trotting along with the gang would answer back and say:

"You bet it is."

When we got to the house, the street in front of it was packed, and the three girls was standing in the door. Mary Jane *was* red-headed, but that don't make no difference, she was most awful beautiful, and her face and her eyes was all lit up like glory, she was so glad her uncles was come. The king he spread his arms, and Mary Jane she jumped for them, and the hare-lip jumped for the duke, and there they *had* it! Everybody most, leastways women, cried for joy to see them meet again at last and have such good times.

Then the king he hunched the duke, private—I see him do it—and then he looked around and see the coffin, over in the corner on two chairs; so then, him and the duke, with a hand across each other's shoulder, and t'other hand to their eyes, walked slow and solemn over there, everybody dropping back to give them room, and all the talk and noise stopping, people saying "Sh!" and all the men taking their hats off and drooping their heads, so you could a heard a pin fall. And when they got there, they bent over and looked in the coffin, and took one sight, and then they bust out a crying so you could a heard them to Orleans, most; and then they put their arms around each other's necks, and hung their chins over each other's shoulders; and then for three minutes, or maybe four, I never see two men leak the way they done. And mind you, everybody was doing the same; and the place was that damp I never see anything like it. Then one of them got on one side of the coffin, and t'other on t'other side, and they kneeled down and rested their foreheads on the coffin, and let on to pray all to themselves. Well, when it come to that, it worked the crowd like you never see anything like it, and so everybody broke down and went to sobbing right out loud—the poor girls, too; and every woman, nearly, went up to the girls, without saying a word, and kissed them, solemn, on the forehead, and then put their hand on their head, and looked up towards the sky, with the tears running down, and then busted out and went off sobbing and swabbing, and give the next woman a show. I never see anything so disgusting.

Well, by and by the king he gets up and comes forward a little, and works himself up and slobbers out a speech, all full of tears and flapdoodle about its being a sore trial for him and his poor brother to lose the diseased, and to miss seeing diseased alive, after the long journey of four thousand mile, but it's a trial that's sweetened and sanctified to us by this dear sympathy and these holy tears, and so he thanks them out of his heart and out of his brother's heart, because out of their mouths they can't, words being too weak and cold, and all that kind of rot and slush, till it was just sickening; and then he blubbers out a pious goody-goody Amen, and turns himself loose and goes to crying fit to bust.

And the minute the words were out of his mouth somebody over in the crowd struck up the doxolojer, and everybody joined in with all their might, and it just warmed you up and made you feel as good as church letting out. Music *is* a good thing; and after all that soul-butter and hogwash, I never see it freshen up things so, and sound so honest and bully.

Then the king begins to work his jaw again, and says how him and his nieces would be glad if a few of the main principal friends of the family would take supper here with them this evening, and help set up with the ashes of the diseased; and says if his poor brother laying yonder could speak, he knows who he would name, for they was names that was very dear to him, and mentioned often in his letters; and so he will name the same, to-wit, as follows, vizz.:—Rev. Mr. Hobson, and Deacon Lot Hovey, and Mr. Ben Rucker, and Abner Shackleford, and Levi Bell, and Dr. Robinson, and their wives, and the widow Bartley.

Rev. Hobson and Dr. Robinson was down to the end of the town, a-hunting together; that is, I mean the doctor was shipping a sick man to t'other world, and the preacher was pinting him right. Lawyer Bell was away up to Louisville on business. But the rest was on hand, and so they all come and shook hands with the king and thanked him and talked to him; and then they shook hands with the duke, and didn't say nothing, but just kept a-smiling and bobbing their heads like a passel of sapheads whilst he made all sorts of signs with his hands and said "Goo-goo—goo-goo-goo," all the time, like a baby that can't talk.

So the king he blatted along, and managed to inquire about pretty much everybody and dog in town, by his name, and mentioned all sorts of little things that happened one time or another in the town, or to George's family, or to Peter—and he always let on that Peter wrote him the things, but that was a lie, he got every blessed one of them out of that young flathead that we canoed up to the steamboat.

Then Mary Jane she fetched the letter her father left behind, and the king he read it out loud and cried over it. It give the dwelling-house and three thousand dollars, gold, to the girls; and it give the tanyard (which was doing a good business), along with some other houses and land (worth about seven thousand), and three thousand dollars in gold to Harvey and William, and told where the six thousand cash was hid, down cellar.[141] So

---

141. This is a lot of money, perhaps an implausible amount, for an old tanner to accumulate. Tanning animal hides was an important business but apparently a fairly easy one to

these two frauds said they'd go and fetch it up, and have everything square and above-board; and told me to come with a candle. We shut the cellar door behind us, and when they found the bag they spilt it out on the floor, and it was a lovely sight, all them yaller-boys. My, the way the king's eyes did shine! He slaps the duke on the shoulder and says:

"Oh, *this* ain't bully nor noth'n! Oh, no, I reckon not! Why, Biljy, it beats the Nonesuch, *don't* it?"

The duke allowed it did. They pawed the yaller-boys, and sifted them through their fingers and let them jingle down on the floor; and the king says:

"It ain't no use talkin'; bein' brothers to a rich dead man, and representatives of furrin heirs that's got left, is the line for you and me, Bilge. Thish-yer comes of trust'n to Providence. It's the best way, in the long run. I've tried 'em all, and ther' ain't no better way."

Most everybody would a been satisfied with the pile, and took it on trust; but no, they must count it. So they counts it, and it comes out four hundred and fifteen dollars short. Says the king:

"Dern him, I wonder what he done with that four hunderd and fifteen dollars?"

They worried over that a while, and ransacked all around for it. Then the duke says:

"Well, he was a pretty sick man, and likely he made a mistake—I reckon that's the way of it. The best way's to let it go, and keep still about it. We can spare it."

"Oh, shucks, yes, we can *spare* it. I don't k'yer noth'n 'bout that—it's the *count* I'm thinkin' about. We want to be awful square and open and above-board, here, you know. We want to lug thish-yer money up stairs

---

enter. The typical tannery in the antebellum South was very small, with just a few employees and little capital invested. In Mississippi, where the Wilks scenes appear to take place, almost all of the tanneries had just one employee, and the average amount of capital invested was under $600 (Fischer et al. 2010, 366, 369; United States Department of State 1841, 362).

Again multiplying by 30 to put the figures into today's values, the $13,000 ($6,000 in gold and $7,000 in land) equate to $390,000 in today's money. And we learn that the tanyard is still going, so none of this money came from selling it. My guess is that Twain knew these figures were implausibly high but wanted a large amount to pique the greed of the duke and the king. Twain also may have liked the symmetry of there being $6,000 in gold, just as Huck has $6,000 in gold back home.

Note that the gold pieces are referred to as "cash." Gold and silver coins circulated freely for most of the 19th century, though paper money and base-metal coins were used for smaller transactions. Paper money was less bulky and hence more convenient, but the money was issued by private banks, not the government, and its value was often uncertain. Checks did not become common until after the Civil War.

and count it before everybody—then ther' ain't noth'n suspicious. But when the dead man says ther's six thous'n dollars, you know, we don't want to—"

"Hold on," says the duke. "Less make up the deffisit"—and he begun to haul out yaller-boys out of his pocket.

"It's a most amaz'n' good idea, duke—you *have* got a rattlin' clever head on you," says the king. "Blest if the old Nonesuch ain't a heppin' us out agin"—and *he* begun to haul out yaller-jackets and stack them up.

It most busted them, but they made up the six thousand clean and clear.

"Say," says the duke, "I got another idea. Le's go up stairs and count this money, and then take and *give it to the girls.*"

"Good land, duke, lemme hug you! It's the most dazzling idea 'at ever a man struck. You have cert'nly got the most astonishin' head I ever see. Oh, this is the boss dodge, ther' ain't no mistake 'bout it. Let 'em fetch along their suspicions now, if they want to—this'll lay 'em out."

When we got up stairs everybody gethered around the table, and the king he counted it and stacked it up, three hundred dollars in a pile—twenty elegant little piles. Everybody looked hungry at it, and licked their chops. Then they raked it into the bag again, and I see the king begin to swell himself up for another speech. He says:

"Friends all, my poor brother that lays yonder, has done generous by them that's left behind in the vale of sorrers. He has done generous by these-yer poor little lambs that he loved and sheltered, and that's left fatherless and motherless. Yes, and we that knowed him, knows that he would a done *more* generous by 'em if he hadn't ben afeard o' woundin' his dear William and me. Now, *wouldn't* he? Ther' ain't no question 'bout it in *my* mind. Well, then—what kind o' brothers would it be, that 'd stand in his way at sech a time? And what kind o' uncles would it be that 'd rob—yes, *rob*—sech poor sweet lambs as these 'at he loved so, at sech a time? If I know William—and I *think* I do—he—well, I'll jest ask him." He turns around and begins to make a lot of signs to the duke with his hands; and the duke he looks at him stupid and leather-headed a while, then all of a sudden he seems to catch his meaning, and jumps for the king, goo-gooing with all his might for joy, and hugs him about fifteen times before he lets up. Then the king says, "I knowed it; I reckon *that*'ll convince anybody the way *he* feels about it. Here, Mary Jane, Susan, Joanner, take the money—take it *all.* It's the gift of him that lays yonder, cold but joyful."

Mary Jane she went for him, Susan and the hare-lip went for the duke, and then such another hugging and kissing I never see yet. And everybody crowded up with the tears in their eyes, and most shook the hands off of them frauds, saying all the time:

"You *dear* good souls!—how *lovely!*—how *could* you!"

Well, then, pretty soon all hands got to talking about the diseased again, and how good he was, and what a loss he was, and all that; and before long a big iron-jawed man worked himself in there from outside, and stood a-listening and looking, and not saying anything; and nobody saying anything to him either, because the king was talking and they was all busy listening. The king was saying—in the middle of something he'd started in on—

"—they bein' partickler friends o' the diseased. That's why they're invited here this evenin'; but to-morrow we want *all* to come—everybody; for he respected everybody, he liked everybody, and so it's fitten that his funeral orgies sh'd be public."

And so he went a-mooning on and on, liking to hear himself talk, and every little while he fetched in his funeral orgies again, till the duke he couldn't stand it no more; so he writes on a little scrap of paper, "*obsequies,* you old fool," and folds it up and goes to goo-gooing and reaching it over people's heads to him. The king he reads it, and puts it in his pocket, and says:

"Poor William, afflicted as he is, his *heart's* aluz right. Asks me to invite everybody to come to the funeral—wants me to make 'em all welcome. But he needn't a worried—it was jest what I was at."

Then he weaves along again, perfectly ca'm, and goes to dropping in his funeral orgies again every now and then, just like he done before. And when he done it the third time, he says:

"I say orgies, not because it's the common term, because it ain't—obsequies bein' the common term—but because orgies is the right term. Obsequies ain't used in England no more, now—it's gone out. We say orgies now, in England. Orgies is better, because it means the thing you're after, more exact. It's a word that's made up out'n the Greek *orgo,* outside, open, abroad; and the Hebrew *jeesum,* to plant, cover up; hence in*ter.* So, you see, funeral orgies is an open er public funeral."

He was the *worst* I ever struck. Well, the iron-jawed man he laughed right in his face. Everybody was shocked. Everybody says, "Why *doctor!*" and Abner Shackleford says:

"Why, Robinson, hain't you heard the news? This is Harvey Wilks."

The king he smiled eager, and shoved out his flapper, and says:

"*Is* it my poor brother's dear good friend and physician? I—"

"Keep your hands off of me!" says the doctor. "*You* talk like an Englishman—*don't* you? It's the worst imitation I ever heard. *You* Peter Wilks's brother. You're a fraud, that's what you are!"

Well, how they all took on! They crowded around the doctor, and tried to quiet him down, and tried to explain to him, and tell him how Harvey'd showed in forty ways that he *was* Harvey, and knowed everybody by name, and the names of the very dogs, and begged and *begged* him not to hurt Harvey's feelings and the poor girls' feelings, and all that; but it warn't no use, he stormed right along, and said any man that pretended to be an Englishman and couldn't imitate the lingo no better than what he did, was a fraud and a liar. The poor girls was hanging to the king and crying; and all of a sudden the doctor ups and turns on *them.* He says:

"I was your father's friend, and I'm your friend; and I warn you *as* a friend, and an honest one, that wants to protect you and keep you out of harm and trouble, to turn your backs on that scoundrel, and have nothing to do with him, the ignorant tramp, with his idiotic Greek and Hebrew, as he calls it. He is the thinnest kind of an impostor—has come here with a lot of empty names and facts which he picked up somewheres, and you take them for *proofs,* and are helped to fool yourselves by these foolish friends here, who ought to know better. Mary Jane Wilks, you know me for your friend, and for your unselfish friend, too. Now listen to me; turn this pitiful rascal out—I *beg* you to do it. Will you?"

Mary Jane straightened herself up, and my, but she was handsome! She says:

"*Here* is my answer." She hove up the bag of money and put it in the king's hands, and says, "Take this six thousand dollars, and invest for me and my sisters any way you want to, and don't give us no receipt for it."

Then she put her arm around the king on one side, and Susan and the hare-lip done the same on the other. Everybody clapped their hands and stomped on the floor like a perfect storm, whilst the king held up his head and smiled proud. The doctor says:

"All right; I wash *my* hands of the matter. But I warn you all that a time's coming when you're going to feel sick whenever you think of this day"—and away he went.

"All right, doctor," says the king, kinder mocking him, "we'll try and get 'em to send for you"—which made them all laugh, and they said it was a prime good hit.

CHAPTER XXVI.

WELL, when they was all gone, the king he asks Mary Jane how they was off for spare rooms, and she said she had one spare room, which would do for Uncle William, and she'd give her own room to Uncle Harvey, which was a little bigger, and she would turn into the room with her sisters and sleep on a cot; and up garret was a little cubby, with a pallet in it. The king said the cubby would do for his valley—meaning me.

So Mary Jane took us up, and she showed them their rooms, which was plain but nice. She said she'd have her frocks and a lot of other traps took out of her room if they was in Uncle Harvey's way, but he said they warn't. The frocks was hung along the wall, and before them was a curtain made out of calico that hung down to the floor. There was an old hair trunk in one corner, and a guitar box in another, and all sorts of little knick-knacks and jimcracks around, like girls brisken up a room with. The king said it was all the more homely and more pleasanter for these fixings, and so don't disturb them. The duke's room was pretty small, but plenty good enough, and so was my cubby.

That night they had a big supper, and all them men and women was there, and I stood behind the king and the duke's chairs and waited on them, and the niggers waited on the rest. Mary Jane she set at the head of the table, with Susan alongside of her, and said how bad the biscuits was, and how mean the preserves was, and how ornery and tough the fried chickens was—and all that kind of rot, the way women always do for to force out compliments; and the people all knowed everything was tip-top, and said so—said "How *do* you get biscuits to brown so nice?" and "Where, for the land's sake, *did* you get these amaz'n pickles?" and all that kind of humbug talky-talk, just the way people always does at a supper, you know.

And when it was all done, me and the hare-lip had supper in the kitchen off of the leavings, whilst the others was helping the niggers clean up the things. The hare-lip she got to pumping me about England, and blest if I didn't think the ice was getting mighty thin, sometimes. She says:

"Did you ever see the king?"

"Who? William Fourth? Well, I bet I have—he goes to our church." I knowed he was dead years ago, but I never let on. So when I says he goes to our church, she says:

"What—regular?"

"Yes—regular. His pew's right over opposite ourn—on t'other side the pulpit."

"I thought he lived in London?"

"Well, he does. Where *would* he live?"

"But I thought *you* lived in Sheffield?"

I see I was up a stump. I had to let on to get choked with a chicken bone, so as to get time to think how to get down again. Then I says:

"I mean he goes to our church regular when he's in Sheffield. That's only in the summer time, when he comes there to take the sea baths."

"Why, how you talk—Sheffield ain't on the sea."

"Well, who said it was?"

"Why, you did."

"I *didn't* nuther."

"You did!"

"I didn't."

"You did."

"I never said nothing of the kind."

"Well, what *did* you say, then?"

"Said he come to take the sea *baths*—that's what I said."

"Well, then! how's he going to take the sea baths if it ain't on the sea?"

"Looky here," I says; "did you ever see any Congress-water?"

"Yes."

"Well, did you have to go to Congress to get it?"

"Why, no."

"Well, neither does William Fourth have to go to the sea to get a sea bath."

"How does he get it, then?"

"Gets it the way people down here gets Congress-water—in barrels. There in the palace at Sheffield they've got furnaces, and he wants his water hot. They can't bile that amount of water away off there at the sea. They haven't got no conveniences for it."

"Oh, I see, now. You might a said that in the first place and saved time."

When she said that, I see I was out of the woods again, and so I was comfortable and glad. Next, she says:

"Do you go to church, too?"

"Yes—regular."

"Where do you set?"

"Why, in our pew."

"*Whose* pew?"

"Why, *ourn*—your Uncle Harvey's."

"His'n? What does *he* want with a pew?"

"Wants it to set in. What did you *reckon* he wanted with it?"

"Why, I thought he'd be in the pulpit."

Rot him, I forgot he was a preacher. I see I was up a stump again, so I played another chicken bone and got another think. Then I says:

"Blame it, do you suppose there ain't but one preacher to a church?"

"Why, what do they want with more?"

"What!—to preach before a king? I never did see such a girl as you. They don't have no less than seventeen."

"Seventeen! My land! Why, I wouldn't set out such a string as that, not if I *never* got to glory. It must take 'em a week."

"Shucks, they don't *all* of 'em preach the same day—only *one* of 'em."

"Well, then, what does the rest of 'em do?"

"Oh, nothing much. Loll around, pass the plate—and one thing or another. But mainly they don't do nothing."

"Well, then, what are they *for*?"

"Why, they're for *style*. Don't you know nothing?"

"Well, I don't *want* to know no such foolishness as that.[142] How is servants treated in England? Do they treat 'em better 'n we treat our niggers?"

"*No!* A servant ain't nobody there. They treat them worse than dogs."

"Don't they give 'em holidays, the way we do, Christmas and New Year's week, and Fourth of July?"

"Oh, just listen! A body could tell *you* hain't ever been to England, by that. Why, Hare-l—why, Joanna, they never see a holiday from year's end to year's end; never go to the circus, nor theatre, nor nigger shows, nor nowheres."

"Nor church?"

"Nor church."[143]

"But *you* always went to church."

Well, I was gone up again. I forgot I was the old man's servant. But next minute I whirled in on a kind of an explanation how a valley was different from a common servant and *had* to go to church whether he wanted

---

142. Joanna "the hare-lip" is clever and has no trouble seeing through her visitor's ruse, just like Judith Loftus in an earlier chapter saw through Huck's ruse. Twain again may be raising the issue of how women in those times, with few exceptions, were not really allowed to use their brains outside the home.

Joanna's case is special because of her cleft palate (called a "hare-lip" because it resembled the split upper lip of a rabbit; the term is now considered offensive). Today, cosmetic surgery is routinely performed on babies born with cleft palates, but in Twain's time the disfigurement was permanent. Joanna has already devoted herself to "good works," the implication being that marriage and paid work is out of her reach. Even eating supper with the rest of the family appears to be forbidden. The "domestic code" of the time was that women stopped working outside the home once they got married. Unmarried women could work in female-dominated occupations such as teaching and domestic service, but even today homely women are less likely to be in the workforce (Hamermesh and Biddle 1994, 1188–1189), and the disparity was probably much greater in the 19th century.

143. Huck is correct that slaves did have holidays. A Christmas holiday of several days was typical, and an Easter Monday holiday and a day off during the summer appear common. Sunday was a day off for everybody, and slave attendance at church services, either in a white church or at a special service led by a white minister, was customary (Phillips 1963, 181, 248, 272, 289; Stampp 1956, 364–374).

As for circuses, theater, and "nigger shows" (Huck's term for minstrel shows), these came to town infrequently. Slaves had less opportunity to attend these events than whites did but could go if they had the day off, permission to leave the plantation, and the price of admission. Stampp notes that "In Virginia a visitor observed that many bondsmen spent Sundays 'strolling about the fields and streets' finding joy in their relative freedom of movement" (1956, 365). While it is commonly thought that slaves were never paid, there were many exceptions to that rule. Skilled artisans were often allowed to hire themselves out in their spare time. Cash bonuses were sometimes given to all of the slaves on a plantation, and some masters are said to have used money incentives on a regular basis (that last point is controversial; see Fogel and Engerman 1974; Gutman 1988; David et al. 1976).

to or not, and set with the family, on account of its being the law. But I didn't do it pretty good, and when I got done I see she warn't satisfied. She says:

"Honest injun, now, hain't you been telling me a lot of lies?"

"Honest injun," says I.[144]

"None of it at all?"

"None of it at all. Not a lie in it," says I.

"Lay your hand on this book and say it."

I see it warn't nothing but a dictionary, so I laid my hand on it and said it. So then she looked a little better satisfied, and says:

"Well, then, I'll believe some of it; but I hope to gracious if I'll believe the rest."

"What is it you won't believe, Joe?" says Mary Jane, stepping in with Susan behind her. "It ain't right nor kind for you to talk so to him, and him a stranger and so far from his people. How would you like to be treated so?"

"That's always your way, Maim—always sailing in to help somebody before they're hurt. I hain't done nothing to him. He's told some stretchers, I reckon; and I said I wouldn't swallow it all; and that's every bit and grain I *did* say. I reckon he can stand a little thing like that, can't he?"

"I don't care whether 'twas little or whether 'twas big; he's here in our house and a stranger, and it wasn't good of you to say it. If you was in his place, it would make you feel ashamed; and so you oughtn't to say a thing to another person that will make *them* feel ashamed."

"Why, Maim, he said—"

"It don't make no difference what he *said*—that ain't the thing. The thing is for you to treat him *kind,* and not be saying things to make him remember he ain't in his own country and amongst his own folks."

I says to myself, *this* is a girl that I'm letting that old reptle rob her of her money!

Then Susan *she* waltzed in; and if you'll believe me, she did give Hare-lip hark from the tomb!

Says I to myself, And this is *another* one that I'm letting him rob her of her money!

---

144. "Honest Injun" is a colloquial version of "honest Indian," which dates back to one of the bloodiest Indian wars of all time, King Philip's War of 1675–1676. The main antagonists in King Philip's War were New England colonists and Wampanoag Indians, and other various tribes were allied with each. General John Talcott used "honest Indian" to mean Indians who were colonial allies or at least were neither threatening nor treacherous: "We sent 27 women and children to Norwich under cover of what we call honest Indians" (qtd. in Temple 1887, 126). The war had an estimated death toll of 7,500 colonists and Indians (Perdue and Green 2010, 31). Depending on the estimates, King Philip's War may have been the bloodiest war ever on American soil relative to the population (Loewen 1996, 119, 337).

Then Mary Jane she took another inning, and went in sweet and lovely again—which was her way—but when she got done there warn't hardly anything left o' poor Hare-lip. So she hollered.

"All right, then," says the other girls, "you just ask his pardon."

She done it, too; and she done it beautiful. She done it so beautiful it was good to hear; and I wished I could tell her a thousand lies, so she could do it again.

I says to myself, this is *another* one that I'm letting him rob her of her money. And when she got through, they all jest laid theirselves out to make me feel at home and know I was amongst friends. I felt so ornery and low down and mean that I says to myself, My mind's made up; I'll hive that money for them or bust.

So then I lit out—for bed, I said, meaning some time or another. When I got by myself, I went to thinking the thing over. I says to myself, shall I go to that doctor, private, and blow on these frauds? No—that won't do. He might tell who told him; then the king and the duke would make it warm for me. Shall I go, private, and tell Mary Jane? No—I dasn't do it. Her face would give them a hint, sure; they've got the money, and they'd slide right out and get away with it. If she was to fetch in help, I'd get mixed up in the business, before it was done with, I judge. No; there ain't no good way but one. I got to steal that money, somehow; and I got to steal it some way that they won't suspicion that I done it. They've got a good thing, here; and they ain't agoing to leave till they've played this family and this town for all they're worth, so I'll find a chance time enough. I'll steal it, and hide it; and by and by, when I'm away down the river, I'll write a letter and tell Mary Jane where it's hid. But I better hive it tonight, if I can, because the doctor maybe hasn't let up as much as he lets on he has; he might scare them out of here yet.

So, thinks I, I'll go and search them rooms. Up stairs the hall was dark, but I found the duke's room, and started to paw around it with my hands; but I recollected it wouldn't be much like the king to let anybody else take care of that money but his own self; so then I went to his room and begun to paw around there. But I see I couldn't do nothing without a candle, and I dasn't light one, of course. So I judged I'd got to do the other thing—lay for them, and eavesdrop. About that time, I hears their footsteps coming, and was going to skip under the bed; I reached for it, but it wasn't where I thought it would be; but I touched the curtain that hid Mary Jane's frocks, so I jumped in behind that and snuggled in amongst the gowns, and stood there perfectly still.

They come in and shut the door; and the first thing the duke done was to get down and look under the bed. Then I was glad I hadn't found the bed when I wanted it. And yet, you know, it's kind of natural to hide under the bed when you are up to anything private. They sets down, then, and the king says:

"Well, what is it? And cut it middlin' short, because it's better for us to be down there a whoopin' up the mournin', than up here givin' 'em a chance to talk us over."

"Well, this is it, Capet. I ain't easy; I ain't comfortable. That doctor lays on my mind. I wanted to know your plans. I've got a notion, and I think it's a sound one."

"What is it, duke?"

"That we better glide out of this, before three in the morning, and clip it down the river with what we've got. Specially, seeing we got it so easy—*given* back to us, flung at our heads, as you may say, when of course we allowed to have to steal it back. I'm for knocking off and lighting out."

That made me feel pretty bad. About an hour or two ago it would a been a little different, but now it made me feel bad and disappointed, The king rips out and says:

"What! And not sell out the rest o' the property? March off like a passel o' fools and leave eight or nine thous'n' dollars' worth o' property layin' around jest sufferin' to be scooped in?—and all good salable stuff, too."

The duke he grumbled; said the bag of gold was enough, and he didn't want to go no deeper—didn't want to rob a lot of orphans of *everything* they had.

"Why, how you talk!" says the king. "We sha'n't rob 'em of nothing at all but jest this money. The people that *buys* the property is the suff'rers; because as soon's it's found out 'at we didn't own it—which won't be long after we've slid—the sale won't be valid, and it'll all go back to the estate. These-yer orphans 'll git their house back agin, and that's enough for *them;* they're young and spry, and k'n easy earn a livin'. *They* ain't agoing to suffer. Why, jest think—there's thous'n's and thous'n's that ain't nigh so well off. Bless you, *they* ain't got noth'n' to complain of."

Well, the king he talked him blind; so at last he give in, and said all right, but said he believed it was blame foolishness to stay, and that doctor hanging over them. But the king says:

"Cuss the doctor! What do we k'yer for *him*? Hain't we got all the fools in town on our side? and ain't that a big enough majority in any town?"

So they got ready to go down stairs again. The duke says:

"I don't think we put that money in a good place."

That cheered me up. I'd begun to think I warn't going to get a hint of no kind to help me. The king says:

"Why?"

"Because Mary Jane 'll be in mourning from this out; and first you know the nigger that does up the rooms will get an order to box these duds up and put 'em away; and do you reckon a nigger can run across money and not borrow some of it?"

"Your head's level, agin, duke," says the king; and he comes a fumbling under the curtain two or three foot from where I was. I stuck tight to the wall, and kept mighty still, though quivery; and I wondered what them fellows would say to me if they catched me; and I tried to think what I'd better do if they did catch me. But the king he got the bag before I could think more than about a half a thought, and he never suspicioned I was around. They took and shoved the bag through a rip in the straw tick that was under the feather bed, and crammed it in a foot or two amongst the straw and said it was all right now, because a nigger only makes up the feather bed, and don't turn over the straw tick only about twice a year, and so it warn't in no danger of getting stole, now.

But I knowed better. I had it out of there before they was half-way down stairs. I groped along up to my cubby, and hid it there till I could get a chance to do better. I judged I better hide it outside of the house somewheres, because if they missed it they would give the house a good ransacking. I knowed that very well. Then I turned in, with my clothes all on; but I couldn't a gone to sleep, if I'd a wanted to, I was in such a sweat to get through with the business. By and by I heard the king and the duke come up; so I rolled off my pallet and laid with my chin at the top of my ladder and waited to see if anything was going to happen. But nothing did.

So I held on till all the late sounds had quit and the early ones hadn't begun, yet; and then I slipped down the ladder.

CHAPTER XXVII.

I crept to their doors and listened; they was snoring, so I tip-toed along, and got down stairs all right. There warn't a sound anywheres. I peeped through a crack of the dining-room door, and see the men that was watching the corpse all sound asleep on their chairs. The door was open into the parlor, where the corpse was laying, and there was a candle in both rooms. I passed along, and the parlor door was open; but I see there warn't nobody in there but the remainders of Peter; so I shoved on by; but the front door was locked, and the key wasn't there. Just then I heard somebody coming down the stairs, back behind me. I run in the parlor and took a swift look around, and the only place I see to hide the bag was in the coffin.[145] The lid

---

145. The front parlor was commonly used for preburial viewings and funerals of dead family members in the 19th century. Although the parlor was also used for receiving and entertaining guests, it was sometimes called "the death room" because of these morbid associations. Death rooms in people's houses gave way to funeral parlors and professional funeral homes, in a trend that was accelerated by the staggering numbers of diseased

was shoved along about a foot, showing the dead man's face down in there, with a wet cloth over it, and his shroud on. I tucked the money-bag in under the lid, just down beyond where his hands was crossed, which made me creep, they was so cold, and then I run back across the room and in behind the door.

The person coming was Mary Jane. She went to the coffin, very soft, and kneeled down and looked in; then she put up her handkerchief and I see she begun to cry, though I couldn't hear her, and her back was to me. I slid out, and as I passed the dining-room I thought I'd make sure them watchers hadn't seen me; so I looked through the crack and everything was all right. They hadn't stirred.

I slipped up to bed, feeling ruther blue, on accounts of the thing playing out that way after I had took so much trouble and run so much resk about it. Says I, if it could stay where it is, all right; because when we get down the river a hundred mile or two, I could write back to Mary Jane, and she could dig him up again and get it; but that ain't the thing that's going to happen; the thing that's going to happen is, the money 'll be found when they come to screw on the lid. Then the king 'll get it again, and it'll be a long day before he gives anybody another chance to smouch it from him. Of course I *wanted* to slide down and get it out of there, but I dasn't try it. Every minute it was getting earlier, now, and pretty soon some of them watchers would begin to stir, and I might get catched—catched with six thousand dollars in my hands that nobody hadn't hired me to take care of. I don't wish to be mixed up in no such business as that, I says to myself.

When I got down stairs in the morning, the parlor was shut up, and the watchers was gone. There warn't nobody around but the family and the widow Bartley and our tribe. I watched their faces to see if anything had been happening, but I couldn't tell.

Towards the middle of the day the undertaker come, with his man, and they set the coffin in the middle of the room on a couple of chairs, and then set all our chairs in rows, and borrowed more from the neighbors till the

---

corpses from the Civil War and the 1918 worldwide influenza epidemic. The death tolls have no equals in American history: 800,000 Civil War dead—the standard estimate of 620,000 soldiers plus rough lower-bound estimates of about 130,000 uncounted soldiers and 50,000 civilians, mostly Southern (Hacker 2011; McPherson 1988, 619n)—and 675,000 American deaths from the flu pandemic (Barry 2005, 4, 238). By the 1920s, living rooms had gradually replaced parlors. The grim association between parlors and death appears to have been one reason, but another was that in most houses the parlor room was largely unused, so a multipurpose living room would be less wasteful (Wajda 2008, 337). In the pages of the *Ladies' Home Journal* at the turn of the century, editor Edward Bok led an influential long-term campaign to replace parlors with living rooms in small houses, architectural plans for which could be purchased through the journal (Ferraro 1998, 55–56).

hall and the parlor and the dining-room was full. I see the coffin lid was the way it was before, but I dasn't go to look in under it, with folks around.

Then the people begun to flock in, and the beats and the girls took seats in the front row at the head of the coffin, and for a half an hour the people filed around slow, in single rank, and looked down at the dead man's face a minute, and some dropped in a tear, and it was all very still and solemn, only the girls and the beats holding handkerchiefs to their eyes and keeping their heads bent, and sobbing a little. There warn't no other sound but the scraping of the feet on the floor and blowing noses—because people always blows them more at a funeral than they do at other places except church.

When the place was packed full, the undertaker he slid around in his black gloves with his softy soothering ways, putting on the last touches, and getting people and things all ship-shape and comfortable, and making no more sound than a cat. He never spoke; he moved people around, he squeezed in late ones, he opened up passage-ways, and done it with nods, and signs with his hands. Then he took his place over against the wall. He was the softest, glidingest, stealthiest man I ever see; and there warn't no more smile to him than there is to a ham.

They had borrowed a melodeum—a sick one; and when everything was ready, a young woman set down and worked it, and it was pretty skreeky and colicky, and everybody joined in and sung, and Peter was the only one that had a good thing, according to my notion. Then the Reverend Hobson opened up, slow and solemn, and begun to talk; and straight off the most outrageous row busted out in the cellar a body ever heard; it was only one dog, but he made a most powerful racket, and he kept it up, right along; the parson he had to stand there, over the coffin, and wait—you couldn't hear yourself think. It was right down awkward, and nobody didn't seem to know what to do. But pretty soon they see that long-legged undertaker make a sign to the preacher as much as to say, "Don't you worry—just depend on me." Then he stooped down and begun to glide along the wall, just his shoulders showing over the people's heads. So he glided along, and the pow-wow and racket getting more and more outrageous all the time; and at last, when he had gone around two sides of the room, he disappears down cellar. Then, in about two seconds we heard a whack, and the dog he finished up with a most amazing howl or two, and then everything was dead still, and the parson begun his solemn talk where he left off. In a minute or two here comes this undertaker's back and shoulders gliding along the wall again; and so he glided and glided around three sides of the room, and then rose up, and shaded his mouth with his hands, and stretched his neck out towards the preacher, over the people's heads, and says, in a kind of a coarse whisper, "*He had a rat!*" Then he drooped down and glided along the wall again to his place. You could see it was a great satisfaction to the people, because naturally they wanted to know. A little thing like that don't cost nothing, and it's just the little things that makes a man to be looked up to and liked. There warn't no more popular man in town than what that undertaker was.

Well, the funeral sermon was very good, but pison long and tiresome; and then the king he shoved in and got off some of his usual rubbage, and at last the job was through, and the undertaker begun to sneak up on the coffin with his screw-driver. I was in a sweat then, and watched him pretty keen. But he never meddled at all; just slid the lid along, as soft as mush, and screwed it down tight and fast. So there I was! I didn't know whether the money was in there or not. So, says I, spose somebody has hogged that bag on the sly?—now how do *I* know whether to write to Mary Jane or not? Spose she dug him up and didn't find nothing—what would she think of me? Blame it, I says, I might get hunted up and jailed; I'd better lay low and keep dark, and not write at all; the thing's awful mixed now; trying to better it, I've worsened it a hundred times, and I wish to goodness I'd just let it alone, dad fetch the whole business!

They buried him, and we come back home, and I went to watching faces again—I couldn't help it, and I couldn't rest easy. But nothing come of it; the faces didn't tell me nothing.

The king he visited around, in the evening, and sweetened everybody up, and made himself ever so friendly; and he give out the idea that his congregation over in England would be in a sweat about him, so he must hurry and settle up the estate right away, and leave for home. He was very sorry he was so pushed, and so was everybody; they wished he could stay longer, but they said they could see it couldn't be done. And he said of course him and William would take the girls home with them; and that pleased everybody too, because then the girls would be well fixed and amongst their own relations; and it pleased the girls, too—tickled them so they clean forgot they ever had a trouble in the world; and told him to sell out as quick as he wanted to, they would be ready. Them poor things was that glad and happy it made my heart ache to see them getting fooled and lied to so, but I didn't see no safe way for me to chip in and change the general tune.

Well, blamed if the king didn't bill the house and the niggers and all the property for auction straight off—sale two days after the funeral; but anybody could buy private beforehand if they wanted to.

So the next day after the funeral, along about noontime, the girls' joy got the first jolt; a couple of nigger traders come along, and the king sold them the niggers reasonable, for three-day drafts as they called it, and away they went, the two sons up the river to Memphis, and their mother down the river to Orleans. I thought them poor girls and them niggers would break their hearts for grief; they cried around each other, and took on so it most made me down sick to see it. The girls said they hadn't ever dreamed of seeing the family separated or sold away from the town. I can't ever get it out of my memory, the sight of them poor miserable girls and niggers hanging around each other's necks and crying; and I reckon I couldn't a stood it all but would a had to bust out and tell on our gang if I hadn't knowed the sale warn't no account and the niggers would be back home in a week or two.

The thing made a big stir in the town, too, and a good many come out flatfooted and said it was scandalous to separate the mother and the children that way. It injured the frauds some; but the old fool he bulled right along, spite of all the duke could say or do, and I tell you the duke was powerful uneasy.

Next day was auction day. About broad-day in the morning, the king and the duke come up in the garret and woke me up, and I see by their look that there was trouble. The king says:

"Was you in my room night before last?"

"No, your majesty"—which was the way I always called him when nobody but our gang warn't around.

"Was you in there yisterday er last night?"

"No, your majesty."

"Honor bright, now—no lies."

"Honor bright, your majesty, I'm telling you the truth. I hain't been anear your room since Miss Mary Jane took you and the duke and showed it to you."

The duke says:

"Have you seen anybody else go in there?"

"No, your grace, not as I remember, I believe."

"Stop and think."

I studied a while, and see my chance; then I says:

"Well, I see the niggers go in there several times."

Both of them give a little jump; and looked like they hadn't ever expected it, and then like they *had*. Then the duke says:

"What, *all* of them?"

"No—leastways, not all at once. That is, I don't think I ever see them all come *out* at once but just one time."

"Hello—when was that?"

"It was the day we had the funeral. In the morning. It warn't early, because I overslept. I was just starting down the ladder, and I see them."

"Well, go on, *go* on—what did they do? How'd they act?"

"They didn't do nothing. And they didn't act anyway, much, as fur as I see. They tip-toed away; so I seen, easy enough, that they'd shoved in there to do up your majesty's room, or something, sposing you was up; and found you *warn't* up, and so they was hoping to slide out of the way of trouble without waking you up, if they hadn't already waked you up."

"Great guns, *this* is a go!" says the king; and both of them looked pretty sick, and tolerable silly. They stood there a thinking and scratching their heads, a minute, and then the duke he bust into a kind of a little raspy chuckle, and says:

"It does beat all, how neat the niggers played their hand. They let on to be *sorry* they was going out of this region! and I believed they *was* sorry. And so did you, and so did everybody. Don't ever tell *me* any more that a nigger ain't got any histrionic talent. Why, the way they played that thing, it would fool *anybody*. In my opinion, there's a fortune in 'em. If I had capital and a theater, I wouldn't want a better layout than that—and here we've gone and sold 'em for a song. Yes, and ain't privileged to sing the song, yet. Say, where *is* that song—that draft."

"In the bank for to be collected. Where *would* it be?"

"Well, *that's* all right then, thank goodness."

Says I, kind of timid-like:

"Is something gone wrong?"

The king whirls on me and rips out:

"None o' your business! You keep your head shet, and mind y'r own affairs—if you got any. Long as you're in this town, don't you forget *that*, you hear?" Then he says to the duke, "We got to jest swaller it, and say noth'n': mum's the word for *us*."

As they was starting down the ladder, the duke he chuckles again, and says:

"Quick sales *and* small profits! It's a good business—yes."

The king snarls around on him and says:

"I was trying to do for the best, in sellin' 'm out so quick. If the profits has turned out to be none, lackin' considable, and none to carry, is it my fault any more'n it's yourn?"

"Well, *they'd* be in this house yet, and we *wouldn't* if I could a got my advice listened to."

The king sassed back, as much as was safe for him, and then swapped around and lit into *me* again. He give me down the banks for not coming and *telling* him I see the niggers come out of his room acting that way—said any fool would a *knowed* something was up. And then waltzed in and cussed *himself* a while; and said it all come of him not laying late and taking his natural rest that morning, and he'd be blamed if he'd ever do it again. So they went off a-jawing; and I felt dreadful glad I'd worked it all off on to the niggers and yet hadn't done the niggers no harm by it.

CHAPTER XXVIII.

BY and by it was getting-up time; so I come down the ladder and started for down stairs; but as I come to the girls' room, the door was open, and I see Mary Jane setting by her old hair trunk, which was open and she'd been packing things in it—getting ready to go to England. But she had stopped now, with a folded gown in her lap, and had her face in her hands, crying. I felt awful bad to see it; of course anybody would. I went in there, and says:

"Miss Mary Jane, you can't abear to see people in trouble, and *I* can't—most always. Tell me about it."

So she done it. And it was the niggers—I just expected it. She said the beautiful trip to England was most about spoiled for her; she didn't know *how* she was ever going to be happy there, knowing the mother and the children warn't ever going to see each other no more—and then busted out bitterer than ever, and flung up her hands, and says:

"Oh, dear, dear, to think they ain't *ever* going to see each other any more!"

"But they *will*—and inside of two weeks—and I *know* it!" says I.

Laws, it was out before I could think!—and before I could budge, she throws her arms around my neck, and told me to say it *again,* say it *again,* say it *again!*

I see I had spoke too sudden, and said too much, and was in a close place. I asked her to let me think a minute; and she set there, very impatient and excited and handsome, but looking kind of happy and eased-up, like a person that's had a tooth pulled out. So I went to studying it out. I says to myself, I reckon a body that ups and tells the truth when he is in a tight place, is taking considerable many resks, though I ain't had no experience, and can't say for certain; but it looks so to me, anyway; and yet here's a case where I'm blest if it don't look to me like the truth is better and actly *safer*, than a lie. I must lay it by in my mind, and think it over some time or other, it's so kind of strange and unregular. I never see nothing like it. Well, I says to myself at last, I'm agoing to chance it; I'll up and tell the truth this time, though it does seem most like setting down on a kag of powder and touching it off just to see where you'll go to. Then I says:

"Miss Mary Jane, is there any place out of town a little ways, where you could go and stay three or four days?"

"Yes—Mr. Lothrop's. Why?"

"Never mind why, yet. If I'll tell you how I know the niggers will see each other again—inside of two weeks—here in this house—and *prove* how I know it—will you go to Mr. Lothrop's and stay four days?"

"Four days!" she says; "I'll stay a year!"

"All right," I says, "I don't want nothing more out of *you* than just your word—I druther have it than another man's kiss-the-Bible." She smiled, and reddened up very sweet, and I says, "If you don't mind it, I'll shut the door—and bolt it."

Then I come back and set down again, and says:

"Don't you holler. Just set still, and take it like a man. I got to tell the truth, and you want to brace up, Miss Mary, because it's a bad kind, and going to be hard to take, but there ain't no help for it. These uncles of yourn ain't no uncles at all—they're a couple of frauds—regular dead-beats. There, now we're over the worst of it—you can stand the rest middling easy."

It jolted her up like everything, of course; but I was over the shoal water now, so I went right along, her eyes a-blazing higher and higher all the time, and told her every blame thing, from where we first struck that young fool going up to the steamboat, clear through to where she flung herself on to the king's breast at the front door and he kissed her sixteen or seventeen times—and then up she jumps, with her face afire like sunset, and says:

"The brute! Come—don't waste a minute—not a *second*—we'll have them tarred and feathered, and flung in the river!"

Says I:

"Cert'nly. But do you mean, *before* you go to Mr. Lothrop's, or—"

"Oh," she says, "what am I *thinking* about!" she says, and set right down again. "Don't mind what I said—please don't—you *won't*, now, *will* you?" laying her silky hand on mine in that kind of a way that I said I would die first. "I never thought, I was so stirred up," she says; "now go on, and I won't do so any more. You tell me what to do, and whatever you say, I'll do it."

"Well," I says, "it's a rough gang, them two frauds, and I'm fixed so I got to travel with them a while longer, whether I want to or not—I druther not tell you why—and if you was to blow on them this town would get me out of their claws, and *I*'d be all right, but there'd be another person that you don't know about who'd be in big trouble. Well, we got to save *him,* hain't we? Of course. Well, then, we won't blow on them."

Saying them words put a good idea in my head. I see how maybe I could get me and Jim rid of the frauds; get them jailed here, and then leave. But I didn't want to run the raft in the daytime, without anybody aboard to answer questions but me; so I didn't want the plan to begin working till pretty late to-night. I says:

"Miss Mary Jane, I'll tell you what we'll do—and you won't have to stay at Mr. Lothrop's so long, nuther. How fur is it?"

"A little short of four miles—right out in the country, back here."

"Well, that'll answer. Now you go along out there, and lay low till nine or half-past, to-night, and then get them to fetch you home again—tell them you've thought of something. If you get here before eleven, put a candle in this window, and if I don't turn up, wait *till* eleven, and *then* if I don't turn up it means I'm gone, and out of the way, and safe. Then you come out and spread the news around, and get these beats jailed."

"Good," she says, "I'll do it."

"And if it just happens so that I don't get away, but get took up along with them, you must up and say I told you the whole thing beforehand, and you must stand by me all you can."

"Stand by you, indeed I will. They sha'n't touch a hair of your head!" she says, and I see her nostrils spread and her eyes snap when she said it, too.

"If I get away, I sha'n't be here," I says, "to prove these rapscallions ain't your uncles, and I couldn't do it if I *was* here. I could swear they was beats and bummers, that's all; though that's worth something. Well, there's others can do that better than what I can—and they're people that ain't going to be doubted as quick as I'd be. I'll tell you how to find them. Gimme a pencil and a piece of paper. There—'*Royal Nonesuch, Bricksville.*' Put it away, and don't lose it. When the court wants to find out something about these two, let them send up to Bricksville and say they've got the men that played the Royal Nonesuch, and ask for some witnesses— why, you'll have that entire town down here before you can hardly wink, Miss Mary. And they'll come a-biling, too."

I judged we had got everything fixed about right, now. So I says:

"Just let the auction go right along, and don't worry. Nobody don't have to pay for the things they buy till a whole day after the auction, on accounts of the short notice, and they ain't going out of this till they get that money—and the way we've fixed it the sale ain't going to count, and they ain't going to *get* no money. It's just like the way it was with the niggers—it warn't no sale, and the niggers will be back before long. Why, they can't collect the money for the *niggers*, yet—they're in the worst kind of a fix, Miss Mary."

"Well," she says, "I'll run down to breakfast now, and then I'll start straight for Mr. Lothrop's."

"'Deed, *that* ain't the ticket, Miss Mary Jane," I says, "by no manner of means; go *before* breakfast."

"Why?"

"What did you reckon I wanted you to go at all for, Miss Mary?"

"Well, I never thought—and come to think, I don't know. What was it?"

"Why, it's because you ain't one of these leather-face people. I don't want no better book than what your face is. A body can set down and read it off like coarse print. Do you reckon you can go and face your uncles, when they come to kiss you good-morning, and never—"

"There, there, don't! Yes, I'll go before breakfast—I'll be glad to. And leave my sisters with them?"

"Yes—never mind about them. They've got to stand it yet a while. They might suspicion something if all of you was to go. I don't want you to see them, nor your sisters, nor nobody in this town—if a neighbor was to ask how is your uncles this morning, your face would tell something. No, you go right along, Miss Mary Jane, and I'll fix it with all of them. I'll tell Miss Susan to give your love to your uncles and say you've went away for a few hours for to get a little rest and change, or to see a friend, and you'll be back to-night or early in the morning."

"Gone to see a friend is all right, but I won't have my love given to them."

"Well, then, it sha'n't be." It was well enough to tell *her* so—no harm in it. It was only a little thing to do, and no trouble; and it's the little things that smoothes people's roads the most, down here below; it would make Mary Jane comfortable, and it wouldn't cost nothing. Then I says: "There's one more thing—that bag of money."

"Well, they've got that; and it makes me feel pretty silly to think *how* they got it."

"No, you're out, there. They hain't got it."

"Why, who's got it?"

"I wish I knowed, but I don't. I *had* it, because I stole it from them; and I stole it to give to you; and I know where I hid it, but I'm afraid it ain't there no more. I'm awful sorry, Miss Mary Jane, I'm just as sorry as I can be; but I done the best I could; I did, honest. I come nigh getting caught, and I had to shove it into the first place I come to, and run—and it warn't a good place."

"Oh, stop blaming yourself—it's too bad to do it, and I won't allow it—you couldn't help it; it wasn't your fault. Where did you hide it?"

I didn't want to set her to thinking about her troubles again; and I couldn't seem to get my mouth to tell her what would make her see that corpse laying in the coffin with that bag of money on his stomach. So for a minute I didn't say nothing—then I says:

"I'd ruther not *tell* you where I put it, Miss Mary Jane, if you don't mind letting me off; but I'll write it for you on a piece of paper, and you can read it along the road to Mr. Lothrop's, if you want to. Do you reckon that 'll do?"

"Oh, yes."

So I wrote: "I put it in the coffin. It was in there when you was crying there, away in the night. I was behind the door, and I was mighty sorry for you, Miss Mary Jane."

It made my eyes water a little, to remember her crying there all by herself in the night, and them devils laying there right under her own roof, shaming her and robbing her; and when I folded it up and give it to her, I see the water come into her eyes, too; and she shook me by the hand, hard, and says:

"*Good*-bye. I'm going to do everything just as you've told me; and if I don't ever see you again, I sha'n't ever forget you, and I'll think of you a many and a many a time, and I'll *pray* for you, too!"—and she was gone.

Pray for me! I reckoned if she knowed me she'd take a job that was more nearer her size. But I bet she done it, just the same—she was just that kind. She had the grit to pray for Judus if she took the notion—there warn't no back-down to her, I judge. You may say what you want to, but in my opinion she had more sand in her than any girl I ever see; in my opinion she was just full of sand. It sounds like flattery, but it ain't no flattery. And when it comes to beauty—and goodness too—she lays over them all. I hain't ever seen her since that time that I see her go out of that door; no, I hain't ever seen her since, but I reckon I've thought of her a many and a many a million times, and of her saying she would pray for me; and if ever I'd a thought it would do any good for me to pray for *her,* blamed if I wouldn't a done it or bust.

Well, Mary Jane she lit out the back way, I reckon; because nobody see her go. When I struck Susan and the hare-lip, I says:

"What's the name of them people over on t'other side of the river that you all goes to see sometimes?"

They says:

"There's several; but it's the Proctors, mainly."

"That's the name," I says; "I most forgot it. Well, Miss Mary Jane she told me to tell you she's gone over there in a dreadful hurry—one of them's sick."

"Which one?"

"I don't know; leastways I kinder forget; but I thinks it's—"

"Sakes alive, I hope it ain't *Hanner?*"

"I'm sorry to say it," I says, "but Hanner's the very one."

"My goodness—and she so well only last week! Is she took bad?"

"It ain't no name for it. They set up with her all night, Miss Mary Jane said, and they don't think she'll last many hours."

"Only think of that, now! What's the matter with her?"

I couldn't think of anything reasonable, right off that way, so I says:

"Mumps."

"Mumps your granny! They don't set up with people that's got the mumps."

"They don't, don't they? You better bet they do with *these* mumps. These mumps is different. It's a new kind, Miss Mary Jane said."

"How's it a new kind?"

"Because it's mixed up with other things."

"What other things?"

"Well, measles, and whooping-cough, and erysiplas, and consumption, and yaller janders, and brain fever, and I don't know what all."

"My land! And they call it the *mumps?*"

"That's what Miss Mary Jane said."

"Well, what in the nation do they call it the *mumps* for?"

"Why, because it *is* the mumps. That's what it starts with."

"Well, ther' ain't no sense in it. A body might stump his toe, and take pison, and fall down the well, and break his neck, and bust his brains out, and somebody come along and ask what killed him, and some numskull up and say, 'Why, he stumped his *toe.*' Would ther' be any sense in that? *No.* And ther' ain't no sense in *this,* nuther. Is it ketching?"

"Is it *ketching*? Why, how you talk. Is a *harrow* catching—in the dark? If you don't hitch onto one tooth, you're bound to on another, ain't you? And you can't get away with that tooth without fetching the whole harrow along, can you? Well, these kind of mumps is a kind of a harrow, as you may say—and it ain't no slouch of a harrow, nuther, you come to get it hitched on good."

"Well, it's awful, *I* think," says the hare-lip. "I'll go to Uncle Harvey and—"

"Oh, yes," I says, "I *would*. Of *course* I would. I wouldn't lose no time."

"Well, why wouldn't you?"

"Just look at it a minute, and maybe you can see. Hain't your uncles obleeged to get along home to England as fast as they can? And do you reckon they'd be mean enough to go off and leave you to go all that journey by yourselves? *You* know they'll wait for you. So fur, so good. Your uncle Harvey's a preacher, ain't he? Very well, then; is a *preacher* going to deceive a steamboat clerk? is he going to deceive a *ship clerk*?—so as to get them to let Miss Mary Jane go aboard? Now *you* know he ain't. What *will* he do, then? Why, he'll say, 'It's a great pity, but my church matters has got to get along the best way they can; for my niece has been exposed to the dreadful pluribus-unum mumps, and so it's my bounden duty to set down here and wait the three months it takes to show on her if she's got it.' But never mind, if you think it's best to tell your uncle Harvey—"

"Shucks, and stay fooling around here when we could all be having good times in England whilst we was waiting to find out whether Mary Jane's got it or not? Why, you talk like a muggins."

"Well, anyway, maybe you'd better tell some of the neighbors."

"Listen at that, now. You do beat all for natural stupidness. Can't you *see* that *they'd* go and tell? Ther' ain't no way but just to not tell anybody at *all*."

"Well, maybe you're right—yes, I judge you *are* right."

"But I reckon we ought to tell Uncle Harvey she's gone out a while, anyway, so he won't be uneasy about her?"

"Yes, Miss Mary Jane she wanted you to do that. She says, 'Tell them to give Uncle Harvey and William my love and a kiss, and say I've run over the river to see Mr.—Mr.—what *is* the name of that rich family your uncle Peter used to think so much of?—I mean the one that—"

"Why, you must mean the Apthorps, ain't it?"

"Of course; bother them kind of names, a body can't ever seem to re-member them, half the time, somehow. Yes, she said, say she has run over for to ask the Apthorps to be sure and come to the auction and buy this house, because she allowed her uncle Peter would ruther they had it than anybody else; and she's going to stick to them till they say they'll come, and then, if she ain't too tired, she's coming home; and if she is, she'll be home in the morning anyway. She said, don't say nothing about the Proc-tors, but only about the Apthorps—which'll be perfectly true, because she *is* going there to speak about their buying the house; I know it, because she told me so herself."

"All right," they said, and cleared out to lay for their uncles, and give them the love and the kisses, and tell them the message.

Everything was all right now. The girls wouldn't say nothing because they wanted to go to England; and the king and the duke would ruther Mary Jane was off working for the auction than around in reach of Doctor Robinson. I felt very good; I judged I had done it pretty neat—I reckoned Tom Sawyer couldn't a done it no neater himself. Of course he would a throwed more style into it, but I can't do that very handy, not being brung up to it.

Well, they held the auction in the public square, along towards the end of the afternoon, and it strung along, and strung along, and the old man he was on hand and looking his level pisonest, up there longside of the auc-tioneer, and chipping in a little Scripture, now and then, or a little goody-goody saying, of some kind, and the duke he was around goo-gooing for sympathy all he knowed how, and just spreading himself generly.

But by and by the thing dragged through, and everything was sold. Everything but a little old trifling lot in the graveyard. So they'd got to work *that* off—I never see such a girafft as the king was for wanting to swallow *everything*. Well, whilst they was at it, a steamboat landed, and in about two minutes up comes a crowd a whooping and yelling and laughing and carrying on, and singing out:

"*Here's* your opposition line! here's your two sets o' heirs to old Peter Wilks—and you pays your money and you takes your choice!"

CHAPTER XXIX.

THEY was fetching a very nice looking old gentleman along, and a nice looking younger one, with his right arm in a sling. And my souls, how the people yelled and laughed, and kept it up. But I didn't see no joke about it, and I judged it would strain the duke and the king some to see any. I reckoned they'd turn pale. But no, nary a pale did *they* turn. The duke he never let on he suspicioned what was up, but just went a goo-gooing around, happy and satisfied, like a jug that's googling out buttermilk; and as for the king, he just gazed and gazed down sorrowful on them new-comers like it give him the stomach-ache in his very heart to think there could be such frauds and rascals in the world. Oh, he done it admira-ble. Lots of the principal people gethered around the king, to let him see they was on his side. That old gentleman that had just come looked all puzzled to death. Pretty soon he begun to speak, and I see, straight off, he pronounced *like* an Englishman, not the king's way, though the king's *was* pretty good for an imitation. I can't give the old gent's words, nor I can't imitate him; but he turned around to the crowd, and says, about like this:

"This is a surprise to me which I wasn't looking for; and I'll acknowledge, candid and frank, I ain't very well fixed to meet it and answer it; for my brother and me has had misfortunes; he's broke his arm, and our baggage got put off at a town above here, last night in the night by a mistake. I am Peter Wilks' brother Harvey, and this is his brother William, which can't hear nor speak—and can't even make signs to amount to much, now't he's only got one hand to work them with. We are who we say we are; and in a day or two, when I get the baggage, I can prove it. But, up till then, I won't say nothing more, but go to the hotel and wait."

So him and the new dummy started off; and the king he laughs, and blethers out:

"Broke his arm—*very* likely, *ain't* it?—and very convenient, too, for a fraud that's got to make signs, and ain't learnt how. Lost their baggage! That's *mighty* good!—and mighty ingenious—under the *circumstances*!"

So he laughed again; and so did everybody else, except three or four, or maybe half a dozen. One of these was that doctor; another one was a sharp looking gentleman, with a carpet-bag of the old-fashioned kind made out of carpet-stuff, that had just come off of the steamboat and was talking to him in a low voice, and glancing towards the king now and then and nodding their heads—it was Levi Bell, the lawyer that was gone up to Louisville;[146] and another one was a big rough husky that come along and listened to all the old gentleman said, and was listening to the king now. And when the king got done, this husky up and says:

---

146. Twain exploited the trashy carpetbagger stereotype when he introduced the king and the duke, but here the respected lawyer Levi Bell also carries a carpetbag. The difference is that Levi Bell is not an outsider who carries all of his worldly possessions in the bag but instead is a pillar of the community returning from a business trip to Louisville.

Louisville, like Cincinnati, was an Ohio River city that had risen to prominence. It was a valuable trading port for Kentucky, which by 1840 had become the 6th-largest state in the union, with a slightly larger population than Massachusetts. Kentucky was a big exporter of tobacco, hogs, corn, and wheat. The state had one of the South's more diversified economies, especially in Louisville, where more than half the workforce was engaged in manufacturing and related trades (United States Department of State 1841, 75, 358–368; Sexton 1986–1987, 159–166). Access to the Ohio and Mississippi Rivers was vital to the prosperity of both Louisville and Kentucky. In 1840 Louisville was the 17th-largest city in America, with over 21,000 people, almost 5,000 more than St. Louis (United States Census 1998).

"Say, looky here; if you are Harvey Wilks, when'd you come to this town?"

"The day before the funeral, friend," says the king.

"But what time o' day?"

"In the evenin'—'bout an hour er two before sundown."

"*How'd* you come?"

"I come down on the *Susan Powell* from Cincinnati."

"Well, then, how'd you come to be up at the Pint in the *mornin'*—in a canoe?"

"I warn't up at the Pint in the mornin'."

"It's a lie."

Several of them jumped for him and begged him not to talk that way to an old man and a preacher.

"Preacher be hanged, he's a fraud and a liar. He was up at the Pint that mornin'. I live up there, don't I? Well, I was up there, and he was up there. I *see* him there. He come in a canoe, along with Tim Collins and a boy."

The doctor he up and says:

"Would you know the boy again if you was to see him, Hines?"

"I reckon I would, but I don't know. Why, yonder he is, now. I know him perfectly easy."

It was me he pointed at. The doctor says:

"Neighbors, I don't know whether the new couple is frauds or not; but if *these* two ain't frauds, I am an idiot, that's all. I think it's our duty to see that they don't get away from here till we've looked into this thing. Come along, Hines; come along, the rest of you. We'll take these fellows to the tavern and affront them with t'other couple, and I reckon we'll find out *something* before we get through."

It was nuts for the crowd, though maybe not for the king's friends; so we all started. It was about sundown. The doctor he led me along by the hand, and was plenty kind enough, but he never let go my hand.

We all got in a big room in the hotel, and lit up some candles, and fetched in the new couple. First, the doctor says:

"I don't wish to be too hard on these two men, but *I* think they're frauds, and they may have complices that we don't know nothing about. If they have, won't the complices get away with that bag of gold Peter Wilks left? It ain't unlikely. If these men ain't frauds, they won't object to sending for that money and letting us keep it till they prove they're all right—ain't that so?"

Everybody agreed to that. So I judged they had our gang in a pretty tight place, right at the outstart. But the king he only looked sorrowful, and says:

"Gentlemen, I wish the money was there, for I ain't got no disposition to throw anything in the way of a fair, open, out-and-out investigation o' this misable business; but alas, the money ain't there; you k'n send and see, if you want to."

"Where is it, then?"

"Well, when my niece give it to me to keep for her, I took and hid it inside o' the straw tick o' my bed, not wishin' to bank it for the few days we'd be here, and considerin' the bed a safe place, we not bein' used to niggers, and suppos'n' 'em honest, like servants in England. The niggers stole it the very next mornin' after I had went down stairs; and when I sold 'em I hadn't missed the money yit, so they got clean away with it. My servant here k'n tell you 'bout it, gentlemen."

The doctor and several said "Shucks!" and I see nobody didn't altogether believe him. One man asked me if I see the niggers steal it. I said no, but I see them sneaking out of the room and hustling away, and I never thought nothing, only I reckoned they was afraid they had waked up my master and was trying to get away before he made trouble with them. That was all they asked me. Then the doctor whirls on me and says:

"Are *you* English, too?"

I says yes; and him and some others laughed, and said, "Stuff!"

Well, then they sailed in on the general investigation, and there we had it, up and down, hour in, hour out, and nobody never said a word about supper, nor ever seemed to think about it—and so they kept it up, and kept it up; and it *was* the worst mixed-up thing you ever see. They made the king tell his yarn, and they made the old gentleman tell his'n; and anybody but a lot of prejudiced chuckleheads would a *seen* that the old gentleman was spinning truth and t'other one lies. And by and by they had me up to tell what I knowed. The king he give me a left-handed look out of the corner of his eye, and so I knowed enough to talk on the right side. I begun to tell about Sheffield, and how we lived there, and all about the English Wilkses, and so on; but I didn't get pretty fur till the doctor begun to laugh; and Levi Bell, the lawyer, says:

"Set down, my boy; I wouldn't strain myself, if I was you. I reckon you ain't used to lying, it don't seem to come handy; what you want is practice. You do it pretty awkward."

I didn't care nothing for the compliment, but I was glad to be let off, anyway.

The doctor he started to say something, and turns and says:

"If you'd been in town at first, Levi Bell—"

The king broke in and reached out his hand, and says:

"Why, is this my poor dead brother's old friend that he's wrote so often about?"

The lawyer and him shook hands, and the lawyer smiled and looked pleased, and they talked right along awhile, and then got to one side and talked low; and at last the lawyer speaks up and says:

"That'll fix it. I'll take the order and send it, along with your brother's, and then they'll know it's all right."

So they got some paper and a pen, and the king he set down and twisted his head to one side, and chawed his tongue, and scrawled off something; and then they give the pen to the duke—and then for the first time, the duke looked sick. But he took the pen and wrote. So then the lawyer turns to the new old gentleman and says:

"You and your brother please write a line or two and sign your names."

The old gentleman wrote, but nobody couldn't read it. The lawyer looked powerful astonished, and says:

"Well, it beats *me*"—and snaked a lot of old letters out of his pocket, and examined them, and then examined the old man's writing, and then *them* again; and then says: "These old letters is from Harvey Wilks; and here's *these* two's handwritings, and anybody can see *they* didn't write them" (the king and the duke looked sold and foolish, I tell you, to see how the lawyer had took them in), "and here's *this* old gentleman's handwriting, and anybody can tell, easy enough, *he* didn't write them—fact is, the scratches he makes ain't properly *writing* at all. Now, here's some letters from—"

The new old gentleman says:

"If you please, let me explain. Nobody can read my hand but my brother there—so he copies for me. It's *his* hand you've got there, not mine."

"*Well!*" says the lawyer, "this *is* a state of things. I've got some of William's letters, too; so if you'll get him to write a line or so we can com—"

"He *can't* write with his left hand," says the old gentleman. "If he could use his right hand, you would see that he wrote his own letters and mine too. Look at both, please—they're by the same hand."

The lawyer done it, and says:

"I believe it's so—and if it ain't so, there's a heap stronger resemblance than I'd noticed before, anyway. Well, well, well! I thought we was right on the track of a slution, but it's gone to grass, partly. But anyway, *one* thing is proved—*these* two ain't either of 'em Wilkses"—and he wagged his head towards the king and the duke.

Well, what do you think?—that muleheaded old fool wouldn't give in *then!* Indeed he wouldn't. Said it warn't no fair test. Said his brother William was the cussedest joker in the world, and hadn't *tried* to write—*he* see William was going to play one of his jokes the minute he put the pen to paper. And so he warmed up and went warbling and warbling right along, till he was actuly beginning to believe what he was saying, *himself*—but pretty soon the new gentleman broke in, and says:

"I've thought of something. Is there anybody here that helped to lay out my br—helped to lay out the late Peter Wilks for burying?"

"Yes," says somebody, "me and Ab Turner done it. We're both here."

Then the old man turns towards the king, and says:

"Perhaps this gentleman can tell me what was tattooed on his breast?"

Blamed if the king didn't have to brace up mighty quick, or he'd a squshed down like a bluff bank that the river has cut under, it took him so sudden—and, mind you, it was a thing that was calculated to make most *anybody* sqush to get fetched such a solid one as that without any notice—because how was *he* going to know what was tattooed on the man? He whitened a little; he couldn't help it; and it was mighty still in there, and everybody bending a little forwards and gazing at him. Says I to myself, *Now* he'll throw up the sponge—there ain't no more use. Well, did he? A body can't hardly believe it, but he didn't. I reckon he thought he'd keep the thing up till he tired them people out, so they'd thin out, and him and the duke could break loose and get away. Anyway, he set there, and pretty soon he begun to smile, and says:

"Mf! It's a *very* tough question, *ain't* it! *Yes,* sir, I k'n tell you what's tattooed on his breast. It's jest a small, thin, blue arrow—that's what it is; and if you don't look clost, you can't see it. *Now* what do you say—hey?"

Well, *I* never see anything like that old blister for clean out-and-out cheek.

The new old gentleman turns brisk towards Ab Turner and his pard, and his eye lights up like he judged he'd got the king *this* time, and says:

"There—you've heard what he said! Was there any such mark on Peter Wilks' breast?"

Both of them spoke up and says:

"We didn't see no such mark."

"Good!" says the old gentleman. "Now, what you *did* see on his breast was a small dim P, and a B (which is an initial he dropped when he was young), and a W, with dashes between them, so: P—B—W"—and he marked them that way on a piece of paper. "Come—ain't that what you saw?"

Both of them spoke up again, and says:

"No, we *didn't.* We never seen any marks at all."

Well, everybody *was* in a state of mind, now, and they sings out:

"The whole *bilin'* of 'm 's frauds! Le's duck 'em! le's drown 'em! le's ride 'em on a rail!" and everybody was whooping at once, and there was a rattling pow-wow. But the lawyer he jumps on the table and yells, and says:

"Gentlemen—gentle*men!* Hear me just a word—just a *single* word—if you PLEASE! There's one way yet—let's go and dig up the corpse and look."

That took them.

"Hooray!" they all shouted, and was starting right off; but the lawyer and the doctor sung out:

"Hold on, hold on! Collar all these four men and the boy, and fetch *them* along, too!"

"We'll do it!" they all shouted; "and if we don't find them marks we'll lynch the whole gang!"

I *was* scared, now, I tell you. But there warn't no getting away, you know. They gripped us all, and marched us right along, straight for the graveyard, which was a mile and a half down the river, and the whole town at our heels, for we made noise enough, and it was only nine in the evening.

As we went by our house I wished I hadn't sent Mary Jane out of town; because now if I could tip her the wink, she'd light out and save me, and blow on our dead-beats.

Well, we swarmed along down the river road, just carrying on like wildcats; and to make it more scary, the sky was darking up, and the lightning beginning to wink and flitter, and the wind to shiver amongst the leaves. This was the most awful trouble and most dangersome I ever was in; and I was kinder stunned; everything was going so different from what I had allowed for; stead of being fixed so I could take my own time, if I wanted to, and see all the fun, and have Mary Jane at my back to save me and set me free when the close-fit come, here was nothing in the world betwixt me and sudden death but just them tattoo-marks. If they didn't find them—

I couldn't bear to think about it; and yet, somehow, I couldn't think about nothing else. It got darker and darker, and it was a beautiful time to give the crowd the slip; but that big husky had me by the wrist—Hines—and a body might as well try to give Goliar the slip. He dragged me right along, he was so excited; and I had to run to keep up.

When they got there they swarmed into the graveyard and washed over it like an overflow. And when they got to the grave, they found they had about a hundred times as many shovels as they wanted, but nobody hadn't thought to fetch a lantern. But they sailed into digging, anyway, by the flicker of the lightning, and sent a man to the nearest house a half a mile off, to borrow one.

So they dug and dug, like everything; and it got awful dark, and the rain started, and the wind swished and swushed along, and the lightning come brisker and brisker, and the thunder boomed; but them people never took no notice of it, they was so full of this business; and one minute you could see everything and every face in that big crowd, and the shovelfuls of dirt sailing up out of the grave, and the next second the dark wiped it all out, and you couldn't see nothing at all.

At last they got out the coffin, and begun to unscrew the lid, and then such another crowding, and shouldering and shoving as there was, to scrouge in and get a sight, you never see; and in the dark, that way, it was awful. Hines he hurt my wrist dreadful, pulling and tugging so, and I reckon he clean forgot I was in the world, he was so excited and panting.

All of a sudden the lightning let go a perfect sluice of white glare, and somebody sings out:

"By the living jingo, here's the bag of gold on his breast!"

Hines let out a whoop, like everybody else, and dropped my wrist and give a big surge to bust his way in and get a look, and the way I lit out and shinned for the road in the dark, there ain't nobody can tell.

I had the road all to myself, and I fairly flew—leastways, I had it all to myself except the solid dark, and the now-and-then glares, and the buzzing of the rain, and the thrashing of the wind, and the splitting of the thunder; and sure as you are born I did clip it along!

When I struck the town, I see there warn't nobody out in the storm, so I never hunted for no back streets, but humped it straight through the main one; and when I begun to get towards our house I aimed my eye and set it. No light there; the house all dark—which made me feel sorry and disappointed, I didn't know why. But at last, just as I was sailing by, *flash* comes the light in Mary Jane's window! and my heart swelled up sudden, like to bust; and the same second the house and all was behind me in the dark, and wasn't ever going to be before me no more in this world. She *was* the best girl I ever see, and had the most sand.

The minute I was far enough above the town to see I could make the towhead, I begun to look sharp for a boat to borrow; and the first time the lightning showed me one that wasn't chained, I snatched it and shoved. It was a canoe, and warn't fastened with nothing but a rope. The towhead was a rattling big distance off, away out there in the middle of the river, but I didn't lose no time; and when I struck the raft at last, I was so fagged I would a just laid down to blow and gasp if I could afforded it. But I didn't. As I sprung aboard I sung out:

"Out with you, Jim, and set her loose! Glory be to goodness, we're shut of them!"

Jim lit out, and was a coming for me with both arms spread, he was so full of joy; but when I glimpsed him in the lightning, my heart shot up in my mouth, and I went overboard backwards; for I forgot he was old King Lear and a drownded A-rab all in one, and it most scared the livers and lights out of me. But Jim fished me out, and was going to hug me and bless me, and so on, he was so glad I was back and we was shut of the king and the duke, but I says:

"Not now—have it for breakfast, have it for breakfast! Cut loose and let her slide!"

So, in two seconds, away we went a sliding down the river, and it *did* seem so good to be free again and all by ourselves on the big river and nobody to bother us. I had to skip around a bit, and jump up and crack my heels a few times, I couldn't help it; but about the third crack, I noticed a sound that I knowed mighty well—and held my breath and listened and waited—and sure enough, when the next flash busted out over the water, here they come!—and just a laying to their oars and making their skiff hum! It was the king and the duke.

So I wilted right down on to the planks, then, and give up; and it was all I could do to keep from crying.

CHAPTER XXX.

W<small>HEN</small> they got aboard, the king went for me, and shook me by the collar, and says:

"Tryin' to give us the slip, was ye, you pup! Tired of our company—hey?"

I says:

"No, your majesty, we warn't—*please* don't, your majesty!"

"Quick, then, and tell us what *was* your idea, or I'll shake the insides out o' you!"

"Honest, I'll tell you everything, just as it happened, your majesty. The man that had aholt of me was very good to me, and kept saying he had a boy about as big as me that died last year, and he was sorry to see a boy in such a dangerous fix; and when they was all took by surprise by finding the gold, and made a rush for the coffin, he lets go of me and whispers, 'Heel it, now, or they'll hang ye, sure!' and I lit out. It didn't seem no good for *me* to stay—*I* couldn't do nothing, and I didn't want to be hung if I could get away. So I never stopped running till I found the canoe; and when I got here I told Jim to hurry, or they'd catch me and hang me yet, and said I was afeard you and the duke wasn't alive, now, and I was awful sorry, and so was Jim, and was awful glad when we see you coming, you may ask Jim if I didn't."

Jim said it was so; and the king told him to shut up, and said, "Oh, yes, it's *mighty* likely!" and shook me up again, and said he reckoned he'd drownd me. But the duke says:

"Leggo the boy, you old idiot! Would *you* a done any different? Did you inquire around for *him*, when you got loose? *I* don't remember it."

So the king let go of me, and begun to cuss that town and everybody in it. But the duke says:

"You better a blame sight give *yourself* a good cussing, for you're the one that's entitled to it most. You hain't done a thing, from the start, that had any sense in it, except coming out so cool and cheeky with that imaginary blue-arrow mark. That *was* bright—it was right down bully; and it was the thing that saved us. For if it hadn't been for that, they'd a jailed us till them Englishmen's baggage come—and then—the penitentiary, you bet! But that trick took 'em to the graveyard, and the gold done us a still bigger kindness; for if the excited fools hadn't let go all holts and made that rush to get a look, we'd a slept in our cravats to-night—cravats warranted to *wear*, too—longer than *we'd* need 'em."

They was still a minute—thinking—then the king says, kind of absent-minded like:

"Mf! And we reckoned the *niggers* stole it!"

That made me squirm!

"Yes," says the duke, kinder slow, and deliberate, and sarcastic, "*we* did."

After about a half a minute, the king drawls out:

"Leastways—*I* did."

The duke says, the same way:

"On the contrary—*I* did."

The king kind of ruffles up, and says:

"Looky here, Bilgewater, what'r you referrin' to?"

The duke says, pretty brisk:

"When it comes to that, maybe you'll let me ask, what was *you* referring to?"

"Shucks!" says the king, very sarcastic; "but *I* don't know—maybe you was asleep, and didn't know what you was about."

The duke bristles up, now, and says:

"Oh, let *up* on this cussed nonsense—do you take me for a blame' fool? Don't you reckon *I* know who hid that money in that coffin?"

"*Yes*, sir! I know you *do* know—because you done it yourself!"

"It's a lie!"—and the duke went for him. The king sings out:

"Take y'r hands off!—leggo my throat!—I take it all back!"

The duke says:

"Well, you just own up, first, that you *did* hide that money there, intending to give me the slip one of these days, and come back and dig it up, and have it all to yourself."

"Wait jest a minute, duke—answer me this one question, honest and fair; if you didn't put the money there, say it, and I'll b'lieve you, and take back everything I said."

"You old scoundrel, I didn't, and you know I didn't. There, now!"

"Well, then, I b'lieve you. But answer me only jest this one more—now *don't* git mad; didn't you have it in your *mind* to hook the money and hide it?"

The duke never said nothing for a little bit; then he says:

"Well—I don't care if I *did*, I didn't *do* it, anyway. But you not only had it in mind to do it, but you *done* it."

"I wisht I may never die if I done it, duke, and that's honest. I won't say I warn't *goin'* to do it, because I *was*; but you—I mean somebody—got in ahead o' me."

"It's a lie! You done it, and you got to *say* you done it, or—"

The king began to gurgle, and then he gasps out:

"'Nough!—*I own up!*"

I was very glad to hear him say that, it made me feel much more easier than what I was feeling before. So the duke took his hands off, and says:

"If you ever deny it again I'll drown you. It's *well* for you to set there and blubber like a baby—it's fitten for you, after the way you've acted. I never see such an old ostrich for wanting to gobble everything—and I a trusting you all the time, like you was my own father. You ought to been ashamed of yourself to stand by and hear it saddled on to a lot of poor niggers and you never say a word for 'em. It makes me feel ridiculous to think I was soft enough to *believe* that rubbage. Cuss you, I can see, now, why you was so anxious to make up the deffesit—you wanted to get what money I'd got out of the Nonesuch and one thing or another, and scoop it *all!*"

The king says, timid, and still a snuffling:

"Why, duke, it was you that said make up the deffersit; it warn't me."

"Dry up! I don't want to hear no more *out* of you!" says the duke. "And *now* you see what you *got* by it. They've got all their own money back, and all of *ourn* but a shekel or two, *besides.* G'long to bed—and don't you deffersit *me* no more deffersits, long 's *you* live!"

So the king sneaked into the wigwam, and took to his bottle for comfort; and before long the duke tackled *his* bottle; and so in about a half an hour they was as thick as thieves again, and the tighter they got the lovinger they got; and went off a-snoring in each other's arms. They both got powerful mellow, but I noticed the king didn't get mellow enough to forget to remember to not deny about hiding the money-bag again. That made me feel easy and satisfied. Of course when they got to snoring, we had a long gabble, and I told Jim everything.

CHAPTER XXXI.

We dasn't stop again at any town, for days and days; kept right along down the river. We was down south in the warm weather, now, and a mighty long ways from home. We begun to come to trees with Spanish moss on them, hanging down from the limbs like long gray beards. It was the first I ever see it growing, and it made the woods look solemn and dismal. So now the frauds reckoned they was out of danger, and they begun to work the villages again.

First they done a lecture on temperance; but they didn't make enough for them both to get drunk on. Then in another village they started a dancing-school; but they didn't know no more how to dance than a kangaroo does; so the first prance they made, the general public jumped in and pranced them out of town. Another time they tried a go at yellocution; but they didn't yellocute long till the audience got up and give them a solid good cussing and made them skip out. They tackled missionarying, and mesmerizing, and doctoring, and telling fortunes, and a little of every-thing; but they couldn't seem to have no luck.[147] So at last they got just about dead broke, and laid around the raft, as she floated along, thinking and thinking, and never saying nothing, by the half a day at a time, and dreadful blue and desperate.

And at last they took a change and begun to lay their heads together in the wigwam and talk low and confidential two or three hours at a time. Jim and me got uneasy. We didn't like the look of it. We judged they was studying up some kind of worse deviltry than ever. We turned it over and over, and at last we made up our minds they was going to break into some-body's house or store, or was going into the counterfeit-money business, or something. So then we was pretty scared, and made up an agreement that we wouldn't have nothing in the world to do with such actions, and if we ever got the least show we would give them the cold shake, and clear out and leave them behind. Well, early one morning we hid the raft in a good, safe place about two mile below a little bit of a shabby village, named Pikesville, and the king he went ashore, and told us all to stay hid whilst he went up to town and smelt around to see if anybody had got any wind of the Royal Nonesuch there yet. ("House to rob, you *mean*," says I to myself; "and when you get through robbing it you'll come back here and wonder what has become of me and Jim and the raft—and you'll have to take it out in wondering.") And he said if he warn't back by midday, the duke and me would know it was all right, and we was to come along.

So we staid where we was. The duke he fretted and sweated around, and was in a mighty sour way. He scolded us for everything, and we couldn't seem to do nothing right; he found fault with every little thing. Something was a-brewing, sure. I was good and glad when midday, come and no king; we could have a change, anyway—and maybe a chance for *the* change, on top of it. So me and the duke went up to the village, and hunted around there for the king, and by and by we found him in the back

---

147. The king and the duke run the gamut of traveling show scams, starting with a bogus temperance lecture. Twain could have been thinking of P. T. Barnum, the legendary circus promoter and hustler whose early career was famous for freak show hoaxes such as General Tom Thumb, the world's smallest man (actually a four-year-old dwarf), whom he exhibited in a tour that included several stops on the Mississippi River. Barnum gave count-less temperance lectures, sometimes with an admission charge, but unlike Twain's charac-ters was a true believer and does not appear to have pocketed the money. Barnum did, however, dig himself out of debt at one point with such lectures as "The Art of Money-Getting" (Barnum 1855, 112, 141; Harris 1981, 155–158, 216). Twain found the cause of tem-perance ridiculous, but he enjoyed Barnum's oddball humor, and the two became friends (Scharnhorst 2006, 221; Powers 2005, 371–372).

room of a little low doggery, very tight, and a lot of loafers bullyragging him for sport, and he a cussing and threatening with all his might, and so tight he couldn't walk, and couldn't do nothing to them. The duke he begun to abuse him for an old fool, and the king begun to sass back; and the minute they was fairly at it, I lit out, and shook the reefs out of my hind legs, and spun down the river road like a deer—for I see our chance; and I made up my mind that it would be a long day before they ever see me and Jim again. I got down there all out of breath but loaded up with joy, and sung out:

"Set her loose, Jim! we're all right, now!"

But there warn't no answer, and nobody come out of the wigwam. Jim was gone! I set up a shout—and then another—and then another one; and run this way and that in the woods, whooping and screeching; but it warn't no use—old Jim was gone. Then I set down and cried; I couldn't help it. But I couldn't set still long. Pretty soon I went out on the road, trying to think what I better do, and I run across a boy walking, and asked him if he'd seen a strange nigger, dressed so and so, and he says:

"Yes."

"Whereabouts?" says I.

"Down to Silas Phelps' place, two mile below here. He's a runaway nigger, and they've got him. Was you looking for him?"

"You bet I ain't! I run across him in the woods about an hour or two ago, and he said if I hollered he'd cut my livers out—and told me to lay down and stay where I was; and I done it. Been there ever since; afeard to come out."

"Well," he says, "you needn't be afeard no more, becuz they've got him. He run off f'm down South, som'ers."

"It's a good job they got him."

"Well, I *reckon*! There's two hunderd dollars reward on him. It's like picking up money out'n the road."

"Yes, it is—and *I* could a had it if I'd been big enough; I see him *first.* Who nailed him?"

"It was an old fellow—a stranger—and he sold out his chance in him for forty dollars, becuz he's got to go up the river and can't wait. Think o' that, now! You bet *I'd* wait, if it was seven year."

"That's me, every time," says I. "But maybe his chance ain't worth no more than that, if he'll sell it so cheap. Maybe there's something ain't straight about it."

"But it *is,* though—straight as a string. I see the handbill myself. It tells all about him, to a dot—paints him like a picture, and tells the plantation he's frum, below Newr*leans.* No-sirree-*bob,* they ain't no trouble 'bout *that* speculation, you bet you. Say, gimme a chaw tobacker, won't ye?"

I didn't have none, so he left. I went to the raft, and set down in the wigwam to think. But I couldn't come to nothing. I thought till I wore my head sore, but I couldn't see no way out of the trouble. After all this long journey, and after all we'd done for them scoundrels, here it was all come to nothing, everything all busted up and ruined, because they could have the heart to serve Jim such a trick as that, and make him a slave again all his life, and amongst strangers, too, for forty dirty dollars.

Once I said to myself it would be a thousand times better for Jim to be a slave at home where his family was, as long as he'd *got* to be a slave, and so I'd better write a letter to Tom Sawyer and tell him to tell Miss Watson where he was. But I soon give up that notion for two things: she'd be mad and disgusted at his rascality and ungratefulness for leaving her, and so she'd sell him straight down the river again; and if she didn't, everybody naturally despises an ungrateful nigger, and they'd make Jim feel it all the time, and so he'd feel ornery and disgraced. And then think of *me!* It would get all around, that Huck Finn helped a nigger to get his freedom; and if I was ever to see anybody from that town again, I'd be ready to get down and lick his boots for shame. That's just the way: a person does a low-down thing, and then he don't want to take no consequences of it. Thinks as long as he can hide it, it ain't no disgrace. That was my fix exactly. The more I studied about this, the more my conscience went to grinding me, and the more wicked and low-down and ornery I got to feeling. And at last, when it hit me all of a sudden that here was the plain hand of Providence slapping me in the face and letting me know my wickedness was being watched all the time from up there in heaven, whilst I was stealing a poor old woman's nigger that hadn't ever done me no harm, and now was show-ing me there's One that's always on the lookout, and ain't agoing to allow no such miserable doings to go only just so fur and no further, I most dropped in my tracks I was so scared. Well, I tried the best I could to kinder soften it up somehow for myself, by saying I was brung up wicked, and so I warn't so much to blame; but something inside of me kept saying, "There was the Sunday school, you could a gone to it; and if you'd a done it they'd a learnt you, there, that people that acts as I'd been acting about that nigger goes to everlasting fire."[148]

---

148. Huck's conflicted thoughts in this paragraph say a lot about the nature of the slave society he lived in. In the first sentence he recognizes, perhaps for the first time, that Jim would be better off as a free man than as a slave. As obvious as that sounds, white south-erners were told again and again, often from the pulpit, that blacks were better off under slavery. Huck has not completely abandoned that view, because even though Miss Watson has decided to sell Jim down the river and separate him from his family, Huck still sees Jim as "an ungrateful nigger" for escaping. Huck even thinks that Jim, once reenslaved, will forever feel the shame of his ingratitude. Huck worries for himself too, because he'll be shunned in society for his "low-down" sinful act. What is his sin, exactly? He is disobeying the commandment "Thou shall not steal" by "stealing" Jim and is going against the bibli-cally sanctioned system of slavery. Slavery's defenders constantly cited Scripture and used

It made me shiver. And I about made up my mind to pray; and see if I couldn't try to quit being the kind of a boy I was, and be better. So I kneeled down. But the words wouldn't come. Why wouldn't they? It warn't no use to try and hide it from Him. Nor from *me,* neither. I knowed very well why they wouldn't come. It was because my heart warn't right; it was because I warn't square; it was because I was playing double. I was letting *on* to give up sin, but away inside of me I was holding on to the biggest one of all. I was trying to make my mouth *say* I would do the right thing and the clean thing, and go and write to that nigger's owner and tell where he was; but deep down in me I knowed it was a lie—and He knowed it. You can't pray a lie—I found that out.

So I was full of trouble, full as I could be; and didn't know what to do. At last I had an idea; and I says, I'll go and write the letter—and *then* see if I can pray. Why, it was astonishing, the way I felt as light as a feather, right straight off, and my troubles all gone. So I got a piece of paper and a pencil, all glad and excited, and set down and wrote:

Miss Watson your runaway nigger Jim is down here two mile below Pikesville and Mr. Phelps has got him and he will give him up for the reward if you send.

HUCK FINN.

I felt good and all washed clean of sin for the first time I had ever felt so in my life, and I knowed I could pray now. But I didn't do it straight off, but laid the paper down and set there thinking—thinking how good it was all this happened so, and how near I come to being lost and going to hell. And went on thinking. And got to thinking over our trip down the river; and I see Jim before me, all the time, in the day, and in the night-time, sometimes moonlight, sometimes storms, and we a floating along, talking, and singing, and laughing. But somehow I couldn't seem to strike no places to harden me against him, but only the other kind. I'd see him standing my watch on top of his'n, stead of calling me, so I could go on sleeping; and see him how glad he was when I come back out of the fog; and when I come to him again in the swamp, up there where the feud was; and such-like times; and would always call me honey, and pet me, and do everything he could think of for me, and how good he always was; and at last I struck the time I saved him by telling the men we had small-pox aboard, and he was so grateful, and said I was the best friend old Jim ever

Paul's letter to Philemon, in which he returns the runaway slave Onesimus, as proof that "slaves should not be taken or detained from their master, without their master's consent," as a South Carolina Episcopal clergyman put it in 1823 (Morrison 1980–1981, 20).

had in the world, and the *only* one he's got now; and then I happened to look around and see that paper.

It was a close place. I took it up, and held it in my hand. I was a trembling, because I'd got to decide, forever, betwixt two things, and I knowed it. I studied a minute, sort of holding my breath, and then says to myself:

"All right, then, I'll *go* to hell"—and tore it up.[149]

It was awful thoughts, and awful words, but they was said. And I let them stay said; and never thought no more about reforming. I shoved the whole thing out of my head; and said I would take up wickedness again, which was in my line, being brung up to it, and the other warn't. And for a starter, I would go to work and steal Jim out of slavery again; and if I could think up anything worse, I would do that, too; because as long as I was in, and in for good, I might as well go the whole hog.

Then I set to thinking over how to get at it, and turned over some considerable many ways in my mind; and at last fixed up a plan that suited me. So then I took the bearings of a woody island that was down the river a piece, and as soon as it was fairly dark I crept out with my raft and went for it, and hid it there, and then turned in. I slept the night through, and got up before it was light, and had my breakfast, and put on my store clothes, and tied up some others and one thing or another in a bundle, and took the canoe and cleared for shore. I landed below where I judged was Phelps's place, and hid my bundle in the woods, and then filled up the canoe with water, and loaded rocks into her and sunk her where I could find her again when I wanted her, about a quarter of a mile below a little steam sawmill that was on the bank.

Then I struck up the road, and when I passed the mill I see a sign on it, "Phelps's Sawmill," and when I come to the farm-houses, two or three hundred yards further along, I kept my eyes peeled, but didn't see nobody around, though it was good daylight now. But I didn't mind, because I didn't want to see nobody just yet—I only wanted to get the lay of the land. According to my plan, I was going to turn up there from the village, not from below. So I just took a look, and shoved along, straight for town. Well, the very first man I see, when I got there, was the duke. He was

---

149. This might be the most quoted line in the entire novel. While Huck has still internalized his society's teachings about how slaves should be grateful and how helping to free a slave is an act of theft deserving of eternal hellfire, he has an internal conscience—his "heart"—that is in conflict with the proslavery external conscience that has been handed down to him. A few paragraphs ago his external conscience had won the battle, and he was informing on Jim in a letter to Miss Watson. Now Huck's internal conscience has won out, though he expects to get the ultimate punishment for it. He is making the greatest sacrifice imaginable—an eternity spent in Hell.

sticking up a bill for the Royal Nonesuch—three-night performance—like that other time. *They* had the cheek, them frauds! I was right on him, before I could shirk. He looked astonished, and says:

"Hel-*lo!* Where'd *you* come from?" Then he says, kind of glad and eager, "Where's the raft?—got her in a good place?"

I says:

"Why, that's just what I was agoing ask your grace."

Then he didn't look so joyful—and says:

"What was your idea for asking *me*?" he says.

"Well," I says, "when I see the king in that doggery yesterday, I says to myself, we can't get him home for hours, till he's soberer; so I went a loafing around town to put in the time, and wait. A man up and offered me ten cents to help him pull a skiff over the river and back to fetch a sheep, and so I went along; but when we was dragging him to the boat, and the man left me aholt of the rope and went behind him to shove him along, he was too strong for me, and jerked loose and run, and we after him. We didn't have no dog, and so we had to chase him all over the country till we tired him out. We never got him till dark, then we fetched him over, and I started down for the raft. When I got there and see it was gone, I says to myself, 'They've got into trouble and had to leave; and they've took my nigger, which is the only nigger I've got in the world, and now I'm in a strange country, and ain't got no property no more, nor nothing, and no way to make my living;' so I set down and cried. I slept in the woods all night. But what *did* become of the raft, then?—and Jim, poor Jim!"

"Blamed if *I* know—that is, what's become of the raft. That old fool had made a trade and got forty dollars, and when we found him in the doggery the loafers had matched half dollars with him and got every cent but what he'd spent for whisky; and when I got him home late last night and found the raft gone, we said, 'That little rascal has stole our raft and shook us, and run off down the river.'"

"I wouldn't shake my *nigger,* would I?—the only nigger I had in the world, and the only property."

"We never thought of that. Fact is, I reckon we'd come to consider him *our* nigger; yes, we did consider him so—goodness knows we had trouble enough for him. So when we see the raft was gone, and we flat broke, there warn't anything for it but to try the Royal Nonesuch another shake. And I've pegged along ever since, dry as a powder-horn. Where's that ten cents? Give it here."

I had considerable money, so I give him ten cents, but begged him to spend it for something to eat, and give me some, because it was all the money I had, and I hadn't had nothing to eat since yesterday. He never said nothing. The next minute he whirls on me and says:

"Do you reckon that nigger would blow on us? We'd skin him if he done that!"

"How can he blow? Hain't he run off?"

"No! That old fool sold him, and never divided with me, and the money's gone."

"*Sold* him?" I says, and begun to cry; "why, he was *my* nigger, and that was my money. Where is he?—I want my nigger."

"Well, you can't *get* your nigger, that's all—so dry up your blubbering. Looky here—do you think *you'd* venture to blow on us? Blamed if I think I'd trust you. Why, if you *was* to blow on us—"

He stopped, but I never see the duke look so ugly out of his eyes before. I went on a-whimpering, and says:

"I don't want to blow on nobody; and I ain't got no time to blow, no-how. I got to turn out and find my nigger."

He looked kinder bothered, and stood there with his bills fluttering on his arm, thinking, and wrinkling up his forehead. At last he says:

"I'll tell you something. We got to be here three days. If you'll promise you won't blow, and won't let the nigger blow, I'll tell you where to find him."

So I promised, and he says:

"A farmer by the name of Silas Ph—" and then he stopped. You see, he started to tell me the truth; but when he stopped, that way, and begun to study and think again, I reckoned he was changing his mind. And so he was. He wouldn't trust me; he wanted to make sure of having me out of the way the whole three days. So pretty soon he says:

"The man that bought him is named Abram Foster—Abram G. Foster—and he lives forty mile back here in the country, on the road to Lafayette."

"All right," I says, "I can walk it in three days. And I'll start this very afternoon."

"No you won't, you'll start *now;* and don't you lose any time about it, neither, nor do any gabbling by the way. Just keep a tight tongue in your head and move right along, and then you won't get into trouble with *us,* d'ye hear?"

That was the order I wanted, and that was the one I played for. I wanted to be left free to work my plans.

"So clear out," he says; "and you can tell Mr. Foster whatever you want to. Maybe you can get him to believe that Jim *is* your nigger—some idiots don't require documents—leastways I've heard there's such down South here.[150] And when you tell him the handbill and the reward's bogus,

---

150. The duke touches on one of the worst nightmares for blacks in antebellum America: the possibility of reenslavement, as "some idiots don't require documents." In many free states, free blacks were required to have documentation of their legal status. Even when they had the documents, there was still the possibility of kidnapping and sale into

maybe he'll believe you when you explain to him what the idea was for getting 'em out. Go 'long now, and tell him anything you want to; but mind you don't work your jaw any *between* here and there."

So I left, and struck for the back country. I didn't look around, but I kinder felt like he was watching me. But I knowed I could tire him out at that. I went straight out in the country as much as a mile, before I stopped; then I doubled back through the woods towards Phelps's. I reckoned I better start in on my plan straight off, without fooling around, because I wanted to stop Jim's mouth till these fellows could get away. I didn't want no trouble with their kind. I'd seen all I wanted to of them, and wanted to get entirely shut of them.

CHAPTER XXXII.

WHEN I got there it was all still and Sunday-like, and hot and sunshiny—the hands was gone to the fields; and there was them kind of faint dronings of bugs and flies in the air that makes it seem so lonesome and like everybody's dead and gone; and if a breeze fans along and quivers the leaves, it makes you feel mournful, because you feel like it's spirits whispering—spirits that's been dead ever so many years—and you always think they're talking about *you*. As a general thing it makes a body wish *he* was dead, too, and done with it all.

Phelps's was one of these little one-horse cotton plantations; and they all look alike. A rail fence round a two-acre yard; a stile, made out of logs sawed off and up-ended, in steps, like barrels of a different length, to climb over the fence with, and for the women to stand on when they are going to jump onto a horse; some sickly grass-patches in the big yard, but mostly it was bare and smooth, like an old hat with the nap rubbed off; big double log house for the white folks—hewed logs, with the chinks stopped up with mud or mortar, and these mud-stripes been whitewashed some time or another; round-log kitchen, with a big broad, open but roofed passage joining it to the house; log smoke-house back of the kitchen; three little log nigger-cabins in a row t'other side the smoke-house; one little hut all by itself away down against the back fence, and some outbuildings down a piece the other side; ash-hopper, and big kettle to bile soap in, by the little

slavery; the most famous case was that of Solomon Northup, who was kidnapped in upstate New York in 1841 and enslaved in Louisiana for the next 12 years. His memoir *12 Years a Slave* became a book in 1853 and an Academy Award–winning movie in 2013. After the passage of the Fugitive Slave Act of 1850, a slave catcher could apprehend any black person in the North and go to court to argue that he or she was an escaped slave. Judges were paid a higher fee for ruling in favor of the slave catcher.

hut; bench by the kitchen door, with bucket of water and a gourd; hound asleep there, in the sun; more hounds asleep, round about; about three shade trees away off in a corner; some currant bushes and gooseberry bushes in one place by the fence; outside of the fence a garden and a watermelon patch; then the cotton fields begins, and after the fields, the woods.

I went around and clumb over the back stile by the ash-hopper, and started for the kitchen. When I got a little ways, I heard the dim hum of a spinning-wheel wailing along up and sinking along down again; and then I knowed for certain I wished I was dead—for that *is* the lonesomest sound in the whole world.

I went right along, not fixing up any particular plan, but just trusting to Providence to put the right words in my mouth when the time come; for I'd noticed that Providence always did put the right words in my mouth, if I left it alone.

When I got half-way, first one hound and then another got up and went for me, and of course I stopped and faced them, and kept still. And such another pow-wow as they made! In a quarter of a minute I was a kind of a hub of a wheel, as you may say—spokes made out of dogs—circle of fifteen of them packed together around me, with their necks and noses stretched up towards me, a-barking and howling; and more a-coming; you could see them sailing over fences and around corners from everywheres.

A nigger woman come tearing out of the kitchen with a rolling-pin in her hand, singing out, "Begone *you* Tige! you Spot! begone, sah!" and she fetched first one and then another of them a clip and sent them howling, and then the rest followed; and the next second, half of them come back, wagging their tails around me, and making friends with me. There ain't no harm in a hound, nohow.

And behind the woman comes a little nigger girl and two little nigger boys, without anything on but tow-linen shirts, and they hung on to their mother's gown, and peeped out from behind her at me, bashful, the way they always do. And here comes the white woman running from the house, about forty-five or fifty year old, bareheaded, and her spinning-stick in her hand;[151]

---

151. A spinning wheel and stick, for turning raw fibers such as wool and cotton into thread or yarn, was a staple of American homes into the early 19th century. The women of the house or female slaves would then weave, knit, and sew the yarn and thread into clothes for the family. Clothing was the most important of home manufactures in early America. With the spread of textile and clothing factories, homemade clothing was rapidly displaced, as noted earlier, but along the frontier and even in areas with ready access to markets, many women still made much of the family's clothing. As Rolla M. Tyron noted, "After the spinning and weaving industries had become established in the home, it was difficult to crowd them out. In fact even after the factory came to do the work of the handicraft system, its development along the line of textile industries was retarded by the tenacity with which the women held on to their spinning wheels and looms" (1966, 191).

and behind her comes her little white children, acting the same way the little niggers was doing. She was smiling all over so she could hardly stand—and says:

"It's *you,* at last!—*ain't* it?"

I out with a "Yes'm" before I thought.

She grabbed me and hugged me tight; and then gripped me by both hands and shook and shook; and the tears come in her eyes, and run down over; and she couldn't seem to hug and shake enough, and kept saying, "You don't look as much like your mother as I reckoned you would, but law sakes, I don't care for that, I'm *so* glad to see you! Dear, dear, it does seem like I could eat you up! Children, it's your cousin Tom!—tell him howdy."

But they ducked their heads, and put their fingers in their mouths, and hid behind her. So she run on:

"Lize, hurry up and get him a hot breakfast, right away—or did you get your breakfast on the boat?"

I said I had got it on the boat. So then she started for the house, leading me by the hand, and the children tagging after. When we got there, she set me down in a split-bottomed chair, and set herself down on a little low stool in front of me, holding both of my hands, and says:

"Now I can have a *good* look at you; and, laws-a-me, I've been hungry for it a many and a many a time, all these long years, and it's come at last! We been expecting you a couple of days and more. What kep' you?—boat get aground?"

"Yes'm—she—"

"Don't say yes'm—say Aunt Sally. Where'd she get aground?"

I didn't rightly know what to say, because I didn't know whether the boat would be coming up the river or down. But I go a good deal on instinct; and my instinct said she would be coming up—from down towards Orleans. That didn't help me much, though; for I didn't know the names of bars down that way. I see I'd got to invent a bar, or forget the name of the one we got aground on—or—Now I struck an idea, and fetched it out:

"It warn't the grounding—that didn't keep us back but a little. We blowed out a cylinder-head."

"Good gracious! anybody hurt?"

"No'm. Killed a nigger."

"Well, it's lucky; because sometimes people do get hurt.[152] Two years ago last Christmas, your uncle Silas was coming up from Newrleans on

---

152. This appalling exchange, where Huck casually implies that "a nigger" is not a person and Aunt Sally does the same, is in keeping with how blacks were perceived by most whites in antebellum America. When the U.S. Constitution was written, blacks "had for more than a century before been regarded as beings of an inferior order, and altogether

the old *Lally Rook*, and she blowed out a cylinder-head and crippled a man. And I think he died afterwards. He was a Baptist. Your uncle Silas knowed a family in Baton Rouge that knowed his people very well. Yes, I remember now, he *did* die. Mortification set in, and they had to amputate him. But it didn't save him. Yes, it was mortification—that was it. He turned blue all over, and died in the hope of a glorious resurrection. They say he was a sight to look at. Your uncle's been up to the town every day to fetch you. And he's gone again, not more'n an hour ago; he'll be back any minute now. You must a met him on the road, didn't you?—oldish man, with a—"

"No, I didn't see nobody, Aunt Sally. The boat landed just at daylight, and I left my baggage on the wharf-boat and went looking around the town and out a piece in the country, to put in the time and not get here too soon; and so I come down the back way."

"Who'd you give the baggage to?"

"Nobody."

"Why, child, it'll be stole!"

"Not where *I* hid it I reckon it won't," I says.

"How'd you get your breakfast so early on the boat?"

It was kinder thin ice, but I says:

"The captain see me standing around, and told me I better have something to eat before I went ashore; so he took me in the texas to the officers' lunch, and give me all I wanted."

I was getting so uneasy I couldn't listen good. I had my mind on the children all the time; I wanted to get them out to one side, and pump them a little, and find out who I was. But I couldn't get no show, Mrs. Phelps kept it up and run on so. Pretty soon she made the cold chills streak all down my back, because she says:

"But here we're a running on this way, and you hain't told me a word about Sis, nor any of them. Now I'll rest my works a little, and you start up yourn; just tell me *everything*—tell me all about 'm all—every one of 'm; and how they are, and what they're doing, and what they told you to tell me; and every last thing you can think of."

---

unfit to associate with the white race, either in social or political relations; and so far inferior, that they had no rights which the white man was bound to respect; and that the negro might justly and lawfully be reduced to slavery. . . . He was bought and sold, and treated as an ordinary article of merchandise and traffic, whenever a profit could be made by it." The quotation comes from the U.S. Supreme Court's infamous *Dred Scott* decision of 1857—involving a Missouri slave seeking his freedom—in which the court ruled that blacks could not be citizens and were not entitled to freedom even in nonslave states. The racism of the time was so rarely questioned that there was not even a word for it; the term "racism" was not coined until 1902 (Demby 2014).

Well, I see I was up a stump—and up it good. Providence had stood by me this fur, all right, but I was hard and tight aground, now. I see it warn't a bit of use to try to go ahead—I'd *got* to throw up my hand. So I says to myself, here's another place where I got to resk the truth. I opened my mouth to begin; but she grabbed me and hustled me in behind the bed, and says:

"Here he comes! Stick your head down lower—there, that'll do; you can't be seen, now. Don't you let on you're here. I'll play a joke on him. Children, don't you say a word."

I see I was in a fix, now. But it warn't no use to worry; there warn't nothing to do but just hold still, and try and be ready to stand from under when the lightning struck.

I had just one little glimpse of the old gentleman when he come in, then the bed hid him. Mrs. Phelps she jumps for him, and says:

"Has he come?"

"No," says her husband.

"Good-*ness* gracious!" she says, "what in the world *can* have become of him?"

"I can't imagine," says the old gentleman; "and I must say, it makes me dreadful uneasy."

"Uneasy!" she says; "I'm ready to go distracted! He *must* a come; and you've missed him along the road. I *know* it's so—something *tells* me so."

"Why Sally, I *couldn't* miss him along the road—*you* know that."

"But oh, dear, dear, what *will* Sis say! He must a come! You must a missed him. He—"

"Oh, don't distress me any more'n I'm already distressed. I don't know what in the world to make of it. I'm at my wit's end, and I don't mind acknowledging 't I'm right down scared. But there's no hope that he's come; for he *couldn't* come and me miss him. Sally, it's terrible—just terrible—something's happened to the boat, sure!"

"Why, Silas! Look yonder!—up the road!—ain't that somebody coming?"

He sprung to the window at the head of the bed, and that give Mrs. Phelps the chance she wanted. She stooped down quick, at the foot of the bed, and give me a pull, and out I come; and when he turned back from the window, there she stood, a-beaming and a-smiling like a house afire, and I standing pretty meek and sweaty alongside. The old gentleman stared, and says:

"Why, who's that?"

"Who do you reckon 't is?"

"I hain't no idea. Who *is* it?"

"It's *Tom Sawyer!*"

By jings, I most slumped through the floor! But there warn't no time to swap knives; the old man grabbed me by the hand and shook, and kept on shaking; and all the time, how the woman did dance around and laugh and cry; and then how they both did fire off questions about Sid, and Mary, and the rest of the tribe.

But if they was joyful, it warn't nothing to what I was; for it was like being born again, I was so glad to find out who I was. Well, they froze to me for two hours; and at last, when my chin was so tired it couldn't hardly go, any more, I had told them more about my family—I mean the Sawyer family—than ever happened to any six Sawyer families. And I explained all about how we blowed out a cylinder-head at the mouth of White River and it took us three days to fix it. Which was all right, and worked first-rate; because *they* didn't know but what it would take three days to fix it. If I'd a called it a bolt-head it would a done just as well.

Now I was feeling pretty comfortable all down one side, and pretty uncomfortable all up the other. Being Tom Sawyer was easy and comfortable; and it stayed easy and comfortable till by and by I hear a steamboat coughing along down the river—then I says to myself, s'pose Tom Sawyer comes down on that boat? And s'pose he steps in here any minute, and sings out my name before I can throw him a wink to keep quiet? Well, I couldn't *have* it that way—it wouldn't do at all. I must go up the road and waylay him. So I told the folks I reckoned I would go up to the town and fetch down my baggage. The old gentleman was for going along with me, but I said no, I could drive the horse myself, and I druther he wouldn't take no trouble about me.

CHAPTER XXXIII.

So I started for town, in the wagon, and when I was half-way I see a wagon coming, and sure enough it was Tom Sawyer, and I stopped and waited till he come along. I says "Hold on!" and it stopped alongside, and his mouth opened up like a trunk, and staid so; and he swallowed two or three times like a person that's got a dry throat, and then says:

"I hain't ever done you no harm. You know that. So, then, what you want to come back and ha'nt *me* for?"

I says:

"I hain't come back—I hain't been *gone*."

When he heard my voice, it righted him up some, but he warn't quite satisfied yet. He says:

"Don't you play nothing on me, because I wouldn't on you. Honest injun, now, you ain't a ghost?"

"Honest injun, I ain't," I says.

"Well—I—I—well, that ought to settle it, of course; but I can't some-how seem to understand it, no way. Looky here, warn't you ever murdered *at all?*"

"No. I warn't ever murdered at all—I played it on them. You come in here and feel of me if you don't believe me."

So he done it; and it satisfied him; and he was that glad to see me again, he didn't know what to do. And he wanted to know all about it right off; because it was a grand adventure, and mysterious, and so it hit him where he lived. But I said, leave it alone till by and by; and told his driver to wait, and we drove off a little piece, and I told him the kind of a fix I was in, and what did he reckon we better do? He said, let him alone a minute, and don't disturb him. So he thought and thought, and pretty soon he says:

"It's all right; I've got it. Take my trunk in your wagon, and let on it's your'n; and you turn back and fool along slow, so as to get to the house about the time you ought to; and I'll go towards town a piece, and take a fresh start, and get there a quarter or a half an hour after you; and you needn't let on to know me, at first."

I says:

"All right; but wait a minute. There's one more thing—a thing that *nobody* don't know but me. And that is, there's a nigger here that I'm a trying to steal out of slavery—and his name is *Jim*—old Miss Watson's Jim."

He says:

"What! Why, Jim is—"

He stopped and went to studying. I says:

"*I* know what you'll say. You'll say it's dirty, low-down business; but what if it is? *I'*m low down; and I'm agoing to steal him, and I want you keep mum and not let on. Will you?"

His eye lit up, and he says:

"I'll *help* you steal him!"

Well, I let go all holts then, like I was shot. It was the most astonishing speech I ever heard—and I'm bound to say Tom Sawyer fell, considerable, in my estimation. Only I couldn't believe it. Tom Sawyer a *nigger stealer*![153]

---

153. Here Huck returns to his community's proslavery morality, which he has still internalized. Many southern churches did not merely condone slavery but also condemned abolitionists. A prominent Methodist clergyman in Twain's hometown of Hannibal held that abolitionism was the worst of all sins (Dempsey 2003, 63–64). Helping Jim escape is perhaps a bigger risk for Tom than for Huck, because Tom, unlike Huck, presumably plans to go back to St. Petersburg. Abetting a fugitive slave was not only considered a mortal sin in Missouri but was also subject to severe punishment. When Twain was six years old, the citizens of Hannibal were up in arms about the "capture" of five slaves by three abolitionists who took them across the river to Illinois. His father, as foreman of a jury, earned the town's gratitude for getting them convicted and sentenced to 12 years of hard labor (Pettit 1974, 18).

"Oh, shucks!" I says; "you're joking."

"I ain't joking, either."

"Well, then," I says, "joking or no joking, if you hear anything said about a runaway nigger, don't forget to remember that *you* don't know nothing about him, and *I* don't know nothing about him."

Then we took the trunk and put it in my wagon, and he drove off his way, and I drove mine. But of course I forgot all about driving slow, on accounts of being glad and full of thinking; so I got home a heap too quick for that length of a trip. The old gentleman was at the door, and he says:

"Why, this is wonderful! Whoever would a thought it was in that mare to do it? I wish we'd a timed her. And she hain't sweated a hair—not a hair. It's wonderful. Why, I wouldn't take a hundred dollars for that horse now; I wouldn't, honest; and yet I'd a sold her for fifteen before, and thought 'twas all she was worth."

That's all he said. He was the innocentest, best old soul I ever see. But it warn't surprising; because he warn't only just a farmer, he was a preacher, too, and had a little one-horse log church down back of the plantation, which he built it himself at his own expense, for a church and schoolhouse, and never charged nothing for his preaching, and it was worth it, too. There was plenty other farmer-preachers like that, and done the same way, down South.

In about half an hour Tom's wagon drove up to the front stile, and Aunt Sally she see it through the window because it was only about fifty yards, and says:

"Why, there's somebody come! I wonder who 'tis? Why, I do believe it's a stranger. Jimmy" (that's one of the children), "run and tell Lize to put on another plate for dinner."

Everybody made a rush for the front door, because, of course, a stranger don't come *every* year, and so he lays over the yaller fever, for interest, when he does come. Tom was over the stile and starting for the house; the wagon was spinning up the road for the village, and we was all bunched in the front door. Tom had his store clothes on, and an audience—and that was always nuts for Tom Sawyer. In them circumstances it warn't no trouble to him to throw in an amount of style that was suitable. He warn't a boy to meeky along up that yard like a sheep; no, he come ca'm and important, like the ram. When he got afront of us, he lifts his hat ever so gracious and dainty, like it was the lid of a box that had butterflies asleep in it and he didn't want to disturb them, and says:

"Mr. Archibald Nichols, I presume?"

"No, my boy," says the old gentleman, "I'm sorry to say 't your driver has deceived you; Nichols's place is down a matter of three mile more. Come in, come in."

Tom he took a look back over his shoulder, and says, "Too late—he's out of sight."

"Yes, he's gone, my son, and you must come in and eat your dinner with us; and then we'll hitch up and take you down to Nichols's."

"Oh, I *can't* make you so much trouble; I couldn't think of it. I'll walk—I don't mind the distance."

"But we won't *let* you walk—it wouldn't be Southern hospitality to do it. Come right in."

"Oh, *do,*" says Aunt Sally; "it ain't a bit of trouble to us, not a bit in the world. You *must* stay. It's a long, dusty three mile, and we *can't* let you walk. And besides, I've already told 'em to put on another plate, when I see you coming; so you mustn't disappoint us. Come right in, and make yourself at home."

So Tom he thanked them very hearty and handsome, and let himself be persuaded, and come in; and when he was in, he said he was a stranger from Hicksville, Ohio, and his name was William Thompson—and he made another bow.

Well, he run on, and on, and on, making up stuff about Hicksville and everybody in it he could invent, and I getting a little nervous, and wondering how this was going to help me out of my scrape; and at last, still talking along, he reached over and kissed Aunt Sally right on the mouth, and then settled back again in his chair, comfortable, and was going on talking; but she jumped up and wiped it off with the back of her hand, and says:

"You owdacious puppy!"

He looked kind of hurt, and says:

"I'm surprised at you, m'am."

"You're s'rp—Why, what do you reckon *I* am? I've a good notion to take and—say, what do you mean by kissing me?"

He looked kind of humble, and says:

"I didn't mean nothing, m'am. I didn't mean no harm. I—I—thought you'd like it."

"Why, you born fool!" She took up the spinning stick, and it looked like it was all she could do to keep from giving him a crack with it. "What made you think I'd like it?"

"Well, I don't know. Only, they—they—told me you would."

"*They* told you I would. Whoever told you 's *another* lunatic. I never heard the beat of it. Who's *they?*"

"Why—everybody. They all said so, m'am."

It was all she could do to hold in; and her eyes snapped, and her fingers worked like she wanted to scratch him; and she says:

"Who's 'everybody'? Out with their names—or ther'll be an idiot short."

He got up and looked distressed, and fumbled his hat, and says:

"I'm sorry and I warn't expecting it. They told me to. They all told me to. They all said kiss her; and said she'll like it. They all said it—every one of them. But I'm sorry, m'am, and I won't do it no more—I won't, honest."

"You won't, won't you? Well, I sh'd *reckon* you won't!"

"No'm, I'm honest about it; I won't ever do it again. Till you ask me."

"Till I *ask* you! Well, I never see the beat of it in my born days! I lay you'll be the Methusalem-numskull of creation before ever *I* ask you—or the likes of you."

"Well," he says, "it does surprise me so. I can't make it out, somehow. They said you would, and I thought you would. But—" He stopped and looked around slow, like he wished he could run across a friendly eye, somewheres; and fetched up on the old gentleman's, and says, "Didn't *you* think she'd like me to kiss her, sir?"

"Why, no, I—I—well, no, I b'lieve I didn't."

Then he looks on around, the same way, to me—and says:

"Tom, didn't *you* think Aunt Sally 'd open out her arms and say, 'Sid Sawyer—'"

"My land!" she says, breaking in and jumping for him, "you impudent young rascal, to fool a body so—" and was going to hug him, but he fended her off, and says:

"No, not till you've asked me, first."

So she didn't lose no time, but asked him; and hugged him and kissed him, over and over again, and then turned him over to the old man, and he took what was left. And after they got a little quiet again, she says:

"Why, dear me, I never see such a surprise. We warn't looking for *you*, at all, but only Tom. Sis never wrote to me about anybody coming but him."

"It's because it warn't *intended* for any of us to come but Tom," he says; "but I begged and begged, and at the last minute she let me come, too; so, coming down the river, me and Tom thought it would be a first-rate surprise for him to come here to the house first, and for me to by and by tag along and drop in and let on to be a stranger. But it was a mistake, Aunt Sally. This ain't no healthy place for a stranger to come."

"No—not impudent whelps, Sid. You ought to had your jaws boxed; I hain't been so put out since I don't know when. But I don't care, I don't mind the terms—I'd be willing to stand a thousand such jokes to have you here. Well, to think of that performance! I don't deny it, I was most putri-fied with astonishment when you give me that smack."

We had dinner out in that broad open passage betwixt the house and the kitchen; and there was things enough on that table for seven families—and all hot, too; none of your flabby tough meat that's laid in a cupboard in a damp cellar all night and tastes like a hunk of old cold cannibal in the morning. Uncle Silas he asked a pretty long blessing over it, but it was worth it; and it didn't cool it a bit, neither, the way I've seen them kind of interruptions do, lots of times.

There was a considerable good deal of talk, all the afternoon, and me and Tom was on the lookout all the time, but it warn't no use, they didn't happen to say nothing about any runaway nigger, and we was afraid to try to work up to it. But at supper, at night, one of the little boys says:

"Pa, mayn't Tom and Sid and me go to the show?"

"No," says the old man, "I reckon there ain't going to be any; and you couldn't go if there was; because the runaway nigger told Burton and me all about that scandalous show, and Burton said he would tell the people; so I reckon they've drove the owdacious loafers out of town before this time."

So there it was!—but *I* couldn't help it. Tom and me was to sleep in the same room and bed; so, being tired, we bid good-night and went up to bed, right after supper, and clumb out of the window and down the lightning-rod, and shoved for the town; for I didn't believe anybody was going to give the king and the duke a hint, and so if I didn't hurry up and give them one they'd get into trouble sure.

On the road Tom he told me all about how it was reckoned I was murdered, and how pap disappeared, pretty soon, and didn't come back no more, and what a stir there was when Jim run away; and I told Tom all about our Royal Nonesuch rapscallions, and as much of the raft-voyage as I had time to; and as we struck into the town and up through the the middle of it—it was as much as half after eight, then—here comes a raging rush of people, with torches, and an awful whooping and yelling, and banging tin pans and blowing horns; and we jumped to one side to let them go by; and as they went by, I see they had the king and the duke astraddle of a rail— that is, I knowed it *was* the king and the duke, though they was all over tar and feathers, and didn't look like nothing in the world that was human— just looked like a couple of monstrous big soldier-plumes. Well, it made me sick to see it; and I was sorry for them poor pitiful rascals, it seemed like I couldn't ever feel any hardness against them any more in the world. It was a dreadful thing to see. Human beings *can* be awful cruel to one another.

We see we was too late—couldn't do no good. We asked some stragglers about it, and they said everybody went to the show looking very innocent; and laid low and kept dark till the poor old king was in the middle of his cavortings on the stage; then somebody give a signal, and the house rose up and went for them.

So we poked along back home, and I warn't feeling so brash as I was before, but kind of ornery, and humble, and to blame, somehow—though *I* hadn't done nothing. But that's always the way; it don't make no difference whether you do right or wrong, a person's conscience ain't got no sense, and just goes for him *anyway*. If I had a yaller dog that didn't know no more than a person's conscience does, I would pison him. It takes up

TRAVELLING BY RAIL.

(Illustration by Edward W. Kemble. From Mark Twain, *Adventures of Huckleberry Finn*. New York: C. L. Webster, 1885. Digitized by the University of Virginia Library.)

more room than all the rest of a person's insides, and yet ain't no good, nohow. Tom Sawyer he says the same.

CHAPTER XXXIV.

WE stopped talking, and got to thinking. By and by Tom says:

"Looky here, Huck, what fools we are, to not think of it before! I bet I know where Jim is."

"No! Where?"

"In that hut down by the ash-hopper. Why, looky here. When we was at dinner, didn't you see a nigger man go in there with some vittles?"

"Yes."

"What did you think the vittles was for?"

"For a dog."

"So 'd I. Well, it wasn't for a dog."

"Why?"

"Because part of it was watermelon."

"So it was—I noticed it. Well, it does beat all, that I never thought about a dog not eating watermelon. It shows how a body can see and don't see at the same time."

"Well, the nigger unlocked the padlock when he went in, and he locked it again when he came out. He fetched uncle a key, about the time we got up from table—same key, I bet. Watermelon shows man, lock shows prisoner; and it ain't likely there's two prisoners on such a little plantation, and where the people's all so kind and good. Jim's the prisoner. All right—I'm glad we found it out detective fashion; I wouldn't give shucks for any other way. Now you work your mind and study out a plan to steal Jim, and I will study out one, too; and we'll take the one we like the best."

What a head for just a boy to have! If I had Tom Sawyer's head, I wouldn't trade it off to be a duke, nor mate of a steamboat, nor clown in a circus, nor nothing I can think of. I went to thinking out a plan, but only just to be doing something; I knowed very well where the right plan was going to come from. Pretty soon, Tom says:

"Ready?"

"Yes," I says.

"All right—bring it out."

"My plan is this," I says. "We can easy find out if it's Jim in there. Then get up my canoe to-morrow night, and fetch my raft over from the island. Then the first dark night that comes, steal the key out of the old man's britches, after he goes to bed, and shove off down the river on the raft, with Jim, hiding daytimes and running nights, the way me and Jim used to do before. Wouldn't that plan work?"

"*Work?* Why, cert'nly, it would work, like rats a-fighting. But it's too blame' simple; there ain't nothing *to* it. What's the good of a plan that ain't no more trouble than that? It's as mild as goose-milk. Why, Huck, it wouldn't make no more talk than breaking into a soap factory."

I never said nothing, because I warn't expecting nothing different; but I knowed mighty well that whenever he got *his* plan ready it wouldn't have none of them objections to it.

And it didn't. He told me what it was, and I see in a minute it was worth fifteen of mine for style, and would make Jim just as free a man as mine would, and maybe get us all killed besides. So I was satisfied, and said we would waltz in on it. I needn't tell what it was, here, because I knowed it wouldn't stay the way it was. I knowed he would be changing it around, every which way, as we went along, and heaving in new bullinesses wherever he got a chance. And that is what he done.

Well, one thing was dead sure; and that was, that Tom Sawyer was in earnest, and was actuly going to help steal that nigger out of slavery. That was the thing that was too many for me. Here was a boy that was respectable, and well brung up; and had a character to lose; and folks at home that had characters; and he was bright and not leather-headed; and knowing and not ignorant; and not mean, but kind; and yet here he was, without any more pride, or rightness, or feeling, than to stoop to this business, and make himself a shame, and his family a shame, before everybody. I *couldn't* understand it, no way at all. It was outrageous, and I knowed I ought to just up and tell him so; and so be his true friend, and let him quit the thing right where he was, and save himself. And I *did* start to tell him; but he shut me up, and says:

"Don't you reckon I know what I'm about? Don't I generly know what I'm about?"

"Yes."

"Didn't I *say* I was going to help steal the nigger?"

"Yes."

"*Well,* then."

That's all he said, and that's all I said. It warn't no use to say any more; because when he said he'd do a thing, he always done it. But *I* couldn't make out how he was willing to go into this thing; so I just let it go, and never bothered no more about it. If he was bound to have it so, *I* couldn't help it.

When we got home, the house was all dark and still; so we went on down to the hut by the ash-hopper, for to examine it. We went through the yard, so as to see what the hounds would do. They knowed us, and didn't make no more noise than country dogs is always doing when anything comes by in the night. When we got to the cabin, we took a look at the front and the two sides; and on the side I warn't acquainted with—which was the north side—we found a square window-hole, up tolerable high, with just one stout board nailed across it. I says:

"Here's the ticket. This hole's big enough for Jim to get through, if we wrench off the board."

Tom says:

"It's as simple as tit-tat-toe, three-in-a-row, and as easy as playing hooky. I should *hope* we can find a way that's a little more complicated than *that,* Huck Finn."

"Well, then," I says, "how 'll it do to saw him out, the way I done before I was murdered, that time?"

"That's more *like,*" he says. "It's real mysterious, and troublesome, and good," he says; "but I bet we can find a way that's twice as long. There ain't no hurry; le's keep on looking around."

Betwixt the hut and the fence, on the back side, was a lean-to that joined the hut at the eaves, and was made out of plank. It was as long as the hut, but narrow—only about six foot wide. The door to it was at the south end, and was padlocked. Tom he went to the soap kettle, and searched around and fetched back the iron thing they lift the lid with; so he took it and prized out one of the staples. The chain fell down, and we opened the door and went in, and shut it, and struck a match, and see the shed was only built against a cabin and hadn't no connection with it; and there warn't no floor to the shed, nor nothing in it but some old rusty played-out hoes, and spades, and picks, and a crippled plow. The match went out, and so did we, and shoved in the staple again, and the door was locked as good as ever. Tom was joyful. He says:

"Now we're all right. We'll *dig* him out. It'll take about a week!"

Then we started for the house, and I went in the back door—you only have to pull a buckskin latch-string, they don't fasten the doors—but that warn't romantical enough for Tom Sawyer; no way would do him but he must climb up the lightning-rod. But after he got up half way about three times, and missed fire and fell every time, and the last time most busted his brains out, he thought he'd got to give it up; but after he was rested, he allowed he would give her one more turn for luck, and this time he made the trip.

In the morning we was up at break of day, and down to the nigger cabins to pet the dogs and make friends with the nigger that fed Jim—if it *was* Jim that was being fed. The niggers was just getting through breakfast and starting for the fields; and Jim's nigger was piling up a tin pan with bread and meat and things; and whilst the others was leaving, the key come from the house.

This nigger had a good-natured, chuckleheaded face, and his wool was all tied up in little bunches with thread. That was to keep witches off. He said the witches was pestering him awful, these nights, and making him see all kinds of strange things, and hear all kinds of strange words and noises, and he didn't believe he was ever witched so long, before, in his life. He got so worked up, and got to running on so about his troubles, he forgot all about what he'd been agoing to do. So Tom says:

"What's the vittles for? Going to feed the dogs?"

The nigger kind of smiled around gradly over his face, like when you heave a brickbat in a mud puddle, and he says:

"Yes, Mars Sid, *a* dog. Cur'us dog, too. Does you want to go en look at 'im?"

"Yes."

I hunched Tom, and whispers:

"You going, right here in the daybreak? *That* warn't the plan."

"No, it warn't—but it's the plan *now*."

So, drat him, we went along, but I didn't like it much. When we got in, we couldn't hardly see anything, it was so dark; but Jim was there, sure enough, and could see us; and he sings out:

"Why, *Huck!* En good *lan'!* ain' dat Misto Tom?"

I just knowed how it would be; I just expected it. *I* didn't know nothing to do; and if I had, I couldn't a done it; because that nigger busted in and says:

"Why, de gracious sakes! do he know you genlmen?"

We could see pretty well, now. Tom he looked at the nigger, steady and kind of wondering, and says:

"Does *who* know us?"

"Why, dis-yer runaway nigger."

"I don't reckon he does; but what put that into your head?"

"What *put* it dar? Didn' he jis' dis minute sing out like he knowed you?"

Tom says, in a puzzled-up kind of way:

"Well, that's mighty curious. *Who* sung out? *When* did he sing out? *What* did he sing out?" And turns to me, perfectly ca'm, and says, "Did *you* hear anybody sing out?"

Of course there warn't nothing to be said but the one thing; so I says:

"No; *I* ain't heard nobody say nothing."

Then he turns to Jim, and looks him over like he never see him before; and says:

"Did you sing out?"

"No, sah," says Jim; "*I* hain't said nothing, sah."

"Not a word?"

"No, sah, I hain't said a word."

"Did you ever see us before?"

"No, sah; not as *I* knows on."

So Tom turns to the nigger, which was looking wild and distressed, and says, kind of severe:

"What do you reckon's the matter with you, anyway? What made you think somebody sung out?"

"Oh, it's de dad-blame' witches, sah, en I wisht I was dead, I do. Dey's awluz at it, sah, en dey do mos' kill me, dey sk'yers me so. Please to don't tell nobody 'bout it sah, er ole Mars Silas he'll scole me; 'kase he say dey *ain't* no witches. I jis' wish to goodness he was heah now—*den* what would he say! I jis' bet he couldn' fine no way to git aroun' it *dis* time. But it's awluz jis' so; people dat's *sot,* stays sot; dey won't look into noth'n'en fine it out f'r deyselves, en when *you* fine it out en tell um 'bout it, dey doan' b'lieve you."

Tom give him a dime, and said we wouldn't tell nobody; and told him to buy some more thread to tie up his wool with; and then looks at Jim, and says:

"I wonder if Uncle Silas is going to hang this nigger. If I was to catch a nigger that was ungrateful enough to run away, *I* wouldn't give him up,

I'd hang him."[154] And whilst the nigger stepped to the door to look at the dime and bite it to see if it was good,[155] he whispers to Jim, and says:

"Don't ever let on to know us. And if you hear any digging going on nights, it's us; we're going to set you free."

Jim only had time to grab us by the hand and squeeze it, then the nigger come back, and we said we'd come again some time if the nigger wanted us to; and he said he would, more particular if it was dark, because the witches went for him mostly in the dark, and it was good to have folks around then.

CHAPTER XXXV.

It would be most an hour, yet, till breakfast, so we left, and struck down into the woods; because Tom said we got to have *some* light to see how to dig by, and a lantern makes too much, and might get us into trouble; what we must have was a lot of them rotten chunks that's called fox-fire, and just makes a soft kind of a glow when you lay them in a dark place. We fetched an armful and hid it in the weeds, and set down to rest, and Tom says, kind of dissatisfied:

"Blame it, this whole thing is just as easy and awkward as it can be. And so it makes it so rotten difficult to get up a difficult plan. There ain't no watchman to be drugged—now there *ought* to be a watchman. There ain't even a dog to give a sleeping-mixture to. And there's Jim chained by one leg, with a ten-foot chain, to the leg of his bed: why, all you got to do is to lift up the bedstead and slip off the chain. And Uncle Silas he trusts everybody; sends the key to the punkin-headed nigger, and don't send nobody to watch the nigger. Jim could a got out of that window-hole

---

154. Tom's morality is still that of the slaveholding class, expecting slaves to be grateful and regarding the ingratitude of a runaway slave as a capital crime. Note that Tom says "I'd hang him," claiming the right to kill a slave as his own right, not the state's. Huck, although a child of the underclass and an ally of an escaped slave, does not seem at all perturbed by Tom's comments; the ideology of slavery and white supremacy was so thoroughly ingrained as to be unquestioned.

155. Counterfeiting was common in the antebellum United States. With hundreds of banks spread across the country and all issuing their own paper-money banknotes with no uniform appearance, counterfeiting was easy, and proving the legitimacy of a given banknote was difficult. Not surprisingly, people tended to prefer hard money in the form of gold and silver coins. Yet these too were often counterfeited, partly because they were in high demand. Among the most notorious counterfeiters was a bogus bank in Boston, Ohio, that set up 10 satellite companies, some of which minted counterfeit coin. The opening of the Ohio and Erie Canal in 1827 extended the reach of the Ohio counterfeiters into the South and West, indeed nationwide (Mihm 2009, 167–171).

before this, only there wouldn't be no use trying to travel with a ten-foot chain on his leg. Why, drat it, Huck, it's the stupidest arrangement I ever see. You got to invent *all* the difficulties. Well, we can't help it, we got to do the best we can with the materials we've got. Anyhow, there's one thing—there's more honor in getting him out through a lot of difficulties and dangers, where there warn't one of them furnished to you by the people who it was their duty to furnish them, and you had to contrive them all out of your own head. Now look at just that one thing of the lantern. When you come down to the cold facts, we simply got to *let on* that a lantern's resky. Why, we could work with a torchlight procession if we wanted to, *I* believe. Now, whilst I think of it, we got to hunt up something to make a saw out of the first chance we get."

"What do we want of a saw?"

"What do we *want* of it? Hain't we got to saw the leg of Jim's bed off, so as to get the chain loose?"

"Why, you just said a body could lift up the bedstead and slip the chain off."

"Well, if that ain't just like you, Huck Finn. You *can* get up the infant-schooliest ways of going at a thing. Why, hain't you ever read any books at all?—Baron Trenck, nor Casanova, nor Benvenuto Chelleeny, nor Henri IV., nor none of them heroes? Whoever heard of getting a prisoner loose in such an old-maidy way as that? No; the way all the best authorities does, is to saw the bed-leg in two, and leave it just so, and swallow the sawdust, so it can't be found, and put some dirt and grease around the sawed place so the very keenest seneskal can't see no sign of its being sawed, and thinks the bed-leg is perfectly sound. Then, the night you're ready, fetch the leg a kick, down she goes; slip off your chain, and there you are. Nothing to do but hitch your rope-ladder to the battlements, shin down it, break your leg in the moat—because a rope-ladder is nineteen foot too short, you know—and there's your horses and your trusty vassles, and they scoop you up and fling you across a saddle and away you go, to your native Languedoc, or Navarre, or wherever it is. It's gaudy, Huck. I wish there was a moat to this cabin. If we get time, the night of the escape, we'll dig one."

I says:

"What do we want of a moat, when we're going to snake him out from under the cabin?"

But he never heard me. He had forgot me and everything else. He had his chin in his hand, thinking. Pretty soon, he sighs, and shakes his head; then sighs again, and says:

"No, it wouldn't do—there ain't necessity enough for it."

"For what?" I says.

"Why, to saw Jim's leg off," he says.

"Good land!" I says, "why, there ain't *no* necessity for it. And what would you want to saw his leg off for, anyway?"

"Well, some of the best authorities has done it. They couldn't get the chain off, so they just cut their hand off and shoved. And a leg would be better still. But we got to let that go. There ain't necessity enough in this case; and besides, Jim's a nigger and wouldn't understand the reasons for it, and how it's the custom in Europe; so we'll let it go. But there's one thing—he can have a rope ladder; we can tear up our sheets and make him a rope ladder easy enough. And we can send it to him in a pie; it's mostly done that way. And I've et worse pies."

"Why, Tom Sawyer, how you talk," I says; "Jim ain't got no use for a rope ladder."

"He *has* got use for it. How *you* talk, you better say; you don't know nothing about it. He's *got* to have a rope ladder; they all do."

"What in the nation can he *do* with it?"

"*Do* with it? He can hide it in his bed, can't he? That's what they all do; and *he's* got to, too. Huck, you don't ever seem to want to do anything that's regular; you want to be starting something fresh all the time. S'pose he *don't* do nothing with it? ain't it there in his bed, for a clew, after he's gone? and don't you reckon they'll want clews? Of course they will. And you wouldn't leave them any? That would be a *pretty* howdy-do, *wouldn't* it! I never heard of such a thing."

"Well," I says, "if it's in the regulations, and he's got to have it, all right, let him have it; because I don't wish to go back on no regulations; but there's one thing, Tom Sawyer—if we go to tearing up our sheets to make Jim a rope ladder, we're going to get into trouble with Aunt Sally, just as sure as you're born. Now, the way I look at it, a hickry-bark ladder don't cost nothing, and don't waste nothing, and is just as good to load up a pie with, and hide in a straw tick, as any rag ladder you can start; and as for Jim, he ain't had no experience, and so *he* don't care what kind of a—"

"Oh, shucks, Huck Finn, if I was as ignorant as you, I'd keep still— that's what *I'd* do. Who ever heard of a state prisoner escaping by a hickry-bark ladder? Why, it's perfectly ridiculous."

"Well, all right, Tom, fix it your own way; but if you'll take my advice, you'll let me borrow a sheet off of the clothes line."

He said that would do. And that gave him another idea, and he says:

"Borrow a shirt, too."

"What do we want of a shirt, Tom?"

"Want it for Jim to keep a journal on."

"Journal your granny—*Jim* can't write."

"S'pose he *can't* write—he can make marks on the shirt, can't he, if we make him a pen out of an old pewter spoon or a piece of an old iron barrel-hoop?"

"Why, Tom, we can pull a feather out of a goose and make him a better one; and quicker, too."

"*Prisoners* don't have geese running around the donjon-keep to pull pens out of, you muggins. They *always* make their pens out of the hardest, toughest, troublesomest piece of old brass candlestick or something like that they can get their hands on; and it takes them weeks and weeks, and months and months to file it out, too, because they've got to do it by rubbing it on the wall. *They* wouldn't use a goose-quill if they had it. It ain't regular."

"Well, then, what'll we make him the ink out of?"

"Many makes it out of iron-rust and tears; but that's the common sort and women; the best authorities uses their own blood. Jim can do that; and when he wants to send any little common ordinary mysterious message to let the world know where he's captivated, he can write it on the bottom of a tin plate with a fork and throw it out of the window. The Iron Mask always done that, and it's a blame' good way, too."

"Jim ain't got no tin plates. They feed him in a pan."

"That ain't nothing; we can get him some."

"Can't nobody *read* his plates."

"That ain't got anything to *do* with it, Huck Finn. All *he's* got to do is to write on the plate and throw it out. You don't *have* to be able to read it. Why, half the time you can't read anything a prisoner writes on a tin plate, or anywhere else."

"Well, then, what's the sense in wasting the plates?"

"Why, blame it all, it ain't the *prisoner's* plates."

"But it's *somebody's* plates, ain't it?"

"Well, spos'n it is? What does the *prisoner* care whose—"

He broke off there, because we heard the breakfast-horn blowing. So we cleared out for the house.

Along during the morning I borrowed a sheet and a white shirt off of the clothes-line; and I found an old sack and put them in it, and we went down and got the fox-fire, and put that in too. I called it borrowing, because that was what pap always called it; but Tom said it warn't borrowing, it was stealing. He said we was representing prisoners; and prisoners don't care how they get a thing so they get it, and nobody don't blame them for it, either. It ain't no crime in a prisoner to steal the thing he needs to get away with, Tom said; it's his right; and so, as long as we was representing a prisoner, we had a perfect right to steal anything on this place we had the least use for, to get ourselves out of prison with. He said if we warn't prisoners it would be a very different thing, and nobody but a mean ornery person would steal when he warn't a prisoner. So we allowed we would steal everything there was that come handy. And yet he made a mighty fuss, one day, after that, when I stole a watermelon out of the nigger patch and eat it; and he made me go and give the niggers a dime, without telling them what it was for. Tom said that what he meant was, we could steal anything we *needed*. Well, I says, I needed the watermelon. But he said I didn't need it to get out of prison with, there's where the difference was. He said if I'd a wanted it to hide a knife in, and smuggle it to Jim to kill the seneskal with, it would a been all right. So I let it go at that, though I couldn't see no advantage in my representing a prisoner if I got to set down and chaw over a lot of gold-leaf distinctions like that, every time I see a chance to hog a watermelon.

Well, as I was saying, we waited that morning till everybody was settled down to business, and nobody in sight around the yard; then Tom he carried the sack into the lean-to whilst I stood off a piece to keep watch. By and by he come out, and we went and set down on the woodpile to talk. He says:

"Everything's all right, now, except tools; and that's easy fixed."

"Tools?" I says.

"Yes."

"Tools for what?"

"Why, to dig with. We ain't agoing to *gnaw* him out, are we?"

"Ain't them old crippled picks and things in there good enough to dig a nigger out with?" I says.

He turns on me, looking pitying enough to make a body cry, and says:

"Huck Finn, did you *ever* hear of a prisoner having picks and shovels, and all the modern conveniences in his wardrobe to dig himself out with? Now I want to ask you—if you got any reasonableness in you at all—what kind of a show would *that* give him to be a hero? Why, they might as well lend him the key, and done with it. Picks and shovels—why, they wouldn't furnish 'em to a king."

"Well, then," I says, "if we don't want the picks and shovels, what do we want?"

"A couple of case-knives."

"To dig the foundations out from under that cabin with?"

"Yes."

"Confound it, it's foolish, Tom."

"It don't make no difference how foolish it is, it's the *right* way—and it's the regular way. And there ain't no *other* way, that ever *I* heard of, and I've read all the books that gives any information about these things. They always dig out with a case-knife—and not through dirt, mind you; generly it's through solid rock. And it takes them weeks and weeks and weeks, and for ever and ever. Why, look at one of them prisoners in the bottom dungeon of the Castle Deef, in the harbor of Marseilles, that dug himself out that way; how long was *he* at it, you reckon?"

"I don't know."

"Well, guess."

"I don't know. A month and a half."

"*Thirty-seven year*—and he come out in China. *That's* the kind. I wish the bottom of *this* fortress was solid rock."

"*Jim* don't know nobody in China."[156]

"What's *that* got to do with it? Neither did that other fellow. But you're always a-wandering off on a side issue. Why can't you stick to the main point?"

"All right—*I* don't care where he comes out, so he *comes* out; and Jim don't, either, I reckon. But there's one thing, anyway—Jim's too old to be dug out with a case-knife. He won't last."

"Yes he will *last,* too. You don't reckon it's going to take thirty-seven years to dig out through a *dirt* foundation, do you?"

"How long will it take, Tom?"

"Well, we can't resk being as long as we ought to, because it mayn't take very long for Uncle Silas to hear from down there by New Orleans. He'll hear Jim ain't from there. Then his next move will be to advertise Jim, or something like that. So we can't resk being as long digging him out as we ought to. By rights I reckon we ought to be a couple of years; but we can't. Things being so uncertain, what I recommend is this: that we really dig right in, as quick as we can; and after that, we can *let on,* to ourselves, that we was at it thirty-seven years. Then we can snatch him out and rush him away the first time there's an alarm. Yes, I reckon that'll be the best way."

"Now, there's *sense* in that," I says. "Letting on don't cost nothing; letting on ain't no trouble; and if it's any object, I don't mind letting on we was at it a hundred and fifty year. It wouldn't strain me none, after I got my hand in. So I'll mosey along now, and smouch a couple of case-knives."

"Smouch three," he says; "we want one to make a saw out of."

"Tom, if it ain't unregular and irreligious to sejest it," I says, "there's an old rusty saw-blade around yonder sticking under the weather boarding behind the smoke-house."

He looked kind of weary and discouraged-like, and says:

"It ain't no use to try to learn you nothing, Huck. Run along and smouch the knives—three of them." So I done it.

CHAPTER XXXVI.

As soon as we reckoned everybody was asleep, that night, we went down the lightning-rod, and shut ourselves up in the lean-to, and got out

---

156. Huck, perhaps inadvertently, makes an important point about slave escapes. A successful escape required having abettors of some kind, which usually were people one already knew or knew about, and the typical slave likely lacked such contacts. Historians have long since debunked the notion of the underground railroad as a "great and intricate network" (Foner 2015, 12).

our pile of fox-fire, and went to work. We cleared everything out of the way, about four or five foot along the middle of the bottom log. Tom said he was right behind Jim's bed now, and we'd dig in under it, and when we got through there couldn't nobody in the cabin ever know there was any hole there, because Jim's counterpin hung down most to the ground, and you'd have to raise it up and look under to see the hole. So we dug and dug with the case-knives, till most midnight; and then we was dog-tired, and our hands was blistered, and yet you couldn't see we'd done anything, hardly. At last I says:

"This ain't no thirty-seven year job, this is a thirty-eight year job, Tom Sawyer."

He never said nothing. But he sighed, and pretty soon he stopped digging, and then for a good little while I knowed that he was thinking. Then he says:

"It ain't no use, Huck, it ain't agoing to work. If we was prisoners it would, because then we'd have as many years as we wanted, and no hurry; and we wouldn't get but a few minutes to dig, every day, while they was changing watches, and so our hands wouldn't get blistered, and we could keep it up right along, year in and year out, and do it right, and the way it ought to be done. But *we* can't fool along, we got to rush; we ain't got no time to spare. If we was to put in another night this way, we'd have to knock off for a week to let our hands get well—couldn't touch a case-knife with them sooner."

"Well, then, what we going to do, Tom?"

"I'll tell you. It ain't right, and it ain't moral, and I wouldn't like it to get out—but there ain't only just the one way: we got to dig him out with the picks, and *let on* it's case-knives."

"*Now* you're *talking!*" I says; "your head gets leveler and leveler all the time, Tom Sawyer," I says. "Picks is the thing, moral or no moral; and as for me, I don't care shucks for the morality of it, nohow.[157] When I start in to steal a nigger, or a watermelon, or a Sunday-school book, I ain't no ways particular how it's done so it's done. What I want is my nigger; or what I want is my watermelon; or what I want is my Sunday-school book;

---

157. Tom's "morality" here is thoughtless at best and sadistic at worst, involving a good deal of torture and the prolonging of Jim's imprisonment. The best that can be said for Tom's actions here is that he seems to be taking his cues from chivalric romantic literature, just like he did with his highwaymen fantasies early in the book, as opposed to being intentionally malevolent. In Chapters 33 and 34, Huck said that Tom was far too respectable, with "a character to lose," to get mixed up in scheme to free a slave (or "steal a nigger," as they keep putting it). Huck is not being intentionally ironic, but Twain surely is. Tom's "respectability" in a racist slave society and his cruel tricks on Jim have a common root.

and if a pick's the handiest thing, that's the thing I'm agoing to dig that nigger or that watermelon or that Sunday-book out with; and I don't give a dead rat what the authorities thinks about it nuther."

"Well," he says, "there's excuse for picks and letting-on in a case like this; if it warn't so, I wouldn't approve of it, nor I wouldn't stand by and see the rules broke—because right is right, and wrong is wrong, and a body ain't got no business doing wrong when he ain't ignorant and knows better. It might answer for *you* to dig Jim out with a pick, *without* any letting-on, because you don't know no better; but it wouldn't for me, be- cause I do know better. Gimme a case-knife."

He had his own by him, but I handed him mine. He flung it down, and says:

"Gimme a *case-knife.*"

I didn't know just what to do—but then I thought. I scratched around amongst the old tools, and got a pick-axe and give it to him, and he took it and went to work, and never said a word.

He was always just that particular. Full of principle.

So then I got a shovel, and then we picked and shoveled, turn about, and made the fur fly. We stuck to it about a half an hour, which was as long as we could stand up; but we had a good deal of a hole to show for it. When I got up stairs, I looked out at the window and see Tom doing his level best with the lightning-rod, but he couldn't come it, his hands was so sore. At last he says:

"It ain't no use, it can't be done. What you reckon I better do? Can't you think up no way?"

"Yes," I says, "but I reckon it ain't regular. Come up the stairs, and let on it's a lightning-rod."

So he done it.

Next day Tom stole a pewter spoon and a brass candlestick in the house, for to make some pens for Jim out of, and six tallow candles; and I hung around the nigger cabins, and laid for a chance, and stole three tin plates. Tom says it wasn't enough; but I said nobody wouldn't ever see the plates that Jim throwed out, because they'd fall in the dog- fennel and jimpson weeds under the window-hole—then we could tote them back and he could use them over again. So Tom was satisfied. Then he says:

"Now, the thing to study out is, how to get the things to Jim."

"Take them in through the hole," I says, "when we get it done."

He only just looked scornful, and said something about nobody ever heard of such an idiotic idea, and then he went to studying. By and by he said he had ciphered out two or three ways, but there warn't no need to decide on any of them yet. Said we'd got to post Jim first.

That night we went down the lightning-rod a little after ten, and took one of the candles along, and listened under the window-hole, and heard

Jim snoring; so we pitched it in, and it didn't wake him. Then we whirled in with the pick and shovel, and in about two hours and a half the job was done. We crept in under Jim's bed and into the cabin, and pawed around and found the candle and lit it, and stood over Jim a while, and found him looking hearty and healthy, and then we woke him up gentle and gradual. He was so glad to see us he most cried; and called us honey, and all the pet names he could think of; and was for having us hunt up a cold chisel to cut the chain off of his leg with, right away, and clearing out without losing any time. But Tom he showed him how unregular it would be, and set down and told him all about our plans, and how we could alter them in a minute any time there was an alarm; and not to be the least afraid, because we would see he got away, *sure.* So Jim he said it was all right, and we set there and talked over old times a while, and then Tom asked a lot of questions, and when Jim told him Uncle Silas come in every day or two to pray with him, and Aunt Sally come in to see if he was comfortable and had plenty to eat, and both of them was kind as they could be, Tom says:

"*Now* I know how to fix it. We'll send you some things by them."

I said, "Don't do nothing of the kind; it's one of the most jackass ideas I ever struck;" but he never paid no attention to me; went right on. It was his way when he'd got his plans set.

So he told Jim how we'd have to smuggle in the rope-ladder pie, and other large things, by Nat, the nigger that fed him, and he must be on the lookout, and not be surprised, and not let Nat see him open them; and we would put small things in uncle's coat pockets and he must steal them out; and we would tie things to aunt's apron strings or put them in her apron pocket, if we got a chance; and told him what they would be and what they was for. And told him how to keep a journal on the shirt with his blood, and all that. He told him everything. Jim he couldn't see no sense in the most of it, but he allowed we was white folks and knowed better than him; so he was satisfied, and said he would do it all just as Tom said.

Jim had plenty corn-cob pipes and tobacco; so we had a right down good sociable time; then we crawled out through the hole, and so home to bed, with hands that looked like they'd been chawed. Tom was in high spirits. He said it was the best fun he ever had in his life, and the most intellectural; and said if he only could see his way to it we would keep it up all the rest of our lives and leave Jim to our children to get out; for he believed Jim would come to like it better and better the more he got used to it. He said that in that way it could be strung out to as much as eighty year, and would be the best time on record. And he said it would make us all celebrated that had a hand in it.

In the morning we went out to the woodpile and chopped up the brass candlestick into handy sizes, and Tom put them and the pewter spoon in his pocket. Then we went to the nigger cabins, and while I got Nat's notice off, Tom shoved a piece of candlestick into the middle of a corn-pone that was in Jim's pan, and we went along with Nat to see how it would work, and it just worked noble; when Jim bit into it it most mashed all his teeth out; and there warn't ever anything could a worked better. Tom said so himself. Jim he never let on but what it was only just a piece of rock or something like that that's always getting into bread, you know; but after that he never bit into nothing but what he jabbed his fork into it in three or four places, first.

And whilst we was a standing there in the dimmish light, here comes a couple of the hounds bulging in, from under Jim's bed; and they kept on piling in till there was eleven of them, and there warn't hardly room in there to get your breath. By jings, we forgot to fasten that lean-to door. The nigger Nat he only just hollered "witches!" once, and keeled over on to the floor amongst the dogs, and begun to groan like he was dying. Tom jerked the door open and flung out a slab of Jim's meat, and the dogs went for it, and in two seconds he was out himself and back again and shut the door, and I knowed he'd fixed the other door too. Then he went to work on the nigger, coaxing him and petting him, and asking him if he'd been imagining he saw something again. He raised up, and blinked his eyes around, and says:

"Mars Sid, you'll say I's a fool, but if I didn't b'lieve I see most a million dogs, er devils, er some'n, I wisht I may die right heah in dese tracks. I did, mos' sholy. Mars Sid, I *felt* um—I *felt* um, sah; dey was all over me. Dad fetch it, I jis' wisht I could git my han's on one er dem witches jis' wunst—on'y jis' wunst—it's all *I'*d ast. But mos'ly I wisht dey'd lemme 'lone, I does."

Tom says:

"Well, I tell you what *I* think. What makes them come here just at this runaway nigger's breakfast-time? It's because they're hungry; that's the reason. You make them a witch pie; that's the thing for *you* to do."

"But my lan', Mars Sid, how's *I* gwyne to make 'm a witch pie? I doan' know how to make it. I hain't ever hearn er sich a thing b'fo'."

"Well, then, I'll have to make it myself."

"Will you do it, honey?—will you? I'll wusshup de groun' und' yo' foot, I will!"

"All right, I'll do it, seeing it's you, and you've been good to us and showed us the runaway nigger. But you got to be mighty careful. When we come around, you turn your back; and then whatever we've put in the pan, don't you let on you see it at all. And don't you look when Jim unloads the pan—something might happen, I don't know what. And above all, don't you *handle* the witch-things."

"*Hannel* 'm, Mars Sid? What *is* you a talkin' 'bout? I wouldn' lay de weight er my finger on um, not f'r ten hund'd thous'n billion dollars, I wouldn't."

CHAPTER XXXVII.

THAT was all fixed. So then we went away and went to the rubbage-pile in the back yard where they keep the old boots, and rags, and pieces of bottles, and wore-out tin things, and all such truck, and scratched around and found an old tin washpan and stopped up the holes as well as we could, to bake the pie in, and took it down cellar and stole it full of flour, and started for breakfast, and found a couple of shingle-nails that Tom said would be handy for a prisoner to scrabble his name and sorrows on the dungeon walls with, and dropped one of them in Aunt Sally's apron pocket which was hanging on a chair, and t'other we stuck in the band of Uncle Silas's hat, which was on the bureau, because we heard the children say their pa and ma was going to the runaway nigger's house this morning, and then went to breakfast, and Tom dropped the pewter spoon in Uncle Silas's coat pocket, and Aunt Sally wasn't come yet, so we had to wait a little while.

And when she come she was hot, and red, and cross, and couldn't hardly wait for the blessing; and then she went to sluicing out coffee with one hand and cracking the handiest child's head with her thimble with the other, and says:

"I've hunted high, and I've hunted low, and it does beat all, what *has* become of your other shirt."

My heart fell down amongst my lungs and livers and things, and a hard piece of corn-crust started down my throat after it and got met on the road with a cough and was shot across the table and took one of the children in the eye and curled him up like a fishing-worm, and let a cry out of him the size of a war-whoop, and Tom he turned kinder blue around the gills, and it all amounted to a considerable state of things for about a quarter of a minute or as much as that, and I would a sold out for half price if there was a bidder. But after that we was all right again—it was the sudden surprise of it that knocked us so kind of cold. Uncle Silas he says:

"It's most uncommon curious, I can't understand it. I know perfectly well I took it *off,* because—"

"Because you hain't got but one *on.* Just *listen* at the man! *I* know you took it off, and know it by a better way than your wool-gethering memory, too, because it was on the clo'es-line yesterday—I see it there myself. But it's gone—that's the long and the short of it, and you'll just have to change to a red flann'l one till I can get time to make a new one. And it'll be the third I've made in two years; it just keeps a body on the jump to keep you in shirts; and whatever you do manage to *do* with 'm all is more'n *I* can make out. A body 'd think you *would* learn to take some sort of care of 'em at your time of life."

"I know it, Sally, and I do try all I can. But it oughtn't to be altogether my fault, because, you know I don't see them nor have nothing to do with them except when they're on me; and I don't believe I've ever lost one of them *off* of me."

"Well, it ain't *your* fault if you haven't, Silas—you'd a done it if you could, I reckon. And the shirt ain't all that's gone, nuther. Ther's a spoon gone; and *that* ain't all. There was ten, and now ther's only nine. The calf got the shirt, I reckon, but the calf never took the spoon, *that's* certain."

"Why, what else is gone, Sally?"

"Ther's six *candles* gone—that's what. The rats could a got the candles, and I reckon they did; I wonder they don't walk off with the whole place, the way you're always going to stop their holes and don't do it; and if they warn't fools they'd sleep in your hair, Silas—*you'd* never find it out; but you can't lay the *spoon* on the rats, and that I *know*."

"Well, Sally, I'm in fault, and I acknowledge it; I've been remiss; but I won't let to-morrow go by without stopping up them holes."

"Oh, I wouldn't hurry; next year'll do. Matilda Angelina Araminta *Phelps!*"

Whack comes the thimble, and the child snatches her claws out of the sugar-bowl without fooling around any. Just then, the nigger woman steps onto the passage, and says:

"Missus, dey's a sheet gone."

"A *sheet* gone! Well, for the land's sake!"

"I'll stop up them holes *to-day*," says Uncle Silas, looking sorrowful.

"Oh, *do* shet up!—s'pose the rats took the *sheet? Where's* it gone, Lize?"

"Clah to goodness I hain't no notion, Miss' Sally. She wuz on de clo'sline yistiddy, but she done gone: she ain' dah no mo', now."

"I reckon the world *is* coming to an end. I *never* see the beat of it, in all my born days. A shirt, and a sheet, and a spoon, and six can—"

"Missus," comes a young yaller wench, "dey's a brass cannelstick miss'n."

"Cler out from here, you hussy, er I'll take a skillet to ye!"

Well, she was just a biling. I begun to lay for a chance; I reckoned I would sneak out and go for the woods till the weather moderated. She kept a-raging right along, running her insurrection all by herself, and everybody else mighty meek and quiet; and at last Uncle Silas, looking kind of foolish, fishes up that spoon out of his pocket. She stopped, with her mouth open and her hands up; and as for me, I wished I was in Jeruslem or somewheres. But not long; because she says:

"It's *just* as I expected. So you had it in your pocket all the time; and like as not you've got the other things there, too. How'd it get there?"

"I reely don't know, Sally," he says, kind of apologizing, "or you know I would tell. I was a-studying over my text in Acts Seventeen, before breakfast, and I reckon I put it in there, not noticing, meaning to put my Testament in, and it must be so, because my Testament ain't in, but I'll go and see, and if the Testament is where I had it, I'll know I didn't put it in, and that will show that I laid the Testament down and took up the spoon, and—"

"Oh, for the land's sake! Give a body a rest! Go 'long now, the whole kit and biling of ye; and don't come nigh me again till I've got back my peace of mind."

I'd a heard her, if she'd a said it to herself, let alone speaking it out; and I'd a got up and obeyed her, if I'd a been dead. As we was passing through the setting-room, the old man he took up his hat, and the shingle-nail fell out on the floor, and he just merely picked it up and laid it on the mantel-shelf, and never said nothing, and went out. Tom see him do it, and remembered about the spoon, and says:

"Well, it ain't no use to send things by *him* no more, he ain't reliable." Then he says: "But he done us a good turn with the spoon, anyway, without knowing it, and so we'll go and do him one without *him* knowing it—stop up his rat-holes."

There was a noble good lot of them, down cellar, and it took us a whole hour, but we done the job tight and good, and ship-shape. Then we heard steps on the stairs, and blowed out our light, and hid; and here comes the old man, with a candle in one hand and a bundle of stuff in t'other, looking as absent-minded as year before last. He went a mooning around, first to one rat-hole and then another, till he'd been to them all. Then he stood about five minutes, picking tallow-drip off of his candle and thinking. Then he turns off slow and dreamy towards the stairs, saying:

"Well, for the life of me I can't remember when I done it. I could show her now that I warn't to blame on account of the rats. But never mind—let it go. I reckon it wouldn't do no good."

And so he went on a-mumbling up stairs, and then we left. He was a mighty nice old man. And always is.

Tom was a good deal bothered about what to do for a spoon, but he said we'd got to have it; so he took a think. When he had ciphered it out, he told me how we was to do; then we went and waited around the spoon-basket till we see Aunt Sally coming, and then Tom went to counting the spoons and laying them out to one side, and I slid one of them up my sleeve, and Tom says:

"Why, Aunt Sally, there ain't but nine spoons, *yet.*"

She says:

"Go 'long to your play, and don't bother me. I know better, I counted 'm myself."

"Well, I've counted them twice, Aunty, and *I* can't make but nine."

She looked out of all patience, but of course she come to count—anybody would.

"I declare to gracious ther' *ain't* but nine!" she says. "Why, what in the world—plague *take* the things, I'll count 'm again."

So I slipped back the one I had, and when she got done counting, she says:

"Hang the troublesome rubbage, ther's *ten* now!" and she looked huffy and bothered both. But Tom says:

"Why, Aunty, *I* don't think there's ten."

"You numskull, didn't you see me *count* 'm?"

"I know, but—"

"Well, I'll count 'm *again*."

So I smouched one, and they come out nine, same as the other time. Well, she *was* in a tearing way—just a trembling all over, she was so mad. But she counted and counted, till she got that addled she'd start to count-in the *basket* for a spoon, sometimes; and so, three times they come out right, and three times they come out wrong. Then she grabbed up the basket and slammed it across the house and knocked the cat galley-west; and she said cle'r out and let her have some peace, and if we come bothering around her again betwixt that and dinner, she'd skin us. So we had the odd spoon, and dropped it in her apron pocket whilst she was a-giving us our sailing-orders, and Jim got it all right, along with her shingle-nail, before noon. We was very well satisfied with this business, and Tom allowed it was worth twice the trouble it took, because he said *now* she couldn't ever count them spoons twice alike again to save her life; and wouldn't believe she'd counted them right, if she *did;* and said that after she'd about counted her head off, for the next three days, he judged she'd give it up and offer to kill anybody that wanted her to ever count them any more.

So we put the sheet back on the line, that night, and stole one out of her closet; and kept on putting it back and stealing it again, for a couple of days, till she didn't know how many sheets she had, any more, and she didn't *care,* and warn't agoing to bullyrag the rest of her soul out about it, and wouldn't count them again not to save her life, she druther die first.

So we was all right now, as to the shirt and the sheet and the spoon and the candles, by the help of the calf and the rats and the mixed-up counting; and as to the candlestick, it warn't no consequence, it would blow over by and by.

But that pie was a job; we had no end of trouble with that pie. We fixed it up away down in the woods, and cooked it there; and we got it done at last, and very satisfactory, too; but not all in one day; and we had to use up three washpans full of flour, before we got through, and we got burnt pretty much all over, in places, and eyes put out with the smoke; because, you see, we didn't want nothing but a crust, and we couldn't prop it up right, and she would always cave in. But of course we thought of the right way at last; which was to cook the ladder, too, in the pie. So then we laid in with Jim, the second night, and tore up the sheet all in little strings, and twisted them together, and long before daylight we had a lovely rope, that you could a hung a person with. We let on it took nine months to make it.

And in the forenoon we took it down to the woods, but it wouldn't go in the pie. Being made of a whole sheet, that way, there was rope enough for forty pies, if we'd a wanted them, and plenty left over for soup, or sausage, or anything you choose. We could a had a whole dinner.

But we didn't need it. All we needed was just enough for the pie, and so we throwed the rest away. We didn't cook none of the pies in the wash-pan, afraid the solder would melt; but Uncle Silas he had a noble brass warming-pan which he thought considerable of, because it belonged to one of his ancestors with a long wooden handle that come over from England with William the Conqueror in the *Mayflower* or one of them early ships[158] and was hid away up garret with a lot of other old pots and things that was valuable, not on account of being any account, because they warn't, but on account of them being relicts, you know, and we snaked her out, private, and took her down there, but she failed on the first pies, because we didn't know how, but she come up smiling on the last one. We took and lined her with dough, and set her in the coals, and loaded her up with rag-rope, and put on a dough roof, and shut down the lid, and put hot embers on top, and stood off five foot, with the long handle, cool and comfortable, and in fifteen minutes she turned out a pie that was a satisfaction to look at. But the person that et it would want to fetch a couple of kags of toothpicks along, for if that rope-ladder wouldn't cramp him down to business, I don't know nothing what I'm talking about, and lay him in enough stomach-ache to last him till next time, too.

Nat didn't look, when we put the witch-pie in Jim's pan; and we put the three tin plates in the bottom of the pan under the vittles; and so Jim got everything all right, and as soon as he was by himself he busted into the pie and hid the rope-ladder inside of his straw tick, and scratched some marks on a tin plate and throwed it out of the window-hole.

---

158. Huck's royal history is again a bit off. William the Conqueror, previously the Duke of Normandy in the Kingdom of France, ruled England from 1066 until his death in 1087. His victory at the Battle of Hastings in 1066 is also known as the Norman Conquest of England. The Norman dynasty ruled England for nearly a century and brought many changes, including the elimination of slavery.

Huck seems to understand that Uncle Silas and Aunt Sally are from the respectable class. They do not seem to be rich—one could hardly eke out a living from a two-acre farm—but he owns some slaves and, apparently, the "little" local sawmill. If he is in fact descended from the early English settlers in America, that only adds to his social cachet. The Phelpses are a bit like Twain's own parents, who were far from wealthy but clearly from the educated, respectable class and with deep roots in America, dating back to their grandfathers' arrival in the colonies in the 1730s.

CHAPTER XXXVIII.

MAKING them pens was a distressid tough job, and so was the saw; and Jim allowed the inscription was going to be the toughest of all. That's the one which the prisoner has to scrabble on the wall. But he had to have it; Tom said he'd *got* to; there warn't no case of a state prisoner not scrabbling his inscription to leave behind, and his coat of arms.

"Look at Lady Jane Grey," he says; "look at Gilford Dudley; look at old Northumberland! Why, Huck, s'pose it *is* considerble trouble?—what you going to do?—how you going to get around it? Jim's *got* to do his inscription and coat of arms. They all do."

Jim says:

"Why, Mars Tom, I hain't got no coat o' arm; I hain't got nuffn but dish-yer ole shirt, en you knows I got to keep de journal on dat."

"Oh, you don't understand, Jim; a coat of arms is very different."

"Well," I says, "Jim's right, anyway, when he says he ain't got no coat of arms, because he hain't."

"I reckon *I* knowed that," Tom says, "but you bet he'll have one before he goes out of this—because he's going out *right,* and there ain't going to be no flaws in his record."

So whilst me and Jim filed away at the pens on a brickbat apiece, Jim a making his'n out of the brass and I making mine out of the spoon, Tom set to work to think out the coat of arms. By and by he said he'd struck so many good ones he didn't hardly know which to take, but there was one which he reckoned he'd decide on. He says:

"On the scutcheon we'll have a bend *or* in the dexter base, a saltire *murrey* in the fess, with a dog, couchant, for common charge, and under his foot a chain embattled, for slavery, with a chevron *vert* in a chief engrailed, and three invected lines on a field *azure,* with the nombril points rampant on a dancette indented; crest, a runaway nigger, *sable,* with his bundle over his shoulder on a bar sinister; and a couple of gules for supporters, which is you and me; motto, *Maggiore fretta, minore otto.* Got it out of a book—means, the more haste, the less speed."

"Geewhillikins," I says, "but what does the rest of it mean?"

"We ain't got no time to bother over that," he says; "we got to dig in like all git-out."

"Well, anyway," I says, "what's *some* of it? What's a fess?"

"A fess—a fess is—*you* don't need to know what a fess is. I'll show him how to make it when he gets to it."

"Shucks, Tom," I says, "I think you might tell a person. What's a bar sinister?"

"Oh, *I* don't know. But he's got to have it. All the nobility does."

That was just his way. If it didn't suit him to explain a thing to you, he wouldn't do it. You might pump at him a week, it wouldn't make no difference.

He'd got all that coat of arms business fixed, so now he started in to finish up the rest of that part of the work, which was to plan out a mournful inscription—said Jim got to have one, like they all done. He made up a lot, and wrote them out on a paper, and read them off, so:

1.   *Here a captive heart busted.*
2.   *Here a poor prisoner, forsook by the world and friends, fretted his sorrowful life.*
3.   *Here a lonely heart broke, and a worn spirit went to its rest, after thirty-seven years of solitary captivity.*
4.   *Here, homeless and friendless, after thirty-seven years of bitter captivity, perished a noble stranger, natural son of Louis XIV.*[159]

Tom's voice trembled, whilst he was reading them, and he most broke down. When he got done, he couldn't no way make up his mind which one for Jim to scrabble onto the wall, they was all so good; but at last he allowed he would let him scrabble them all on. Jim said it would take him a year to scrabble such a lot of truck on to the logs with a nail, and he didn't know how to make letters, besides; but Tom said he would block them out for him, and then he wouldn't have nothing to do but just follow the lines. Then pretty soon he says:

"Come to think, the logs ain't agoing to do; they don't have log walls in a dungeon: we got to dig the inscriptions into a rock. We'll fetch a rock."

Jim said the rock was worse than the logs; he said it would take him such a pison long time to dig them into a rock, he wouldn't ever get out. But Tom said he would let me help him do it. Then he took a look to see

---

159. Tom appears to have in mind a romantic legend concerning a famous French prisoner who became known as the Man in the Iron Mask. The prisoner, known as Marchioly at the time of his death in 1703, was incarcerated for his last 34 years during Louis XIV's reign. Marchioly wore a mask of black velvet cloth, and rumors about him and his identity swept the nation and the world long after his death. The philosopher Voltaire claimed that the prisoner wore an iron mask and was Louis XIV's older illegitimate half brother. The Man in the Iron Mask was immortalized in the last book of Alexander Dumas's popular historical romance trilogy that included *The Three Musketeers* and continues to be the subject of novels, movies, and other adaptations. Another rumor, similar to rumors about Louis XVI's heir apparent "the dolphin," was that the prisoner was one of Louis XIV's illegitimate sons. John Noone's *The Man behind the Iron Mask* (1994) provides a comprehensive look at this myth and its many forms.

how me and Jim was getting along with the pens. It was most pesky tedious hard work and slow, and didn't give my hands no show to get well of the sores, and we didn't seem to make no headway, hardly. So Tom says:

"I know how to fix it. We got to have a rock for the coat of arms and mournful inscriptions, and we can kill two birds with that same rock. There's a gaudy big grindstone down at the mill, and we'll smouch it, and carve the things on it, and file out the pens and the saw on it, too."[160]

It warn't no slouch of an idea; and it warn't no slouch of a grindstone nuther; but we allowed we'd tackle it. It warn't quite midnight, yet, so we cleared out for the mill, leaving Jim at work. We smouched the grindstone, and set out to roll her home, but it was a most nation tough job. Sometimes, do what we could, we couldn't keep her from falling over, and she come mighty near mashing us, every time. Tom said she was going to get one of us, sure, before we got through. We got her half way; and then we was plumb played out, and most drownded with sweat. We see it warn't no use, we got to go and fetch Jim. So he raised up his bed and slid the chain off of the bed-leg, and wrapt it round and round his neck, and we crawled out through our hole and down there, and Jim and me laid into that grindstone and walked her along like nothing; and Tom superintended. He could out-superintend any boy I ever see. He knowed how to do everything.

Our hole was pretty big, but it warn't big enough to get the grindstone through; but Jim he took the pick and soon made it big enough. Then Tom marked out them things on it with the nail, and set Jim to work on them, with the nail for a chisel and an iron bolt from the rubbage in the lean-to for a hammer, and told him to work till the rest of his candle quit on him, and then he could go to bed, and hide the grindstone under his straw tick and sleep on it. Then we helped him fix his chain back on the bed-leg, and was ready for bed ourselves. But Tom thought of something, and says:

"You got any spiders in here, Jim?"

"No, sah, thanks to goodness I hain't, Mars Tom."

"All right, we'll get you some."

"But bless you, honey, I doan' *want* none. I's afeard un um. I jis' 's soon have rattlesnakes aroun'."

Tom thought a minute or two, and says:

---

160. Grindstones were heavy rotating disks that could be used for sharpening tools, such as the blades of a saw. The mill is evidently Silas Phelps's sawmill, mentioned earlier.

A TOUGH JOB

(Illustration by Edward W. Kemble. From Mark Twain, *Adventures of Huckleberry Finn*. New York: C. L. Webster, 1885. Digitized by the University of Virginia Library.)

"It's a good idea. And I reckon it's been done. It *must* a been done; it stands to reason. Yes, it's a prime good idea. Where could you keep it?"

"Keep what, Mars Tom?"

"Why, a rattlesnake."

"De goodness gracious alive, Mars Tom! Why, if dey was a rattlesnake to come in heah, I'd take en bust right out thoo dat log wall, I would, wid my head."

"Why, Jim, you wouldn't be afraid of it, after a little. You could tame it."

"*Tame* it!"

"Yes—easy enough. Every animal is grateful for kindness and petting, and they wouldn't *think* of hurting a person that pets them. Any book will tell you that. You try—that's all I ask; just try for two or three days. Why, you can get him so, in a little while, that he'll love you; and sleep with you;

and won't stay away from you a minute; and will let you wrap him round your neck and put his head in your mouth."

"*Please,* Mars Tom—*doan'* talk so! I can't *stan'* it! He'd *let* me shove his head in my mouf—fer a favor, hain't it? I lay he'd wait a pow'ful long time 'fo' I *ast* him. En mo' en dat, I doan' *want* him to sleep wid me."

"Jim, don't act so foolish. A prisoner's *got* to have some kind of a dumb pet, and if a rattlesnake hain't ever been tried, why, there's more glory to be gained in your being the first to ever try it than any other way you could ever think of to save your life."

"Why, Mars Tom, I doan' *want* no sich glory. Snake take 'n bite Jim's chin off, den *whah* is de glory? No, sah, I doan' want no sich doin's."

"Blame it, can't you *try?* I only *want* you to try—you needn't keep it up if it don't work."

"But de trouble all *done,* ef de snake bite me while I's a tryin' him. Mars Tom, I's willin' to tackle mos' anything 'at ain't onreasonable, but ef you en Huck fetches a rattlesnake in heah for me to tame, I's gwyne to *leave,* dat's *shore.*"

"Well, then, let it go, let it go, if you're so bullheaded about it. We can get you some garter-snakes and you can tie some buttons on their tails, and let on they're rattlesnakes, and I reckon that 'll have to do."

"I k'n stan' *dem,* Mars Tom, but blame' 'f I couldn' get along widout um, I tell you dat. I never knowed b'fo', 't was so much bother and trouble to be a prisoner."

"Well, it *always* is, when it's done right. You got any rats around here?"

"No, sah, I hain't seed none."

"Well, we'll get you some rats."

"Why, Mars Tom, I doan' *want* no rats. Dey's de dadblamedest creturs to 'sturb a body, en rustle roun' over 'im, en bite his feet, when he's tryin' to sleep, I ever see. No, sah, gimme g'yarter-snakes, 'f I's got to have 'm, but doan' gimme no rats; I ain' got no use f'r um, skasely."

"But, Jim, you *got* to have 'em—they all do. So don't make no more fuss about it. Prisoners ain't ever without rats. There ain't no instance of it. And they train them, and pet them, and learn them tricks, and they get to be as sociable as flies. But you got to play music to them. You got anything to play music on?"

"I ain' got nuffn but a coase comb en a piece o' paper, en a juice-harp; but I reck'n dey wouldn' take no stock in a juice-harp."

"Yes they would. *They* don't care what kind of music 'tis. A jews-harp's plenty good enough for a rat. All animals like music—in a prison they dote on it. Specially, painful music; and you can't get no other kind out of a jews-harp. It always interests them; they come out to see what's the matter with you. Yes, you're all right; you're fixed very well. You want to set on your bed, nights, before you go to sleep, and early in the mornings, and play your jews-harp; play 'The Last Link is Broken'—that's the thing that'll scoop a rat quicker'n anything else; and when you've played about two minutes, you'll see all the rats, and the snakes, and spiders, and things begin to feel worried about you, and come. And they'll just fairly swarm over you, and have a noble good time."

"Yes, *dey* will, I reck'n, Mars Tom, but what kine er time is *Jim* havin'? Blest if I kin see de pint. But I'll do it ef I got to. I reck'n I better keep de animals satisfied, en not have no trouble in de house."

Tom waited to think it over, and see if there wasn't nothing else; and pretty soon he says:

"Oh—there's one thing I forgot. Could you raise a flower here, do you reckon?"

"I doan know but maybe I could, Mars Tom; but it's tolable dark in heah, en I ain' got no use f'r no flower, nohow, en she'd be a pow'ful sight o' trouble."

"Well, you try it, anyway. Some other prisoners has done it."

"One er dem big cat-tail-lookin' mullen-stalks would grow in heah, Mars Tom, I reck'n, but she wouldn't be wuth half de trouble she'd coss."

"Don't you believe it. We'll fetch you a little one, and you plant it in the corner, over there, and raise it. And don't call it mullen, call it Pitchi-ola—that's its right name, when it's in a prison. And you want to water it with your tears."

"Why, I got plenty spring water, Mars Tom."

"You don't *want* spring water; you want to water it with your tears. It's the way they always do."

"Why, Mars Tom, I lay I kin raise one er dem mullen-stalks twyste wid spring water whiles another man's a *start'n* one wid tears."

"That ain't the idea. You *got* to do it with tears."

"She'll die on my han's, Mars Tom, she sholy will; kase I doan' skasely ever cry."

So Tom was stumped. But he studied it over, and then said Jim would have to worry along the best he could with an onion. He promised he would go to the nigger cabins and drop one, private, in Jim's coffee-pot, in the morning. Jim said he would "jis' 's soon have tobacker in his coffee;" and found so much fault with it, and with the work and bother of raising the mullen, and jews-harping the rats, and petting and flattering up the snakes and spiders and things, on top of all the other work he had to do on pens, and inscriptions, and journals, and things, which made it more trou-ble and worry and responsibility to be a prisoner than anything he ever undertook, that Tom most lost all patience with him; and said he was just loadened down with more gaudier chances than a prisoner ever had in the world to make a name for himself, and yet he didn't know enough to appreciate them, and they was just about wasted on him. So Jim he was sorry, and said he wouldn't behave so no more, and then me and Tom shoved for bed.

CHAPTER XXXIX.

In the morning we went up to the village and bought a wire rat trap and fetched it down, and unstopped the best rat hole, and in about an hour we had fifteen of the bulliest kind of ones; and then we took it and put it in a safe place under Aunt Sally's bed. But while we was gone for spiders, little Thomas Franklin Benjamin Jefferson Elexander Phelps found it there, and opened the door of it to see if the rats would come out, and they did; and Aunt Sally she come in, and when we got back she was a standing on top of the bed raising Cain, and the rats was doing what they could to keep off the dull times for her. So she took and dusted us both with the hickry, and we was as much as two hours catching another fifteen or sixteen, drat that meddlesome cub, and they warn't the likeliest, nuther, because the first haul was the pick of the flock. I never see a likelier lot of rats than what that first haul was.

We got a splendid stock of sorted spiders, and bugs, and frogs, and caterpillars, and one thing or another; and we like-to got a hornet's nest, but we didn't. The family was at home. We didn't give it right up, but staid with them as long as we could; because we allowed we'd tire them out or they'd got to tire us out, and they done it. Then we got allycumpain and rubbed on the places, and was pretty near all right again, but couldn't set down convenient. And so we went for the snakes, and grabbed a couple of dozen garters and house-snakes, and put them in a bag, and put it in our room, and by that time it was supper time, and a rattling good honest day's work: and hungry?—oh, no, I reckon not! And there warn't a blessed snake up there, when we went back—we didn't half tie the sack, and they worked out somehow, and left. But it didn't matter much, because they was still on the premises somewheres. So we judged we could get some of them again. No, there warn't no real scarcity of snakes about the house for a considerable spell. You'd see them dripping from the rafters and places, every now and then; and they generly landed in your plate, or down the back of your neck, and most of the time where you didn't want them. Well, they was handsome, and striped, and there warn't no harm in a million of them; but that never made no difference to Aunt Sally; she despised snakes, be the breed what they might, and she couldn't stand them no way you could fix it; and every time one of them flopped down on her, it didn't make no difference what she was doing, she would just lay that work down and light out. I never see such a woman. And you could hear her whoop to Jericho. You couldn't get her to take aholt of one of them with the tongs. And if she turned over and found one in bed, she would scramble out and lift a howl that you would think the house was afire. She disturbed the old man so, that he said he could most wish there hadn't ever been no snakes created. Why, after every last snake had been gone clear out of the house for as much as a week, Aunt Sally warn't over it yet; she warn't near over it; when she was setting thinking about something, you could touch her on the back of her neck with a feather and she would jump right out of her stockings. It was very curious. But Tom said all women was just so. He said they was made that way; for some reason or other.

We got a licking every time one of our snakes come in her way; and she allowed these lickings warn't nothing to what she would do if we ever loaded up the place again with them. I didn't mind the lickings, because they didn't amount to nothing; but I minded the trouble we had, to lay in another lot. But we got them laid in, and all the other things; and you never see a cabin as blithesome as Jim's was when they'd all swarm out for music and go for him. Jim didn't like the spiders, and the spiders didn't like Jim; and so they'd lay for him, and make it mighty warm for him. And he said that between the rats, and the snakes, and the grindstone, there warn't no room in bed for him, skasely; and when there was, a body couldn't sleep, it was so lively, and it was always lively, he said, because *they* never all slept at one time, but took turn about, so when the snakes was asleep the rats was on deck, and when the rats turned in the snakes come on watch, so he always had one gang under him, in his way, and t'other gang having a circus over him, and if he got up to hunt a new place, the spiders would take a chance at him as he crossed over. He said if he ever got out, this time, he wouldn't ever be a prisoner again, not for a salary.[161]

---

161. Jim's prolonged imprisonment and torture by Tom and Huck, the same people who are supposedly trying to help him escape to freedom, make these chapters extremely problematic. Literature scholars typically regard them as the book's main flaw, a case of Twain abandoning his narrative for the sake of a few cheap laughs.

Some have suggested that these chapters provide a parable of the treatment of blacks after the Civil War and especially after the early years of Reconstruction. Tom and Huck are supposed to be helping Jim escape, but Tom is clearly more interested in using Jim to act out grisly prison scenes from historical romance books, and Huck is under Tom's sway. Twain himself was apparently more interested in bashing those historical romances, a recurring pet peeve of his, than in commenting on the abandonment of Reconstruction, but the parallels are there. The federal government freed most of the slaves in 1863 with the Emancipation Proclamation, freed all of them in 1865 with the Thirteenth Amendment, and then granted them basic civil rights with the two Reconstruction amendments to the U.S. Constitution. But enforcing all of these amendments was a different story. Ex-slaveholders and white southerners in general fiercely resisted full civil rights for blacks. The North-dominated government kept troops in the South to enforce those amendments and establish schools and other institutions for blacks, but the political will to keep them there quickly faded. By 1877 the last troops had been withdrawn from the South, essentially turning the

Well, by the end of three weeks, everything was in pretty good shape. The shirt was sent in early, in a pie, and every time a rat bit Jim he would get up and write a little in his journal whilst the ink was fresh; the pens was made, the inscriptions and so on was all carved on the grindstone; the bed-leg was sawed in two, and we had et up the sawdust, and it give us a most amazing stomach-ache. We reckoned we was all going to die, but didn't. It was the most undigestible sawdust I ever see; and Tom said the same. But as I was saying, we'd got all the work done, now, at last; and we was all pretty much fagged out, too, but mainly Jim. The old man had wrote a couple of times to the plantation below Orleans to come and get their runaway nigger, but hadn't got no answer, because there warn't no such plantation; so he allowed he would advertise Jim in the St. Louis and New Orleans papers; and when he mentioned the St. Louis ones, it give me the cold shivers, and I see we hadn't no time to lose. So Tom said, now for the nonnamous letters.

"What's them?" I says.

"Warnings to the people that something is up. Sometimes it's done one way, sometimes another. But there's always somebody spying around, that gives notice to the governor of the castle. When Louis XVI. was going to light out of the Tooleries, a servant girl done it.[162] It's a very good way, and so is the nonnamous letters. We'll use them both. And it's usual for the prisoner's mother to change clothes with him, and she stays in, and he slides out in her clothes. We'll do that, too."

---

freed slaves (and their children) over to their former masters. The mass of white northerners were far more interested in reconciliation with white southerners than with enforcing the Reconstruction amendments that gave blacks citizenship, the rights of equal protection and due process, and voting rights. While a return to outright slavery was out of the question, so was an open labor market for black workers. Northern employers were generally unwelcoming, preferring to hire European immigrants. Southern states passed broad breach of contract laws that made it a criminal offense for blacks to switch employers. Blacks could be easily and arbitrarily incarcerated under those laws and equally broad vagrancy laws, and the Thirteenth Amendment actually allowed involuntary servitude for convicts. More than 100,000 blacks in the decades after the Civil War toiled as de facto slaves for states or for private companies that paid the states for the labor of their inmates (Blackmon 2009, 7). Black voting rights were suppressed to the point of disenfranchisement, black schools were severely underfunded, and Jim Crow segregation became the law of the land in southern states. The federal government could have done more to guarantee the civil rights of African Americans, but by 1877 this was not a priority. Genuine enforcement of the Reconstruction amendments would have to wait until the 1960s.

162. The Tuileries was the French imperial palace in Paris before the royal court moved to Versailles. Following the French Revolution, Louis XVI and the royal family were moved back to the Tuileries in October 1789 and placed under house arrest. The royal family attempted unsuccessfully to escape in June 1791.

"But looky here, Tom, what do we want to *warn* anybody for, that something's up? Let them find it out for themselves—it's their lookout."

"Yes, I know; but you can't depend on them. It's the way they've acted from the very start—left us to do *everything*. They're so confiding and mullet-headed they don't take notice of nothing at all. So if we don't *give* them notice, there won't be nobody nor nothing to interfere with us, and so after all our hard work and trouble this escape 'll go off perfectly flat; won't amount to nothing—won't be nothing *to* it."

"Well, as for me, Tom, that's the way I'd like."

"Shucks!" he says, and looked disgusted. So I says:

"But I ain't going to make no complaint. Any way that suits you suits me. What you going to do about the servant-girl?"

"You'll be her. You slide in, in the middle of the night, and hook that yaller girl's frock."

"Why, Tom, that'll make trouble next morning; because of course she prob'bly hain't got any but that one."

"I know; but you don't want it but fifteen minutes, to carry the nonnamous letter and shove it under the front door."

"All right, then, I'll do it; but I could carry it just as handy in my own togs."

"You wouldn't look like a servant-girl *then,* would you?"

"No, but there won't be nobody to see what I look like, *anyway.*"

"That ain't got nothing to do with it. The thing for us to do, is just to do our *duty,* and not worry about whether anybody *sees* us do it or not. Hain't you got no principle at all?"

"All right, I ain't saying nothing; I'm the servant-girl. Who's Jim's mother?"

"I'm his mother. I'll hook a gown from Aunt Sally."

"Well, then, you'll have to stay in the cabin when me and Jim leaves."

"Not much. I'll stuff Jim's clothes full of straw and lay it on his bed to represent his mother in disguise, and Jim 'll take the nigger woman's gown off of me and wear it, and we'll all evade together. When a prisoner of style escapes, it's called an evasion. It's always called so when a king escapes, frinstance. And the same with a king's son; it don't make no difference whether he's a natural one or an unnatural one."

So Tom he wrote the nonnamous letter, and I smouched the yaller wench's frock, that night, and put it on, and shoved it under the front door, the way Tom told me to. It said:

Beware. Trouble is brewing. Keep a sharp lookout. UNKNOWN FRIEND.

Next night we stuck a picture which Tom drawed in blood, of a skull and crossbones, on the front door; and next night another one of a coffin, on the back door. I never see a family in such a sweat. They couldn't a been worse scared if the place had a been full of ghosts laying for them behind everything and under the beds and shivering through the air. If a door banged, Aunt Sally she jumped, and said "ouch!" if anything fell, she jumped and said "ouch!" if you happened to touch her, when she warn't noticing, she done the same; she couldn't face noway and be satisfied, because she allowed there was something behind her every time—so she was always a whirling around, sudden, and saying "ouch," and before she'd got two-thirds around, she'd whirl back again, and say it again; and she was afraid to go to bed, but she dasn't set up. So the thing was working very well, Tom said; he said he never see a thing work more satisfactory. He said it showed it was done right.

So he said, now for the grand bulge! So the very next morning at the streak of dawn we got another letter ready, and was wondering what we better do with it, because we heard them say at supper they was going to have a nigger on watch at both doors all night. Tom he went down the lightning-rod to spy around; and the nigger at the back door was asleep, and he stuck it in the back of his neck and come back. This letter said:

> *Don't betray me, I wish to be your friend. There is a desprate gang of cutthroats from over in the Ingean Territory going to steal your runaway nigger to-night,*[163] *and they have been trying to scare you so as*

---

163. At the time Indian Territory consisted of most of the present state of Oklahoma and eastern portions of the territories of Kansas and Nebraska. It was the area that had been reserved for Indian tribes following the 1830 Indian Removal Act and the forced relocation, also known as the Trail of Tears, of eastern Indian tribes to the west. Some two dozen tribes had allotments, usually small and often shared with another tribe, in this territory (Howe 2009, 418). Many if not most Indians in the area that is now the United States lived farther west, in the northern and western territories of the United States and in western areas that still belonged to Britain and Mexico and had little white settlement. There was no guarantee, and probably not much expectation, that any of these areas would remain Indian areas for much longer. With rapid westward settlement of whites, aided by the transportation revolution, the Mexican-American War, and the prevailing manifest destiny ideology that held that the United States should expand all the way to the Pacific Ocean, Indian Territory was short-lived. Over the course of the 19th century the territory shrunk to what is now Oklahoma, then to half of Oklahoma, and finally to a scattering of reservations.

The Indian areas had a reputation for lawlessness, mostly because of cultural stereotypes but partly because they had their own laws and were little policed by white American authorities, which made them potential hideouts for criminals. A federal law passed in 1871 prohibited murder and other major crimes in the territories, but in the decades before that law and perhaps even after it, white Americans often associated Indian Territory with crime and wildness. Twain plays on this stereotype in *The Adventures of Tom Sawyer*, inventing a murderous villain named Injun Joe. Huck does not specify whether his fake "cutthroats" are Indian or not.

you will stay in the house and not bother them. I am one of the gang, but have got religgion and wish to quit it and lead an honest life again, and will betray the helish design. They will sneak down from northards, along the fence, at midnight exact, with a false key, and go in the nigger's cabin to get him. I am to be off a piece and blow a tin horn if I see any danger; but stead of that, I will BA *like a sheep soon as they get in and not blow at all; then whilst they are getting his chains loose, you slip there and lock them in, and can kill them at your leasure. Don't do anything but just the way I am telling you, if you do they will suspicion something and raise whoop-jamboreehoo. I do not wish any reward but to know I have done the right thing.*

UNKNOWN FRIEND.

CHAPTER XL.

WE was feeling pretty good, after breakfast, and took my canoe and went over the river a-fishing, with a lunch, and had a good time, and took a look at the raft and found her all right, and got home late to supper, and found them in such a sweat and worry they didn't know which end they was standing on, and made us go right off to bed the minute we was done supper, and wouldn't tell us what the trouble was, and never let on a word about the new letter, but didn't need to, because we knowed as much about it as anybody did, and as soon as we was half up stairs and her back was turned, we slid for the cellar cupboard and loaded up a good lunch and took it up to our room and went to bed, and got up about half-past eleven, and Tom put on Aunt Sally's dress that he stole and was going to start with the lunch, but says:

"Where's the butter?"

"I laid out a hunk of it," I says, "on a piece of a corn-pone."

"Well, you *left* it laid out, then—it ain't here."

"We can get along without it," I says.

"We can get along *with* it, too," he says; "just you slide down cellar and fetch it. And then mosey right down the lightning-rod and come along. I'll go and stuff the straw into Jim's clothes to represent his mother in disguise, and be ready to *ba* like a sheep and shove soon as you get there."

So out he went, and down cellar went I. The hunk of butter, big as a person's fist, was where I had left it, so I took up the slab of corn-pone with it on, and blowed out my light, and started up stairs very stealthy, and got up to the main floor all right, but here comes Aunt Sally with a candle, and I clapped the truck in my hat, and clapped my hat on my head, and the next second she see me; and she says:

"You been down cellar?"

"Yes'm."

"What you been doing down there?"

"Noth'n."

"Noth'n!"

"No'm."

"Well, then, what possessed you to go down there, this time of night?"

"I don't know 'm."

"You don't *know?* Don't answer me that way, Tom, I want to know what you been *doing* down there."

"I hain't been doing a single thing, Aunt Sally, I hope to gracious if I have."

I reckoned she'd let me go, now, and as a generl thing she would; but I s'pose there was so many strange things going on she was just in a sweat about every little thing that warn't yard-stick straight; so she says, very decided:

"You just march into that setting-room and stay there till I come. You been up to something you no business to, and I lay I'll find out what it is before *I'm* done with you."

So she went away as I opened the door and walked into the setting-room. My, but there was a crowd there! Fifteen farmers, and every one of them had a gun. I was most powerful sick, and slunk to a chair and set down. They was setting around, some of them talking a little, in a low voice, and all of them fidgety and uneasy, but trying to look like they warn't; but I knowed they was, because they was always taking off their hats, and putting them on, and scratching their heads, and changing their seats, and fumbling with their buttons. I warn't easy myself, but I didn't take my hat off, all the same.

I did wish Aunt Sally would come, and get done with me, and lick me, if she wanted to, and let me get away and tell Tom how we'd overdone this thing, and what a thundering hornet's nest we'd got ourselves into, so we could stop fooling around, straight off, and clear out with Jim before these rips got out of patience and come for us.

At last she come, and begun to ask me questions, but I *couldn't* answer them straight, I didn't know which end of me was up; because these men was in such a fidget now, that some was wanting to start right *now* and lay for them desperadoes, and saying it warn't but a few minutes to midnight; and others was trying to get them to hold on and wait for the sheep-signal; and here was aunty pegging away at the questions, and me a shaking all over and ready to sink down in my tracks I was that scared; and the place getting hotter and hotter, and the butter beginning to melt and run down my neck and behind my ears; and pretty soon, when one of them says, *"I'm* for going and getting in the cabin *first,* and right *now,* and catching them when they come," I most dropped; and a streak of butter come a trickling down my forehead, and Aunt Sally she see it, and turns white as a sheet, and says:

EVERY ONE HAD A GUN.

(Illustration by Edward W. Kemble. From Mark Twain, *Adventures of Huckleberry Finn*. New York: C. L. Webster, 1885. Digitized by the University of Virginia Library.)

"For the land's sake, what *is* the matter with the child!—he's got the brain fever as shore as you're born, and they're oozing out!"

And everybody runs to see, and she snatches off my hat, and out comes the bread, and what was left of the butter, and she grabbed me, and hugged me, and says:

"Oh, what a turn you did give me! and how glad and grateful I am it ain't no worse; for luck's against us, and it never rains but it pours, and when I see that truck I thought we'd lost you, for I knowed by the color and all, it was just like your brains would be if—Dear, dear, whyd'nt you *tell* me that was what you'd been down there for, *I* wouldn't a cared. Now cler out to bed, and don't lemme see no more of you till morning!"

I was up stairs in a second, and down the lightning-rod in another one, and shinning through the dark for the lean-to. I couldn't hardly get my words out, I was so anxious; but I told Tom as quick as I could, we must jump for it, now, and not a minute to lose—the house full of men, yonder, with guns!

His eyes just blazed; and he says:

"No!—is that so? *Ain't* it bully! Why, Huck, if it was to do over again, I bet I could fetch two hundred! If we could put it off till—"

"Hurry! *hurry!*" I says. "Where's Jim?"

"Right at your elbow; if you reach out your arm you can touch him. He's dressed, and everything's ready. Now we'll slide out and give the sheep-signal."

But then we heard the tramp of men, coming to the door, and heard them begin to fumble with the padlock, and heard a man say:

"I *told* you we'd be too soon; they haven't come—the door is locked. Here, I'll lock some of you into the cabin, and you lay for 'em in the dark and kill 'em when they come; and the rest scatter around a piece, and listen if you can hear 'em coming."

So in they come, but couldn't see us in the dark, and most trod on us whilst we was hustling to get under the bed. But we got under all right, and out through the hole, swift but soft—Jim first, me next, and Tom last, which was according to Tom's orders. Now we was in the lean-to, and heard trampings close by outside. So we crept to the door, and Tom stopped us there and put his eye to the crack, but couldn't make out nothing, it was so dark; and whispered and said he would listen for the steps to get further, and when he nudged us Jim must glide out first, and him last. So he set his ear to the crack and listened, and listened, and listened, and the steps a scraping around, out there, all the time; and at last he nudged us, and we slid out, and stooped down, not breathing, and not making the least noise, and slipped stealthy towards the fence, in Injun file, and got to it, all right, and me and Jim over it; but Tom's britches catched fast on a splinter on the top rail, and then he hear the steps coming, so he had to pull loose, which snapped the splinter and made a noise; and as he dropped in our tracks and started somebody sings out:

"Who's that? Answer, or I'll shoot!"

But we didn't answer; we just unfurled our heels and shoved. Then there was a rush, and a *bang, bang, bang!* and the bullets fairly whizzed around us! We heard them sing out:

"Here they are! They've broke for the river! after 'em, boys! And turn loose the dogs!"

So here they come, full tilt. We could hear them, because they wore boots, and yelled, but we didn't wear no boots, and didn't yell. We was in the path to the mill; and when they got pretty close on to us, we dodged into the bush and let them go by, and then dropped in behind them. They'd had all the dogs shut up, so they wouldn't scare off the robbers; but by this time somebody had let them loose, and here they come, making pow-wow enough for a million; but they was our dogs; so we stopped in our tracks till they catched up; and when they see it warn't nobody but us, and no excitement to offer them, they only just said howdy, and tore right ahead towards the shouting and clattering; and then we up steam again and whizzed along after them till we was nearly to the mill, and then struck up through the bush to where my canoe was tied, and hopped in and pulled for dear life towards the middle of the river, but didn't make no more noise than we was obleeged to. Then we struck out, easy and comfortable, for the island where my raft was; and we could hear them yelling and barking at each other all up and down the bank, till we was so far away the sounds got dim and died out. And when we stepped on to the raft, I says:

"*Now,* old Jim, you're a free man *again,* and I bet you won't ever be a slave no more."

"En a mighty good job it wuz, too, Huck. It 'uz planned beautiful, en it 'uz *done* beautiful; en dey ain't *nobody* kin git up a plan dat's mo' mixed-up en splendid den what dat one wuz."

We was all glad as we could be, but Tom was the gladdest of all, because he had a bullet in the calf of his leg.

When me and Jim heard that, we didn't feel so brash as what we did before. It was hurting him considerable, and bleeding; so we laid him in the wigwam and tore up one of the duke's shirts for to bandage him, but he says:

"Gimme the rags; I can do it myself. Don't stop, now; don't fool around here, and the evasion booming along so handsome; man the sweeps, and set her loose! Boys, we done it elegant!—'deed we did. I wish *we'd* a had the handling of Louis XVI., there wouldn't a been no 'Son of Saint Louis, ascend to heaven!' wrote down in *his* biography;[164] no, sir, we'd a whooped him over the *border*—that's what we'd a done with *him*—and done it just as slick as nothing at all, too. Man the sweeps—man the sweeps!"

But me and Jim was consulting—and thinking. And after we'd thought a minute, I says:

"Say it, Jim."

So he says:

"Well, den, dis is de way it look to me, Huck. Ef it wuz *him* dat 'uz bein' sot free, en one er de boys wuz to git shot, would he say, 'Go on en save me, nemmine 'bout a doctor f'r to save dis one?' Is dat like Mars Tom Sawyer? Would he say dat? You *bet* he wouldn't! *Well,* den, is *Jim* gywne to say it? No, sah—I doan' budge a step out'n dis place 'dout a *doctor,* not if it's forty year!"

---

164. "Son of Saint Louis, ascend to heaven!" is the blessing that Henry Essex Edgeworth, a Catholic priest who was Louis XVI's confessor, reportedly gave to Louis just before he was guillotined. Saint Louis was Louis XVI's ancestor Louis IX, who ruled France from 1226 to 1270 and was canonized by Pope Boniface VIII in 1297. The city of St. Louis, founded in 1764 by two Frenchmen, was named for him.

I knowed he was white inside, and I reckoned he'd say what he did say—so it was all right, now, and I told Tom I was agoing for a doctor. He raised considerable row about it, but me and Jim stuck to it and wouldn't budge; so he was for crawling out and setting the raft loose himself; but we wouldn't let him. Then he give us a piece of his mind—but it didn't do no good.

So when he sees me getting the canoe ready, he says:

"Well, then, if you're bound to go, I'll tell you the way to do when you get to the village. Shut the door, and blindfold the doctor tight and fast, and make him swear to be silent as the grave, and put a purse full of gold in his hand, and then take and lead him all around the back alleys and every-wheres, in the dark, and then fetch him here in the canoe, in a roundabout way amongst the islands, and search him and take his chalk away from him, and don't give it back to him till you get him back to the village, or else he will chalk this raft so he can find it again. It's the way they all do."

So I said I would, and left, and Jim was to hide in the woods when he see the doctor coming, till he was gone again.

CHAPTER XLI.

THE doctor was an old man; a very nice, kind-looking old man, when I got him up. I told him me and my brother was over on Spanish Island hunting, yesterday afternoon, and camped on a piece of a raft we found, and about midnight he must a kicked his gun in his dreams, for it went off and shot him in the leg, and we wanted him to go over there and fix it and not say nothing about it, nor let anybody know, because we wanted to come home this evening, and surprise the folks.

"Who is your folks?" he says.

"The Phelpses, down yonder."

"Oh," he says. And after a minute, he says: "How'd you say he got shot?"

"He had a dream," I says, "and it shot him."

"Singular dream," he says.

So he lit up his lantern, and got his saddle-bags, and we started. But when he sees the canoe, he didn't like the look of her—said she was big enough for one, but didn't look pretty safe for two. I says:

"Oh, you needn't be afeard, sir, she carried the three of us, easy enough."

"What three?"

"Why, me and Sid, and—and—and *the guns;* that's what I mean."

"Oh," he says.

But he put his foot on the gunnel, and rocked her; and shook his head, and said he reckoned he'd look around for a bigger one. But they was all locked and chained; so he took my canoe, and said for me to wait till he come back, or I could hunt around further, or maybe I better go down home and get them ready for the surprise, if I wanted to. But I said I didn't; so I told him just how to find the raft, and then he started.

I struck an idea, pretty soon. I says to myself, spos'n he can't fix that leg just in three shakes of a sheep's tail, as the saying is? spos'n it takes him three or four days? What are we going to do?—lay around there till he lets the cat out of the bag? No, sir, I know what *I'll* do. I'll wait, and when he comes back, if he says he's got to go any more, I'll get down there, too, if I swim; and we'll take and tie him, and keep him, and shove out down the river; and when Tom's done with him, we'll give him what it's worth, or all we got, and then let him get ashore.

So then I crept into a lumber pile to get some sleep; and next time I waked up the sun was away up over my head! I shot out and went for the doctor's house, but they told me he'd gone away in the night, some time or other, and warn't back yet. Well, thinks I, that looks powerful bad for Tom, and I'll dig out for the island, right off. So away I shoved, and turned the corner, and nearly rammed my head into Uncle Silas's stomach! He says:

"Why, *Tom!* Where you been, all this time, you rascal?"

"*I* hain't been nowheres," I says, "only just hunting for the runaway nigger—me and Sid."

"Why, where ever did you go?" he says. "Your aunt's been mighty uneasy."

"She needn't," I says, "because we was all right. We followed the men and the dogs, but they outrun us, and we lost them; but we thought we heard them on the water, so we got a canoe and took out after them, and crossed over, but couldn't find nothing of them; so we cruised along up-shore till we got kind of tired and beat out; and tied up the canoe and went to sleep, and never waked up till about an hour ago, then we paddled over here to hear the news, and Sid's at the post-office to see what he can hear, and I'm a-branching out to get something to eat for us, and then we're going home."

So then we went to the post-office to get "Sid"; but just as I suspicioned, he warn't there; so the old man he got a letter out of the office, and we waited a while longer, but Sid didn't come; so the old man said come along, let Sid foot it home, or canoe-it, when he got done fooling around—but we would ride. I couldn't get him to let me stay and wait for Sid; and he said there warn't no use in it, and I must come along, and let Aunt Sally see we was all right.

When we got home, Aunt Sally was that glad to see me she laughed and cried both, and hugged me, and give me one of them lickings of hern that don't amount to shucks, and said she'd serve Sid the same when he come.

And the place was plum full of farmers and farmers' wives, to dinner; and such another clack a body never heard. Old Mrs. Hotchkiss was the worst; her tongue was agoing all the time. She says:

"Well, Sister Phelps, I've ransacked that-air cabin over, an' I b'lieve the nigger was crazy. I says to Sister Damrell—didn't I, Sister Damrell?—s'I, he's crazy, s'I—them's the very words I said. You all hearn me: he's crazy, s'I; everything shows it, s'I. Look at that-air grindstone, s'I; want to tell *me* 't any cretur 'ts in his right mind 's a goin' to scrabble all them crazy things onto a grindstone, s'I? Here sich 'n' sich a person busted his heart; 'n' here so 'n' so pegged along for thirty-seven year, 'n' all that—natcherl son o' Louis somebody, 'n' sich everlast'n rubbage. He's plumb crazy, s'I; it's what I says in the fust place, it's what I says in the middle, 'n' it's what I says last 'n' all the time—the nigger's crazy—crazy 's Nebokoodneezer, s'I."

"An' look at that-air ladder made out'n rags, Sister Hotchkiss," says old Mrs. Damrell, "what in the name o' goodness *could* he ever want of—"

"The very words I was a-sayin' no longer ago th'n this minute to Sister Utterback, 'n' she'll tell you so herself. Sh-she, look at that-air rag ladder, sh-she; 'n' s'I, yes, *look* at it, s'I—what *could* he a wanted of it, s'I. Sh-she, Sister Hotchkiss, sh-she—"

"But how in the nation'd they ever *git* that grindstone *in* there, *any-way?* 'n' who dug that-air *hole?* 'n' who—"

"My very *words,* Brer Penrod! I was a-sayin'—pass that-air sasser o' m'lasses, won't ye?—I was a-sayin' to Sister Dunlap, jist this minute, how *did* they git that grindstone in there, s'I. Without *help,* mind you—'thout *help!* Thar's wher 'tis. Don't tell *me,* s'I; there *wuz* help, s'I; 'n' ther' wuz a *plenty* help, too, s'I; ther's ben a *dozen* a-helpin' that nigger, 'n' I lay I'd skin every last nigger on this place, but *I'd* find out who done it, s'I; 'n' moreover, s'I—"

"A *dozen* says you!—*forty* couldn't a done everything that's been done. Look at them case-knife saws and things, how tedious they've been made; look at that bed-leg sawed off with 'm, a week's work for six men; look at that nigger made out'n straw on the bed; and look at—"[165]

---

165. An enduring myth in the Old South was that of the contented slave. Defenders of slavery insisted on it to keep the antislavery forces at bay and perhaps to ease their consciences. Even well after emancipation, popular works such as Margaret Mitchell's *Gone with the Wind* told a similar story about happy slaves. Twain clearly did not buy into this myth, and the slave-owning Phelpses don't seem to either. They seem to recognize that slaves will help a fugitive escape rather than cooperate with efforts to recapture and return the slave.

"You may *well* say it, Brer Hightower! It's jist as I was a-sayin' to Brer Phelps, his own self. S'e, what do *you* think of it, Sister Hotchkiss, s'e? think o' what, Brer Phelps, s'I? think o' that bed-leg sawed off that a way, s'e? *think* of it, s'I? I lay it never sawed *itself* off, s'I—somebody *sawed* it, s'I; that's my opinion, take it or leave it, it mayn't be no 'count, s'I, but sich as 't is, it's my opinion, s'I, 'n' if anybody k'n start a better one, s'I, let him *do* it, s'I, that's all. I says to Sister Dunlap, s'I—"

"Why, dog my cats, they must a ben a house-full o' niggers in there every night for four weeks, to a done all that work, Sister Phelps. Look at that shirt—every last inch of it kivered over with secret African writ'n done with blood! Must a ben a raft uv 'm at it right along, all the time, amost. Why, I'd give two dollars to have it read to me; 'n' as for the niggers that wrote it, I 'low I'd take 'n' lash 'm t'll—"

"People to *help* him, Brother Marples! Well, I reckon you'd *think* so, if you'd a been in this house for a while back. Why, they've stole everything they could lay their hands on—and we a watching all the time, mind you. They stole that shirt right off o' the line! and as for that sheet they made the rag ladder out of, ther' ain't no telling how many times they *didn't* steal that; and flour, and candles, and candlesticks, and spoons, and the old warming-pan, and most a thousand things that I disremember, now, and my new calico dress; and me, and Silas, and my Sid and Tom on the constant watch day *and* night, as I was a-telling you, and not a one of us could catch hide nor hair, nor sight nor sound of them; and here at the last minute, lo and behold you, they slides right in under our noses, and fools us, and not only fools *us* but the Injun Territory robbers too, and actly gets *away* with that nigger, safe and sound, and that with sixteen men and twenty-two dogs right on their very heels at that very time! I tell you, it just bangs anything I ever *heard* of. Why, *sperits* couldn't a done better, and been no smarter. And I reckon they must a *been* sperits—because, *you* know our dogs, and ther' ain't no better; well, them dogs never even got on the *track* of 'm, once! You explain *that* to me, if you can!—*any* of you!"

"Well, it does beat—"

"Laws alive, I never—"

"So help me, I wouldn't a be—"

"*House*-thieves as well as—"

"Goodnessgracioussakes, I'd a ben afeard to *live* in sich a—"

"'Fraid to *live*!—why, I was that scared I dasn't hardly go to bed, or get up, or lay down, or *set* down, Sister Ridgeway. Why, they'd steal the very—why, goodness sakes, you can guess what kind of a fluster *I* was in by the time midnight come, last night. I hope to gracious if I warn't afraid they'd steal some o' the family! I was just to that pass, I didn't have no reasoning faculties no more. It looks foolish enough, *now,* in the daytime; but I says to myself, there's my two poor boys asleep, 'way up stairs in that lonesome room, and I declare to goodness I was that uneasy 't I crep' up there and locked 'em in! I *did*. And anybody would. Because, you know, when you get scared, that way, and it keeps running on, and getting worse and worse, all the time, and your wits gets to addling, and you get to doing all sorts o' wild things, and by and by you think to yourself, spos'n *I* was a boy, and was away up there, and the door ain't locked, and you—" She stopped, looking kind of wondering, and then she turned her head around slow, and when her eye lit on me—I got up and took a walk.

Says I to myself, I can explain better how we come to not be in that room this morning, if I go out to one side and study over it a little. So I done it. But I dasn't go fur, or she'd a sent for me. And when it was late in the day, the people all went, and then I come in and told her the noise and shooting waked up me and "Sid," and the door was locked, and we wanted to see the fun, so we went down the lightning-rod, and both of us got hurt a little, and we didn't never want to try *that* no more. And then I went on and told her all what I told Uncle Silas before; and then she said she'd forgive us, and maybe it was all right enough anyway, and about what a body might expect of boys, for all boys was a pretty harum-scarum lot, as fur as she could see; and so, as long as no harm hadn't come of it, she judged she better put in her time being grateful we was alive and well and she had us still, stead of fretting over what was past and done. So then she kissed me, and patted me on the head, and dropped into a kind of a brown study; and pretty soon jumps up, and says:

"Why, lawsamercy, it's most night, and Sid not come yet! What *has* become of that boy?"

I see my chance; so I skips up and says:

"I'll run right up to town and get him," I says.

"No you won't," she says. "You'll stay right wher' you are; *one's* enough to be lost at a time. If he ain't here to supper, your uncle 'll go."

Well, he warn't there to supper; so right after supper uncle went.

He come back about ten, a little bit uneasy; hadn't run across Tom's track. Aunt Sally was a good *deal* uneasy; but Uncle Silas he said there warn't no occasion to be—boys will be boys, he said, and you'll see this one turn up in the morning all sound and right. So she had to be satisfied. But she said she'd set up for him a while, anyway, and keep a light burning, so he could see it.

And then when I went up to bed she come up with me and fetched her candle, and tucked me in, and mothered me so good I felt mean, and like I couldn't look her in the face; and she set down on the bed and talked with me a long time, and said what a splendid boy Sid was, and didn't seem to want to ever stop talking about him; and kept asking me every now and then, if I reckoned he could a got lost, or hurt, or maybe drownded, and might be laying at this minute, somewheres, suffering or dead, and she not by him to help him, and so the tears would drip down, silent, and I would tell her that Sid was all right, and would be home in the morning, sure; and she would squeeze my hand, or maybe kiss me, and tell me to say it again, and keep on saying it, because it done her good, and she was in so much trouble. And when she was going away, she looked down in my eyes so steady and gentle, and says:

"The door ain't going to be locked, Tom; and there's the window and the rod; but you'll be good, *won't* you? And you won't go? For *my* sake."

Laws knows I *wanted* to go, bad enough, to see about Tom, and was all intending to go; but after that I wouldn't a went, not for kingdoms.

But she was on my mind, and Tom was on my mind; so I slept very restless. And twice I went down the rod, away in the night, and slipped around front, and see her setting there by her candle in the window with her eyes towards the road and the tears in them; and I wished I could do something for her, but I couldn't, only to swear that I wouldn't never do nothing to grieve her any more. And the third time, I waked up at dawn, and slid down, and she was there yet, and her candle was most out, and her old gray head was resting on her hand, and she was asleep.

CHAPTER XLII.

THE old man was up town again, before breakfast, but couldn't get no track of Tom; and both of them set at the table, thinking, and not saying nothing, and looking mournful, and their coffee getting cold, and not eating anything. And by and by the old man says:

"Did I give you the letter?"

"What letter?"

"The one I got yesterday out of the post-office."

"No, you didn't give me no letter."

"Well, I must a forgot it."

So he rummaged his pockets, and then went off somewheres where he had laid it down, and fetched it, and give it to her. She says:

"Why, it's from St. Petersburg—it's from Sis."

I allowed another walk would do me good; but I couldn't stir. But before she could break it open, she dropped it and run—for she see something. And so did I. It was Tom Sawyer on a mattress; and that old doctor; and Jim, in *her* calico dress, with his hands tied behind him; and a lot of people. I hid the letter behind the first thing that come handy, and rushed. She flung herself at Tom, crying, and says:

"Oh, he's dead, he's dead, I know he's dead!"

And Tom he turned his head a little, and muttered something or other, which showed he warn't in his right mind; then she flung up her hands, and says:

"He's alive, thank God! And that's enough!" and she snatched a kiss of him, and flew for the house to get the bed ready, and scattering orders right and left at the niggers and everybody else, as fast as her tongue could go, every jump of the way.

I followed the men to see what they was going to do with Jim; and the old doctor and Uncle Silas followed after Tom into the house. The men was very huffy, and some of them wanted to hang Jim, for an example to all the other niggers around there, so they wouldn't be trying to run away like Jim done, and making such a raft of trouble, and keeping a whole family scared most to death for days and nights. But the others said, don't do it, it wouldn't answer at all, he ain't our nigger, and his owner would turn up and make us pay for him, sure. So that cooled them down a little, because the people that's always the most anxious for to hang a nigger that hain't done just right, is always the very ones that ain't the most anxious to pay for him when they've got their satisfaction out of him.[166]

They cussed Jim considerble, though, and give him a cuff or two, side the head, once in a while, but Jim never said nothing, and he never let on to know me, and they took him to the same cabin, and put his own clothes on him, and chained him again, and not to no bed-leg this time, but to a big staple drove into the bottom log, and chained his hands, too, and both legs, and said he warn't to have nothing but bread and water to eat, after this, till his owner come or he was sold at auction because he didn't come in a certain length of time, and filled up our hole, and said a couple of farmers with guns must stand watch around about the cabin every night, and a bulldog tied to the door in the daytime; and about this time they was through with the job and was tapering off with a kind of generl good-bye cussing, and then the old doctor comes and takes a look, and says:

"Don't be no rougher on him than you're obleeged to, because he ain't a bad nigger. When I got to where I found the boy, I see I couldn't cut the bullet out without some help, and he warn't in no condition for me to leave, to go and get help; and he got a little worse and a little worse, and after a long time he went out of his head, and wouldn't let me come anigh him any more, and said if I chalked his raft he'd kill me, and no end of wild foolishness like that, and I see I couldn't do anything at all with him; so I says, I got to have *help*, somehow; and the minute I says it, out crawls this nigger from somewheres, and says he'll help, and he done it, too, and done it very well. Of course I judged he must be a runaway nigger, and there I *was*! and there I had to stick, right straight along all the rest of the day, and all night. It was a fix, I tell you! I had a couple of patients with the chills,

---

166. Although all southern states made it a crime to murder a slave, convictions were often difficult to obtain. Yet lynchings of slaves, except for extreme offenses such as rape or insurrection, were uncommon (Stampp 1956, 190–191, 219–224). Huck explains why: slaves were valuable, legally recognized property, and the murderers would be expected to make restitution to the slave's owner.

and of course I'd of liked to run up to town and see them, but I dasn't, because the nigger might get away, and then I'd be to blame; and yet never a skiff come close enough for me to hail. So there I had to stick, plumb until daylight this morning; and I never see a nigger that was a better nuss or faithfuller, and yet he was resking his freedom to do it, and was all tired out, too, and I see plain enough he'd been worked main hard, lately. I liked the nigger for that; I tell you, gentlemen, a nigger like that is worth a thousand dollars—and kind treatment, too. I had everything I needed, and the boy was doing as well there as he would a done at home—better, maybe, because it was so quiet; but there I *was,* with both of 'm on my hands; and there I had to stick, till about dawn this morning; then some men in a skiff come by, and as good luck would have it, the nigger was setting by the pallet with his head propped on his knees, sound asleep; so I motioned them in quiet, and they slipped up on him and grabbed him and tied him before he knowed what he was about, and we never had no trouble. And the boy being in a kind of a flighty sleep, too, we muffled the oars and hitched the raft on, and towed her over very nice and quiet, and the nigger never made the least row nor said a word, from the start. He ain't no bad nigger, gentlemen; that's what I think about him."

Somebody says:

"Well, it sounds very good, doctor, I'm obleeged to say."

Then the others softened up a little, too, and I was mighty thankful to that old doctor for doing Jim that good turn; and I was glad it was according to my judgment of him, too; because I thought he had a good heart in him and was a good man, the first time I see him. Then they all agreed that Jim had acted very well, and was deserving to have some notice took of it, and reward. So every one of them promised, right out and hearty, that they wouldn't cuss him no more.

Then they come out and locked him up. I hoped they was going to say he could have one or two of the chains took off, because they was rotten heavy, or could have meat and greens with his bread and water, but they didn't think of it, and I reckoned it warn't best for me to mix in, but I judged I'd get the doctor's yarn to Aunt Sally, somehow or other, as soon as I'd got through the breakers that was laying just ahead of me. Explanations, I mean, of how I forgot to mention about Sid being shot when I was telling how him and me put in that dratted night paddling around hunting the runaway nigger.

But I had plenty time. Aunt Sally she stuck to the sick-room all day and all night; and every time I see Uncle Silas mooning around, I dodged him.

Next morning I heard Tom was a good deal better, and they said Aunt Sally was gone to get a nap. So I slips to the sick-room, and if I found him awake I reckoned we could put up a yarn for the family that would wash. But he was sleeping, and sleeping very peaceful, too; and pale, not fire-faced the way he was when he come. So I set down and laid for him to wake. In about half an hour, Aunt Sally comes gliding in, and there I was, up a stump again! She motioned me to be still, and set down by me, and begun to whisper, and said we could all be joyful now, because all the symptoms was first rate, and he'd been sleeping like that for ever so long, and looking better and peacefuller all the time, and ten to one he'd wake up in his right mind.

So we set there watching, and by and by he stirs a bit, and opened his eyes very natural, and takes a look, and says:

"Hello, why, I'm at *home!* How's that? Where's the raft?"

"It's all right," I says.

"And *Jim?*"

"The same," I says, but couldn't say it pretty brash. But he never noticed, but says:

"Good! Splendid! *Now* we're all right and safe! Did you tell Aunty?"

I was going to say yes; but she chipped in and says:

"About what, Sid?"

"Why, about the way the whole thing was done."

"What whole thing?"

"Why, *the* whole thing. There ain't but one; how we set the runaway nigger free—me and Tom."

"Good land! Set the run—What *is* the child talking about! Dear, dear, out of his head again!"

"*No,* I ain't out of my *head;* I know all what I'm talking about. We *did* set him free—me and Tom. We laid out to do it, and we *done* it. And we done it elegant, too." He'd got a start, and she never checked him up, just set and stared and stared, and let him clip along, and I see it warn't no use for *me* to put in. "Why, Aunty, it cost us a power of work—weeks of it—hours and hours, every night, whilst you was all asleep. And we had to steal candles, and the sheet, and the shirt, and your dress, and spoons, and tin plates, and case-knives, and the warming-pan, and the grindstone, and flour, and just no end of things, and you can't think what work it was to make the saws, and pens, and inscriptions, and one thing or another, and you can't think *half* the fun it was. And we had to make up the pictures of coffins and things, and nonnamous letters from the robbers, and get up and down the lightning-rod, and dig the hole into the cabin, and make the rope-ladder and send it in cooked up in a pie, and send in spoons and things to work with, in your apron pocket—"

"Mercy sakes!"

"—and load up the cabin with rats and snakes and so on, for company for Jim; and then you kept Tom here so long with the butter in his hat that you come near spiling the whole business, because the men come before we was out of the cabin, and we had to rush, and they heard us and let drive at us, and I got my share, and we dodged out of the path and let them go by, and when the dogs come they warn't interested in us, but went for the most noise, and we got our canoe, and made for the raft, and was all safe, and Jim was a free man, and we done it all by ourselves, and *wasn't* it bully, Aunty!"

"Well, I never heard the likes of it in all my born days! So it was *you*, you little rapscallions, that's been making all this trouble, and turned everybody's wits clean inside out and scared us all most to death. I've as good a notion as ever I had in my life, to take it out o' you this very minute. To think, here I've been, night after night, a—*you* just get well once, you young scamp, and I lay I'll tan the Old Harry out o' both o' ye!"

But Tom, he *was* so proud and joyful, he just *couldn't* hold in, and his tongue just *went* it—she a-chipping in, and spitting fire all along, and both of them going it at once, like a cat-convention; and she says:

"*Well,* you get all the enjoyment you can out of it *now,* for mind I tell you if I catch you meddling with him again—"

"Meddling with *who?*" Tom says, dropping his smile and looking surprised.

"With *who?* Why, the runaway nigger, of course. Who'd you reckon?"

Tom looks at me very grave, and says:

"Tom, didn't you just tell me he was all right? Hasn't he got away?"

"*Him?*" says Aunt Sally; "the runaway nigger? 'Deed he hasn't. They've got him back, safe and sound, and he's in that cabin again, on bread and water, and loaded down with chains, till he's claimed or sold!"

Tom rose square up in bed, with his eye hot, and his nostrils opening and shutting like gills, and sings out to me:

"They hain't no *right* to shut him up! *Shove!*—and don't you lose a minute. Turn him loose! he ain't no slave; he's as free as any cretur that walks this earth!"

"What *does* the child mean?"

"I mean every word I *say,* Aunt Sally, and if somebody don't go, *I'll* go. I've knowed him all his life, and so has Tom, there. Old Miss Watson died two months ago, and she was ashamed she ever was going to sell him down the river, and *said* so; and she set him free in her will."[167]

---

167. A relatively benevolent master might free his slaves on his own accord; "manu-mission" was the term for this. This practice was rare. Famous cases include George Washington freeing all of his slaves in his will and Thomas Jefferson freeing all members of the Hemings family, who may have been his blood relations. According to the 1850 census, manumissions were somewhat more common than slaves escapes, though both were rare; manumitted slaves outnumbered fugitive slaves 1,467 to 1,011 (United States Senate 1854, 64). Missouri and the other border states allowed it with few restrictions, although manu-missions were almost unheard of in Missouri except in St. Louis County (Trexler 1914, 224). The remaining Upper South states and Louisiana allowed it as long as the free slave left the state soon thereafter, and the remaining Lower South states had essentially outlawed it altogether (Stampp 1956, 232–235).

"Then what on earth did *you* want to set him free for, seeing he was already free?"

"Well, that *is* a question, I must say; and *just* like women! Why, I wanted the *adventure* of it; and I'd a waded neck-deep in blood to—goodness alive, Aunt Polly!"[168]

If she warn't standing right there, just inside the door, looking as sweet and contented as an angel half-full of pie, I wish I may never!

Aunt Sally jumped for her, and most hugged the head off of her, and cried over her, and I found a good enough place for me under the bed, for it was getting pretty sultry for *us*, seemed to me. And I peeped out, and in a little while Tom's Aunt Polly shook herself loose and stood there looking across at Tom over her spectacles—kind of grinding him into the earth, you know. And then she says:

"Yes, you *better* turn y'r head away—I would if I was you, Tom."

"Oh, deary me!" says Aunt Sally; "*is* he changed so? Why, that ain't *Tom,* it's Sid; Tom's—Tom's—why, where is Tom? He was here a minute ago."

"You mean where's Huck *Finn*—that's what you mean! I reckon I hain't raised such a scamp as my Tom all these years, not to know him when I *see* him. That *would* be a pretty howdy-do. Come out from under that bed, Huck Finn."

So I done it. But not feeling brash.

Aunt Sally she was one of the mixed-upest looking persons I ever see; except one, and that was Uncle Silas, when he come in, and they told it all to him. It kind of made him drunk, as you may say, and he didn't know nothing at all the rest of the day, and preached a prayer-meeting sermon that night that gave him a rattling ruputation, because the oldest man in the world couldn't a understood it. So Tom's Aunt Polly, she told all about who I was, and what; and I had to up and tell how I was in such a tight place that when Mrs. Phelps took me for Tom Sawyer—she chipped in and says, "Oh, go on and call me Aunt Sally, I'm used to it, now, and 'tain't no need to change"—that when Aunt Sally took me for Tom Sawyer, I had to stand it—there warn't no other way, and I knowed he wouldn't

---

168. Once again, Tom makes clear that Jim's freedom matters little to him next to the "adventure" of putting obstacles in Jim's way to make his plight more like something from an adventure book. The news that Tom could have freed Jim upon arrival, with the news of Miss Watson's will, underscores that Tom—and Huck, who like the others says nothing about the cruelty of prolonging Jim's bondage—is not much of an agent of deliverance. While not Twain's apparent intention, these later chapters work well as a parable of the end of Reconstruction and of postbellum whites' limited interest in the cause of black liberty in general.

"THIS IS A WHITE MAN'S GOVERNMENT."

"We regard the Reconstruction Acts (so called) of Congress as usurpations, and unconstitutional, revolutionary, and void."—Democratic Platform.

This 1868 cartoon by Thomas Nast highlights the opposition to Reconstruction, which sought to guarantee basic civil rights for blacks. It shows a Democratic coalition of an urban immigrant (depicted in racist fashion as a chimp), a Confederate general, and a corrupt capitalist, standing on a black man and preventing him from reaching a ballot box. White Southern and Democratic resistance undermined Reconstruction, and its end in 1877 meant that slavery was ultimately replaced not by freedom but by decades of segregation and legal oppression of blacks. (Library of Congress)

mind, because it would be nuts for him, being a mystery, and he'd make an adventure out of it, and be perfectly satisfied. And so it turned out, and he let on to be Sid, and made things as soft as he could for me.

And his Aunt Polly she said Tom was right about old Miss Watson setting Jim free in her will; and so, sure enough, Tom Sawyer had gone and took all that trouble and bother to set a free nigger free! and I couldn't ever understand, before, until that minute and that talk, how he *could* help a body set a nigger free, with his bringing-up.

Well, Aunt Polly she said that when Aunt Sally wrote to her that Tom and *Sid* had come, all right and safe, she says to herself:

"Look at that, now! I might have expected it, letting him go off that way without anybody to watch him. So now I got to go and trapse all the way down the river, eleven hundred mile, and find out what that creetur's up to, *this* time, as long as I couldn't seem to get any answer out of you about it."

"Why, I never heard nothing from you," says Aunt Sally.

"Well, I wonder! Why, I wrote you twice, to ask you what you could mean by Sid being here."

"Well, I never got 'em, Sis."

Aunt Polly she turns around slow and severe, and says:

"You, Tom!"

"Well—*what*?" he says, kind of pettish.

"Don't you what *me,* you impudent thing—hand out them letters."

"What letters?"

"*Them* letters. I be bound, if I have to take aholt of you I'll—"

"They're in the trunk. There, now. And they're just the same as they was when I got them out of the office. I hain't looked into them, I hain't touched them. But I knowed they'd make trouble, and I thought if you warn't in no hurry, I'd—"

"Well, you *do* need skinning, there ain't no mistake about it. And I wrote another one to tell you I was coming; and I s'pose he—"

"No, it come yesterday; I hain't read it yet, but *it's* all right, I've got that one."[169]

---

169. The spread of mail delivery was another aspect of the 19th-century communications revolution. By 1840 the nation had more than 13,000 post offices, up from 75 in 1790, and more than 84,000 miles of post roads, including waterways. Besides its greater reach, mail delivery had gotten faster as steamboats and railroads replaced or complemented horses and wagons. People took advantage of these improvements—postal revenues per person were 27 times higher in 1840 than a half century earlier. Frontier and rural Americans were connected to the rest of the country to a degree that was scarcely imaginable a few decades earlier (Blumin 2000, 828–829; United States Postal Service 2012, 7, 10, 12, 15).

I wanted to offer to bet two dollars she hadn't, but I reckoned maybe it was just as safe to not to. So I never said nothing.

CHAPTER THE LAST.

THE first time I catched Tom, private, I asked him what was his idea, time of the evasion?—what it was he'd planned to do if the evasion worked all right and he managed to set a nigger free that was already free before? And he said, what he had planned in his head, from the start, if we got Jim out all safe, was for us to run him down the river, on the raft, and have adventures plumb to the mouth of the river, and then tell him about his being free, and take him back up home on a steamboat, in style, and pay him for his lost time, and write word ahead and get out all the niggers around, and have them waltz him into town with a torchlight procession and a brass band, and then he would be a hero, and so would we. But I reckoned it was about as well the way it was.

We had Jim out of the chains in no time, and when Aunt Polly and Uncle Silas and Aunt Sally found out how good he helped the doctor nurse Tom, they made a heap of fuss over him, and fixed him up prime, and give him all he wanted to eat, and a good time, and nothing to do. And we had him up to the sick-room; and had a high talk; and Tom give Jim forty dollars for being prisoner for us so patient, and doing it up so good, and Jim was pleased most to death, and busted out, and says:

"*Dah*, now, Huck, what I tell you?—what I tell you up dah on Jackson islan'? I *tole* you I got a hairy breas', en what's de sign un it; en I *tole* you I ben rich wunst, en gwineter to be rich *agin;* en it's come true; en heah she is! *Dah,* now! doan' talk to *me*—signs is *signs,* mine I tell you; en I knowed jis' 's well 'at I 'uz gwineter be rich agin as I's a stannin' heah dis minute!"

And then Tom he talked along, and talked along, and says, le's all three slide out of here, one of these nights, and get an outfit, and go for howling adventures amongst the Injuns, over in the Territory, for a couple of weeks or two; and I says, all right, that suits me, but I ain't got no money for to buy the outfit, and I reckon I couldn't get none from home, because it's likely pap's been back before now, and got it all away from Judge Thatcher and drunk it up.

"No he hain't," Tom says; "it's all there, yet—six thousand dollars and more; and your pap hain't ever been back since. Hadn't when I come away, anyhow."

Jim says, kind of solemn:

"He ain't a-comin' back no mo', Huck."

I says:

OUT OF BONDAGE.

(Illustration by Edward W. Kemble. From Mark Twain, *Adventures of Huckleberry Finn*. New York: C. L. Webster, 1885. Digitized by the University of Virginia Library.)

"Why, Jim?"

"Nemmine why, Huck—but he ain't comin' back no mo'."

But I kept at him; so at last he says:

"Doan' you 'member de house dat was float'n down de river, en dey wuz a man in dah, kivered up, en I went in en unkivered him and didn' let you come in? Well, den, you k'n git yo' money when you wants it; kase dat wuz him."

Tom's most well, now, and got his bullet around his neck on a watch-guard for a watch, and is always seeing what time it is, and so there ain't nothing more to write about, and I am rotten glad of it, because if I'd a knowed what a trouble it was to make a book I wouldn't a tackled it and

This map shows the Indian lands near Missouri in the early 1840s. The "Injun Territory" that Huck wants to "light out for" could be the tribal lands in Iowa (though Iowa was in the process of relocating its Indians in preparation for statehood in 1846) or the various designated Indian territories to the west of Missouri, Iowa, and Arkansas. The federal government granted those small, separate areas to about a dozen different tribes, several of which had traveled the "Trail of Tears" in the 1830s from their previous lands in the east. (Map by Steven J. York Productions.)

ain't agoing to no more. But I reckon I got to light out for the Territory ahead of the rest, because Aunt Sally she's going to adopt me and sivilize me and I can't stand it.[170] I been there before.

THE END. YOURS TRULY, HUCK FINN.

---

170. White Americans' stereotypes of Indians and their territory were two-sided: wild and lawless but also wild and free. To Huck the territory means adventure and another welcome escape from "sivilization." The words recall the federal government during George Washington's administration, when Secretary of War Henry Knox attempted to "civilize" the Indians, chiefly by pushing them to replace hunting with animal husbandry, which conveniently would require less land, creating a surplus that could be sold to Americans. Knox lamented that most of his countrymen seemed to favor extermination under the pretext that it would "be impracticable to civilize the Indians of North America" (Perdue and Green 2010, 43–45; Wallace 2009, 168). But that "uncivilized" lifestyle—hunting and fishing, living in the wilderness—appealed to many white Americans. Daniel Boone was perhaps the most famous white American in the 19th century who adopted the Indian life-style. Benjamin Franklin said much earlier that "No European who has tasted Savage Life can afterward bear to live in our societies" (Wright 1988, 88).

Bibliography

Anderson, Terry L., and Peter J. Hill. "Are Government Giveaways Really Free?" In *Second Thoughts: Myths and Morals of U.S. Economic History,* edited by Donald N. McCloskey, 109–113. New York: Oxford University Press, 1993.

Anderson, Terry L., and Fred S. McChesney. "The Political Economy of Indian Wars." In *The Other Side of the Frontier: Economic Explorations into Native American History,* edited by Linda Barrington, 206–223. Boulder, CO: Westview, 1999.

Appleby, Joyce. *The Relentless Revolution: A History of Capitalism.* New York: Norton, 2010.

"ARKan-SAW or Ar-KANSAS." Arkansas Secretary of State, n.d., http://www.sos .arkansas.gov/educational/students/Documents/arkansasorarkansaw.pdf.

Atack, Jeremy, and Peter Passell. *A New Economic View of American History.* 2nd ed. New York: Norton, 1994.

Banner, Stuart. *How the Indians Lost Their Land: Law and Power on the Frontier.* Cambridge, MA: Belknap Press of Harvard University Press, 2005.

Barnum, Phineas Taylor. *The Autobiography of P. T. Barnum.* 2nd ed. London: Ward and Lock, 1855.

Barry, John M. *The Great Influenza: The Story of the Deadliest Pandemic in History.* New York: Penguin, 2005.

Bateman, Fred, and Thomas Weiss. *A Deplorable Scarcity: The Failure of Industrialization in the Slave Economy.* Chapel Hill: University of North Carolina Press, 1981.

Benson, Lee. *Toward the Scientific Study of History.* Philadelphia: J. B. Lippincott, 1972.

Berger, Max. *The British Traveller in America, 1836–1860.* Gloucester, MA: Peter Smith, 1964.

Between Two Rivers. Directed by Jacob Cartwright and Nick Jordan. Manchester, UK: Wurstundgritz, 2012.

Blackmon, Douglas A. *Slavery by Another Name: The Re-enslavement of Black Americans from the Civil War to World War II.* New York: Anchor Books, 2009.

Blumin, Stuart M. "The Social Implications of U.S. Economic Development." In *The Cambridge Economic History of the United States,* Vol. 2, *The Long*

Nineteenth Century, edited by Stanley L. Engerman and Robert E. Gallman Pages, 813–863. New York: Cambridge University Press, 2000.

Brown, William W. *The Narrative of William W. Brown, a Fugitive Slave.* 1848; reprint, Mineola, NY: Dover, 2003.

Bryan, William Jennings. "Cross of Gold." The American Experience, Speech, July 9, 1896, http://www.pbs.org/wgbh/amex/1900/filmmore/reference/primary/crossofgold.html.

Buchanan, Thomas C. *Slaves, Free Blacks, and the Western Steamboat World.* Chapel Hill: University of North Carolina Press, 2004.

Byrne, Frank. *Becoming Bourgeois: Merchant Culture in the South, 1820–1865.* Lexington: University of Kentucky Press, 2006.

Campanella, Richard. *Lincoln in New Orleans: The 1828–1831 Flatboat Voyages and Their Place in History.* Lafayette: University of Louisiana at Lafayette Press, 2010.

Carnegie, Andrew. *The Empire of Business.* New York: Doubleday, 1913.

Carter, Susan B., et al., eds. *Historical Statistics of the United States: Earliest Times to the Present; Millennial Edition.* 5 vols. Cambridge: Cambridge University Press, 2006.

Chernow, Ron. *The House of Morgan: An American Banking Dynasty and the Rise of Modern Finance.* New York: Grove Press, 2010.

Cimprich, John. "Self-Purchase." In *Dictionary of Afro-American Slavery,* edited by Randall M. Miller and John David Smith, 661–663. Westport, CT: Greenwood, 1988.

Coates, Ta-Nehisi. "People often say to me 'My great-great-great grandfather didn't own slaves.' And I tell them, 'Yes, but he wanted to.'" Twitter, June 23, 2015, https://twitter.com/tanehisicoates/status/613546022514630656.

Cochran, Thomas C., and William Miller. *The Age of Enterprise: A Social History of Industrial America.* New York: Harper and Row, 1961.

Coffin, Levi. *Reminiscences of Levi Coffin, the Reputed President of the Underground Railroad; Being a Brief History of the Labors of a Lifetime in Behalf of the Slave, with the Stories of Numerous Fugitives, Who Gained Their Freedom through His Instrumentality, and Many Other Incidents.* Cincinnati: Robert Clarke and Co., 1880.

Daempfle, Peter. *Good Science, Bad Science, Pseudoscience, and Just Plain Bunk: How to Tell the Difference.* Lanham, MD: Rowman and Littlefield, 2013.

Daley, Suzanne. "Genetics Offers Denouement to Mystery of Prince's Death." *New York Times,* April 20, 2000, A1, A8, http://www.nytimes.com/2000/04/20/world/genetics-offers-denouement-to-mystery-of-prince-s-death.html.

Dallek, Robert. *Lone Star Rising: Lyndon Johnson and His Times, 1908–1960.* New York: Oxford University Press, 1991.

David, Paul, et al. *Reckoning with Slavery.* New York: Oxford University Press, 1976.

Davis, James E. *Frontier Illinois.* Bloomington: Indiana University Press, 1998.

Demby, Gene. "The Ugly, Fascinating History of the Word Racism." National Public Radio, January 6, 2014, http://www.npr.org/blogs/codeswitch/2014/01/05/260006815/the-ugly-fascinating-history-of-the-word-racism.

Dempsey, Terrell. *Searching for Jim: Slavery in Sam Clemens's World.* Columbia: University of Missouri Press, 2003.

Dickens, Charles. *American Notes.* 1842; reprint, New York: Oxford University Press, 1997.

Dictionary.com, http://dictionary.reference.com/.

Dinnerstein, Leonard, and David M. Reimers. *Ethnic Americans: A History of Immigration.* New York: Columbia University Press, 1999.

Dobeck, Mark F., and Euel Elliott. *Money.* Westport, CT: Greenwood, 2007.

Doddington, David. "Slavery and Dogs in the Antebellum South." Sniffing the Past, February 23, 2012, https://sniffingthepast.wordpress.com/2012/02/23/slavery-and-dogs-in-the-antebellum-south/.

Douglass, Frederick. *Narrative of the Life of Frederick Douglass, an American Slave.* 1845; reprint, New York: Penguin, 1982.

Douglas, George H. *The Golden Age of the Newspaper.* Westport: CT: Greenwood, 1999.

Egnal, Marc. *A Mighty Empire: The Origins of the American Revolution.* Ithaca, NY: Cornell University Press, 1988.

Elbaum, Bernard. "Why Apprenticeship Persisted in Britain but Not in the United States." *Journal of Economic History* 49(2) (June 1989): 337–349.

Federal Deposit Insurance Corporation. *A Brief History of Deposit Insurance in the United States.* Washington, DC: FDIC, 1998, https://www.fdic.gov/bank/historical/brief/brhist.pdf.

Ferraro, Sharon. "*Ladies' Home Journal* Houses [1895–1919]." *Old-House Journal* 26(2) (March–April 1998): 52–57.

Finke, Roger, and Rodney Stark. *The Churching of America 1776–1990: Winners and Losers in Our Religious Economy.* New Brunswick, NJ: Rutgers University Press, 1994.

Fischer, Victor, and Lin Salamo, with Harriet Elinor Smith and Walter Blair, eds. *Mark Twain: Adventures of Huckleberry Finn.* 125th anniversary ed. Berkeley: University of California Press, 2010.

Fisher, James. *Historical Dictionary of American Theater: Beginnings.* Lanham, MD: Rowman and Littlefield, 2015.

Fogel, Robert W., and Stanley L. Engerman. *Time on the Cross: The Economics of American Negro Slavery,* Vol. 1. Boston: Little, Brown, 1974.

Foner, Eric. *Gateway to Freedom: The Hidden History of the Underground Railroad.* New York: Norton, 2015.

Foner, Eric. *Nothing but Freedom: Emancipation and Its Legacy.* Baton Rouge: Louisiana State University Press, 1983.

Foner, Eric. Review of Stuart Banner, *How the Indians Lost Their Land: Law and Power on the Frontier* (Harvard University Press, 2005). *London Review of Books* 28(3) (February 9, 2006): 17–18.

Fraser, Steve. *Every Man a Speculator: A History of Wall Street in American Life.* New York: Harper Perennial, 2006.

Galbraith, John Kenneth. *A Short History of Financial Euphoria.* New York: Penguin, 1994.

Gates, Henry Louis. "Did Dogs Really Eat Slaves, Like in Django?" The Root, January 14, 2013, http://www.theroot.com/articles/history/2013/01/how_accurate_is_django_unchained_on_riding_horses_mandingo_fighting_and_dogs_eating_slaves.3.html.

Gates, Paul W. *The Farmer's Age: Agriculture.* New York: Holt, Rinehart and Winston, 1960.

Genovese, Eugene D. *The Political Economy of Slavery.* 1965; reprint, New York: Vintage Books, 1967.

Genovese, Eugene D. *Roll, Jordan, Roll: The World the Slaves Made.* New York: Vintage Books, 1974.

Goldin, Claudia. "America's Graduation from High School: The Evolution and Spread of Secondary Schooling in the Twentieth Century." *Journal of Economic History* 58(2) (June 1998): 345–374.

Goldin, Claudia, and Lawrence F. Katz. "The 'Virtues' of the Past: Education in the First Hundred Years of the New Republic." National Bureau of Economic Research Working Paper 9958, September 2003.

Gordon, John Steele. *An Empire of Wealth.* New York: HarperCollins, 2004.

Gross, Daniel A. "The History of the Humble Suitcase." Smithsonian.com, May 9, 2014, http://www.smithsonianmag.com/history/history-humble-suitcase -180951376/.

Gutman, Herbert G. *Slavery and the Numbers Game.* 1975; reprint, Chicago: University of Illinois Press, 1988.

Hacker, J. David. "A Census-Based Count of the Civil War Dead." *Civil War History* 57(4) (December 2011): 307–348.

Hagedorn, Hermann. *Roosevelt in the Bad Lands,* Vol. 1. Boston: Houghton Mifflin, 1921.

Hahn, Steven. *The Roots of Southern Populism: Yeoman Farmers and the Transformation of the Georgia Upcountry, 1850–1890.* New York: Oxford University Press, 1983.

Haines, Michael R., Lee A. Craig, and Thomas Weiss. "The Short and the Dead: Nutrition, Mortality, and the 'Antebellum Puzzle' in the United States." *Journal of Economic History* 63(2) (June 2003): 382–413.

Haites, Erik F., James Mak, and Gary M. Walton. *Western River Transportation: The Era of Early Internal Development, 1810–1860.* Baltimore: Johns Hopkins University Press, 1975.

Hamermesh, Daniel S., and Jeff E. Biddle. "Beauty and the Labor Market." *American Economic Review* 84(5) (December 1994): 1174–1194.

Harris, Leslie M. *In the Shadow of Slavery: African Americans in New York City, 1626–1863.* Chicago: University of Chicago Press, 2003.

Harris, Neil. *Humbug: The Art of P. T. Barnum.* Chicago: University of Chicago Press, 1981.

Hartsock, Ralph. "Women's Christian Temperance Movement (WCTU)." In *Encyclopedia of Populism in America: A Historical Encyclopedia,* Vol. 2, edited by Alexandra Kindell and Elizabeth S. Demers, 816–818. Santa Barbara, CA: ABC-CLIO, 2014.

Hawk, Emory Q. *Economic History of the South.* New York: Prentice-Hall, 1934.

Henriques, Antonio. "Plenty of Land, Land of Plenty: The Agrarian Output of Portugal (1311–20)." *European Review of Economic History* 19(2) (May 2015): 149–170.

Herndon, Ruth Wallis, and John E. Murray, eds. *Children Bound to Labor: The Pauper Apprentice System in Early America.* Ithaca, NY: Cornell University Press, 2009.

Higgs, Robert. "Accumulation of Property by Southern Blacks before World War I." *American Economic Review* 72(4) (September 1982): 236–245.

Higgs, Robert. *The Transformation of the American Economy, 1865–1914.* New York: Wiley, 1971.

Holcombe, R. I. *History of Marion County, Missouri.* St. Louis: E. F. Perkins, 1884.

Holmes, Oliver Wendell. *Currents and Counter-Currents in Medical Science.* Boston: Ticknor and Fields, 1861.

Hopkins, Donald R. *The Greatest Killer: Smallpox in History.* Chicago: University of Chicago Press, 2002.

Howe, Daniel Walker. *What Hath God Wrought: The Transformation of America, 1815–1848.* New York: Oxford University Press, 2009.

Hughes, Glenn. *A History of the American Theatre, 1700–1950.* New York: Samuel French, 1951, http://archive.org/stream/historyoftheamer030363mbp /historyoftheamer030363mbp_djvu.txt.

Hummel, Jeffrey Rogers. *Emancipating Slaves, Enslaving Free Men: A History of the American Civil War.* Chicago: Open Court, 1996.

Irwin, Douglas A., and Peter Temin. "The Antebellum Tariff on Textiles Revisited." *Journal of Economic History* 61(3) (September 2001): 777–798.

Johnston, Louis, and Samuel H. Williamson. "What Was the U.S. GDP Then?" MeasuringWorth, 2015, http://www.measuringworth.org/usgdp/.

Kaplan, Fred. *The Singular Mark Twain.* New York: Anchor, 2005.

Kennedy, Randall. *Nigger: The Strange Career of a Troublesome Word.* New York: Pantheon, 2002.

Kessler-Harris, Alice. *Out to Work: A History of Wage-Earning Women in the United States.* New York: Oxford University Press, 1982.

Ketcham, Steve. "Celebrity Endorsements Are a Thing of the Past (and Present)." *Old Times,* February 2001.

Khan, B. Zorina. *The Democratization of Invention: Patents and Copyrights in American Economic Development, 1790–1920.* New York: Cambridge University Press, 2005.

Klein Christopher. "8 Reasons Why We Forget Some Historical Events." *The Boston Globe.* April 26, 2015. Accessed May 14. 2015. http://www .bostonglobe.com/ideas/2015/04/25/reasons-why-forget-some-historical -events/qKW3yebxed5NV1kwPVL2bK/story.html.

Kotlikoff, Laurence. "The Structure of Slave Prices in Antebellum New Orleans, 1804 to 1862." *Economic Inquiry* 17(4) (October 1979): 496– 518.

Lamoreaux, Naomi. "Entrepreneurship in the United States, 1865–1920." In *The Invention of Enterprise: Entrepreneurship from Ancient Mesopotamia to Modern Times,* edited by David S. Landes, 367–400. Princeton, NJ: Princeton University Press, 2010.

Lansden, John M. *A History of the City of Cairo, Illinois.* 1910; reprint, Carbondale: Southern Illinois University Press, 2009.

Larson, Agnes M. *The White Pine Industry in Minnesota: A History.* Minneapolis: University of Minnesota Press, 1949.

Lemons, J. Stanley. "Black Stereotypes as Reflected in Popular Culture, 1880– 1920." *The American Quarterly* 29(1) (Spring, 1977): 102–116.

Lender, Mark Edward, and James Kirby Martin. *Drinking in America: A History.* New York: Free Press, 1982.

Leonard, James S., ed. *Making Mark Twain Work in the Classroom*. Durham, NC: Duke University Press, 1999.

Levy, Andrew. *Huck Finn's America: Mark Twain and the Era That Shaped His Masterpiece*. New York: Simon and Schuster, 2014.

Licht, Walter. *Industrializing America: The Nineteenth Century*. Baltimore: Johns Hopkins University Press, 1995.

Lindert, Peter H. *Growing Public: Social Spending and Economic Growth since the Eighteenth Century*, Vol. 1. New York: Cambridge University Press, 2004.

Lindert, Peter H., and Jeffrey G. Williamson. "American Incomes before and after the Revolution." *Journal of Economic History* 73(3) (September 2013): 725–765.

Litwack, Leon F. *Been in the Storm So Long: The Aftermath of Slavery*. New York: Vintage Books, 1979.

Litwack, Leon F. *North of Slavery: The Negro in the Free States 1790–1865*. Chicago: University of Chicago Press, 1965.

Lloyd, James T. *Lloyd's Steamboat Directory, and Disasters on the Western Waters*. Cincinnati: J. T. Lloyd and Company, 1856.

Loewen, James W. *Lies My Teacher Told Me: Everything Your American History Textbook Got Wrong*. New York: Touchstone, 1996.

Marks, Ken, and Lisa Marks. *Hannibal, Missouri: A Brief History*. Charleston, SC: History Press, 2011.

McGovern, Charles F. *Sold American: Consumption and Citizenship, 1890–1945*. Chapel Hill: University of North Carolina Press, 2006.

McGuire, Robert A. *To Form a More Perfect Union: A New Economic Interpretation of the United States Constitution*. New York: Oxford University Press, 2003.

McManus, Edgar J. *Black Bondage in the North*. Syracuse, NY: Syracuse University Press, 1973.

McPherson, James M. *Battle Cry of Freedom*. New York: Oxford University Press, 1988.

McWhiney, Grady. *Cracker Culture: Celtic Ways in the Old South*. Tuscaloosa: University of Alabama Press, 1988.

Mensh, Elaine, and Harry Mensh. *Black, White, and Huckleberry Finn: Reimagining the American Dream*. Tuscaloosa: University of Alabama Press, 2001.

Mihm, Stephen. *A Nation of Counterfeiters: Capitalists, Con Men, and the Making of the United States*. Cambridge, MA: Harvard University Press, 2009.

Miller, Roger LeRoy, and Robert L. Sexton. *Issues in American Economic History*. Mason, OH: Thomson South-Western, 2005.

Mintz, Steven. *Huck's Raft: A History of American Childhood*. Cambridge, MA: Harvard University Press, 2004.

Mintz, Steven, and Sarah McNeil. "Rise of Democratic Politics." Digital History, 2013, http://www.digitalhistory.uh.edu/disp_textbook.cfm?smtid =2&psid=3541.

Montesquieu. *The Spirit of Laws*, Vol. 1. 1748; reprint, Cincinnati: Robert Clarke and Company, 1873.

Moran, Joe. *Star Authors: Literary Celebrity in America*. London: Pluto, 2000.

Morone, James. *Hellfire Nation: The Politics of Sin in American History.* New Haven, CT: Yale University Press, 2003.

Morris, Charles R. *The Tycoons: How Andrew Carnegie, John D. Rockefeller, Jay Gould, and J. P. Morgan Invented the American Supereconomy.* New York: Owl Books, 2006.

Morrison, Larry R. "The Religious Defense of American Slavery before 1830." *Journal of Religious Thought* 37(2) (Fall–Winter 1980–1981): 16–29.

National Park Service. "Aboard the Underground Railroad," Dr. Richard Eells House, n.d., http://www.nps.gov/nr/travel/underground/il3.htm.

Noone, John. *The Man behind the Iron Mask.* New York: St. Martin's, 1994.

Northup, Solomon. *Twelve Years a Slave.* 1853; reprint, Mineola, NY: Dover, 2000.

Nugent, Walter. *Crossings: The Great Transatlantic Migrations, 1870–1914.* Indianapolis: Indiana University Press, 1995.

Nugent, Walter. *Habits of Empire: A History of American Expansion.* New York: Vintage Books, 2009.

Officer, Lawrence H., and Samuel H. Williamson. "The Annual Consumer Price Index for the United States, 1774–2014." MeasuringWorth, 2015, http://www.measuringworth.com/uscpi/.

Olmstead, Alan L., and Paul W. Rhode. "Biological Innovation and Productivity Growth in the Antebellum Cotton Economy." *Journal of Economic History* 68(4) (December 2008): 1123–1171.

Online Etymology Dictionary, http://www.etymonline.com/.

OpenStax College. *U.S. History.* OpenStax CNX, May 15, 2015, http://cnx.org/contents/a7ba2fb8-8925-4987-b182-5f4429d48daa@3.15.

Owsley, Frank Lawrence. *Plain Folk of the Old South.* Baton Rouge: Louisiana State University Press, 1949.

Paskoff, Paul F. *Troubled Waters: Steamboat Disasters, River Improvements, and American Public Policy, 1821–1860.* Baton Rouge: Louisiana State University Press, 2007.

Pegram, Thomas R. *Battling Demon Rum: The Struggle for a Dry America, 1800–1933.* Chicago: Ivan R. Dee, 1998.

Perdue, Theda, and Michael D. Green. *North American Indians: A Very Short Introduction.* New York: Oxford University Press, 2010.

Perkins, Edwin J. *The Economy of Colonial America.* New York: Columbia University Press, 1980.

Perkins, Edwin J. "The Entrepreneurial Spirit in Colonial America." *Business History Review* 63 (Spring 1989): 169–186.

Perrottet, Tony. *The Sinner's Grand Tour: A Journey through the Historical Underbelly of Europe.* New York: Crown Archetype, 2011.

Pettit, Arthur G. *Mark Twain and the South.* Lexington: University Press of Kentucky, 1974.

Phillips, Ulrich Bonnell. *Life and Labor in the Old South.* 1929; reprint, Boston: Little, Brown, 1963.

Piketty, Thomas. *Capital in the Twenty-First Century.* Cambridge, MA: Belknap Press of Harvard University Press, 2014.

Pitney, John J., Jr., and John-Clark Levin. *Private Anti-Piracy Navies: How Warships for Hire Are Changing Maritime Security.* Lanham, MD: Lexington Books, 2013.

Powers, Ron. *Mark Twain: A Life.* New York: Free Press, 2005.

Railton, Stephen. *Mark Twain: A Short Introduction.* Malden, MA: Blackwell, 2004.

Ransom, Roger, and Richard Sutch. *One Kind of Freedom: The Economic Consequences of Emancipation.* 2nd ed. New York: Cambridge University Press, 2001.

Rasmussen, R. Kent. "Introduction and Notes" to Mark Twain, *Adventures of Huckleberry Finn.* New York: Penguin, 2014.

Richards, Leonard L. "The Jacksonians and Slavery." In *Antislavery Reconsidered: New Perspectives on the Abolitionists,* edited by Lewis Perry and Michael Fellman, 99–118. Baton Rouge: Louisiana State University Press, 1979.

Ridgeley, Douglas Clay. *The Geography of Illinois.* Chicago: University of Chicago Press, 1921.

Rodriguez, Junius P., ed. *Slavery in the United States: A Social, Political, and Historical Encyclopedia,* Vol. 1. Santa Barbara, CA: ABC-CLIO, 2007.

Rorabaugh, William J. *The Alcoholic Republic.* New York: Oxford University Press, 1979.

Sandage, Scott A. *Born Losers: A History of Failure in America.* Cambridge, MA: Harvard University Press, 2005.

Sandlin, Lee. *Wicked River: The Mississippi: When It Last Ran Wild.* New York: Pantheon, 2010.

Sante, Luc. *Low Life: Lures and Snares of Old New York.* New York: Farrar, Straus and Giroux, 1991.

Saunders, George. "Introduction." In Mark Twain, *Adventures of Huckleberry Finn,* ix–xxv. New York: Modern Library Classics, 2008.

Scharnhorst, Gary, ed. *Mark Twain: The Complete Interviews.* Tuscaloosa: University of Alabama Press, 2006.

Sexton, Robert L. "Regional Choice and Economic History." *Economic Forum* 16(1) (Winter 1986–1987): 159–166.

Shinn, Josiah Hazen. *Pioneers and Makers of Arkansas.* Baltimore: Genealogical and Historical Publishing Company, 1908.

Shulman, Stanford T. "The History of Pediatric Infectious Diseases." *Pediatric Research* 55 (2004): 163–176.

Sickels, Robert C. *100 Entertainers Who Changed America: An Encyclopedia of Pop Culture Luminaries.* Santa Barbara, CA: ABC-CLIO, 2013.

Siebert, Wilbur H. *The Underground Railroad: From Slavery to Freedom.* 1898; reprint, North Stratford, NH: Ayer Company Publishers, 2000.

Smith, Andrew F. *Food and Drink in American History: A "Full Course" Encyclopedia,* Vol. 2. Santa Barbara, CA: ABC-CLIO, 2013.

Stampp, Kenneth M. *The Peculiar Institution: Slavery in the Ante-Bellum South.* New York: Vintage Books, 1956.

Steckel, Richard H., and Joseph M. Prince. "Tallest in the World: Native Americans of the Great Plains in the Nineteenth Century." *American Economic Review* 91(1) (March 2001): 287–294.

Stewart, David O. *Impeached: The Trial of Andrew Johnson and the Fight for Lincoln's Legacy.* New York: Simon and Schuster, 2009.

Tadman, Michael. *Speculators and Slaves: Masters, Traders, and Slaves in the Old South.* Madison: University of Wisconsin Press, 1989.

Taylor, George Rogers. "American Economic Growth before 1840: An Exploratory Essay." *Journal of Economic History* 24(4) (December 1964): 427–444.

Taylor, George Rogers. *The Transportation Revolution, 1815–1860.* New York: Rinehart, 1951.

Temple, J. H. *History of North Brookfield, Massachusetts: Preceded by an Account of Old Quabaug, Indian and English Occupation, 1647–1676; Brookfield Records, 1686–1783.* Boston: Town of North Brookfield, 1887.

Thornton, Russell. "Population History of Native North Americans." In *A Population History of North America,* edited by Michael R. Haines and Richard H. Steckel, 9–50. Cambridge: Cambridge University Press, 2000.

Tocqueville, Alexis de. *Democracy in America.* 1835; reprint, Chicago: University of Chicago Press, 2000.

Trexler, Harrison Anthony. *Slavery in Missouri, 1804–1865.* Baltimore: Johns Hopkins University Press, 1914.

Twain, Mark. *Adventures of Huckleberry Finn.* 1884; reprint, New York: Penguin, 2014.

Twain, Mark. *The Adventures of Tom Sawyer.* 1876; reprint, New York: Barnes and Noble Classics, 2008.

Twain, Mark. *The Annotated Huckleberry Finn.* Edited with an introduction and notes by Michael Patrick Hearn. New York: Norton, 2001.

Twain, Mark. *Autobiography of Mark Twain.* 2 vols. Berkeley: University of California Press, 2010.

Twain, Mark. *Collected Tales, Sketches, Speeches, and Essays 1891–1910.* New York: Library of America, 1992.

Twain, Mark. *The Complete Short Stories.* New York: Everyman's Library, 2012.

Twain, Mark. *Following the Equator.* Hartford, CT: American Publishing Company, 1897.

Twain, Mark. "The Grand Tour—1. The Sandwich Islands." Speech at Baseball Dinner, Delmonico's, New York, April 8, 1889. In *Mark Twain Speaking,* edited by Paul Fatout, 244–247. Iowa City: University of Iowa Press, 1978.

Twain, Mark. "Greeting to 1900." In *Mark Twain's Notebook,* edited by Albert Bigelow Paine, 372. 1900; reprint, New York: Harper, 1935.

Twain, Mark. *The Innocents Abroad.* 1869; reprint, Pleasantville, NY: Reader's Digest, 1990.

Twain, Mark. "Jane Lampton Clemens." In *Huck Finn and Tom Sawyer among the Indians and Other Unfinished Stories,* 82–92. 1890; reprint, Berkeley: University of California Press, 1989.

Twain, Mark. *Life as I Find It: A Treasury of Mark Twain Rarities.* Edited by Charles Neider. New York: Cooper Square, 2000.

Twain, Mark. *Collected Tales, Sketches, Speeches, and Essays 1891-1910.* New York: Library of America, 1992.

Twain, Mark. *Life on the Mississippi.* 1883; reprint, New York: Bantam Books, 1963.

Twain, Mark. *A Pen Warmed-Up in Hell: Mark Twain in Protest.* Edited by Frederick Anderson. New York: Harper Colophon, 1979.

Twain, Mark. *The Prince and the Pauper.* 1881; reprint, New York: Signet Classic, 1964.

Twain, Mark. *Roughing It.* 1872; reprint, New York: Penguin, 1985.

Twain, Mark. *Tales, Speeches, Essays, and Sketches.* New York: Penguin, 1994.

Twain, Mark. *The Tragedy of Pudd'nhead Wilson.* 1894; reprint, New York: Bantam Books, 1981.

Twain, Mark, and Charles Dudley Warner. *The Gilded Age: A Tale of Today.* 1873; reprint, New York: Meridian, 1994.

Tyron, Rolla M. *Household Manufacturers in the United States, 1640–1860.* Reprint ed. New York: Augustus M. Kelley, 1966.

Tyrrell, Ian. *Sobering Up: From Temperance to Prohibition in Antebellum America, 1815–1860.* Westport, CT: Praeger, 2000.

United States Bureau of the Census. "Table 7. Population of the 100 Largest Urban Places: 1840." United States Census Bureau, June 15, 1998, https://www.census.gov/population/www/documentation/twps0027/tab07.txt.

United States Department of Commerce. *Historical Statistics of the United States.* Washington, DC: U.S. Government Printing Office, 1975.

United States Department of State. *Compendium of the Enumeration of the Inhabitants and Statistics of the United States, as Obtained at the Department of State from the Returns of the Sixth Census of Population.* Washington, DC: Thomas Allen, 1841.

United States Postal Service. *The United States Postal Service: An American History, 1775–2006.* Publication 100, November 2012, https://about.usps.com/publications/pub100.pdf.

United States Senate. *Statistical View of the United States, Embracing Its Territory, Population—White, Free Colored, and Slave—Moral and Social Condition, Industry, Property and Revenue: The Detailed Statistics of Cities, Towns, and Counties, Being a Compendium of the Seventh Census.* Washington, DC: Beverley Tucker, 1854.

Vedder, Henry Clay. *American Writers of To-Day.* New York: Silver, Burdett, 1894.

Wade, Richard C. *Slavery in the Cities: The South, 1820–1860.* New York: Oxford University Press, 1964.

Wade, Richard C. *The Urban Frontier: Pioneer Life in Early Pittsburgh, Cincinnati, Lexington, Louisville, and St. Louis.* 1959; reprint, Chicago: University of Chicago Press, 1976.

Wajda, Shirley Teresa. "The Demise of the Domestic Parlor." In *Material Culture in America: Understanding Everyday Life,* edited by Helen Sheumaker and Shirley Teresa Wajda, 337. Santa Barbara, CA: ABC-CLIO, 2008.

Wallace, Anthony F. C. *Jefferson and the Indians: The Tragic Fate of the First Americans.* Cambridge, MA: Harvard University Press, 2009.

Walton, Gary M., and Hugh Rockoff. *History of the American Economy.* 12th ed. Mason, OH: South-Western, Cengage Learning, 2014.

Webster's Ninth New Collegiate Dictionary. Springfield, MA: Merriam-Webster, 1991.

Weslager, C. A. *The Log Cabin in America: From Pioneer Days to the Present.* New Brunswick, NJ: Rutgers University Press, 1969.

Whaples, Robert. "Where Is There Consensus among American Economic Historians? The Results of a Survey on Forty Propositions." *Journal of Economic History* 55 (1995): 139–154.

Wilde, Oscar. "The American Man." *Court and Society Review* 4(145) (April 13, 1887): 341–343.

Williamson, Jeffrey G. "Unequal Gains: American Growth and Inequality since 1774." Keynote address at the Economic and Business History Conference, La Crosse, Wisconsin, May 29, 2015, http://mymedia.uwlax.edu/Mediasite /Play/14198051eaa245fa96ededc4aa72f3da1d.

Williamson, Jeffrey G., and Peter H. Lindert. *American Inequality: A Macroeconomic History.* New York: Academic Press, 1980.

Williamson, Samuel H. "What Was the U.K. GDP Then?" MeasuringWorth, 2015, http://www.measuringworth.com/ukgdp/.

Winship, Michael. *American Literary Publishing in the Mid-nineteenth Century: The Business of Ticknor and Fields.* New York: Cambridge University Press, 2003.

Wishart, David M. "Indigenous North American Economy." In *The Oxford Encyclopedia of Economic History,* Vol. 1, edited by Joel Mokyr Pages, 117–121. New York: Oxford University Press, 2003.

Wolfram, Walt, and Jeffrey Reaser. *Talkin' Tar Heel: How Our Voices Tell the Story of North Carolina.* Chapel Hill: University of North Carolina Press, 2014.

Work Projects Administration. *Missouri: The WPA Guide to the "Show Me" State.* 1941; reprint, St. Louis: Missouri Historical Society Press, 1998.

Wright, Esmond. *Franklin of Philadelphia.* Cambridge, MA: Harvard University Press, 1988.

Wright, Gavin. "The Origins of American Industrial Success, 1879–1940." *American Economic Review* 80(4) (September 1990): 651–668.

Wright, Gavin. *The Political Economy of the Cotton South.* New York: Norton, 1978.

Wyatt-Brown, Bertram. *Honor and Violence in the Old South.* New York: Oxford University Press, 1986.

Index

About the Annotator

Ranjit S. Dighe, PhD, is professor of economics at the State University of New York at Oswego. His specialty is American social and economic history. He has served as president of the Economic and Business History Society. Dighe is the author of *The Historian's Wizard of Oz: Reading L. Frank Baum's Classic as a Political and Monetary Allegory* and has had his work published in such journals as *Research in Economic History, Essays in Economic and Business History,* and *Social History of Alcohol and Drugs.* He has done extensive research on the Great Depression and Prohibition, among other topics. Dighe holds a doctorate in economics from Yale University and a bachelor's degree in economics from Oberlin College. He blogs at moneyandblogging.wordpress.com.